Contesting
home defence

Manchester University Press

Cultural History of Modern War

Series editors Peter Gatrell, Max Jones,
Penny Summerfield and Bertrand Taithe

Already published

Jeffrey S. Reznick   *Healing the nation: soldiers and the culture of
caregiving in Britain during the Great War*

Centre for the
Cultural History
of War

Contesting home defence

Men, women and the Home Guard in the Second World War

~

PENNY SUMMERFIELD

and CORINNA PENISTON-BIRD

Manchester University Press

Manchester and New York

distributed exclusively in the USA by Palgrave

The right of Penny Summerfield and Corinna Peniston-Bird to be identified as the authors of this work has been asserted by them in accordance with the Copyright, Designs and Patents Act 1988.

Published by Manchester University Press
Oxford Road, Manchester M13 9NR, UK
and Room 400, 175 Fifth Avenue, New York, NY 10010, USA
www.manchesteruniversitypress.co.uk

Distributed exclusively in the USA by Palgrave
175 Fifth Avenue, New York,
NY 10010, USA

Distributed exclusively in Canada by UBC Press
University of British Columbia, 2029 West Mall,
Vancouver, BC, Canada V6T 1Z2

British Library Cataloguing-in-Publication Data
A catalogue record for this book is available from the British Library

Library of Congress Cataloging-in-Publication Data applied for

ISBN   978 0 7190 6201 8 *hardback*
ISBN   978 0 7190 6202 5 *paperback*

First published 2007

16 15 14 13 12 11 10 09 08 07   10 9 8 7 6 5 4 3 2 1

Typeset in Minion
by Koinonia, Manchester
Printed in Great Britain
by Bell & Bain Ltd, Glasgow

For Chloë:
Dad's Army fan

Contents

List of illustrations

List of abbreviations

ACI	Army Council Instruction
ARP	Air Raid Precautions
ARW	Air Raid Warden
ATS	Auxiliary Territorial Service
BBC, WAC	British Broadcasting Corporation, Written Archives Centre
BCL, WA	Birkenhead Central Library, Wirral Archives
CO	commanding officer
CPGB	Communist Party of Great Britain
DCM	Distinguished Conduct Medal
DGHG	Director General Home Guard
ESRC	Economic and Social Research Council
GTE	Gender, Training and Employment (Project)
HG	Home Guard
HGA	Home Guard Auxiliary (secret organisation 1940-45)
HGA	Home Guard Association (formed 2002)
IWM, DD	Imperial War Museum, Documents Department
IWM, PA	Imperial War Museum, Photograph Archive
IWM, SA	Imperial War Museum, Sound Archive
IRA	Irish Republican Army
JP	Justice of the Peace
KCLA	Kings College London Archive
LDV	Local Defence Volunteers
LHC	Liddell Hart Collection (KCLA)
MOA	Mass-Observation Archive
MP	Member of Parliament
MoI	Ministry of Information

List of abbreviations

NA	National Archives
NCO	non-commissioned officer
PI	project interview
RAF	Royal Air Force
ROF	Royal Ordnance Factory
SoS	Secretary of State
TA	Territorial Army
THWA	Tom H. Wintringham Archive (KCLA)
WO	War Office
WAAF	Women's Auxiliary Air Force
WHD	Women's Home Defence
WHGA	Women's Home Guard Auxiliary
WRNS	Women's Royal Naval Service
WVS	Women's Voluntary Services

Preface and acknowledgements

In 1991 I was leading an oral history project on women's experiences during and after the Second World War.[1] One of the interviewees, Yvette Baynes, startled her interviewer, a student researcher, by saying that she felt that she did more for the war effort as a Home Guard than as a secretary in a munitions factory in Birmingham. Yvette explained that the group of five women with whom she joined made their own uniforms and trained with the men. She thought that they might have been the only women Home Guards in the country since she had never heard of others; nor indeed had the interviewer.[2] This evidence that women joined the Home Guard needed further investigation, and I planned to return to it after completing the book based on the 1991 project, published as *Reconstructing Women's Wartime Lives*.[3] The immediate occasion for further research was my professorial inaugural lecture in 1997, for which I needed a case study of the ways in which twentieth-century wars disturbed gender relations and identities by generating pressures (frequently resisted) for women to take on tasks conventionally done by men.[4] I wanted to discuss an area that I had not worked on before and on which there was little published work. Women and the Home Guard met these criteria.

Fragments of that history were recorded in existing accounts. It was referred to by the wartime feminist writers Vera Douie and Elaine Burton, who wrote books in the 1940s indicting the wartime Government for failing to use women to the fullest extent possible because of anachronistic prejudices. They stated, briefly and in passing, that the Labour MP Edith Summerskill had formed an organisation called Women's Home Defence, led a campaign for women's membership of the Home Guard, insisted on joining the House of Commons Home Guard herself and eventually wrung meagre concessions from a reluctant Government.[5] But relatively recent histories of the Home Guard written by men (Norman Longmate, Paul MacKenzie) were dismissive of Summerskill, seeing her campaign as an irritant to the Home Guard which the Government rightly resisted.[6] However, buried in the appendices of a wartime account, Charles Graves's *The Home Guard of Britain* (1943), was evidence that other women were accepted into the ranks of Home Guard units.[7] In the autumn of 1997 a friend spotted an entry in the personal column of *Saga Magazine*. Mrs Gale Sharp of York thanked women former Home Guards 'who wrote to me giving details of their service' in support of her campaign for a place for women in the Remembrance Day parades. So Yvette's group of five was not alone, and other women who had joined the Home Guard were alive and possibly available to interview. Following a meeting in January 1998, Mrs Gale Sharp kindly forwarded my letters requesting interviews to the women who had contacted her through *Saga Magazine*.[8] It was apparent that the topic of women in the Home Guard was more than a 'case': here was a hidden history waiting to be researched and needing to be told.

These investigations also suggested that the Home Guard itself was a complex and fascinating organisation. I had met it before, in a much earlier study of education in the armed forces during the war.[9] Army education, and particularly the creation of the Army Bureau of Current Affairs, were informed by the ideas – progressive in military circles at the time – that soldiers should not be 'automata' but should be trained to think for themselves, because modern warfare demanded alertness and initiative. Not only this, but motivation and commitment were important. In other words, soldiers should understand and believe in what they fought for. Wartime military thinkers such as Basil Liddell Hart and Tom Wintringham wrote in this way. Much of Wintringham's writing was concerned with the Home Guard: he argued that it was vital that both the Home Guard and the British Army should develop 'democratic discipline' as forces of 'men who feel free, and feel themselves by natural right the equals of their fellows; men who accept regulations and order … because they realise the need for these in strengthening their collective actions'.[10] More generally, he argued that soldiers of all sorts 'must be made to feel that their own contribution has value and is accepted, that the war is their war'.[11] Army education based on such principles was warmly supported by the military officials responsible for army welfare, but it was regarded with suspicion by more conventional members of the War Office, notably Captain H. D. R. Margesson and Sir James Grigg, successive Secretaries of State for War between 1940 and 1945. Later, it was seen as a radicalising factor in the British Army, and was held responsible by some Conservative politicians, including Winston Churchill and R. A. Butler, for the leftward swing that produced the Labour victory in the general election of 1945.

The Wintringham connection raised the question of whether the Home Guard was also a site in which wartime radicalism flourished. References to Wintringham's influence in the Home Guard histories referred to above, as well as in work focused specifically on him, suggest that he made a left-wing challenge concerning the character and purpose of the Home Guard, which the Government opposed.[12] As well as prompting questions about the issues at stake, the possibility that the Home Guard contained radical elements, or that it was important to the Government that it should not, invited further investigation. What did it mean, in the most general terms, for men to be members of the Home Guard? If oral history interviewing was an appropriate way to pursue the women's story, it would also help to answer these other questions. The outline of a research project on the Home Guard, embracing both women's and men's experiences, began to take shape.

In the early stages of research one thing became clear: it was not possible to ask questions about the Home Guard without invoking the BBC television situation comedy *Dad's Army*. Recent historians of the Home Guard (or their publishers) refer to the show in their titles or on their covers, using its popularity to help sell copies, but either shrug it off in their discussions of the force or counterpose their histories to it: their work reveals the 'real *Dad's Army*'.[13] The growing body of work on popular memory, which informed the analysis in *Reconstructing Women's Wartime Lives*, suggested that rather than trying to peel off the *Dad's Army* veneer in this way, it would be more important to understand the powerful version of Home Guard history that it presents. How does this version relate to the way that the force had been represented in popular culture during and after the war? And how has it affected the way both men and women remember their own experiences in the Home Guard?

With this cluster of questions, I started a pilot project with funding from Lancaster University, and then applied to the Leverhulme Trust for more substantial funding covering the costs of employing a research associate for fifteen months.[14] This brought Corinna Peniston-Bird into the project in a natural transition from her previous work on the theme of sexual integration in the military and, specifically, the representation of military women in Hollywood films.[15] From the summer of 1999 we engaged in the research together: we explored the political struggles over the shape and character of the Home Guard; we investigated representations of the Home Guard in all kinds of wartime popular culture, and watched all the episodes of *Dad's Army* that we could catch as repeats or buy as video tapes or DVDs; and we interviewed twenty-nine men and women who had been members of the Home Guard, corresponded with others and listened to numerous interviews in the Imperial War Museum's Sound Archive. Fifteen months was not long enough to complete all we had planned: in 2001–2 I gained an Arts and Humanities Research Board Research Leave Award and we both obtained further small grants from our (by then) respective institutions, to augment the research and aid the preparation of the materials for analysis and writing.[16] We wrote and published together on various aspects of the project along the way.[17] As far as this book is concerned, I wrote 7 chapters while Corinna drafted 2, and I redrafted and finalised every chapter in the light of extensive comments and further material from Corinna.

As indicated above, the research was made possible by grants from Lancaster University, the Leverhulme Trust, the Arts and Humanities Research Board and the University of Manchester, which we acknowledge gratefully. The generosity of the men and women who took the time to share their memories of Home Guard service with us in oral history interviews and in correspondence, and who lent us photographs, badges, certificates and other 'ephemera', is sincerely appreciated: their contribution has been both invaluable and inspirational. We are also indebted to the numerous librarians and archivists who made our visits worthwhile and enjoyable. We have presented papers on, and benefited from discussion of, aspects of the research at seminars and conferences in Australia, Britain, France, Germany, Ireland, the Netherlands and the USA. Students, colleagues and friends have loaned us tapes, books and artefacts, have passed on nuggets they discovered in archives that they were mining for other purposes, have found us people to interview and have made valuable critical suggestions: we are truly grateful. We also appreciate the hard work of Bridget Cook and Cheryl Scott who transcribed the interviews, of Tracy Carrington who word-processed fat files of pencil-written notes, of Anne-Marie Hughes who did some archival checking for us, and of Karl Kuroski who helped with the index. Finally we are indebted to all the discussants, colleagues and friends who have read and commented on conference papers and draft chapters at various stages, especially Sarah Barber, Janet Finch, James Hinton, Max Jones, Fred Leventhal, Nick Mansfield, Elizabeth Maslen, David Morgan,

Jeffrey Richards, Sonya Rose and Peter Yeandle. Above all, Oliver Fulton, who has read everything – some of it more than once – deserves especial thanks. The incisive remarks and suggestions of all these commentators have been invaluable, although of course we take final responsibility for what follows on these pages.

Every effort has been made to contact copyright holders for permission to quote their words; pseudonyms have been used wherever requested.

Penny Summerfield

Notes

1 ESRC, Grant R000 23 2048, 1990–92, 'Gender, Training and Employment 1939–1950' (GTE Project).
2 GTE Project, Yvette Baynes (pseud.), interviewed by Hilary Arksey, November 1991, 322–364 and 687–690 (these figures refer to numbered paragraphs).
3 P. Summerfield, *Reconstructing Women's Wartime Lives: Discourse and Subjectivity in Oral Histories of the Second World War* (Manchester: Manchester University Press, 1998).
4 P. Summerfield, '"My Dress for an Army Uniform": Gender Instabilities in the Two World Wars', Lancaster University, *Inaugural Lecture Series*, (1997).
5 E. Burton, *What of the Women? A Study of Women in Wartime* (London: Frederick Muller, 1941), p. 55; V. Douie, *The Lesser Half: A Survey of the Laws, Regulations and Practices Introduced During the Present War Which Embody Discrimination Against Women* (London: Women's Publicity Planning Association, 1943), p. 44.
6 N. Longmate, *The Real Dad's Army: The Story of the Home Guard* (London: Arrow Books, 1974); S. P. MacKenzie, *The Home Guard: A Military and Political History* (Oxford: Oxford University Press, 1995).
7 C. Graves, *The Home Guard of Britain* (London: Hutchinson, 1943), Part 2.
8 *Saga Magazine*, Autumn 1997.
9 P. Summerfield, 'Education and Politics in the British Armed Forces in the Second World War', *International Review of Social History*, 26:2 (1981), pp. 133–158.
10 T. Wintringham, *New Ways of War* (Harmondsworth: Penguin, 1940), pp. 43–44; see also B. H. Liddell Hart, *Dynamic Defence* (London: Faber & Faber, 1940), p. 55.
11 Wintringham, *New Ways*, p. 50.
12 See Longmate, *Real Dad's Army*, p. 88; MacKenzie, *Home Guard*, Ch. 5; D. Fernbach, 'Tom Wintringham and Socialist Defense Strategy', *History Workshop*, 14 (autumn, 1982), pp. 73–78; H. Purcell, *The Last English Revolutionary: Tom Wintringham 1898–1949* (Stroud: Sutton Publishing, 2004), Ch.

12.

13 Longmate, *Real Dad's Army*; MacKenzie, *Home Guard*, on the book cover 'The real story of "Dad's Army"'; S. P. MacKenzie, 'The Real *Dad's Army*: The British Home Guard 1940–1944', P. Addison and A. Calder, *Time to Kill: The Soldier's Experience of War in the West 1939–1945* (London: Pimlico, 1997), pp. 50–59.

14 Lancaster University, Research Support Grant, 'The Gendering of British National Defence 1939–1945', June 1998–July 1999; Leverhulme Trust Research Grant, F/185/AK, 'The Gendering of Home Defence in the Second World War: The Case of the Home Guard', June 1999–August 2000.

15 C. Peniston-Bird, 'Sexual Integration in the Military since 1945: Ambiguity, Contradiction and Possibility' and 'Delilah Shaves Her Hair: Women, the Military and Hollywood', in G. J. DeGroot and C. Peniston-Bird (eds), *A Soldier and a Woman: Sexual Integration in the Military* (Harlow: Pearson, 2000).

16 P. Summerfield, University of Manchester Research Support Grants 2001–2, 2003–4, and AHRB Research Leave Scheme Award RLS/AN4827/APN12197, 'Contesting Home Defence: Men, Women and the Home Guard in Britain in World War Two' 2001–2; C. Peniston-Bird, Lancaster University Research Support Grant, 2002.

17 P. Summerfield and C. Peniston-Bird, 'Women in the Firing Line: the Home Guard and the Defence of Gender Boundaries in Britain in the Second World War', *Women's History Review*, 9:2 (2000), pp. 231–255; C. Peniston-Bird and P. Summerfield ' "Hey, You're Dead!": The Multiple Uses of Humour in Representations of British National Defence in the Second World War', *Journal of European Studies*, 31 (2001), pp. 413–435; P. Summerfield and C. Peniston-Bird, 'The Home Guard in Britain in the Second World War: Uncertain Masculinities?', in P. R. Higate (ed.), *Military Masculinities: Identity and the State* (Westport, CT: Praeger, 2003).

1

Introduction:
contested histories

This book explores the meanings of the Second World War in British popular and personal memory. It does so through the study of one particular field of action, namely 'home defence', the military strategy for the security of the British nation against bombardment, incursion, invasion and occupation. Although home defence has had its historians, of whom more shortly, other aspects of the war, such as the Blitz, the civilian home front, and military organisation and campaigns, have received more attention.[1] In particular, home defence has not, to date, been discussed in terms of its cultural meanings. Yet the Home Guard, the wartime organisation officially created to provide home defence, has featured strongly in popular culture, both during the war and, from the late 1960s to the present day, as the subject of the enormously popular television comedy series *Dad's Army*. In view of this prominence, it is surprising that the place of home defence in contemporary and latter-day understandings of the Second World War has not previously been addressed in depth.

The Home Guard originated in May 1940 as the Local Defence Volunteers (LDV), a voluntary force of civilians who trained and worked as soldiers on a part-time basis, in readiness for full-time mobilisation if necessary. The force was called into being by Anthony Eden, Secretary of State for War, at a time when German advances in Holland and Belgium stimulated fears of an invasion of Britain. This anxious anticipation was intensified by the defeat of France and the evacuation of the British Expeditionary Force from Dunkirk in June 1940. Renamed the Home Guard in July 1940, at Winston Churchill's insistence, the force was maintained and developed as an adjunct to the armed forces after expectations of full-scale invasion had faded. It was 'stood down' in December

1944 and was disbanded a year later, although in the 1950s unsuccessful attempts were made to revive it. This much is agreed in the various available accounts of the Second World War and home defence, but beyond it there are considerable differences of historical interpretation and representation.

We have used a three-part critical strategy to address the changing meanings of home defence over time; it shapes the structure of the book. Thus we explore political challenges to the official concept of home defence (Part I); we investigate the representation of the Home Guard in popular culture during and after the war (Part II); and we scrutinise the recall of wartime participation in home defence in personal memory (Part III).

This chapter offers a brief introduction to our project. We begin by reviewing the evolving historical discourse concerning the cultural and social history of the Second World War and the relationship to it of the history of home defence. Following this, we trace briefly the origins of the Home Guard, and discuss some of the implications of its name. Then we situate our theoretical approach in the recent developments in cultural history on which we draw and to which we aim to contribute. Finally we outline the structure of the book and introduce the sources and the methodologies which we have used.

Histories of the Second World War and of home defence

Historical representations of the social history of Britain in the Second World War can be conveniently divided into two phases which can be linked to shifts in the broader socio-political environment. This phasing should not be thought of, however, as a linear progression: each phase has constituted a discursive terrain on which rival interpretations were debated.

From 1945 to the late 1960s, historians' discussions of the Second World War and social change variously contributed to, and contested, an account of the war that Geoff Eley has referred to as 'a narrative of popular democratic accomplishment'.[2] This story was characterised by two linked elements: the quasi-socialist measures such as rationing, state nurseries, the emergency hospital service and 'manpower budgeting' that the wartime Government introduced in order to mobilise the population for war; and the leftward-leaning response of the population so mobilised, who supposedly welcomed 'equality of sacrifice' and demanded that the principle of 'fair shares for all' should guide not only wartime policy but also postwar reconstruction under a Labour Government.

In 1969, however, Angus Calder's path-breaking study *The People's War* identified and probed the social and political tensions beneath the surface of the apparent national consensus about the war effort and its consequences.[3] Calder's work inaugurated the second historiographical phase, coinciding with and stimulating a range of other studies that sought to understand, variously, the origins of wartime radicalism in pre-war and wartime political formations, its containment by the wartime state, its contestation by contemporary interest groups and its subversion by the advent of the post-war global economy and the Cold War.[4] This phase coincided with the weakening of the traditional Left in the 1980s and 1990s, under the twin pressures of Thatcherism and the collapse of communist regimes in Russia and Eastern Europe. In this context the historiography moved in a number of directions. On the one hand, feminist and socialist historians identified the unfulfilled potential of wartime radicalism for women and the working class. Sites of study included women's wartime participation in war work and in the armed forces, and the putative changes in gender relations and identities that followed from it.[5] Socialist attention also focused on popular desires and aspirations for social reconstruction that went beyond Labour's post-war reforms.[6] On the other hand, a right-wing critique claimed that wartime radicalism led the post-war Labour Government to sacrifice Britain's great-power status for an unsustainable and ultimately destructive programme of social and economic reform.[7] In any case, argued revisionist historians of the 1990s, contrary to the claims of historians of wartime radicalism there was little popular support for welfare reform and little sense of social solidarity in the 1940s.[8]

Simultaneously, in the 1980s and 1990s, a converse popular image gained ascendancy – the Second World War as a period of exemplary national solidarity. This image was invoked by both Right and Left during the Falklands–Malvinas War of 1982, when it was embedded in a nostalgic narrative in which the Second World War represented aggressive British patriotism successfully defending democracy.[9] Historians' critical responses to this construction focused on what were seen as over-emphasised claims of righteous nationalism and national unity. In *The Myth of the Blitz*, published in 1991, for example, Angus Calder exposed the counter-evidence of anti-social and divisive behaviours, and probed the ideological processes by which the myth (as he saw it) of national unity itself became a historical 'truth'.[10] Drawing on the work of Roland Barthes, Calder (and others) recognised that cultural media are vital for the construction of 'myths', such as that of national unity, communicated through symbolic forms, including language and images.[11] In Britain in the Second World War the 'imagined community'[12] of the nation at war had been powerfully portrayed in film, radio, newspapers and magazines. During the 1980s and 1990s, cinema historians analysed the class tensions in such representations,[13] while feminist cultural historians revealed profound tensions between gender and nation in competing models of femininity in cinematic and other cultural imaginings of wartime society.[14] In a recent social and cultural history, *Which People's War?*, Sonya Rose argues that wartime Britain was indeed dominated by 'heroic, populist and utopian constructions of national identity and citizenship'. However, she concludes, these powerful, unifying constructions were so fraught with the contradictions of region, race, gender and class that, far from unproblematically securing social stability, they stimulated contestation.[15]

In any event, as this brief historiographical sketch indicates, there is no danger of the Second World War dropping out of British history: as a number of historians have argued since the 1980s, it is far too salient to contemporary political and social understandings of Britain and the British.[16] Historical writing concerning the Second World War constitutes a 'field of force'[17] crackling with rival interpretations. And central to that lively historiography is the issue of what is included or excluded, centred or marginalised, remembered or forgotten.

The Home Guard has been referred to, albeit in passing, in the debates about the meaning of the Second World War reviewed above. Indeed, Angus Calder's two different treatments of it, in *The People's War* and in *The Myth of the Blitz*, illustrate the historiographical shift that took place between the late 1960s and the 1990s. In *The People's War* (1969) the Home Guard is characterised as 'a People's Army'. There are two central motifs in Calder's analysis: the disruptive effects of social class on the force; and the constraining effects of 'the authorities' on the potentially radical enthusiasm of its members. The former is summed up in the evidence of Home Guard camaraderie blighted by class bias in, for example, the selection of officers, which Calder uses to support George Orwell's assertion that the Home Guard was a 'People's Army officered by Blimps'. The latter is encapsulated in Calder's presentation of the members' liking for 'a "do-it-yourself" offensive spirit' and his claim that 'the authorities were not altogether intoxicated with the idea of arming the lower classes'.[18]

In *The Myth of the Blitz* (1991), in contrast, the focus is on the cultural processes by which the Home Guard was integrated into the 'myth' of wartime unity. Calder suggests that in literary representations during and after the war, the Home Guard symbolised the British mood of resistance and contributed a reassuring sense of historical continuity and social solidarity: 'Kipling's soldiers had joined the Home Guard, along with Hardy's Wessex villagers'; while in postwar literature the 'Heroic Commuter' turned out also to have donned 'the warden's tin helmet, the Home Guard's uniform'.[19] However, Calder implies that these images created a cover for a range of wartime dysfunctionalities in which the Home Guard was implicated, including Britain's lack of military preparedness and its imperialistic bombast. Calder hints at an unattractive role for the Home Guard, in contrast to the populist image: he cites allegations that it was used for socially divisive functions such as strike-breaking and presents evidence that, caught up in the spy paranoia of the summer of 1940, its members were responsible for unnecessary civilian deaths and injuries.[20]

Calder's two accounts of the Home Guard are not directly contradictory, but the approach of each is quite diifferent. In the first, evidence of lower-class enthusiasm and solidarity is counterposed to the socially differentiating effects of class dominance and state control. In the second, the cultural construction of the Home Guard as a repository of wartime popular enthusiasm and solidarity is critically scrutinised, and the resulting 'myth' is contrasted with evidence of disunity and dysfunctionality.

In spite of the relevance of the Home Guard to debates over the meaning of Britain at war, until now it has not been addressed as a case study of Britain's wartime social and cultural history in its own right. Specialist histories of the Home Guard have approached it from within the discursive terrain of political and military history. They have, for example, challenged the claims of political leaders that the Home Guard was militarily effective and important for morale. Thus in 1974 Norman Longmate argued that the utility of the Home Guard for defence was always questionable, and that by 1943 any military justification for it was a thing of the past, but that nevertheless 'the government was not prepared to stand it down and instead constantly tried to find for it some new strategic role'.[21] David Yelton, writing in 1994, underscored the place of the Home Guard in 'the myth of a unified Britain standing firm against Nazi aggression'. He suggested that the Home Guard was primarily a propaganda exercise, designed 'to reassure the British public and to give patriotic civilian men a sense that they were contributing to their country's defence', as well as to show the world, particularly the United States, that Britain would not surrender to Germany.[22] Drawing on the Ministry of

Information's Home Intelligence reports, Yelton argued that, paradoxically, the Home Guard's contribution to morale declined as its military contribution increased. Thus it had the most positive effects on morale from 1940 to 1941, when it was still inadequately armed and trained, but as it became more completely militarised and integrated into the regular army, and as the threat of invasion diminished, it lost its popular appeal.

In 1995 Paul MacKenzie explored, in greater depth than either Longmate or Yelton, 'the origins, nature and significance of the Home Guard as a military and a political phenomenon', and essentially reinforced their conclusions. He argued that the Home Guard was of little use in military terms, but was created and maintained purely for political reasons. MacKenzie claimed that this 'citizen army' was a 'strong political force', since its members had voting rights and so were able to 'pressure the government' into satisfying their demands. The result was that decisions about the Home Guard's role were determined less by the military authorities than by 'influential members of the Home Guard'.[23] A television documentary for which MacKenzie was an adviser and interlocutor, broadcast in Britain in the summer of 1998, elaborated on the expensive military mistakes made by the Home Guard, arguing that its military inefficiency posed a lethal danger to its own members, and that these problems undermined the justification for its existence.[24]

This book seeks to explore the history of the Home Guard not through the lens of politico-military history but from the perspective of the debate about the cultural meanings of the Second World War. Thus we make no attempt to settle questions such as whether the Home Guard would have been capable of repelling an invasion in the summer of 1940, or whether it was a danger either to the public or to itself. Instead, the book addresses the ways in which the Home Guard has been represented and remembered – in political discourse, in popular culture and in personal memory. We are concerned with public narratives of the war in general and the Home Guard in particular, and their relationship to personal understandings.

We avoid use of the term 'myth', however, because of two methodological pitfalls associated with it. The first is one of logic: it concerns the problem of contrasting 'myth' and 'reality'. Post-structuralists have pointed out that it is impossible to separate 'reality' from language and other cultural signifiers.[25] In other words, not only narrative accounts but also all other types of evidence of 'what actually happened' are inseparable from the cultural constructions within which they are articulated and understood. Accounts of 'reality' are themselves constructed, just as are 'myths'.

The second problem relates to the all-consuming tendency of 'myth'. Calder's argument is that 'the myth of the Blitz', and specifically the notion of a united war effort conducted by a people confident of victory, was not only produced by propaganda and by the rhetoric of the Coalition Government (although these were important) but was also spontaneous and emergent, and was as much subscribed to by the Left as by the Right.[26] He draws on both official pronouncements and the commentary of a fascinating range of journalists, broadcasters, literary authors, film-makers, photographers, diarists and other cultural producers to substantiate his argument. But the result tends to flatten an undulating cultural landscape: the tensions, contradictions and differences between the various official, popular and personal constructions of the meaning of the war are diminished because the focus of analysis is on the ways in which they all contributed to the building of 'the myth'. 'Myth', as so used, places unwelcome pressures on analysis of cultural meanings by reducing complex and contested representations to the same status.

Instead, we work with a less totalising understanding of the contribution of culture to popular understandings. Our approach is to see sources of evidence about the past, be they drawn from political rhetoric, official records, popular culture or personal testimony, as cultural repositories of historical meaning, in the sense that they all represent and interpret the phenomena they describe, often in conflicting ways. We analyse the interrelations – and the contradictions – between such sources, and hence the inclusions, exclusions, centering and marginalisation that have taken place in the making of the Home Guard's story. In what follows we explore the process by which dominant repesentations of the Home Guard have been, over time, created, challenged, adopted and modified. Our focus, in short, is the contested process of construction and reconstruction in the creation of the cultural meaning and popular memory of the Home Guard during the war and afterwards.

Wartime rhetoric

A strong story about the Home Guard was communicated through the wartime rhetoric that informed policy-making from the start. The urgency with which the creation of a history and an identity for the Home Guard was undertaken during 1939–45 might have been simply a product of the wartime situation. Wars are particularly intense historical moments, in which the sense of 'history being made' is strong, yet the meaning of events is far from clear. For public commitment to be sustained, wars need to be interpreted and thereby justified as they happen, and the meanings so generated must be communicated rapidly to a wide audience. There were, however, more specific pressures at work as far as the Home Guard in the Second World War was concerned. The idea of a Home Guard for Britain had been relatively late in arriving. The anticipated new feature of the Second World War was heavy aerial bombardment of civilian populations, and steps were taken to prepare for this as early as 1937, by establishing civil defence organisations run by the existing local authorities under the Air Raid Precautions Act passed in that year.[27] The threat of invasion had thus been regarded as much more remote than bombing, and in any case there was confidence among politicians and military planners in 1938 and 1939 that the Royal Navy and the Royal Air Force (RAF) would together be strong enough to repel both aerial attack and seaborne invasion.

During this period the War Office nevertheless considered creating some additional form of defence. From 1936 its policy included the formation of voluntary Home Defence Battalions, consisting of ex-servicemen capable of guarding vulnerable parts of Britain in the event of war. However, according to MacKenzie, these battalions 'existed on paper only': public funds were not spent on them and they never met or drilled.[28] In autumn 1939 the Cabinet revisited the issue. With the regular forces fighting abroad, Britain might need a resident force to defend against invasion. Such a force would have to be separate from and additional to other types of home defence such as Air Raid Precautions and the National Fire Service and anti-aircraft batteries, which had their own specific responsibilities – for protecting the civilian population during air raids, dealing with fires caused by attack and destroying enemy aircraft. The options included retaining part of the Regular Army, which was being expanded by conscription from summer 1939,[29] or using members of the Territorial Army Associations, a trained army reserve. There were objections to both: the Regular Army was expanding only slowly and the Territorials were valuable within it as a trained supplement to the newly conscripted 'raw recruits'. The alternative was to form something new.

In October 1939 Winston Churchill, as First Lord of the Admiralty, wrote to the Home Secretary: 'Why do we not form a Home Guard of half a million men over forty?' He envisaged a force of middle-aged men, 'many of whom served in the last war', which would free younger men for service away from home.[30] In the absence of a manifest threat of invasion nothing official was done between September 1939 and May 1940, although some private citizens organised their own defence forces.[31] The

Nazi occupation of Belgium and Holland in May 1940 transformed the situation. Churchill became Prime Minister and the voices of advocates of a national home defence force were heard, amid official concern about the 'anarchic' formation of bands of armed civilians.[32] As the Dutch Army surrendered to the Germans, Anthony Eden, the new Secretary of State for War, announced the formation of the LDV.

There followed a rush of official representations of the Home Guard as nothing short of a metaphor for Britain in wartime. They conjured a force, and thereby a nation, of loyal citizens inspired by patriotism and youthful enthusiasm (whatever their age), whose shared commitment to the practical task of home defence fuelled binding friendships between men of diverse backgrounds. They evoked an ancient nation that embraced political, social and regional diversity within a solid, purposeful and commonly held determination to protect shared territory and liberty. The claims, elisions and omissions in these constructions, and the challenges to them, are reviewed in Chapter 2. Here we focus briefly on the use made by Churchill, the leading wartime rhetorician in a strong field, of the symbolic potential of the word 'home' in the title 'Home Guard'.

Churchill was unhappy with the name given the new force in May: he thought 'Local Defence Volunteers' sounded too dry. He complained, 'The word "local" is uninspiring' because 'it is associated with local government and local option'.[33] In June 1940, against the opposition of Eden who, as Secretary of State for War, had coined the original title, Churchill insisted on the pithier name of 'Home Guard' that he had first suggested the previous autumn. On 23 July an official announcement in Parliament confirmed the change, even though the expense of replacing the armlets on which 'LDV' had been printed was said to be around £3,500.[34]

Churchill did not identify the source of his inspiration, although he and others wrote of alternatives he had rejected, including Herbert Morrison's suggestion of 'Civic Guard', which Churchill thought too evocative of the 'wild men in the French Revolution'.[35] The name Home Guard served his purposes well. While 'Guard' suggested reliability, security and military status, 'Home' claimed an even more extensive discursive territory. Antonia Lant has argued that the wartime use of the word 'Home' in naming ministries and services represented an attempt by the British Government, faced with the vulnerability of 'home', 'to ensure its continued existence'. She also observes that in every case of such naming, 'the word "home" is virtually interchangeable with the word "national"'.[36] Churchill was particularly adept at eliding 'home' and 'nation' for rhetorical purposes. In his much-quoted 'never surrender' speech of 4 June 1940, immediately after the evacuation of the remnants of the British Army from Dunkirk, he proclaimed: 'I have, myself, full confidence that ... we shall prove ourselves once again able to defend our Island home, to ride out the storm of war, and to outlive the menace of tyranny, if necessary for years, if necessary alone'.[37] 'Our Island home' was a phrase that came readily to Churchill's lips, as a historian of 'the English-speaking peoples'.[38] It was also familiar to the public, because of its use in popular patriotic songs: *Lords Of The Air*, in 1939, gave the Navy, the Army and the Air Force the common purpose of defending 'England our island home/ Land of the free'.[39]

This association of home and nation invested the tangible and affective qualities of home in the otherwise abstract concept of the nation. The concept of the 'nation–home' evoked a place that was comforting, that was the depository of values held dear and that was at the same time vulnerable. The name change on which Churchill insisted harnessed the Home Guard to this nexus: through it he established rhetorically the vital role of the Home Guard in the nation–home's defence. Furthermore, the image suggested by 'our island home' was of the coast delineating Britain, or more precisely the southern edge of England. It evoked the white cliffs of Dover and the green countryside stretching inland from them. 'Our island home' was evocative of a pastoral British identity that became a central motif in the representation of the wartime nation,[40] and that, as we shall see, was closely associated with the Home Guard.

The key occasion on which Churchill elaborated the elision between nation, home and Home Guard was not in the turbulent summer of 1940, but in May 1943, when he insisted that the third anniversary of the formation of the Home Guard should be celebrated to give public recognition to the Home Guard's contribution to defence.[41] Parades, church services and radio programmes were organised,[42] and an officially approved account of the force's first three years, *The Home Guard of Britain* by Charles Graves, was published.[43] Broadcasting on 14 May 1943, with (as so often) an American as well as a British audience in mind, Churchill spoke of the 'indispensable work done by the Home Guard' in its 'unfailing defence [of] our small island home'. He explained the proximity of Great Britain to the enemy and its position as 'the advanced fighting base of the United Nations', bearing the brunt of 'assault by air and sea'. His elaboration of the key features of the 'tense, organised, vibrant' war effort of the British nation–home culminated with: 'In this home there burns the light of freedom – guard it well, Home Guard!'[44]

The Home Guard, then, was rhetorically and culturally constructed by Churchill not only as a force that would defend localities against invasion, but also as a response to the vulnerability and value of 'home' and 'nation' in a total war. Yet, as we shall see in chapters 4 and 5, on representations of the Home Guard in cartoons, plays, films and fiction, 'home' was a complex and ambivalent symbol within the repertoire of wartime popular culture: it was what 'we' were fighting for, the emotional locus of human values. But homes were also key sites of tension: between generations and, above all, between genders. Such tensions were the longstanding critical and comic subjects of popular narratives, and the war provided new sources of conflict. Moreover, experience of home life in wartime was further disrupted not only by enemy bombing, which had destroyed and damaged 100,000 British homes by the beginning of 1943, with more to come,[45] but by the numerous requirements of the state. These included the installation of the blackout; restrictions on the use of bath-water; the rationing of food and clothing; the adoption of 'make-do-and-mend'; the erection of air-raid shelters inside the home or in the garden; the provision of billets for evacuees, war workers and soldiers, and so on. The war effort also had the effect of displacing a large proportion of the population from home, through the mobilisation of men for the armed forces and women for the women's auxiliary forces, and through the direction of workers of both genders into industrial, agricultural and other types of civilian war work. Those who remained at home spent a lot of time out of the house, whether working locally in industry or in civil defence, fire-watching at their place of work, or participating in wartime voluntary organisations.[46] The dangers threatening the home in wartime, coupled with the changes in consumption and production, work and leisure, meant that the pattern of home life was greatly altered. The idealised and emotionally compelling image of the harmonious home that symbolised the nation co-existed with the lived experience of disrupted and dysfunctional wartime homes, and with popular understandings that domestic bliss was by no means the norm.

Cultural history

The theoretical orientation of this book owes much to recent developments in cultural history, notably the insights into the malleability and contestation of historical narratives that have informed the 'cultural turn'. Also important are the concept of popular memory; the theory and method of oral history; the idea of the cultural circuit; and understandings of gender as a social and cultural construct. The cultural turn – that is, the move towards the study of language, semiotics, representations and meanings – has been helpfully defined as a 'concern with the conditions of communication, the terms of representation, the interaction between structures of meaning – narratives, discourses – and the ways in which individuals and groups use them and thus express themselves'.[47] This concern is now seen as legitimate terrain for historical work, and the idea that history is itself a discursive practice is also widely accepted. But historians nevertheless occupy a range of positions on the 'truth claims' that can be made concerning the past. Some reject the possibility that historians can 'tell it as it was' on the grounds that there can be no past that 'was', separate from the past that historians reconstruct.[48] But others are more confident that there were or are 'real' past experiences that can be apprehended. Miri Rubin, for example, insists: 'The cultural turn asks not … "How it really was" but rather "How was it for him, or her, or them?"'[49] To this end, cultural historians study the ways in which ideas and practices are circulated and reproduced through a variety of modes of communication, and they explore the changing cultural and material circumstances within which the agency and subjectivity of individuals are expressed. In particular, cultural historians are committed to the idea that history has social prominence because the meaning of past events matters. Such meanings are central to memory, both popular and personal, and without memory, societies, no less than individuals, have no sense of self: they lose their identity.[50] History-writing is caught up in the cultural processes which constantly subject memory to 'revision, amplification and "forgetting"'.[51] Particular ideas about the past are included and emphasised, others are excluded or at best marginalised; historical viewpoints gain or lose influence according to the contemporary social and political salience of the way the historian organises and interprets the past.

Particularly relevant to the study undertaken here is the process by which discourses or narratives gain ascendancy within popular memory, excluding or marginalising some aspects of experience while stressing others. Recovering what has been lost in this process not only restores omissions to the available picture of the past, but also destabilises that picture, by re-introducing elements that do not fit and by seeking to explain why they have been excluded. In the past twenty years, historians of class, race, women, sexuality and masculinity have demonstrated the possibilities and limitations of such challenges to popular memory.

We use the concept of 'popular memory' to express the idea that there is at any time within any social group a collective consciousness of the past, which is historically and spatially situated. Alternative terms to 'popular memory' include 'collective memory', 'social memory' and 'public memory'. Although they have different intellectual antecedents, these terms have in common the insistence that memory develops in a social framework within which a shared view of the past is generated. Maurice Halbwachs, a Durkheimian sociologist, sees 'collective memory' as an expression of the community of interests of a social group and hence as a unifying force within such groups. Individuals have their own distinctive capacity for memory, 'but individual memory is nevertheless a part or an aspect of group memory, since ... it is connected with the thoughts that come to us from the social milieu'.[52] The Birmingham Popular Memory Group uses 'popular' rather than 'collective memory'. Popular memory is seen as a product of contest: it has a reciprocal relationship with private or personal memory and is shaped by a variety of representations of the past that struggle for dominance in the public domain. Influenced by Gramsci, theorists of popular memory embrace more emphatically than users of 'collective' memory the notion that, in any society at any time, hegemonic claims are made about the view of the past that is collectively remembered.[53] The terms 'popular memory' and 'public memory' are sometimes used interchangeably, but the latter is more appropriately used to refer specifically to instances of commemoration and memorialisation that are conducted in the name of 'the public' in order to strengthen and support collective or popular memory.[54]

The concept 'collective memory' has had its detractors: for example Alon Confino, Felipe Fernandez-Armesto and Alessandro Portelli, who criticise its vagueness, lack of an associated methodology and abstraction from the individual.[55] We have chosen to use 'popular memory', because the theorists who employ it stress the notions of selectivity in the development of dominant versions of the past and of reciprocity between personal and collective memories; and also because the term is suggestive of close connections with popular culture. Our approach in this book is to emphasise popular culture as an important part of the social framework within which popular memory is generated and expressed. Our method is to seek to capture the contributions to structures of meaning not only of political processes but of specific cultural products, such as poetry, novels, cartoons, plays, films and television programmes, and to trace the relationship, defined by some theorists as the 'cultural circuit', between the discourses so generated and individual understandings of the personal and collective past.[56]

Oral history is one of the sources on which we draw throughout. In Chapter 3 we draw on it for information about aspects of the Home Guard which are unrecorded (or make only a marginal appearance) in official documentation. Such testimony is important for revealing what has been collectively forgotten. However, personal testimony is not simply a window on the past: it is a product of the interplay between personal memory and the repertoire of discursively available understandings through which memory is formed and expressed. Although oral history may be useful in revealing, and helping to fill, gaps in the public record, it is not possible to recover from it 'truths' which are wholly independent of culture. Memories are formed through a complex process of interaction between an individual's experiences and publicly available constructs, including prior accounts of similar experiences.[57]

The 'cultural circuit', referred to above, is a helpful theorisation of the relationship between experience and representation. Developed by Richard Johnson and Graham Dawson, it starts from the assumptions that public accounts not only draw on but transform personal stories, and that no personal account is innocent of such wider discourses.[58] But in turn, the accounts of their experience that narrators give to local and particular audiences become incorporated in public versions of the lives and cultures to which they relate, and achieve wider distribution, especially through modern media technology. *Dad's Army*, a compelling interpretation of the Home Guard composed in part from accounts based on personal memory, is a case in point. The production of such powerful representations, according to Dawson, creates 'a tradition of recognizable public forms that tends both to define and to limit imaginative possibilities'.[59] Personal accounts cannot escape such dominant public representations, but must relate to and negotiate them. This does not preclude the possibility of resistance, for, as the Popular Memory Group argues, 'dominant memory is produced in the course of ... struggles and is always open to contestation'.[60] But, so the theory goes, just as it is impossible for public representations to be completely divorced from the experience of individuals, so it is impossible for such representations to be ignored in the formation and articulation of personal narratives.

Memory is central to our work. So, too, is gender. Differentiation between male and female, masculine and feminine, is arguably the most profound divide in the cultural construction of identity and in the operation of social relations. As Alice Kessler-Harris writes, 'Whether it is constructed through language and discourse, the invention and deployment of symbol systems, or social and cultural positioning, the "self" that participates in forming the world around us is gendered.'[61] Popular memory is saturated with gendered interpretations and under-standings, which individual subjectivities cannot ignore and with which they are intimately linked. Furthermore, gender identities, relations and meanings are destabilised by war. This was particularly true of the 'total' wars of the twentieth century, in which attacks on civilian populations blurred the distinction between the territory known as the 'battle front' and the spaces 'behind the lines', including the 'home front'. Govern-ments that engaged in 'mobilising' to produce a 'war effort' – that is, in organising society to wage such wars and to defend against their effects – were inevitably confronted by the problem of gender.[62] The culturally constructed gender divide in pre-war Britain associated masculinity with public life, military service and physically or intellectually demanding work; femininity was allied to domesticity and to varieties of work and public life that could be deemed compatible with it. Mobilisation for war exposed the inconsistencies in such inherently contingent conventions.[63] The war effort required, and patriotism justified, the replacement of men by women in a range of industrial, agricultural and clerical work on the home front. Could women not also join men in military activities? The British Government in both world wars indeed found it necessary to use women as 'auxiliaries', supporting the male armed forces with a range of medical, clerical and technical services: developments that brought women very close to armed involvement in waging war. But the possibility that women might have a genuinely combatant role was hotly contested, notably in the context of home defence.[64]

The meaning of masculinity as well as femininity was plunged into uncertainty by total war. Peacetime ideals of manhood coalesced and elided in wartime into ideal types: the 'soldier hero' in the First World War; the fighter pilot in the Second.[65] But if the military man was the ideal, the status of the male civilian in wartime was thereby rendered uncertain, especially if he was of military age. His insecurities have been documented by several historians in relation to the wars of the twentieth century. Nicoletta Gullace suggests that in the First World War 'the signs of manhood relied on that external emblem of courage – the military uniform', something which the male civilian conspicuously lacked. Similarly, Sonya Rose argues that the 'successful enactment' of 'hegemonic masculinity' in the Second World War 'depended on being visibly a member of the fighting forces'.[66]

This study views home defence in Britain in the Second World War as one of the sites on which these gender instabilities were most visibly played out. The idea that men should fight, and that women should entrust themselves and their children to men's protection, was both robustly upheld and vigorously challenged in the context of home defence. Men's status as soldiers in the Home Guard was far from secure: they wore military uniforms and were part of an armed organisation with military objectives, but they were also civilians who had been debarred from the regular forces by reason of age, fitness or occupation, and they performed their military duties only on a part-time basis. Women, on the other hand, were moving across the civilian–military divide in Britain in the Second World War. They were subject to government direction into war work from April 1941 and (if they were aged 19–31 and single) to conscription from December 1941. Women's war work options included service in the auxiliary forces, for which they wore military uniform full-time and were required to undertake military training, albeit not for combatant roles. Although there was much continuity of gendered work allocation, jobs were available in and out of the military that were novel for women and that challenged traditional assumptions. Both the militarised feminine identities of women in war service and the insecure masculine identities of civilian men had the potential to disturb gender relations and were, in consequence, sensitive issues, as the struggles over the membership and functions of the Home Guard indicate. Gender identities and relationships were also, as we show, central to the ways in which home defence was recalled in personal testimony and in popular memory concerning the Second World War.

Structure, methods and sources

This book is organised in three sections, relating to the three critical strategies that inform the research. The two chapters in Part I address political challenges to the official version of the social and ideological character of the Home Guard. Chapter 2 addresses tensions over the social and political composition and the ideological inspiration of the Home Guard, and their relationship both to the military functions of the force and to its masculine identity. Suspected social and political selectivity was challenged, as was the suggestion that the role of the Home Guard should be limited to that of static guards. Critics on the Left, such as Tom Wintringham, viewed the Home Guard through the lens of an alternative military and political inspiration, quite different from the conservative nationalism that inspired its originators, even though both sides spoke of it as a 'people's army'. The vision of the force fostered on the Left represented a profoundly different approach to the meaning of the war, the war effort and the post-war world from that of Churchill and other political and military leaders.

The history of the contest over the character, composition and functions of the Home Guard is found in a number of official and non-official sources, including the minutes and memoranda of the surviving War Office files in the National Archives (formerly the Public Record Office), Hansard (the record of parliamentary debates) and the press. Instructions addressed to Home Guard commanders (often marked 'Not to Be Published') provide guidance on the official view of the military functions of the Home Guard, while the writing of those who challenged this view, published in newspapers, magazines, books and pamphlets, delineates alternative interpretations.

Official representations of the Home Guard ignored not only the challenge from the Left, but also a major initiative on the part of women to join its ranks, which is explored in Chapter 3. The denial of a place to women was both rhetorical and practical. There was vigorous protest about this formal exclusion, and women, led by Labour MP Dr Edith Summer-skill, asserted their agency through their own home-defence organisation, as well as eliciting support in unexpected places. Until now, historians of the Home Guard have been dismissive of this aspect of Home Guard history, regarding women's aspirations to a combatant role in the Home Guard as ridiculous and overstated.[67] But both the social and political selectivity discussed in Chapter 2 and the exclusion of women explored in Chapter 3 exposed cracks in the rhetorical claim that the Home Guard was emblematic of Britain at war. They reveal the partiality of the wartime rhetoric of inclusiveness, and suggest that the idea of the nation–home united against the threat of an invasion was itself deeply fractured.

The political contest over women's membership of the Home Guard is a history that can only be partly unearthed in the press, in official files and in Hansard. The gaps and silences in the official record are revealed by other types of archive, including personal diaries and memoirs, oral histories, and 'finds' such as papers, photographs and material objects, including badges and certificates, in individuals' personal possession as well as in libraries and museums. We use all of these in reconstructing the hidden history of women's involvement in British home defence.

Part II explores cultural representations of the Home Guard during and after the war. Official accounts, in posters, films and radio broadcasts, for example, had explicit aims: to inform, aid recruitment, raise morale, and counter views officially regarded as impeding the war effort. Many unofficial versions took up the government's message about home defence and, like it, they were selective in their representation of Home Guard experience. Others offered more challenging accounts, that were sometimes serious and very often comic. Chapters 4 and 5 explore the meanings with which the Home Guard was endowed by poets, playwrights, film-makers, broadcasters, fiction writers, cartoonists and comic-sketch writers during the war. The questions we raise include how far accounts that contested the official version were compatible with support for the overall political project of the Home Guard, and how far these popular representations of the Home Guard challenged the project and with it the notion of national unity. We also explore the ways in which constructions of Home Guard identity played on gender insecurities. Chapter 4 investigates the tension in popular culture between the affectionate exploration in representations of the Home Guard of the contradictions within (male) wartime national unity and satirical treatment that represented the Home Guard as an emasculated enterprise and a symbol of everything that was wrong with Britain at war.

In the various types of popular culture discussed in Chapter 4, the Home Guard and the British national character with which it was associated were represented as male. Chapter 5 discusses the guises in which women appeared in representations of home defence. We seek to penetrate the almost complete silence concerning women's participation in the Home Guard, and we show that the depiction of women's roles in relation to home defence, whether in serious propaganda, feature films or fiction, is not as simple as one might expect. We also explore the commentaries put into the mouths of women in humorous accounts of the Home Guard. Were these women's voices intended to recuperate masculine vulnerability and soldierly status or to add to critiques of the Home Guard and the British war effort?

The form and content of the popular representations of the Home Guard that we explore in Chapters 4 and 5 are varied. Each genre has its own conventions although they sometimes work together. Newspaper and magazine cartoons, whether they communicate political opinion or social commentary, express their messages primarily visually, but often with text that underlines the point;[68] word sketches and comic rhymes are short and pithy, telling stories that lead to a punchline and are sometimes supplemented by drawings. Plays, novels, thrillers and films are longer and more complex, communicating a number of messages, in some cases comic and in others serious. Chapters 4 and 5 scrutinise the contribution of different genres to the meaning of the Home Guard as well as analysing those meanings in their own right.

Chapter 6 turns from wartime to later cultural accounts. It explores the continuities and discontinuities in post-war representations of the Home Guard, in particular its reappearance in popular culture in the late 1960s in the BBC television series *Dad's Army*, first broadcast from 1968 to 1977. *Dad's Army* established itself as the dominant popular account of the Home Guard in the late twentieth century and thus has a crucial place in the history of the popular narrative of British home defence in the Second World War. We investigate the operation of the cultural circuit in its development: we analyse its relationship to wartime comic accounts of the Home Guard and also to pre-war non-military comedies and post-war military ones; and we explore the use of personal memory in the making of the series. Finally, we again address the question of satire: to what extent does *Dad's Army* support and celebrate the Home Guard and the British war effort, and to what extent, if any, does it undermine it?

Part III, containing Chapters 7 and 8, explores another stage in the cultural circuit: it scrutinises personal memories of wartime participation in home defence, and their relationship to cultural constructions of the Home Guard, including the *Dad's Army* representation. We draw on oral-history interviews, correspondence and questionnaire responses that we collected between 1998 and 2001, other interviews dating from the 1980s and 1990s that are archived in the Imperial War Museum, and also a variety of written testimony. Chapter 7 explores the relationship of men's memories to popular narratives of the Home Guard in official rhetoric and popular culture. It discusses the 'take-up', by men recalling their wartime experiences of home defence, of the notions of national unity and patriotism, and the incidence in such personal accounts of scepticism about whether the ideals of the people's war were really achieved within the Home Guard. Chapter 8 explores women's revelations of recruitment to and service within the Home Guard. We seek to understand, sympathetically, the misremembering and uncertainty that characterised such accounts, and to highlight the importance, for the expression of personal testimony, of public accounts that offer a framework within which to place memory. The *Dad's Army* construction was a benchmark that could not be avoided by either men or women. We discuss in both chapters the extent to which *Dad's Army* can be said to constitute a dominant discourse that limited imaginative possibilities, and how far it is possible for those remembering the Home Guard to contest the *Dad's Army* version of Home Guard history.

All but one of the men interviewed denied even the possibility that women could have been members of the Home Guard. As we argue, this is indicative of the silencing of a forgotten story of women's participation. But the history of men's involvement is not simple either, and throughout the book we challenge the ways in which it has been represented in the long-running and multifaceted processes of construction and reconstruction that contribute to the formation of popular memory. In particular we draw attention to the disappearance of the Home Guard's radical elements from public representations. Nevertheless, and in contrast to the case of women's membership, there is a recognised history of the male Home Guard and its place in the Second World War, which has been relayed through numerous cultural and historical treatments. There is, in short, a Home Guard legend available to men who recall their experiences of the Home Guard: women are simply not part of the legend. The re-insertion of women in this history challenges not only deeply held cultural norms according to which, until very recently, women have had no place in combat, but also the dominant *Dad's Army* image of the Home Guard as a collection of bumbling, if well-intentioned, male amateurs.

This book explores the circuit between political discourses, cultural products and personal recollections. It traces the complex ways in which the wartime destabilisation of gender articulates with the memory of the Home Guard. It contests the history of home defence in the Second World War by scrutinising that which has been revised and amplified, and seeking to recover that which has been forgotten. In so doing, it joins the historiographical 'field of force' concerning the dominant narrative and the popular memory of Britain in the Second World War.

Notes

1 Examples of recent work on these themes include, on the Blitz and the home front: J. R. Freedman, *Whistling in the Dark: Memory and Culture in Wartime London* (Kentucky: University Press of Kentucky, 1999); J. Hinton, *Women, Social Leadership and the Second World War* (Oxford: Oxford University Press, 2002); C. M. Peniston-Bird, *Blitz: A Pictorial History of Britain Under Attack* (London: Caxton Editions, 2001); S. Rose, *Which People's War? National Identity and Citizenship in Wartime Britain 1939–1945* (Oxford: Oxford University Press, 2003); P. Summerfield, *Reconstructing Women's Wartime Lives: Discourse and Subjectivity in Oral Histories of the Second World War* (Manchester: Manchester University Press, 1998); on military organisation: J. Crang, *The British Army and the People's War 1939–1945* (Manchester: University of Manchester Press, 2000); D. French, *Raising Churchill's Army: The British Army and the War Against Germany 1919–1945* (Oxford: Oxford

University Press, 2000); on military campaigns: A. Beevor, *Berlin: The Downfall, 1945* (Harmondsworth: Penguin, 2003); M. Hastings, *Armageddon: The Battle for Germany 1944–45* (London: Macmillan, 2004); R. Overy, *The Battle of Britain* (Harmondsworth: Penguin, 2004).

2 G. Eley, 'Finding the People's War: Film, British Collective Memory and World War II', Forum, *American Historical Review*, 106 (2001), p. 821.

3 A. Calder, *The People's War: Britain 1939–1945* (London: Cape, 1969, 2000).

4 P. Addison, *The Road to 1945: British Politics and the Second World War* (London: Cape, 1975); I. McLaine, *Ministry of Morale: Home Front Morale and the Ministry of Information in World War II* (London: George Allen & Unwin, 1979); P. Summerfield, 'Education and Politics in the British Armed Forces in the Second World War', *International Review of Social History*, 26:2 (1981), pp. 133–158; R. Croucher, *Engineers at War* (London: Merlin, 1982).

5 P. Summerfield, *Women Workers in the Second World War: Production and Patriarchy in Conflict* (London: Croom Helm, 1984; Routledge, 1989); D. Riley, *War in the Nursery: Theories of the Child and Mother* (London: Virago, 1983); E. Wilson, *Only Halfway to Paradise: Women in Postwar Britain 1945–1968* (London: Tavistock, 1980); G. Braybon and P. Summerfield, *Out of the Cage: Women's Experiences in Two World Wars* (London: Pandora, 1987).

6 J. Hinton, 'Coventry Communism: A Study of Factory Politics in the Second World War', *History Workshop Journal*, 10 (1980), pp. 90–118; J. Hinton, 'Self-Help and Socialism: The Squatters' Movement of 1946', *History Workshop Journal*, 25 (1988), pp. 100–126.

7 C. Barnett, *The Audit of War* (London: Macmillan, 1986).

8 R. Lowe, 'The Second World War, Consensus and the Foundation of the Welfare State' *Twentieth-Century British History*, 1 (1990), p. 175. See also S. Fielding, P. Thompson and N. Tiratsoo, *'England Arise!' The Labour Party and Popular Politics in 1940s Britain* (Manchester: Manchester University Press, 1995); I. Zweiniger-Bargielowska, *Austerity in Britain: Rationing, Controls and Consumption 1939–1955* (Oxford: Oxford University Press, 2000); R. Mackay, *Half the Battle: Civilian Morale in Britain during the Second World War* (Manchester: Manchester University Press, 2002).

9 Eley, 'Finding the People's War', pp. 820–823. See also R. Bromley, *Lost Narratives: Popular Fictions, Politics and Recent History* (London: Routledge, 1988), Introduction; L. Noakes, *War and the British: Gender, Memory and National Identity* (London: I. B. Tauris, 1998), pp. 108–120; K. Foster, *Fighting Fictions: War, Narrative and National Identity* (London: Pluto Press, 1999).

10 A. Calder, *The Myth of the Blitz* (London: Cape, 1991).

11 R. Barthes, *Mythologies* (London: Paladin, 1973), especially pp. 117–138.

12 B. Anderson, *Imagined Communities: Reflections on the Origin and Spread of Nationalism* (London: Verso, 1991).

13 A. Aldgate and J. Richards, *Britain Can Take It: British Cinema in the Second World War* (Edinburgh: Edinburgh University Press, 1994 [1986]); J. Richards, *Films and British National Identity: From Dickens to 'Dad's Army'* (Manchester:

Manchester University Press, 1997); A. Aldgate and J. Richards, *Best of British: Cinema and Society from 1930 to the Present* (London: I. B. Tauris, 1999); J. Chapman, *The British at War: Cinema, State and Propaganda, 1939–1945* (London: I. B. Tauris, 1998).

14 A. Lant, *Blackout: Reinventing Women for Wartime British Cinema* (Princeton: Princeton University Press, 1991); C. Gledhill and G. Swanson (eds), *Nationalising Femininity: Culture, Sexuality and British Cinema in the Second World War* (Manchester: Manchester University Press, 1996).

15 Rose, *Which People's War?*, pp. 25, 293.

16 Bromley, *Lost Narratives*; Noakes, *War and the British*; R. Weight, *Patriots: National Identity in Britain 1940–2000* (London: Pan Books, 2003).

17 K. Jenkins, *Rethinking History* (London: Routledge, 1991), p. 1, n. 1.

18 Calder, *People's War*, pp. 124, 127, 125; see also pp. 343–344.

19 Calder, *Myth of the Blitz*, pp. 181, 173; Calder's reference to wartime evocations of Kipling and Hardy characters is non-specific; that to the 'Heroic Commuter' relates to R. F. Delderfield's *The Avenue at War* (first published London: Hodder & Stoughton, 1958).

20 Calder, *Myth of the Blitz*, pp. 29, 54, 69–70, 109.

21 N. Longmate, *The Real Dad's Army: The Story of the Home Guard* (London: Arrow Books, 1974), pp. 96–98.

22 D. K. Yelton, 'British Public Opinion, the Home Guard, and the Defense of Great Britain 1940–1944', *Journal of Military History*, 58 (July 1994), p. 462.

23 S. P. MacKenzie, *The Home Guard. A Military and Political History* (Oxford: Oxford University Press, 1995), pp. 3–4.

24 *Secret History: Dad's Army*, Channel 4, June 1998.

25 See J. W. Scott, 'Experience', in J. Butler and J. W. Scott (eds), *Feminists Theorize the Political* (London: Routledge, 1992), pp. 31–34.

26 Calder, *Myth of the Blitz*, e.g. pp. 14–15, 125, 179; see also B. Schwarz, Review of Angus Calder, *The Myth of the Blitz*, *History Workshop*, 33 (1992), pp. 281–283.

27 Peniston-Bird, *Blitz*, p. 134.

28 MacKenzie, *Home Guard*, pp. 16–17.

29 The Military Training Act, May 1939, introduced conscription for men aged 20 and 21; the National Service (Armed Forces) Act, 2 September 1939, made all men 18–41 liable for conscription; the National Service (No. 2) Act, 18 December 1941, extended the upper age-limit to 51: Ministry of Labour and National Service, *Report for the Years 1939–1946*, Cmd. 7225 (London: HMSO, 1947), pp. 8–9.

30 W. S. Churchill, *The Second World War*, vol. 1: *The Gathering Storm* (London: Cassell, 1948), First Lord to Home Secretary, 7 October 1939, p. 384.

31 See MacKenzie, *Home Guard*, p. 19; and C. Graves, *The Home Guard of Britain* (London: Hutchinson, 1943), p. 15.

32 B. Collier, *The Defence of the United Kingdom* (London: HMSO, 1957), pp. 103,106; MacKenzie, 'The Real *Dad's Army*', pp. 51–52.

33 W. S. Churchill, *The Second World War*, vol. 2: *Their Finest Hour* (London: Cassell, 1949) p. 148.

34 Hansard, vol. 363, col. 576, 23 July 1940 (name change); vol. 364, col. 224, 7 August, 1940 (cost of armbands).

35 Churchill, *Second World War*, vol. 2, p. 148; H. Morrison, *Herbert Morrison: An Autobiography* (London: Odhams Press, 1960), p. 185.

36 Lant, *Blackout*, p. 44.

37 W. S. Churchill, *Winston S. Churchill: His Complete Speeches 1897–1963*, vol. 6: *1935–1942*, ed. R. Rhodes James (London: Chelsea House, 1974), pp. 6230–6231.

38 R. Jenkins, *Churchill* (London: Pan, 2002), p. 448.

39 M. Leitch (ed.), *Great Songs of World War II* (London: Wise Publications, n.d. [1975]), p. 105.

40 S. Featherstone, 'The Nation as Pastoral in British Literature of the Second World War', *Journal of European Studies*, 16:3 (1986), pp. 155–168.

41 W. S. Churchill, *Second World War*, vol. 4: *The Hinge of Fate* (London: Cassell, 1951), p. 840.

42 BBC, Written Archives Centre (BBC, WAC), R51/231, Talks: HG 1940–44, correspondence 17 and 23 March 1943.

43 Graves, *Home Guard*. In spite of giving Graves permission to write to Commanding Officers for information, the War Office censored some of the material, including an account of internal controversy about the formation of the force: Imperial War Museum, Documents Department (IWM, DD), 77/165/1 Brigadier W. Carden Roe.

44 Churchill, *Complete Speeches*, vol. 7: *1943–1949*, p. 6772.

45 Calder, *People's War*, p. 316.

46 Summerfield, *Women Workers*, Chapter 2; Calder, *People's War*, p. 207; Central Statistical Office, *Fighting with Figures: A Statistical Digest of the Second World War* (London: HMSO, 1995).

47 M. Rubin, 'What Is Cultural History Now?' in D. Cannadine (ed.), *What Is History Now?* (Basingstoke: Palgrave Macmillan, 2004), p. 81.

48 H. White, *Tropics of Discourse: Essays in Cultural Criticism* (Baltimore: Johns Hopkins University Press, 1978); Jenkins, *Rethinking*.

49 Rubin, 'What Is Cultural History Now?', p. 81.

50 D. Lowenthal, *The Past Is a Foreign Country* (Cambridge: Cambridge University Press, 1985), pp. 197–198.

51 Bromley, *Lost Narratives*, p. 1.

52 M. Halbwachs, *On Collective Memory* (Chicago: University of Chicago Press, 1992), p. 53.

53 Popular Memory Group, 'Popular Memory: Theory, Politics, Method', in Centre for Contemporary Cultural Studies, *Making Histories: Studies in History-Writing and Politics* (London: Hutchinson, 1982); Noakes, *War and the British*, pp. 11–14.

54 See L. Coser, Introduction to Halbwachs, *On Collective Memory*, p. 25.

55 A. Confino, 'Collective Memory and Cultural History: Problems of Method', *American Historical Review*, 102:5 (1997), pp. 1386–1403; F. Fernandez-Armesto, 'Epilogue: What Is History *Now*?', in Cannadine (ed.), *What Is History Now?*, pp. 155–156; A. Portelli, *The Battle of Valle Giulia: Oral History and the Art of Dialogue* (Madison: University of Wisconsin Press, 1997), p. 57.

56 Historical work that adopts this approach includes Noakes, *War and the British*; Summerfield, *Reconstructing*; A. Thomson, *Anzac Memories: Living with the Legend* (Oxford: Oxford University Press Australia, 1994).

57 P. Summerfield, 'Culture and Composure: Creating Narratives of the Gendered Self in Oral History Interviews', *Cultural and Social History*, 1 (2004), pp. 65–93.

58 G. Dawson, *Soldier Heroes: British Adventure, Empire and the Imagining of Masculinities* (London: Routledge, 1994), pp. 22–26; R. Johnson, 'The Story So Far and Other Transformations' in D. Punter (ed.), *Introduction to Contemporary Cultural Studies* (Harlow: Longman, 1986).

59 Dawson, *Soldier Heroes*, p. 25.

60 Popular Memory Group, 'Popular Memory', p. 207.

61 A. Kessler-Harris, 'What Is Gender History Now?', in Cannadine (ed.), *What Is History Now?*, p. 100.

62 M. R. Higonnet, J. Jenson, S. Michel and M. C. Weitz (eds), *Behind the Lines: Gender and the Two World Wars* (Yale: Yale University Press, 1987).

63 P. Summerfield, '"My Dress for an Army Uniform": Gender Instabilities in the Two World Wars', Lancaster University, Inaugural Lecture Series (1997).

64 D'Ann Campbell, 'Women in Combat: the World War Two experience in the United States, Great Britain, Germany and the Soviet Union' (1993), in G. Martel (ed.), *The World War Two Reader* (London: Routledge, 2004), pp. 250–269; G. J. DeGroot, 'I Love the Scent of Cordite in Your Hair', *History*, 82:265 (1997), pp. 73–92; G. J. DeGroot, 'Whose Finger on the Trigger? Mixed Anti-Aircraft Batteries and the Female Combat Taboo', *War in History*, 4:4 (1997), pp. 434–453.

65 P. Fussell, *The Great War and Modern Memory* (Oxford: Oxford University Press, 1975); P. Addison and J. A. Crang, *The Burning Blue: A New History of the Battle of Britain* (London: Pimlico, 2000).

66 N. Gullace, 'White Feathers and Wounded Men: Female Patriotism and the Memory of the Great War', *Journal of British Studies* 36:2 (1997), p. 199; Rose, *Which People's War?*, p. 153.

67 Longmate, *The Real Dad's Army*, p. 115: 'Even before the LDV had been set up, a few women had clamoured to be enrolled in an armed force', but (he alleges) few came forward when permitted in 1943, and 'the Home Guard remained, for all practical purposes, an all-male organisation'. MacKenzie, *Home Guard*: 'problems remained' in 1943, one of which was women (pp. 83–84); women were a 'lingering issue' (pp. 125–129), on which Summerskill 'was trying to force the government's hand' (pp. 126–127); and by March 1944, recruitment of women 'was yielding results far below expectation' (p. 147).

PART I

Political challenges

2

The People's Army: competing visions of the Home Guard

The announcement of the formation of the LDV by Anthony Eden, Secretary of State for War, in a BBC radio broadcast on 14 May 1940, attracted a quarter of a million volunteers within a week.[1] This was astonishing, especially in view of the lack of interest in their antecedents, the Home Defence Battalions. The main reason for the change was the escalation of the threat of invasion in the context of the German occupation of Belgium, Holland and France in May to June 1940. But in the absence of prior planning many aspects of the force were unclear. Decisions about who was eligible to join, what military functions they should fulfill and what equipment they could be supplied with were made during the weeks and months following the first surge of volunteers. The lack of an agreed policy meant that the social, military and political characteristics of the new force, and the tradition to which it belonged, were invented hurriedly – and that there were rival versions. Members of the Government made grand rhetorical claims about the Home Guard's symbolism for Britain in total war. These claims were contested by those suspicious that recruitment was selective, as well as by critics of the official account of the ideological character and military purpose of the force. The Home Guard was at once a major new departure as a military organisation and a lively site of wartime controversy.

Home defence and national unity

Eden's broadcast was a remarkable media event. His public statement was transmitted at a time of high tension, and it established in a few dry sentences the intended tone and character of the new force. Eden described how the Germans had dropped troops by parachute in Belgium and Holland to prepare the way for invasion. He claimed that there were 'countless' men aged 17–65 in Britain who were not in military service but who wanted to help to defend their country against such an invasion: now was their opportunity. He invited them to enroll at their local police stations as LDVs, in which capacity they would augment the 'defence already arranged' in order to 'make assurance doubly sure'.[2] By the end of July 1.5 million men were said to have come forward,[3] suggesting that the formation of the force resonated strongly with prevailing values and attitudes. The result also demonstrated the power of the mass media in wartime: the radio carried the message to a listening public of as many as 36 million people out of a British population of 48 million.[4]

In part because there was no blueprint and in part because the new defence force became symbolic of much more than itself, the story of the Home Guard was told by politicians with particular creativity and *élan*, as well as much use of seventeenth-century English.[5] There were two principal themes: the military value of the force and its status as an expression of national identity.

Wartime accounts of the Home Guard emphasised that the force filled the gap left by soldiers fighting abroad, an issue that took on new meaning after the evacuation from Dunkirk in June 1940. Churchill suggested in late June that the Home Guard formed a 'crust' over the parts of the country that were vulnerable to invasion,[6] and throughout the war he talked up its determination and capacity: it 'would devour an invading army'; it would 'take a lot of killing'; its spirit was 'conquer or die' and its watchwords were 'you can always take one with you'.[7] The importance of the force as a vital 'line of defence' – first, second or last – was much emphasised.[8]

Numerous public accounts elided the emblematic identity of the Home Guard as a counter-invasion force with the British character. Eden's original radio announcement emphasised the inclusivity of the force: the 'countless' men who wanted to help to defend their country and who could now volunteer to do so. Although Eden did not prioritise the recruitment of veterans of previous conflicts, he said they should have 'a knowledge of firearms', and Churchill, in an unsuccessful bid to form a home guard in October 1939, had identified ex-servicemen as a suitable core for home defence.[9] The significance of the emphasis on veterans was twofold: it invested rhetorical value in a socially mixed group of older men who could be expected to be both patriotic and keen to volunteer; and it emphasised to the public the presence in Britain of men with military experience, who were not in the regular forces but were capable of providing effective protection. The themes of patriotism, voluntarism, social unity and Britishness embodied by the idealised ex-serviceman were generalised to the Home Guard as a whole.

This was nowhere more strongly accomplished than in a speech in the House of Commons by Sir Edward Grigg, Under-Secretary for War, in November 1940.[10] With a rhetorical flourish that was impressive even by the standards of the time, he extended the idea of the inclusivity of the organisation and emphasised the voluntary spirit which had led to its rapid growth, while maintaining the emphasis on older men as its core. Furthermore, in describing the Home Guard, he enunciated a clearly defined and historically rooted notion of British national identity. He said that 'men of all ages in all parts of the country were eating their hearts out' to serve in a military capacity, and that the Home Guard gave this vast mixed community of 'all sorts and conditions of patriotic men'[11] such an opportunity. Although he referred to 'men of all ages', he implicitly reinforced Churchill's vision of a force of older men by suggesting that they possessed the 'gift of eternal youth'. They belonged to a British tradition of readiness to defend their country. Their forebears were the Fencibles, a militia first formed in the days of the Armada to defend home soil, and the Yeomanry, a volunteer, part-time, cavalry force for local defence; both had been mobilised in the 1790s against the threat of invasion by Napoleon. The patron saints of England, Scotland and Wales, as well as St Crispin, the saint associated in Shakespeare's *Henry V* with the Battle of Agincourt and the unmanliness of English gentlemen 'a-bed' on that day, were marching in the Home Guard's 'democratic ranks'. The Home Guard, according to Grigg, was 'Britain incarnate, an epitome of British character in its gift for comradeship in trouble, its resourcefulness at need, its deep love of its own land, and its surging anger at the thought that any invader should set foot on our soil'.[12]

Sir Edward Grigg's speech offered a stirring portrayal of the Home Guard as the essence of national identity. Its omissions, however, should not be overlooked. Firstly, it was unashamedly nationalist: the contest evoked was a British one, to protect the home turf in the traditional way against a foreign threat, rather than an international struggle against a modern totalitarian power. An alternative inspiration for the Home Guard lay in an understanding of the Second World War as a global conflict: against fascism and for the achievement of a more socially just world thereafter. Secondly, Grigg's evocation of the unity embodied by the Home Guard concealed divisions. The implication that it was a force of older men ignored the roles within it of young and middle-aged men, and the apparently socially encompassing phrase 'all sorts and conditions of men' denied women a place in the force. Chapter 3 demonstrates this exclusion to have been unacceptable to numerous British women.

Thirdly, although political inclusivity was suggested by the term 'British' (rather than 'English'), Grigg's saintly roll-call did not include St Patrick, the patron saint of Ireland. Full Irish independence from Britain was very recent: Eire, which had become a sovereign state in 1937, maintained its neutrality in the Second World War, while the six counties of Northern Ireland remained part of the United Kingdom and the British war effort.[13] By omitting St Patrick, Sir Edward Grigg dodged the problem of evoking the neutrality (and potential treachery) of Eire, but eclipsed the British population of Northern Ireland from his delineation of the nation.

Sir Edward Grigg's account was echoed although never quite matched. Sir James Grigg depicted the Home Guard as a symbol of wartime male solidarity when, in 1944, he described it as 'an outward and visible sign of an inward unity and brotherhood, without distinction of class or calling' and suggested that this unity would be 'carried forward into the future ... to rebuild our national life'.[14] George VI remembered the Irish in December 1944, while reproducing the construction of the Home Guard as an all-male organisation. He wove into his speech the need for a 'citizen force to help in the defence of the homeland' and evoked the enthusiasm of 'men of every age and every calling' 'throughout Britain and Northern Ireland' to form this force to defend freedom, referring to its 'voluntary spirit', its 'comradeship of arms' and its proof of the capacity of 'men from all kinds of homes and many different occupations' to co-operate happily.[15]

Such rhetoric threw a veil over political and social divisions: its purpose was to construct the Home Guard as inclusive and democratic, a symbol of national unity. The initial response to the call for recruits suggested that there was enthusiastic popular take-up of this discourse, indeed that the Home Guard was understood to be even more all-embracing than was officially proclaimed. According to Eden's broadcast, recruits were supposed to be men, British subjects, aged seventeen to sixty-five, 'of reasonable physical fitness' and to have 'a knowledge of firearms'.[16] But those who flocked to volunteer included women, foreign nationals, men who were older and younger than the age limits, and those who were unfit and had never used firearms. Some of each of these groups were accepted, alongside men who conformed to the proclaimed speci-fications, but others were rejected. We explore the special position of women in the next chapter. The focus here is on the vociferous challenges that arose from the uneven application of membership qualifications to other groups, in the face of expectations that the Home Guard should be democratic and all-inclusive.

Contested recruitment

Eden invited men aged 17–65 to join the LDV, even though the National Service (Armed Forces) Act, passed on 2 September 1939, had established in law the idea that only men in a narrower age-range had the right sort of manliness for military service by confining conscription to the army, the navy and the RAF to men aged 18–41. But even the Home Guard age-limits were contested, at both extremes, by those who thought they should be extended. There were protests about the exclusion of fit men over 65 who had military experience, such as Harry Breen, a decorated veteran of the First World War aged 70, rejected by the Greenock Home Guard. Eden responded that the military rigours of Home Guard service were inappropriate for men over 65, while speaking appreciatively of Breen's 'patriotic spirit'.[17] The Government reiterated the rules more than once, however, as the official age-limits continued to be flouted. Charles Graves, in a 1943 account of the force, claimed that the 'oldest L.D.V.' was an 80-year-old veteran of the Egyptian Campaign of 1884–85, Alexander Taylor of the Crieff Home Guard, Perthshire.[18] At the other end of the scale, boys as young as 14 were accepted.[19] The issue of age conveyed mixed messages. As Eden and Grigg acknowledged, defiance of the rules was a sign of the patriotic motivation of the 'men of all ages' who 'were eating their hearts out' to defend their country, whatever the obstacles.[20] But a man's age was also a tag that proclaimed his embodiment of a distinct type of masculinity that changed from one life-stage to the next: youth, old age, as well as infirmity at any age, were not associated with efficient military defence, and the presence of men so marked risked compromising the Home Guard's reputation.

An even more complicated issue was the restriction of recruitment to British nationals. The exclusion of 'enemy aliens' was not due to essentialist assumptions about suitability, competence and aptitude, as it was where age and health were concerned, but was caused by uncertainty about the individual's identification with Britain. The Irish formed the largest proportion of the numerous immigrants living in Britain in 1940. In view of Eire's neutrality, entry controls were imposed after the fall of France, but the wartime labour shortage meant that the British Government encouraged Irish workers to come to Britain for most of the war, and in any case nationals of Eire had joint citizenship.[21] However, applicants with Irish nationality, or whose parents were Irish, were sometimes refused enrolment in the Home Guard as if they were 'enemy aliens'. In December 1940 the Director General Sir Ralph Eastwood stated that 'citizens of Eire are British subjects' and so were eligible, as of course were Britons from Northern Ireland.[22] But there was sensitivity in the Home Office about the possibility of members of the Irish Republican Army joining the Home Guard. The IRA started a bombing campaign on the British mainland in January 1939, in the cause of the unification of Ulster with Eire as an independent republic, which the British Government had barely managed to suppress before the threat of invasion became imminent.[23] In view of the 'large floating population of Eire citizens' in Britain during the war, the Home Office wanted to prevent the enrolment in the Home Guard of its 'disaffected subjects'. However, it decided that, since 'I.R.A. men do not all come from Eire', the secret police ('Special Branch') and the Security Service (MI5) should vet *all* Irish applicants, in spite of the political risks of thereby implying that all Irishmen were potential terrorists.[24] This was a cumbersome and divisive process which alienated 'Irishmen who were loyal and anxious to join the Home Guard'.[25] But although the extent of checking was reduced between 1941 and 1943, MI5's involvement was maintained because of fears that the Home Guard would inadvertently train future members of the IRA and provide them with access to arms and ammunition.[26] These were, in essence, the reasons that the Home Guard was not established in Northern Ireland on the same footing as in the rest of the United Kingdom. Instead, as the 'Ulster Defence Force' it was a branch of the Royal Ulster Constabulary, the predominantly Protestant police force, an extension of sectarianism into the war effort that was bitterly resented by some Catholics.[27]

The 1919 Aliens Act had made the entry of (other) foreign nationals, including Russians, Poles, Germans and Italians (all well-established groups in Britain before the First World War), 'dependent upon the discretion of an immigration officer'.[28] The Act also restricted employment rights and gave the Home Secretary powers of deportation. During the interwar years it governed the entry of refugees from Nazism: the letter and the spirit of the Act meant that they were not treated with any special sympathy.[29] From September 1939, Defence Regulation 18B made possible the detention without trial – internment – not only of 'aliens' from enemy countries but of British subjects with origins in enemy countries.[30]

Cases of exclusion from the Home Guard hit the headlines when foreign nationality was confused with membership of a minority faith or with another social differentiator, and when evidence of loyalty to the British state was ignored. A case in point is that of Jack White, who joined the LDV in May 1940 but was forced to leave the next month. His father, a Russian Jew, had settled in Manchester at the age of 7, but had never been 'naturalised' – that is, he had not applied for and been granted British citizenship – so his British-born son Jack was not a British subject. Jack White, however, had not only fought for Britain in the First World War but held the Victoria Cross for heroic service. The *News Chronicle* took up his case,[31] and official policy was then altered: Sir Edward Grigg announced in Parliament in July 1940, with specific reference to White, that war service could now overrule non-British nationality as a qualification for the Home Guard.[32] Jack White himself, however, believed that he had been excluded because he was a Jew, rather than because he was the son of a Russian father: 'I don't ask for favours for myself, I want the country to let all us Jewish ex-servicemen make ourselves useful.'[33] British anti-semitism was strong in the 1930s and 1940s: contemporary commentators such as George Orwell documented its presence in the Home Guard, and, in spite of the efforts of Eleanor Rathbone and the *Manchester Guardian*, the ending of Jewish oppression under the National Socialist regime was not recognised as an official war aim.[34] The Second World War was popularly interpreted as a war against threatened invasion by an aggressive foreign power – the threat which endowed the Home Guard with importance and accounted for the huge response in its first few weeks. The trans-nationality of Jews, many of whom, like Jack White's father, had been immigrants to Britain, made them targets for the rhetorical 'othering' on which a sense of national unity was built.[35] Jack White reversed the discourse in speaking for 'all us Jewish ex-servicemen': Home Guard membership offered them the chance to play a useful military part in the war effort and affirmed their place in the British polity.

White's case occupied a position at the boundary of the official confidence in national unity which was implied by the government's willingness to recruit and arm civilians for part-time military service. This confidence was constructed proudly as a product of British democratic traditions: a Home Guard officer said in 1943, 'the creation of the Home Guard was one of the finest democratic gestures this country has ever made. It was not only an act of courage, but an act of faith. Can one imagine a Dictator country placing arms and ammunition into the hands of nearly two million civilians?'[36] Cases such as White's indicate the limits of the 'act of faith'. Doubts about the legal or ethnic status of White's national identity were eventually overridden by the evidence of his loyalty to, and personal identification with, the nation. But other non-British subjects were not trusted with 'arms and ammunition'. Possession of enemy nationality (German, Austrian or Italian) or marriage to a woman born in an enemy country officially disqualified a man from enrolment, whether or not the man or his wife were Jewish or had fled from the country concerned.[37] In addition, Home Guard officers were prohibited from employing in their households anyone with enemy nationality, an indication not only of the assumption that officers would be drawn from the servant-employing classes, but also of anxiety that spies would penetrate the very homes that the Home Guard had been created to defend.[38] Nevertheless, such restrictions (as well as others relating to age and, as the next chapter shows, gender) were not always observed at local level.[39]

An associated fear was of the inadvertent recruitment of 'fifth columnists', that is alleged supporters of Nazi Germany living in Britain.[40] Anxiety was sharpened by the understanding that such fifth columnists had facilitated the German occupation of Norway, Holland and Belgium in the spring of 1940.[41] Major Vidkun Quisling, the Norwegian army officer and diplomat who co-operated with the German occupying forces and ruled Norway on their behalf from 1940 to 1945, became symbolic. Parliament was told, in May 1940, that 'Quislings' would be excluded from the British Home Guard by a process of local vetting. Members had to be admitted by those who

> knew their antecedents and character ... it will be extremely difficult for any doubtful character to get into the Force, because each volunteer will have to be vouched for by his commanding officer all the way down the scale, and he will be vouched for personally and from personal experience.[42]

In addition, the Home Guard was instructed to look out for and take action against fifth columnists in the community; a similar application of local knowledge would make these people recognisable by Home Guards.[43] The traitor, in this structure of meanings, was the easily detectable antithesis of the honest British patriot. However, as Richard Thurlow argues, the probability of a fifth-column presence in Britain may have been less than was feared because of the thoroughness of internment under Defence Regulation 18B. This was amended to include 'political dissenters', including fascists, on 22 May 1940, just over a week after the LDV were called into being.[44] Even so, there were allegations in May and August 1940 that British fascists were joining the Home Guard and in some cases being given positions of leadership,[45] and the possible infiltration of the Home Guard by fifth columnists was a powerful component of representations of home defence in popular culture, as Chapters 4 and 5 show.

If the exclusion of fascists could be defined as legitimate, other restrictions were more questionable. Suspicions of class bias in recruitment, particularly to the officer ranks when these were established in the Home Guard in November 1940, were strong. The principles of selection for higher ranks established at that time, which specifically ruled out 'political, business and social connections', suggest that practices since the formation of the LDV in May had followed the well-worn grooves of the local social hierarchy.[46] Indeed, the operation of 'old boy networks' was quite innocently described by enthusiasts in 1943, who spoke of 'clubs' of former army officers combining to vet the lists of volunteers given them by the police, and to form from them the first LDV battalions.[47] Even after the announcement that officer selection must be by merit, specifically 'the ability to command the confidence of all ranks', rather than by social position, old habits died hard.[48] George Orwell, who joined the LDV in London soon after its formation, and rose to the rank of sergeant, wrote in Feburary 1941: 'The Home Guard swells to a million men in a few weeks, and is deliberately organised from above in such a way that only people with private incomes can hold positions of command.'[49] In May 1941, Richard Law, Financial Secretary at the War Office, tried to refute such accusations by stating that 'under ten per cent' of Home Guard commanders were 'peers, baronets, knights or brigadier-generals'.[50] Since analysts of British social structure suggest that at the most 5–7 per cent of the British population belonged in the 'upper class' between 1931 and 1951,[51] Law's figure actually supports the suspicion of social bias. In October 1941 Lt-Col. T. A. Lowe, a regular contributor of articles on the Home Guard to the *Daily Mail*, wrote that social preference was still going on: 'the Home Guard is a democratic force if ever there was one. Yet there can be no doubt that many of the commissions recently granted have had a "social" flavour about them',[52] and Willie Gallacher, Communist MP for West Fife, complained that class bias was working against appointment by merit as late as February 1944.[53] Such critics were openly sceptical of the claims of leading politicians concerning 'unity and brotherhood' and the absence of 'distinction of class or calling' in the Home Guard.

However, the loyalty of critics like Gallacher was itself under suspicion. Before the entry of the USSR to the war in June 1941, the Communist Party of Great Britain (CPGB) was considered potentially obstructive to the war effort because of its line that the war was an imperialist one, like the First World War, and its orchestration of a 'Stop the War' campaign. The CPGB was itself small (18,000 members in July 1939) but its influence on the Left was great. A section of the Labour Party, led by Stafford Cripps, worked closely with it against both international fascism and the British capitalist and class system in the 1930s, and in the autumn of 1939, coinciding with the CPGB's 'Stop the War' campaign, a small group of Labour MPs who had been pacifists in the First World War led the call for a truce, attracting support from more than seventy constituency Labour parties.[54]

The events of the summer of 1940 radically reduced the influence of the anti-war campaign: both the CPGB and particularly the Labour Left shifted their emphasis away from outright opposition to the war, calling instead for the removal from the Cabinet of the 'guilty men' who had supported appeasement in the 1930s and who were suspected of representing the 'vested interests' of the capitalist class in the profits of war.[55] During the rest of 1940 and the first half of 1941, the CPGB demanded the establishment of a 'People's Government' which would be 'truly representative' of the British people and would work for a 'people's peace'.[56] But the Party allegedly remained hostile to the Home Guard until June 1941. Orwell wrote in August 1941 that 'the Communist Party from the first forbade its members to join the Home Guard',[57] and Victor Gollancz claimed that Hugh Slater, who had fought in Spain against the supporters of Franco as a leading member of the International Brigade, was made to leave the CPGB after publishing a training manual for the Home Guard in 1941.[58] Nevertheless, many left-wingers, both communist and socialist, were keen to join.

The authorities responsible for recruitment to the LDV and the Home Guard, however, were told not to admit any political extremists. Chief constables were instructed by the Home Office on 15 May 1940 to make enquiries and inform the headquarters of the military area if 'they have reason to suppose that the applicant has political beliefs which would not be desirable in the Home Guard'. They were told to exclude:

> 1. Men of hostile connections or origin, or whose loyalty there is reason for doubting. 2. Men engaged in subversive activities. 3. Men with serious criminal records.[59]

Since, as we have seen, most of those on the far Right were interned, this focused attention on the Left: not only communists but also (in spite of the inclusion of Labour leaders in Churchill's Coalition Government) some Labour Party members were deemed unacceptable. They were rejected with no reason given other than that they had been deemed unsuitable, in order 'to keep as secret as possible the fact that the police vetted applications'.[60] The War Office and the Home Office were committed to the avoidance of frank explanations when 'the individual in question had political views – extreme Left or extreme Right – which we did not choose to see represented in one of our Armed Forces' because it was feared that 'merely to hint at the reasons for rejection would inevitably lead to controversy and political difficulties'.[61] But when asked in the Commons in July 1940 about whether he was 'sure that political determination is not being made', Eden blithely stated: 'I am absolutely sure. I think the Local Defence Volunteers themselves are quite confident of that.'[62]

Of course, such rejection without explanation invited queries and complaints. Mr J. E. Welsh, a Labour councillor in Gloucester and the local Labour Party agent, was dismissed from the LDV in June 1940, even though he had four years' experience in the Territorial Army: he protested that he was the victim of political discrimination. Two members of the South Wales Miners' Federation were rejected by the Trelewis Home Guard in July 1940. Their political affiliation was not stated, but the SWMF was closely linked to both the CPGB and the Labour Party.[63] George Strauss, Labour MP for Lambeth North, asked Eden with reference to Mr Welsh, 'whether there is any political or social ban on the membership of this body',[64] and Ness Edwards, Labour MP for the Caerphilly Division of Glamorganshire, asked him why the miners had been refused admission.[65] The standard ministerial response to such questions was indirect: enquiries were being made and the MP concerned would receive a written reply. Several cases involved men associated with the International Brigades of the Spanish Civil War of 1936–39. The Brigades, composed of volunteers from various nations, had fought against the coalition of fascist and other right-wing forces led by General Franco, which had attempted to depose the democratically elected Republican Government.[66] Referring to the need for experienced recruits in the Home Guard, Willie Gallacher asked Eden in July: 'Is the Right Hon. Gentleman not aware that the best men are the men of the International Brigade, but that attempts have been made to keep them out?'[67] A case in point was Wogan Philipps, who, as the son of Lord Milford, might appear to have had impeccable upper-class credentials. He was, however, prospective Labour candidate for South Oxfordshire and had driven an ambulance for the Republican Government in the Spanish Civil War.[68] When he applied to join the Home Guard in June 1940 he came up against 'some of the local gentry', as he put it, who threatened to resign if he was admitted.[69] Angry and humiliated, Philipps joined the Merchant Navy Reserve, apparently without difficulty.[70]

In at least some instances, then, left-wing political associations, socialist as well as communist, affected the attitudes both of the 'clubs' of men with 'political, business and social connections' suspected of running the force and of the chief constables who made recommendations about membership to the military authorities. Official intolerance of left-wing membership gradually dwindled after the German invasion of the USSR in June 1941. In January 1942 the Home Office instructed chief constables to 'modify' the earlier practice of exclusion.[71] It later declared, in February 1943, that 'Communists should be enrolled into this service in the same way as they are enrolled into H. M. Forces, where their activities in this connection would be under supervision.'[72] However, this did not equate with official approbation. As Sonya Rose argues, the Ministry of Information endeavoured (largely successfully) to ensure that growing public enthusiasm for 'Russia' as an ally did not 'increase the popularity of the British Communist Party'.[73] As we shall see, critical comparisons between the Soviet war effort and the British Home Guard focused not on reducing suspicion of the Left, but on achieving greater efficiency in the Home Guard, as well as persuading the authorities to admit women to its ranks.

The set of issues around who might or might not belong to the Home Guard exposed cracks and contradictions in British national unity. What was the meaning of 'home defence' if not everyone 'at home' could be involved? Wartime Britain, and by extension the Home Guard, was supposed to have united 'men of every age and every calling' in 'comradeship of arms', as George VI put it. However, not only enthusiasts outside the age-limits, but immigrants, Irishmen, Jews, communists and socialists could find themselves beyond the pale. The exclusion of youths under 17 and men over 65, as well as men deemed physically unfit, suggested that the masculinity of these social groups was impaired. Exclusion on the grounds of nationality and political affiliation indicated the limits of democratic inclusivity. And whatever the rationale, the definition of such groups as marginal to the war effort contradicted the all-embracing rhetoric of the diverse and democratic Britain represented by the Home Guard.

Ideological inspiration

The issue of precisely which social order the Home Guard in practice represented was closely linked to the debate over the political meaning of the war. Was it a nationalist struggle to defend the British parts of the British Isles against invasion? Or was it part of an international struggle

against the rising tide of European fascism? Was the appropriate precedent the British resistance to Napoleon's army in the 1790s or the fight
of the International Brigade and People's Militia against the supporters
of Franco in Spain from 1936 to 1939? Or was a new model, specifically
British but suited to modern war, required?

These questions did not animate only the Left: there was controversy
in the Government about the kind of force the LDV should be. In May
1940 key members of the War Office, notably Frederick Bovenschen,
Deputy Under-Secretary of State for War, argued that General Sir Walter
Kirke, Commander-in-Chief Home Forces, was following the wrong
model. Kirke, who was responsible for rapidly putting together plans
for the structure and organisation of the LDV, cited as an appropriate
antecedent the 'Boer Commando' – that is, the guerrilla fighter operating
in a decentralised structure that gave 'the utmost latitude to local enterprise'. But Bovenschen and others in the War Office frowned on Kirke's
evocation of the Boer rebels who had challenged Britain's imperial power
in South Africa from 1899 to 1902. They advocated the model of the
Territorial, a part-time soldier working within an organised extension
of the British Army's hierarchical and centralised structure.[74] The LDV
were, in fact, initially organised with considerable local autonomy, much
as Kirke wanted: it was the only way to 'bring the scheme into being as
quickly as possible' even though War Office officials continued to voice
concerns about avoiding 'chaos' and establishing 'full discipline'.[75] But
the argument over the kind of force the LDV should be, conventional or
modern, orthodox or unorthodox, clean or dirty, intensified in and out
of the War Office during the summer of 1940.

The Left liked the idea of a popular guerrilla force. It was particularly
excited about the apparent relevance of the recent Republican mobilisation against Franco. Numerous radical commentators urged the LDV to
develop along what were seen as Spanish lines, especially after the British
retreat from Dunkirk in the first week of June 1940. Even though the
three-year war in Spain had fostered sectarian tensions and exposed the
contradictions between socialist aspirations and the dictatorial tenden-
cies of Soviet communism, it symbolised the heroism and moral rectitude of the anti-fascist cause.[76] The official British refusal to aid Spain, on
the other hand, had provoked suspicions of covert government sympathy
with fascism. In 1940 the theme of numerous newspaper articles was
the creation of an all-inclusive 'people's army', which would prevent an
invasion force from exploiting weak points in the nation's defences, as the
Germans had done in Holland, Belgium and France. T. L. Horabin, Liberal

MP for North Cornwall (known for his left-leaning views) published an article in the *News Chronicle* in June 1940 headlined 'Arm the People Now!' above a photograph of women and men bearing rifles, captioned 'They did it in Barcelona':

> The threat of invasion can be met in one way only – by our becoming a Nation in Arms. By turning the resistance to invasion into 'a people's war'. By turning the whole people into one vast army, incorporating every man and boy capable of bearing arms and every woman with the courage to sling a milk-bottle at a cyclist invader. [77]

Age, gender and other social differentiators scarcely mattered in the creation of a People's Army – boys and women could play a part, as well as men of all ages. Inclusivity and voluntarism were imbued with the heroism and radicalism associated with the defence of the Spanish Republic: the Home Guard was, in the minds of many on the Left, the equivalent of the people's militias and International Brigades. This in turn stimulated the suspicions of those on the Right, for whom the Spanish Civil War had been a foreign struggle in which Britain need have little interest.

The LDV force came into being in this political context. Eden's broadcast defined the LDV as a counter-invasion force but did not colour it with a specifically anti-fascist tint. He identified its role as primarily one of defence against airborne invasion by parachutists: the Volunteers were originally known as 'parashots'. This definition had ideological implications. The LDV were officially warned that the invader might adopt a variety of disguises:

> The Germans are … in the habit of dropping spies, saboteurs and agents behind the lines and may do so in this country. Such men are often dressed in mufti, our own uniform, or may assume almost any disguise, e.g. priests and even women. These men are not soldiers and must be treated as spies.[78]

Home Guard patrols, and particularly the road blocks at which they checked identity cards, were meant to enable the detection of such interlopers. Despite the confidentiality of the official instruction, the parachutist disguised as a nun entered the popular discourse of home defence: his subterfuge of appropriating the dress associated with a particularly innocent type of womanhood was a sly trick beneath manly British standards, characteristic of an immoral and ungodly enemy.

The Left likewise constructed the Home Guard as a counter-invasion force, but additionally viewed it as both specifically anti-fascist and also potentially revolutionary: the huge popular response to the call for LDVs was seen as evidence of a people's democracy in action – a replay of the

Spanish Civil War. Left-wing opinion concerning 'the strategy and tactics of people's war in the specific conditions of fascist aggression in Europe' was led by former communist and veteran of the Spanish Civil War Tom Wintringham.[79] His experience of Spain had persuaded him that a civilian army, inspired by democratic ideals and organised on democratic lines, could successfully resist a fascist army: 'Freedom, felt and making a difference, making a people eager, is almost a formula for winning wars', he wrote in July 1940.[80] He saw the 'people's army' as a harbinger of radical change. Rather than recalling the patriotism of the Fencibles and the Yeomanry, as Sir Edward Grigg did in Parliament, Wintringham evoked the radical democratic claims of the Levellers in Cromwell's New Model Army of the 1640s,[81] and he cited not Agincourt (1415) but Crécy (1346) as the iconic British battle – because he regarded it as a victory of autonomous communities of village bowmen against a feudal army.[82]

Even though the Republicans lost the war in Spain, Wintringham argued that they had impeded the advance of the Francoists and their Italian and German allies for nearly three years because they had mobilised a popular army.[83] In an article in *Picture Post* in June 1940, he argued that only such an army could counter the current German tactics of 'deep infiltration' by which parachutists were dropped far behind enemy lines:

> An armed people, with some rifles in every village and every suburb, an armed guard on every important cross-roads, revolvers worn by typists, and signs up in the restaurants 'please leave hand-grenades and machine-guns at the door' – such a people can tackle parachutists before breakfast.[84]

In spite of such enthusiastic hyperbole, Wintringham's practical experience in Spain made him more cautious than other left-wing advocates of arming *all* the people, and more insistent on training and discipline. Fighting a people's war, he wrote,

> does not mean the indiscriminate arming of everyone. It means that the efforts of our army for the defence of this country should be supplemented by some training and some arming of about four million men, who continue to live as civilians and to work at their jobs until invasion occurs or until they are needed.[85]

Elsewhere he indicated that these 4 million men should mostly be ex-servicemen with military experience. In Wintringham's more sober statements, the Regular Army played the lead role. Furthermore, armed typists or, indeed, women of any sort rapidly disappeared from his vision of the militant citizens who would work closely with it.

Wintringham believed in June 1940 that the LDV were not yet an effective 'people's army', but he was convinced that they could become one if their numbers were increased, their organisation and leadership democratised and, above all, if they were trained.[86] In the summer of 1940 he established a private training school for Home Guard members in the grounds of Osterley Park, a stately home just west of London owned by Lord Jersey, a friend of the progressive publisher Edward Hulton, who provided the funds. Wintringham had a regular column in Hulton's popular weekly magazine *Picture Post*. If this gave Wintringham literary space in which to express his ideas to a wide audience, Osterley was the physical space in which he put his ideas into practice. From July to September 1940 the Osterley school trained over 3,000 members of the Home Guard in 2-day courses taken by 100 men at a time, and acquired a revolutionary reputation.

Two aspects of the school account for this image. Firstly, Wintringham construed the Home Guard as a democratic, anti-fascist force that would not stand for a settlement with Hitler in any circumstances short of his complete defeat. Wintringham's teaching at Osterley was imbued with comparisons between the Home Guard and the People's Militia of Republican Spain, 'an army very like their own, the army that for year after year held up Fascism's flood-tide towards world power'.[87] Instructors included a number of veterans of the Spanish Civil War, including Spanish miners and left-wingers such as Wintringham's friends Hugh Slater and Bert ('Yank') Levy. Slater, like George Orwell who had also fought in Spain and was outspoken in his support for Wintringham and the school, believed that the Home Guard would not only resist invasion but would also turn against the British Government if it made any attempt to appease Hitler and sue for a compromise peace.[88]

Secondly, Wintringham was committed to teaching guerrilla warfare, which he believed was the only form of warfare suitable for repelling fascist invasion. He argued that the Home Guard should be a force of 'first class irregulars' organised and trained in different ways from the regular soldiers of the British Army. Hence he recruited the Chief Instructor of the Boy Scouts, Stanley White, to the school, and combined Baden Powell's scouting tradition with the unorthodox warfare recommended before the Second World War by military figures such as T. E. Lawrence and Orde Wingate, and used in some parts of the Spanish Civil War.[89] The heady topics of the Osterley lectures, and of the practical training, included stalking undetected through the countryside, camouflaged knife-attacks, garrotting enemy sentries, sniping at dive-bombers, wires across the road to bring down motor-cyclists, home-made grenades dropped on cars from trees or lobbed under tanks, and house-to-house street-fighting.[90] These were the methods that Wintringham advocated in response to the main means of 'deep infiltration' characteristic of modern warfare: the parachutist who was dropped behind enemy lines; the tank that constituted a mobile fortress; and the aeroplane that delivered not only bombs but also military personnel together with supplies of arms and ammunition. However, Wintringham's approach earned him accusations that he was 'teaching murder rather than teaching war', and soon brought him into conflict with officials in the War Office. He claimed that an 'officer high up in the command of the L.D.V.' called for the closure of the school in its early days, on the grounds that 'crawling around' was unsuitable training for men who would only be required 'to sit in a pill-box and shoot straight'.[91]

S. P. MacKenzie and others have implied that official opposition not only to Wintringham's 'irregular methods' but to his politics was representative of the War Office view and the reason for the school's closure after three months.[92] Indeed the Osterley Park experiment is usually seen as a daring attempt by the Left to train a citizens' guerrilla army, inspired by the ex-communist firebrand Wintringham, and stamped on by the authorities. But the situation was more complex. A private military training school teaching armed warfare could not, any more than could a private army, be tolerated by the state. To survive, such a school needed War Office approval.[93] (In any case, Edward Hulton could not have funded the venture indefinitely.) A War Office official who reported on the school in July 1940 stated that 'while approving of the school in principle, he did not think the Instructors were of a suitable type … owing to the Communistic tendency of Instructors'. In response, the Home Guard Inspectorate asked MI5 to vet the instructors and sent more senior army officers to inspect the school.[94] But rather than simply refusing any recognition to the school and its 'communistic' instructors, and thereby suppressing it, the War Office absorbed the school into its own training system. Osterley Park was officially closed on 30 September 1940, but Home Guard training recommenced two weeks later, in the grounds of another large country house, 'Denbies', in Surrey. Sir Edward Grigg explained in Parliament: 'We have established a Home Guard school based on the admirable school which was first started by Mr Hulton at Osterley.'[95] 'Denbies' had much the same syllabus[96] as well as some of Osterley's 'communistic' personnel, including Hugh Slater and 'Yank' Levy, and Wintringham himself as 'lecturer and adviser'.[97]

The language of the relevant War Office minutes is striking: 'They were keeping on several instructors (toughs) from Osterley Park [...] Home Guard students who had passed through the course like the blood and thunder aspect'.[98] This departure from formal civil service language echoed Wintringham: he described Yank Levy as 'my good tough [...] the best lecturer on rough stuff that I know'.[99] As these linguistic continuities suggest, it was and is a misrepresentation to suggest that all members of the War Office thought that Home Guards needed only to learn to sit in a pill-box and shoot straight. Officials may have disliked the emphasis on militant democracy, but nevertheless approved Ministry of Information plans for three films featuring training in Osterley techniques, two of which included specific references to the Spanish Civil War.[100] The commentary in *Citizen Army* (1940), accompanying a lesson about grenades, includes the statement: 'Among the instructors who are at the School are several men who fought in Spain and who have had experience of the kind of fighting in which Home Guard would be engaged in an invasion.'[101] Wintringham himself was commissioned by the BBC to contribute to at least two broadcasts on the Home Guard in 1941: he presented it as 'a citizen army based on and arising out of a genuine democratic defence movement'.[102]

Nevertheless, the War Office made changes at 'Denbies' with which Wintringham was unhappy. He resigned from his position there in June 1941, owing, in his own words, 'to differences of opinion on the development of the Home Guard'.[103] He believed that members of the Home Guard in the age group 35–40 who had 'proved themselves' as company commanders should be exempt from conscription to the regular forces, as were their civil defence counterparts in the Fire Services and Rescue Squads. He argued that officer appointments in the Home Guard were (still) both class-bound and politically prejudiced;[104] indeed the 'Denbies' regulations indicate conventional expectations of the social standing of the 'platoon commanders and above', now nominated as trainees.[105] And he protested against the view that the Home Guard was 'a fourth rate militia force, not to be trusted with ammunition for fear they shoot themselves, and incapable of learning the intricacies of modern war'. He insisted that the Home Guard should be trained not only to fight for 'islands of defence' but also to be 'active garrisons', capable of sufficient mobility to harass the enemy, while the Regular Army was preparing the counter-attack.[106]

Wintringham's critique of Home Guard policy in the summer of 1941 saw the force as a superb counter to Nazi warfare: it was highly efficient to arm volunteers who were also working productively in war industries and were capable of taking on defence that would otherwise occupy the Regular Army. Like the Home Guard officer quoted earlier, and like Orwell, Wintringham insisted that only a democracy, confident in the active participation of its citizens, as opposed to a totalitarian state dependent on 'blind devotion', could do such a thing.[107] As Miles Taylor argues, this perception of the Home Guard enabled Wintringham, Orwell and others on the Left to regard popular patriotism in wartime not as the irrational force feared by J. A. Hobson in 1902 but as a conscious choice on the part of 'the people'.[108] Orwell wrote exultantly, in April 1941: 'The Home Guard is the most anti-Fascist body existing in England', describing it as 'an astonishing phenomenon, a sort of People's Army officered by Blimps' and stating that 'it is much more democratic and consciously anti-Fascist than some of its commanders would wish'.[109] As the last sentence implies, left-wing enthusiasm maintained a critical stance. Wintringham argued that the potential of the Home Guard could not be realised until the prejudice of 'those who distrust and fear the ordinary people of this country', as well as the outdated military methods still favoured by some senior officers, were swept away, and the Home Guard was thoroughly trained in guerrilla tactics.[110] Orwell agreed that 'the grip of the retired colonel with his pre-machine-gun mentality' must be broken.[111]

Even though Osterley challenged its values, the War Office also approved at least one other such experiment, a Home Guard training camp at Burwash in Sussex inspired by John Langdon-Davies, a journalist who wrote critical articles on the Home Guard for the *Sunday Pictorial*. Langdon-Davies, a Home Guard captain, was Commandant of this school, which was officially recognised in December 1941 as the South-Eastern Command Fieldcraft Training School.[112] Although he had reported from the Republican side on the Spanish Civil War, Langdon-Davies was probably more acceptable to the military authorities than Wintringham, because he had no communist past and was overtly anti-Soviet.[113] Nevertheless, he expressed a similar faith in local democracy and active citizenship, and Burwash taught the same kind of guerrilla tactics as Osterley.[114]

The view that the Home Guard's role should be a mobile one, and hence that traditional army drill was not the most suitable training, was represented in the War Office, even though it was contested. The potential for official commitment to unorthodox methods was complicated, however, by the secrecy surrounding the parallel development of a clandestine organisation known as the Home Guard Auxiliary, unequivocally designed to wage guerrilla warfare in the event of invasion. The nominal link between this Auxiliary and the Home Guard was part of its disguise rather than an organisational reality,[115] but its existence strengthened the position of officials who wanted the Home Guard to concentrate on conventional training for static guard duties, rather than guerrilla techniques.

Military functions

Throughout the years 1940–42 the 'strategy of nodal points' dominated the official version of the Home Guard's role. The 'nodal point' was a defensive position such as a village or a road junction which the Home Guard was supposed to defend 'to the last man and the last round'.[116] In contrast, Wintringham and others, including the respected military theorist Basil Liddell Hart, advised that the Home Guard should use 'the tactics of infiltration and of elastic defence', that is, it should both penetrate beyond the enemy's strong points to strike at its military infrastructure and make tactical retreats in order to lure the enemy forward into positions in which it could be ambushed.[117] Lord Bridgeman, Director General of the Home Guard from the summer of 1941 until the end of the war, suggested in August 1941 and again in January 1942 that the Home Guard could have a role in sabotage and harassment, even if the defence of 'nodal points' remained its main task.[118] But as far as the army leadership was concerned, mobile deployment was impractical for the Home Guard for four reasons: the force lacked military transport and mobile forms of artillery; command and control of the Home Guard were not integrated above battalion level; in their limited opportunities for training, part-time soldiers could only master the techniques of static defence, not the greater complexities of mobility; and mobile bands of Home Guards would cause confusion to regular troops and increase civilian casualties.[119] In June 1942 orders to company commanders stated that guerrilla fighting by the Home Guard 'must not be allowed [...] Instructions issued must NOT detract from the overriding principle that there will be no withdrawal from Nodal Points while there are any men left to defend it [*sic*]'.[120] Nevertheless, reference to guerrilla warfare did not completely disappear from the Home Guard's training. *Home Guard Instruction Number 51*, issued in September 1942, told commanders that guerrilla activity might be permissible in sparsely populated areas where there were no nodal points, and gave details of how to train a Home Guard squad for such a role.[121]

There was another side to a mobile role for the Home Guard, however, one which had more to do with morale than practicalities. Churchill was consistently enthusiastic about the Home Guard, in part because he thought it represented a population activated by the possibility of invasion, inspired to resist and hence committed to all aspects of the war effort. He was aware of dips in Home Guard morale and deliberately 'talked it up' in his speeches, as well as reiterating the possibility of invasion even at moments when this was generally regarded as unlikely, for example in the spring of both 1942 and 1943.[122] As the consistent popularity of the 'blood and thunder' aspects of training suggested, preparing the Home Guard for a mobile role, involving guerrilla tactics such as stalking and unarmed combat, contributed to an 'offensive mentality' which was better for morale than training for a purely static role.

These rival versions of the military role of the Home Guard – static or mobile, conventional or unorthodox – had implications for gender identities.[123] The defence of nodal points involved bearing weapons, being trained in their use and undertaking sentinel responsibilities, and was thus not incompatible with wartime military masculinity. But mobile military duties were more highly esteemed in the Second World War. 'Blood and thunder' stood for unorthodox methods that produced results – garrotting sentries, lobbing grenades – which had been seen as *un*manly before the war, representative of the sneaky tactics of rebellious colonial subjects such as the Boers and deviants like 'Lawrence of Arabia'. Sitting in a pillbox and shooting straight, in contrast, evoked the patriotic heroism of defence to the last man. But it was contaminated by evidence that wars characterised by 'defence of the line', notably the First World War, resulted in a high death toll that was both inglorious and largely futile. In the world of *blitzkrieg*, when the pace of war was faster and less predictable than previously, some military leaders became convinced that the use of initiative, intelligence, stealth and subterfuge to outwit a ruthless enemy was more manly than was obediently taking up a static position. General Sir James Marshall-Cornwall, General Officer in Command of the British Army's Western Command, evoked both military and masculine powerlessness when he took a stand against 'making our Home Guards pillbox-bound and impotent for war'.[124]

The policy of a static guard role for the Home Guard attracted public criticism through the controversial provision of 'pikes', that is bayonets welded to steel tubes, to all Home Guard units at the beginning of 1942. The pike policy was meant to ensure that every Home Guard had a weapon, and was based on a belief in the effectiveness of 'cold steel' in the Home Guard's armory.[125] Bayonet training was thought to have salutary effects on masculine aggression: 'it is "guts and gristle" instruction, with nothing peacetime or "pansy" about it', as an Army training manual put it in 1940.[126] Pikes had their defenders, even from within the 'mobility' camp, on the grounds that they were quieter and lighter than rifles and were good for 'cads' warfare', especially at night.[127] But War Office confidence in the cult of the bayonet was misjudged, as Brigadier-General Lord Page Croft, Under-Secretary for War, discovered when endeavouring to defend the pike policy in Parliament. Complaints were made about the waste of materials and labour in the production of an ineffective weapon, and there was outrage about the pike's symbolic implications: 'The provision of pikes for the Home Guard, if it was not meant to be a joke, was an insult', complained one MP; another quoted a constituent asking 'when may we expect the bows and arrows and slings?'[128] The theme of insulting the Home Guard with 'medieval knicknacks' was echoed in the House of Lords.[129] Chapter 4 shows how cartoonists used the pike to suggest that the Home Guard was run by out-of-date commanders, committed to archaic methods that undermined the military status of the force.

The provision of pikes coincided with the introduction of conscription to the Home Guard under the National Service No. 2 Act of December 1941. Pikes were supplied so that every conscript could be armed, even though, ironically, their provision was also blamed for the declining enthusiasm for the Home Guard that made conscription necessary. In spite of the inference, in Parliament and the press, that the military role of the Home Guard was now limited, the Government justified conscription in terms of the importance of the Home Guard to its defence strategy. Increasing numbers of Home Guards were needed from 1942 to mid-1944, to replace the Regular Army on guard duties and to relieve army personnel on coastal defences and (in conjunction with the women of the Auxiliary Territorial Service) on anti-aircraft batteries.[130] The Home Guard was also required to participate in army training. David French explains in his history of 'Churchill's Army' that in 1942–43 the use of realistic battle drill and field-firing exercises to train the home forces was stepped up, both to raise morale and to 'increase the tempo at which the British army could operate and enable it to compete on equal terms with the Germans'.[131] Accordingly, the Home Guard was drawn into a rigorous army training regime, involving monthly military exercises in which 'the enemy' was expected to be 'as offensive as the Germans will be'.[132] For these functions, its members were armed with more modern weapons than pikes. More fundamentally, the division between static guard duties and a mobile role became untenable: the defence of fixed points such as houses and weapon dumps was necessary, but so too were raids and ambushes. There were even complaints that too much commando-style mobility was expected.[133] From 1942 to 1944 these exercises prepared British troops for D-Day and were also valued for the contribution they made to pre-service training.[134] At the same time, the Home Guard in southern Britain was trained and equipped so that it could almost completely replace the British Army in home defence, before, during and after the re-invasion of Europe in June 1944: its members were required to sleep in full kit, in readiness for an alert, during this period.[135]

Ironically, then, the Home Guard's integration into army training led to its instruction in some of the military techniques that Wintringham and other radicals had advocated. Now, however, these were intended to prepare British forces for the invasion of Europe, rather than to enable the Home Guard to act as an anti-fascist, counter-invasion, 'people's army'. On the other hand, throughout the war, and especially at times and in localities where defence duties and military training were not required, the force was required to co-operate with the Civil Defence Services.[136] This requirement, that the Home Guard swap its role of armed military response to attack, for one of civil protection of life and property from the effects of war, was not always popular with its members.[137]

Conscription

The Government introduced conscription to the Home Guard in December 1941, to ensure that the supply of personnel was sufficient for the guard, defence and training duties required of it. Any male British subject between the ages of 18 and 51 could now be directed to enroll, a step which required the authorities to revisit their previous exclusion of political extremists 'with no reason given'. In keeping with its anxieties about the Home Guard inadvertently training members of the IRA, the Home Office issued secret instructions that Irishmen who had come to work in Britain during the war would not be conscripted.[138] As far as the Left was concerned, on the other hand, internal memoranda acknowledged that the entry of the Soviet Union to the war as an ally had made a difference: 'In the past any active member of the Communist Party has been excluded from the Home Guard, but in the altered circumstances brought about by the attack by Germany on the Soviet Union, it seems right to modify this.'[139]

The official Memorandum of Regulations which accompanied the Act sounded draconian.[140] New disciplinary requirements would apply throughout the Home Guard, even though the compulsory powers of recruitment were to be used only in areas where numbers were too low. Members' attendance was now legally enforced: defaulters were liable to summary conviction in a civil court and a penalty of one month's imprisonment or a fine of up to £10. Periods of training and duty were fixed at a maximum of 48 hours every 4 weeks. In place of earlier arrangements permitting resignation with a fortnight's notice (known as the 'housemaid's clause'), members now had to remain in the Home Guard until their services were dispensed with by the state, and the designation 'Volunteer' was dropped: ordinary members of the Home Guard were henceforth called 'Privates'.[141] Volunteers unwilling to accept the revised conditions of service were given two months after the passing of the Act in which to resign, after which they were bound by the new regulations.

The erosion of the voluntary principle by these requirements was seen by critics as a violation of the meaning of Britain at war. Compulsory recruitment directly contradicted the rhetoric with which the Home Guard had hitherto been celebrated, both by conservative leaders such as Eden, Grigg and Churchill, and on the Left. The Home Guard's prized 'voluntary spirit' was central to the Britishness it was said to embody, and it was also seen as an expression of democracy in action, epitomised by willing co-operation in defence of state and society.[142] Conscription, in contrast, had in the past been associated with Prussian militarism and coerced loyalty,[143] and there was a faint echo of the opposition to its introduction in the First World War. Several Labour MPs expressed the view that 'the introduction of conscription for the Home Guard will destroy the spirit of that body' by making it militarised and bureaucratised, and by undermining local independence, initiative and the 'free association of comradeship in duty'. It might achieve 'a little bit more prompt obedience', but it would 'destroy the spirit which was intended to defend England'.[144]

Conscription, and the more rigorous membership terms introduced at the same time, nevertheless had their supporters. There were three main arguments in favour. Firstly, Home Guard service should be required of all young men, since it provided useful military training prior to their call up.[145] Secondly, it was a way of ensuring the fair distribution of the burdens of war across the population that would counter the tendency for the Home Guard to fill up with 'slackers' and 'Sunday soldiers'.[146] Thirdly, it was important that the Home Guard should be closely comparable with the army, which was itself composed of a mixture of volunteers and conscripts and was subject to strict internal discipline.[147] In making the case for conscription, Churchill combined flattering references to the origins and development of the Home Guard, which had 'become a most powerful, trained, uniformed body', with insistence on its centrality to national defence and hence the importance of maintaining its efficiency.[148]

Parallels with the Red Army were drawn by those in favour as well as those against compulsion. Churchill dodged the continuing difficulties of equipping the Home Guard, which were potentially incompatible with the conscription that he was recommending, by urging improvisation, claiming, 'that is what they are doing in Russia in defending their country'.[149] Henry Charleton, Labour MP for South Leeds, argued on the other hand that 'Russian soldiers' provided such a compelling 'example' for the Home Guard that compulsion was unnecessary.[150] The soldiers of the Red Army were conceptualised in these statements as acceptable 'Russian' patriots rather than the more menacing representatives of international Soviet communism, and idealised 'Russians' were held up as role models. For critics, a particular target of comparison was the enduring obsession of Home Guard officers with parade-ground drill in the months after conscription: 'It might be a good idea to emulate the Russian guerillas and concentrate on how to wipe out as many Germans as possible instead of trying to dazzle them with a blinding array of gleaming brasswork', wrote a Midlands Home Guard to *Reynolds News* in January 1942.[151]

In practice, there was pride in areas where there was no need to apply compulsion because recruitment and attendance were still buoyant and there were no 'slackers'.[152] Some Home Guard commanding officers urged that compulsory service was unnecessary because volunteers were plentiful when there was something worthwhile to do, such as weekend camps or training in mobile methods.[153] But conscription was on balance accepted. Even though some Labour MPs spoke out against it, the far Left appears to have been silent on the issue: Wintringham believed in military discipline within his democratically-inspired 'armies of freemen', and he and others were not opposed (as Socialists had been in the First World War) to conscription to the Army. There were even criticisms, voiced for example by John Langdon-Davies, who had supported tighter discipline in the force from its early days, that compulsion was applied insufficiently rigorously and consistently.[154]

On the other hand, there were public protests when the regulations appeared to be applied unreasonably, for example to men who were patently unfit,[155] and to occupational groups such as miners and agricultural workers, who, as Walter Citrine, General Secretary of the Trades Union Congress, pointed out, were already putting in long hours for the war effort.[156] A widely publicised case was that of Reginald Brown, a farm labourer, who was sentenced to one month's imprisonment with hard labour in October 1942 for failing to attend Home Guard parades. The *Daily Express* protested: 'How can a man do his Home Guard drills if he milks cows, does harvesting, tractor-driving, hoeing, corn-cutting on three farms, and often works from 6 a.m. to 10 p.m. including Sundays?', and the *Daily Herald* received 'scores of letters' that regarded the imprisonment as 'one of the monstrosities of the war' and called for Brown's release.[157] As late as February 1944, at least one commentator bemoaned the damage to the spirit of the British war effort which was inflicted by conscription to the Home Guard: 'It has succeeded in producing men and materials', stated the *News of the World*, 'but its workings stand condemned by public opinion as alien to the spirit and traditions of the nation.'[158]

Compulsion was lifted in September 1944, when the Home Guard returned to its original voluntary status. At this point Orwell asserted that the inclusion of the Home Guard in the National Service Act had been unnecessary: there had been sustained commitment throughout the period 1940–44. He added that members had been motivated not by the democratic spirit and consciousness of 'what the war is about' that he and others had evoked in the days of Osterley, but by 'the primitive instinct to defend one's native soil'.[159] Orwell thus contributed not only to the enduring image of the Home Guard as primarily a counter-invasion force, but also, perversely, to the obliteration from popular memory of the left-wing vision that he had shared, of a democratic, anti-fascist Home Guard.

But in spite of the shift from voluntarism to compulsion, and from counter-insurgent guerrilla force to adjunct of the army, the Home Guard remained a resilient metaphor for the nation at war. Ironically, the legal enforcement of compulsory service in the Home Guard was used, at least once, as an opportunity for an assertion of 'the spirit and traditions of the nation'. Early in 1944, George Roberts, a West Indian who had come to Britain to work as a skilled electrician in a war factory and had joined the Home Guard as a volunteer, was fined £5 by the Liverpool Police Court for failing to attend Home Guard parades. He explained the reason for his non-attendance: he had been refused admission to the Grafton dance hall because of his colour, so he had returned to the hall in his Home Guard uniform only to be turned away again, as a result of which he decided not to go to Home Guard meetings 'because he had been insulted while wearing the uniform'.[160] The Grafton was currently catering for white American troops accustomed to the 'colour bar'. On appeal to the Quarter Sessions, however, Roberts's fine was commuted to one farthing by the Liverpool Recorder, E. G. Hemmerde, KC, who declared: 'People came over here to risk their lives on behalf of what they proudly call the Mother Country'; it was 'impertinence for any country to accept the aid of coloured people from any part of the world and then to say "Our laws do not enable us to deal with you on terms of complete equality."'[161]

The Home Guard was thus recognisably constructed as a force in which people risked their lives, and Britain as a liberal polity in which the law upheld equal treatment regardless of race. The ethos of voluntarism, patriotism, democracy and unity associated with the Home Guard and the war effort was reiterated in this judgment. The occasion was a breach of the law compelling participation in home defence that critics had condemned as alien to these wartime values. But compulsion was not the real issue in Roberts's case: the targets were aberrant members of wartime society, represented by dance-hall proprietors who were placing the expectations of their new clientele of segregated white American servicemen above the British tradition 'of complete equality'.[162] That 'tradition' was clearly vulnerable to racial prejudice, as the case of Jack White in 1940 had suggested. Chapter 3 reveals the limitations, as well as the surprising flexibility, of the tradition in relation to gender.

Conclusion

The Home Guard in official discourse symbolised the unity, purpose and inclusiveness of the British war effort. But this view was contradicted by the exclusion not only of the old and the young, but also of foreign nationals, the Irish, and British communists and socialists. Left-wing political affiliation aroused particular government suspicion, but official prohibition was deliberately muted in order to protect Britain's democratic image. The wartime Left brought to the Home Guard a set of aspirations inspired by the Spanish Civil War and stimulated by the neo-socialism of the war effort. Its vision of the Home Guard as a 'citizens' army' implied that the meaning of the war for British civilians was not only the stoical endurance of living through the Blitz, but the heroic resistance of a militant citizenry.[163] Such an army could be trusted to bear arms for a Britain whose democratic reconstruction the war was already heralding. It should be trained both for operational integration with the regular forces and in modern unorthodox tactics.

The insistence of radical military strategists that the Home Guard could, in such ways, mount an effective defence against invasion, challenged the ideas of those in the War Office who regarded any role for the

Home Guard other than that of the static guard armed with the fixed bayonet as impractical and undesirable. But official rejection was not the only story. British liberalism was better served by containment than by outright repression: the Osterley Park training school was taken over rather than closed down. Considerations of morale and military practicality (especially the need to involve the Home Guard in training the Regular Army for the allied invasion of Europe) ensured that the preparation of the Home Guard for a mobile offensive role continued. Between the beginning of 1942 and the summer of 1944 the Home Guard was trained not only for static defence but also in street-fighting and camouflage. Ironically, given the association of the Home Guard with radical voluntarism, legal compulsion was introduced to secure sufficient numbers. Orwell's 'retired colonel with a pre-machine-gun mentality', the 'Blimp' of Low's cartoons and of the Powell and Pressburger film (which we discuss in Chapter 4), did not dominate the Home Guard. Even so, 'Blimp' was an abiding presence within its leadership, where he expressed his opposition to identifying the Home Guard with modes of warfare that he regarded as ungentlemanly and degenerate.

The conceptualisations of the Home Guard that we have reviewed here raise at least four questions about the masculine status of the force. Firstly, the requirement that the Home Guard recruit only men who were too old or too young for the armed forces, those who had been rejected on medical grounds or those who were in reserved occupations associated it (however unfairly, especially to the last group) with impaired manhood and military inefficiency. Secondly, the uncertainties about the military role of the Home Guard (whether mobile or static), coupled with the slow arrival of uniforms and the provision of anachronistic weapons such as pikes, placed question-marks over the soldierly identity of the force. The popularity of mobility, as against the stasis of guarding fixed points, reflected not only natural impatience with inaction, but also the identification of action, including guerrilla techniques and commando-style warfare, with military manliness. Thirdly, the suggestions throughout its history of the dispensability of the Home Guard (expressed, for example, in the requirement that it swap armed home defence for civil defence when needed), plus the allegations that it was full of 'slackers and Sunday soldiers', cast doubt on its status as a worthwhile military organisation and on the identity of its members as 'real' soldiers. Fourthly and finally, the relationship of the Home Guard to women was ambiguous. According to some radicals, men and women could – and should – be comrades within a civilian army resisting fascism, as they were believed to have been in

Spain. But left-wing conviction concerning women's place in combat did not last beyond the enthusiasm for a 'citizens' army' of the summer of 1940, and the assumption on the part of the War Office was, from the start, that armed home defence was an exclusively male responsibility. In Chapter 3 we explore the hotly contested issue of whether there was a place for women in the Home Guard.

Notes

1 Hansard, vol. 361, col. 239, 22 May 1940.

2 IWM, Sound Archive (SA) 17697, Anthony Eden, recorded 14 May 1940.

3 Hansard, vol. 363, col. 578, 23 July 1940; vol. 376, col. 2178, 18 December 1941.

4 Calder, *People's War*, p. 65; N. Pronay, 'The News Media at War', in N. Pronay and D. W. Spring (eds), *Propaganda, Politics and Film 1918–45* (London: Macmillan, 1982), p. 175.

5 Eden's use of the phrase 'to make assurance doubly sure' echoed Shakespeare's *Macbeth*, Act 4, Scene 1, line 83.

6 Churchill, *Second World War*, vol. 2, pp. 154–155.

7 Churchill, *Second World War*, vol. 2, pp. 235, 357; W. S. Churchill, *The Second World War*, vol. 6: *Triumph and Tragedy* (London: Cassell, 1954), p. 668; Churchill, *Complete Speeches*, vol. 7, p. 6773.

8 Hansard, vol. 376, col. 2114, 18 December 1941, Captain H. Margesson, Secretary of State for War (second); J. Brophy, *Britain's Home Guard. A Character Study*, Foreword by Sir James Grigg (London: Harrap & Co., 1945), p. 5 (second, at times first); *Speeches and Replies to Addresses by His Majesty King George VI, December 1936–February 1952* (H&S Ltd, n.d. [1958]), pp. 53–54 (second, at times first); J. Radnor, *It All Happened Before: The Home Guard Through the Centuries* (London: Harrap & Co., 1945), p. 11 (last).

9 Churchill, *Second World War*, vol. 1, p. 393.

10 Sir Edward Grigg and Sir James Grigg were not related.

11 'Collect or Prayer for All Conditions of Men', *Book of Common Prayer*, 1662.

12 Hansard, vol. 365, cols 1897–1898, 19 November 1940; reference to Shakespeare's *Henry V* (Act IV, Scene 3).

13 R. Fisk, *In Time of War: Ireland, Ulster and the Price of Neutrality 1939–45* (London: Deutsch, 1983).

14 Brophy, *Britain's Home Guard*, p. 5. The Anglican sacrament is 'an outward and visible sign of an inward and spiritual grace': *Book of Common Prayer*, 1662.

15 *Speeches and Replies*, pp. 53–54.

16 National Archives (NA), War Office (WO), 199/3243, History of the Formation and Organization of the Home Guard, 3A, 14 May 1940.

17 Hansard, vol. 363, col. 1188, 30 July 1940; vol 364, col. 589, 13 August 1940.

18 Graves, *Home Guard*, p. 38; also pp. 248, 267.
19 Project interview (PI), Dennis Smith, 11 May 2000 (paragraphs 278, 513); see Chapter 7, n. 1, for details of interviews.
20 IWM, SA, 17697, Eden, 14 May 1940; Hansard, vol. 365, cols 1897–1898, 19 November 1940, Sir Edward Grigg.
21 C. Holmes, *John Bull's Island: Immigration and British Society 1871–1971* (London: Macmillan, 1988), pp. 164–165.
22 NA, WO, 199/3237, 503, 20 December 1940. Eastwood's point was frequently forgotten within the BBC; T. Hajkowski, 'The BBC, the Empire, and the Second World War, 1939–1945', *Historical Journal of Film, Radio and Television*, 22:2 (2002), p. 154.
23 Holmes, *John Bull's Island*, p. 133.
24 NA, Home Office (HO), 45/25009, 'Arrangements for the Enrolment of Eire subjects', 14 and 18 July 1941 and HO Circular 700, 169/29, August 1941.
25 NA, HO, 45/25009, 'Arrangements', Report of Regional Conference of Detective Officers, 12 December 1941.
26 NA, HO, 45/25009, 'Irish Labourers Applying to Join HG', MI5 to Home Office, 1 August 1942; 'Arrangements', MI5 to Home Office, 19 October 1943.
27 MacKenzie, *Home Guard*, pp. 84–85; also E. Dunlop, *John Luke's Home Guard* (Ballymena: Ballymena Borough Council, 1994), p. 7.
28 Holmes, *John Bull's Island*, pp. 113–114.
29 Holmes, *John Bull's Island*, pp. 145–146.
30 Holmes, *John Bull's Island*, p. 192.
31 *News Chronicle*, 24 June 1940.
32 Hansard, vol. 363, col. 1007, 25 July 1940.
33 *News Chronicle*, 24 June 1940.
34 George Orwell, *The Collected Essays, Journalism and Letters of George Orwell*, vol. 2: *My Country Right or Left 1940–43*, ed. S. Orwell and I. Angus (London: Secker & Warburg, 1969), pp. 290–291; T. Kushner, *The Persistence of Prejudice: Antisemitism in British Society during the Second World War* (Manchester: Manchester University Press, 1989), Chapter 5.
35 Rose, *Which People's War?*, pp. 92–106.
36 Graves, *Home Guard*, pp. 356–357, quoting Lt-Col., 8th NR (Middlesbrough), Battalion Home Guard. Orwell stated: 'No authoritarian State would have dared to distribute weapons so freely', *Observer*, 15 October 1944.
37 Hansard, vol. 369, col. 1130, 11 March 1941. Nationals of allied or neutral states were admissable, if vouched for by the local chief constable.
38 Hansard, vol. 370, col. 311, 20 March 1941.
39 Some 'enemy aliens' were allowed to join after release from internment: IWM, SA 3789, Klaus Ernst Hinrichson; SA 4420, Gerhard Kraus.
40 Hansard, vol. 361, cols. 403–404, 28 May 1940.
41 Graves, *Home Guard*, p. 11.
42 Hansard, vol. 361 col. 274, 22 May 1940, Richard Law, Financial Secretary at the War Office.

43 GHQ, Home Forces, Local Defence Volunteers Training Instruction No. 2, 1940, p. 2; NA, WO, 199/3237, Home Guard Instruction No. 10, 1940, p. 3.

44 R. Thurlow 'The Evolution of the Mythical British Fifth Column 1939–46', *Twentieth-Century British History*, 10:4 (1999), p. 483.

45 Hansard, vol. 363, col. 434, 18 July 1940; col. 1189, 30 July 1940.

46 Hansard, vol. 365, cols 1891–1892, 19 November 1940.

47 Graves, *Home Guard*, p. 356.

48 Hansard, vol. 365, cols 1886–1891, 19 November 1940, Sir Edward Grigg.

49 Orwell, *Collected Essays*, 'The Lion and the Unicorn', February 1941, p. 85.

50 Hansard, vol. 371, col. 578, 1 May 1941.

51 A. H. Halsey (ed.), *Trends in British Society since 1900* (London: Macmillan 1972), table 4.1, p. 113.

52 *Daily Mail*, 31 October 1941, 'We Don't Want Women in the Home Guard. We Want Better Officers', Lt-Col. T. A. Lowe; also *Evening Standard*, 8 January 1941, 'Don't Let Colonel Blimp Ruin the Home Guard'.

53 Hansard, vol. 396, cols 1603–1604, 8 February 1944. Gallacher, the only wartime Communist MP, sat for West Fife from 1935 to 1950.

54 Calder, *People's War*, pp. 58–59.

55 'Cato', *Guilty Men* (London: Gollancz, July 1940); G. D. H. Cole, H. Laski, G. Orwell, M. Sutherland and F. Williams, *Victory or Vested Interest?* (London: Routledge, 1942).

56 Calder, *People's War*, pp. 243–244; H. Pelling, *The British Communist Party: A Historical Profile* (London: A.&C. Black, 1975), pp. 116–117.

57 Orwell, *Collected Essays*, vol. 2, p. 152.

58 V. Gollancz, *Russia and Ourselves* (London: Gollancz, 1941), p. 100.

59 NA, HO, 45/25009, 'Police Vetting of Men Who Are to Be Compulsorily Enrolled', HO Circular 700, 170/38, 15 May 1940.

60 NA, HO, 45/25009, 'Home Guard Police Scrutiny of Applications', Memoranda, October–December 1940.

61 NA, HO, 45/25009, 'Police Scrutiny', 30 October 1940.

62 Hansard, vol. 363, col. 6, 16 July 1940.

63 C. Williams, *Capitalism, Community and Conflict. The South Wales Coalfield 1898–1947* (Cardiff: University of Wales Press, 1998), pp. 24, 46, 58.

64 Hansard, vol. 362, col. 601, 27 June 1940.

65 Hansard, vol. 363, col. 6, 16 July 1940.

66 A. Jackson, *British Women and the Spanish Civil War 1936–1939* (London: Routledge, 2002); R. Baxell, *British Volunteers in the Spanish Civil War: The British Battalion in the International Brigades, 1936–1939* (London: Routledge, 2004).

67 Hansard, vol. 362, col. 1053, 9 July 1940.

68 H. Lee, 'Doom and Bloomsbury', *Observer*, Review, 2 June 2002.

69 *Daily Herald*, 29 July 1940, 'Peer's Son Excluded from Home Guard'.

70 S. Hastings, *Rosamond Lehmann* (London: Chatto & Windus, 2002), p. 206.

71 NA, HO, 45/25009, 'Police Vetting', 27 January 1942; HO Circular 700 169/35, 19 February 1942.

72 NA, HO, 45/25009, 'Police Vetting', extract from Minutes of Security Conference, 24 February 1943.
73 Rose, *Which People's War?*, p. 54. The British Institute of Public Opinion recorded that 62 per cent of British people favoured Russia over other allies in mid-1942: S. Nicholas, *The Echo of War: Home Front Propaganda and the Wartime BBC, 1939–45* (Manchester: Manchester University Press, 1996), p. 168.
74 IWM, DD, 77/165/1, Brigadier W. Carden Roe, file containing two censored reports on formation of LDV.
75 Graves, *Home Guard*, p. 11; Hansard, vol.361, col. 275, 22 May 1940.
76 G. Orwell, *Homage to Catalonia* (London: Secker & Warburg, 1938).
77 *News Chronicle*, 15 June 1940; also John Langdon-Davies, 'Arm the People', *Reynolds News*, 16 June 1940.
78 GHQ, Home Forces, Local Defence Volunteers Training Instruction No. 2, 1940, 'Instructions Regarding Role and Status', p. 5.
79 D. Fernbach, 'Tom Wintringham and Socialist Defense Strategy', *History Workshop Journal*, 14, (1982), p. 70; also H. Purcell, *The Last English Revolutionary: Tom Wintringham 1898–1949* (Stroud: Sutton, 2004).
80 T. Wintringham, *Armies of Freemen* (London: Routledge, 1940), p. ix.
81 T. Wintringham, *Mutiny: A Survey of Mutinies from Spartacus to Invergordon* (London: Stanley Nott, 1936).
82 Wintringham, *Armies*, pp. 57–77.
83 Wintringham, *Armies*, chapter 8.
84 T. Wintringham, 'Against Invasion: The Lessons of Spain', *Picture Post*, 15 June 1940, p. 12.
85 T. Wintringham, *New Ways of War* (Harmondsworth: Penguin, 1940), p. 73; also Wintringham, 'Against Invasion', p. 11.
86 Wintringham, *New Ways*, p. 73.
87 T. Wintringham, 'The Home Guard Can Fight', *Picture Post*, 21 September 1940, pp. 9–10.
88 H. Slater, *Home Guard for Victory* (London: Gollancz, 1941), quoted in Purcell, *Last English Revolutionary*, p. 186; Orwell, *Collected Essays*, vol. 2, pp. 116, 153.
89 Purcell, *Last English Revolutionary*, p. 194. Wintringham implies that the Spanish Civil War was conducted as a guerrilla war, but Orwell experienced deadlocked trench warfare on the Aragón front.
90 Wintringham, 'The Home Guard Can Fight', pp. 9–17; King's College London Archive (KCLA), T. H. Wintringham Archive, 5/25, Report on Osterley Park (n.d.); M. Panter-Downes, *Letter from England* (Boston: Little, Brown & Co., 1940), pp. 229–243; 'Home Guards Told Use Sneakthief Methods', *Sunday Express*, 4 August 1940.
91 Wintringham, 'The Home Guard Can Fight', pp. 13, 10; see also Purcell, *Last English Revolutionary*, pp. 192–193; and Orwell, 'Diary', 20 August 1940, in *Collected Essays*, p. 368.

92 MacKenzie, *Home Guard*, pp. 73–76; Purcell, *Last English Revolutionary*, pp. 197–199.

93 NA, WO, 165/92, Inspectorate of Local Defence Volunteers, 6, 12 July 1940; Panter-Downes, *Letter*, p. 230: the War Office 'smiles benignly on the project but hasn't yet given it official standing'.

94 NA, WO, 165/92, Inspectorate of Local Defence Volunteers, 8, 16 July 1940, and 9, 19 July 1940; MI5 appears not to have responded and may have regarded other threats to security as more serious.

95 Hansard, vol. 365, col. 1889, 19 November 1940.

96 NA, WO, 199/3237, 468, Home Guard School, Administrative Instructions.

97 NA, WO, 199/3237, 400, 1 October 1940, 43/Misc/6977 (MT7).

98 NA, WO, 165/92 Inspectorate of Local Defence Volunteers, 21, 10 September 1940, and 22, 17 September 1940.

99 KCLA, Wintringham Archive, 1/34, Wintringham to Lt Gen Andrew Thorne, GOC Scottish Command, 6 December (1941).

100 *Citizen Army* (1940); *Home Guard* (1941); *Unarmed Combat* (1941). Both *Citizen Army* and *Home Guard* were referred to in the official files as 'Osterley Park'; however, the notes stating 'Location: Osterley Park, Nr Dorking' suggest that they were in fact shot at Denbies.

101 NA, INF, 6/446, *Citizen Army*.

102 BBC, WAC, R19/509 Entertainment Home Guard 1940–43, 'We Also Serve', 8 March 1941, repeated 24 April 1941, and 'In Readiness', 3 July 1941.

103 KCLA, Wintringham Archive, 3/32, Wintringham to Buell Hammett, Santa Barbara, 19 December 1941. After leaving, Wintringham worked with Sir Richard Acland to form a new broad-left political party, called Common Wealth. He contested Midlothian North, a Conservative seat, in a bye-election in February 1943, losing by less than 1,000 votes: see Purcell, *Last English Revolutionary*, pp. 216–217.

104 Wintringham, 'Train the Home Guard', *Picture Post*, vol. 11, no. 7, 17 May 1941, pp. 26–27.

105 NA, WO, 199/3237 Regulations and Instructions Related to Local Defence Volunteers and Home Guard, No. 468, Home Guard School. 'Platoon commanders and above' were to comprise the student body; they were told to 'park their cars under the cover of trees'(2 per cent of the population owned cars in 1939) and were permitted to 'bring their own valise and bedding' but not 'servants as no accommodation is available'.

106 Wintringham, 'Train the Home Guard', pp. 24–28.

107 In fact the USSR armed partisans to resist the Nazi invasion in June 1941 and Germany armed the *Volkssturm* as a last-ditch defence against allied invasion in 1944–45.

108 M. Taylor, 'Patriotism, History and the Left in Twentieth-Century Britain', *Historical Journal*, 33:4 (1990), p. 982.

109 Orwell, *Collected Essays*, vol. 2, pp. 116–117.

110 Wintringham, 'Train the Home Guard', p. 28; Wintringham, *New Ways*,

Chapter 2.

111 Orwell, Review of Hugh Slater's *Home Guard for Victory*, in *New Statesman and Nation*, 21 (1941), p. 168, quoted in MacKenzie, *Home Guard*, p. 105. For others who agreed see Mass-Observation Archive (MOA), TC 66, Town and District Survey, Box 22, Worcester Village, HN, 10 September 1940 and 21 October 1940; KCLA, Liddell Hart Collection, 5 4 337, Correspondence and Intelligence, June–July 1941.

112 A. G. Street, *From Dusk Till Dawn* (London: Blandford Press, 1946), p. 92.

113 J. Langdon-Davies, *Parachutes Over Britain* (London: Pilot Press, 1940), p. 19.

114 J. Langdon-Davies, *Home Guard Fieldcraft Manual* (London: John Murray 1942); Street, *From Dusk Till Dawn*, pp. 91–95.

115 D. Lampe, *The Last Ditch: The Secrets of the Nationwide British Resistance Organization and the Nazi Plans for the Occupation of Britain 1940–1944* (London: Cassell, 1968), p. 69.

116 GHQ, Home Forces, Home Guard Instruction No. 51, 'Battlecraft and Battle Drill for the Home Guard', Part 4, November 1943.

117 Wintringham, *New Ways*, p. 28. B. Liddell Hart, *Dynamic Defence* (London: Faber & Faber, 1940), pp. 51–56; 'Are We Wasting the Home Guards' Time?', *Daily Mail*, 11 April 1942.

118 MacKenzie, *Home Guard*, pp. 106–107.

119 MacKenzie, *Home Guard*, pp. 102–105.

120 NA, WO, 199/1869, GOC to Corps Cmdrs, Operational Role of HG, June 1942, quoted in MacKenzie, *Home Guard*, p. 108.

121 GHQ, Home Forces, Home Guard Instruction No. 51, 'Battlecraft and Battle-drill for the Home Guard', Part II, September 1942, p. 1.

122 Churchill, *Complete Speeches*, vol. 6, p. 6519, 2 December 1941; p. 6635, 12 May 1942; Churchill, *Second World War*, vol. 4, p. 833. Liddell Hart, *Daily Mail*, 18 November 1941 and *Manchester Evening News*, 4, 5, 6 November 1942.

123 For the range of masculinities elaborated in the military in modern democracies see D. Morgan, 'Theatre of War: Combat, the Military, and Masculinities', in H. Brod and M. Kaufman (eds), *Theorizing Masculinities* (London: Sage, 1994), pp. 165–182.

124 NA, WO, 199/363 60A, Marshall-Cornwall to Swayne, 27 April 1942, quoted in MacKenzie, *Home Guard*, p. 113.

125 Hansard, vol. 376, col. 1031, 2 December 1941 (Prime Minister).

126 General Staff, Army Training Memorandum No. 35 (War Office, 1940), quoted in D. French, '"You Cannot Hate the Bastard Who Is Trying to Kill You ...": Combat and Ideology in the British Army in the War Against Germany, 1939–45' (2000), reprinted in G. Martel (ed.), *The World War Two Reader* (London: Routledge, 2004), p. 184.

127 'H.G.s Say "Pikes Are Best at Night"', *Daily Express*, 6 February 1942; 'Home Guard Pikes Are Not a War Office Joke', *News Chronicle*, 6 February 1942; 'How to Use That Pike', *Daily Herald*, 7 February 1942.

128 Hansard, vol. 378, cols 1129 (Captain Godfrey Nicholson, Conservative, Farnham, Surrey), 1137 (Willie Gallacher, Communist, West Fife), 11 March 1942; also col. 1147 (Sir Henry Fildes, Liberal Nationalist, Dumfriesshire, who addressed Croft in satirical verse).

129 'Home Guards Deride Pikes', *Daily Telegraph*, 18 March 1942, quoting Lord Mansfield.

130 Numbers rose from 11,000 (May 1942) to c.150,000 (August 1944): MacKenzie, *Home Guard*, pp. 109, 117, 122, 150.

131 D. French, *Raising Churchill's Army: The British Army and the War against Germany 1919–1945* (Oxford: Oxford University Press), p. 206.

132 GHQ, Home Forces, Home Guard Instruction No. 56, February 1943, pp. 7–8, 4. Reports indicating the seriousness of such exercises include: 'Home Guards Like Realism', *Daily Express*, 3 March 1942; 'Civilians to Dig Trenches', *Daily Express*, 9 March 1942; BBC, WAC R42/112/2, Protection, Home Guard 1941–45, Chief Umpire's Report on Exercise 'Scrag' 17/18 April 1943.

133 Hansard, vol. 376, col. 2123, 18 December 1941; 'I'm A Home Guard And (At 50) I Don't Want to Be a Commando!', *Sunday Dispatch*, 29 November 1942.

134 GHQ, Home Forces, Home Guard Instruction No. 56, February 1943, p. 6.

135 Collier, *Defence*, pp. 231, 298–300, 322–323; 'Had There Been No Home Guard We Would Have to Form One Now', *Sunday Dispatch*, 2 April 1944; E. Raymond, *Please You, Draw Near: Autobiography 1922–1968* (London: Cassell, 1969), p. 90.

136 Local Defence Volunteers Training Instuctions No. 6, 1940, 'Relations Between the Civil Defence Services and the Local Defence Volunteers'; NA, WO, 199/3237, Home Guard Instruction No. 10, 1940, sections 1 and 3 (e); NA, WO, 199/3243, G. W. Lambert, War Office, to Commander-in-Chief, Home Forces, 3 May 1944.

137 NA, WO, 199/3243, G. W. Lambert, War Office, to Commander-in-Chief, Home Forces, 3 May 1944.

138 NA, HO, 45/25009, MI5 to Home Office, 11 November 1942.

139 NA, HO, 45/25009, 'Police Vetting', 27 January 1942. The list of prohibited aliens grew however, including, in February 1942, Hungarians, Bulgarians, Roumanians, Finns, Thailanders and Japanese nationals: NA, HO, 45/25009, 'Enrolment of Aliens in the Home Guard', War Office to Army Commanders-in-Chief, 23 February 1942.

140 Parliamentary Papers, *Home Guard: Memorandum on the Principal Measures to Be Provided for by Defence Regulations*, December 1941, Cmd. 6324.

141 'Home Guards Will Be "Privates"', *Daily Express*, 3 February 1942. Home Guard NCO and officer ranks had been brought into line with army ranks as early as February 1941, but the term 'volunteer' for other ranks had remained.

142 E.g. IWM, DD, 72/59/5, Brigadier G. W. Sutton, 'Address to the Home Guard by G.O.C. in C.', South Eastern Command, January 1943.

143 I. R. Bet-El, *Conscripts: Lost Legions of the Great War* (Stroud: Sutton, 1999), p. 3.

144 Hansard, vol. 376, cols 2164–2166, 18 December 1941, Josiah Wedgwood, Labour, Newcastle-under-Lyme; Henry Charleton, Labour, South Leeds, made similar points: vol. 376, cols 2122–2124, 18 December 1941.

145 Hansard, vol. 368, col. 74, 21 January 1941.

146 Lt-Col. T. A. Lowe, 'Slackers in the Home Guard', *Daily Mail*, 16 April 1941; Lt-Col. T. A. Lowe, 'They Still May Try it Here So – Conscript the Home Guard!' *Daily Mail*, 31 May 1941; 'Act Now – Give the Home Guard COMPULSION', *Sunday Graphic*, 22 June 1941; Hansard, vol. 374, col. 1796, 22 October 1941.

147 'Officers Attack Home Guard Dodgers: War Office Urged to Impose Real Army Discipline', *Sunday Chronicle*, 7 September, 1941; 'Sergeant Said "So What?" to H.G. Subaltern', *Daily Mail*, 9 September 1941. Compulsion in the Home Guard raised the issue of medical inspection on army lines, but medical tests were never applied, with the result that the Home Guard was always at risk of over-straining some members as well as being seen as the 'army of the unfit'.

148 Hansard, vol. 376, col. 1031, 2 December 1941.

149 Hansard, vol. 376, col. 1032, 2 December 1941.

150 Hansard, vol. 376, col. 2125, 18 December 1941.

151 'Our Readers Write about Home Guards' Inaction', *Reynolds News*, 11 January 1942; see also 'Court Martialled', *Sunday Express*, 22 March 1942. The accused complained about the emphasis on 'ceremonials' and said they wanted to fight 'like the Russians'.

152 Graves, *Home Guard*, pp. 309, 361.

153 'H.G.s Say: Bands, Flags, and No Brass Hats', *Daily Express*, 29 August 1944

154 J. Langdon-Davies, 'The Truth about Home Guard Conscripts', *Sunday Pictorial*, 4 January 1942.

155 E.g. Arthur Spicer, rejected for military service with the lowest fitness rating but fined for failing to attend the Home Guard: *Daily Express*, 28 September 1943.

156 'Citrine's Criticisms of Home Guard Drills Are Supported', *News Chronicle*, 9 November 1943. For discussion of the injustice to miners see Hansard, vol. 392, cols 800–801, 12 October 1943; vol. 395, cols 219–220, 30 November 1943; for agricultural workers see vol. 380, col. 22, 19 May 1942; vol. 380, cols 1687–1688, 18 June 1942. Also 'Farmers and the Home Guard', *Lake District Herald*, 13 March 1943; 'Farmer Home Guard Fined £12', *Evening Standard*, 7 July 1943.

157 'H.G. Farm Worker Missed Drill', *Daily Express*, 6 October 1942; 'Want Jailed Home Guard Released', *Daily Herald*, 9 October, 1942.

158 'Compulsion: H.G. Poll Yields a Post-War Challenge', *News of the World*, 13 February 1944.

159 G. Orwell, 'Home Guard Lessons for the Future', *Observer*, 15 October, 1944.

160 'Recorder on Colour Bar. Fine on West Indian Reduced', *The Times*, 2 August 1944, p. 2, col. E.
161 *The Times*, 2 August 1944; *News Chronicle*, 2 August 1944.
162 See also Holmes, *John Bull's Island*, p. 203; Rose, *Which People's War?*, p. 248.
163 The term was coined by J. B. Priestley in 1941 to refer to members of new wartime voluntary associations, including the Home Guard, whose circumstances 'favour a sharply democratic outlook': quoted in Calder, *People's War*, p. 163.

3

Women, weapons and home defence

In his broadcast of May 1940 Eden referred to the desire of 'men of all ages ... to do something for the defence of their country' and invited those aged 17–65 to join the LDV. But, from the start, women also asked to join. They did not take rebuff lightly: of all the exclusions discussed in Chapter 2, the one that was most vigorously and persistently challenged was that of women. This chapter traces the contest over women's membership, the nature of the opposition and the creation of an entirely new organisation, Women's Home Defence (WHD). It explores the use made of women by local Home Guard units, and the eventual, but still unstable, official compromise over women's membership of the force. The questions of whether the Home Guard needed women, and, if it did, on what terms, were connected with the bigger issue of women's role in the defence of Britain and in the war effort as a whole. 'Watching and waiting' was a thing of the past, but how far was women's active participation to go, and was their contribution to the war effort to include any form of combat?

Women and the Home Guard: the campaign

While Eden had called for men, the attitude of several MPs to the crisis of the summer of 1940 was that home defence needed all the able-bodied recruits it could attract, including women. For these MPs the question was not so much whether women should be allowed to join the LDV as whether they should have combatant or auxiliary roles. In June 1940 Frederick Seymour Cocks, Labour MP for Nottinghamshire (Broxtowe), asked if women 'who can use a rifle' could be members, and in July, Eleanor Rathbone, Independent MP for the Combined English Universities, asked if 'there was to be a women's force auxiliary to the L.D.V. similar to the auxiliaries to the Army, Navy and Air Force'.[1] The reply to Cocks was a curt 'No, Sir', and to Rathbone that the matter was 'under consideration', although the War Office files indicate that this was not the case. Dr Edith Summerskill backed up both questioners. She asked for reasons for the reply to Cocks and was told that, 'apart from any question of principle ... there are all sorts of questions of organisation which make it impracticable': however, none was spelled out.[2] She followed Rathbone by asking Anthony Eden 'how we are to fight in the hills, in the streets and in the houses ... if women are excluded from the L.D.V.s?', and was told that this was 'a different question'.[3] Summerskill's words echoed those of Churchill following the evacuation of Dunkirk.[4] Her demand for an ungendered understanding of 'we', the British population, who would 'never surrender', set the tone for her prolonged engagement with the Government on the issue of women in the Home Guard: she repeatedly confronted political and military leaders with the inclusive rhetoric of the war effort and asked why women were in practice excluded from it; she also consistently challenged the prohibition on women's use of firearms.

Edith Summerskill was more committed to gender equality than were other parliamentary questioners. Labour MP for Fulham West from 1938 to 1955, and then for Warrington from 1955 until she accepted a life peerage in 1961, she took a leading role in controversial issues concerning women before and during the war. These included the advocacy of birth control, painless childbirth, abortion law reform, equal pay, and equal rights for women at work and in marriage. She was insistent during the war that military service, including combat, was not harmful to women, physically or morally, and she supported women's deployment in a range of *men's* jobs, including work on anti-aircraft gun sites and in heavy and skilled branches of industry.[5]

Summerskill again expressed her outrage at the exclusion of women from the British 'we' during Sir Edward Grigg's effusive speech about the Home Guard of November 1940. When he characterised the new force as 'a lusty infant', she called out 'But it is of only one sex'; and when he listed the all-male litany of saints marching in its ranks she threw in 'What about Boadicea?'[6] In her own speeches she made her egalitarian principles explicit: 'I am not asking for women to be included solely as cooks and clerks in the Home Guard but in the same capacity as men, with equal rights and no privileges'.[7] She dismissed the idea that women were not suitable for military duties like picketing, patrolling, observation, communications and barricading the streets, and insisted that rifle-training was required so that women would not find themselves helpless in an invasion because it 'was not womanly for me to learn how to use a rifle'.[8] Summerskill dismissed the relevance of conventional gender roles to combat, yet evoked them in relation to the domestic and local focus of Home Guard activity, emphasising (in the period prior to women's direction and call-up) the special suitability for the Home Guard of women 'who can remain in their own homes and in their own towns and villages'.[9] At the heart of the nation was the home, and within the home was a woman: who better to arm and train for home defence, then, than women?

There were two ostensible reasons for the Government's refusal to consider women's membership of the Home Guard: shortage of resources (instructors, respirators, rifles, steel helmets, uniforms);[10] and the demand for women in other aspects of the war effort (civil defence, factories, nursing and voluntary organisations).[11] Summerskill and others responded that ways of sharing scant resources could be found,[12] and that the most suitable members of both sexes must be recruited for these various types of work: 'it is better for a C3 man to do the washing up and for an A1 woman ... to be on the gun site'.[13] Rarely expressed, but underlying the official objections, was the notion that it was not appropriate for women to bear arms. One Director General of the Home Guard after another repeated this view, but with a circularity that threw no light on the reasons for the prohibition. Lieut.-General Sir Ralph Eastwood wrote in December 1940, 'Under no circumstances should women be enrolled in the Home Guard ... it is undesirable for women to bear arms in the Home Guard, and I do not think anyone should be enrolled in the Home Guard who is not under obligation to bear arms.' The argument was still being repeated in October 1941: Major-General Lord Bridgeman stated that everyone in the Home Guard must be 'trained in the use of arms ... to prevent Conscientious Objectors and others being able to slide into the Home Guard to get the protection of the uniform and yet decline to prepare themselves to fight the King's battles'. Women could not bear arms (even if they wanted to fight the King's battles) and therefore could not be admitted.[14]

However, the emergence of a women's home-defence movement bore out Summerskill's insistence that women were keen to serve – in an armed capacity – in home defence, and were prepared to defy such War Office pronouncements.[15] Some of them had joined rifle clubs and learned to shoot before the war.[16] In the summer of 1940 a group was formed under the leadership of Venetia Foster in the West End of London called the

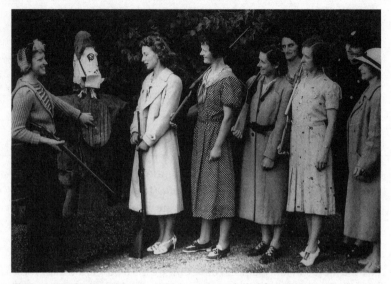

Figure 1 Mrs Venetia Foster training women excluded from LDV in the Amazon Defence Corps

Amazon Defence Corps, a choice of name celebrating a feminine warrior identity which (as we shall see) male politicians derided. Its objectives were 'to obtain training for women in the use and handling of firearms and other weapons of defence' and to secure equal membership of the LDV.[17]

A similar group was formed in Bristol under the title Women's Home Defence Corps. In December 1940 its leader, Miss Watson-Williams, elicited the help of Mavis Tate, Conservative MP for Frome, who forwarded a petition signed by one hundred people from the Bristol area to the Secretary of State for War, demanding equal membership of the Home Guard and 'that women of the Home Guard shall be trained in the use of handling of firearms, and that arms shall be issued to them'.[18] From these beginnings a new national wartime organisation developed, with Venetia Foster of the Amazon Defence Corps as Treasurer and Edith Summerskill as Chairman.[19] As we shall see in the next section, there was mounting evidence of its local co-operation with the Home Guard.

In response to such infringements, the War Office explicitly banned women's involvement with the Home Guard. In November 1941 the following announcement appeared in *The Times* and elsewhere:

> The War Office has sent an order to all Home Guard units that the training of
> women as unofficial Home Guard units has not been authorized. Weapons
> and ammunition in the charge of the Army or of Home Guard units must
> not be used for the instruction of women and the use of the name Home
> Guard is not permitted.[20]

Growing shortages of military personnel, however, as well as technological
changes that blurred the line between combatant and non-combatant
roles, were putting pressure on such thinking, in the army if not the
Home Guard. General Sir Frederick Pile, General Officer Commanding
Anti-Aircraft Command, devised a scheme to release 40,000 servicemen
on anti-aircraft batteries for more active forms of service by replacing
them with women from the Auxiliary Territorial Service (ATS). But Sir
James Grigg, as Under-Secretary of State for War in 1941, described Pile's
scheme (disapprovingly) as 'breath-taking and revolutionary'[21] and the
military hierarchy strove to ensure that the operational deployment
of women on anti-aircraft gun batteries did not breach the prohibition against women's use of lethal weapons. Officially, men loaded and
fired the guns, while women operated the height and range finders that
enabled them to be aimed, and were not classified as combatants. General
Pile, who favoured interchangeable roles, said crossly that the government 'was prepared to allow women to do anything to kill the enemy
except pull the trigger.'[22] In practice, the distinction between *aiming* and
firing the guns was increasingly spurious, but attempts to maintain the
divide between combatant men and non-combatant women continued.
Women were required to give their consent in writing to perform any
work in the Forces that required handling lethal weapons (which they
were not allowed to fire), whereas it was taken for granted that men would
do such work.[23]

Summerskill thought that the underlying causes of the opposition to
women's involvement in combat lay in persistent 'nineteenth-century'
attitudes to femininity, notably 'this idea that women are still weak, gentle
creatures who must be protected', which was particularly strong in the
'masculine' War Office.[24] She insisted that such beliefs had been vitiated by
the conditions of modernity: twentieth-century forms of warfare, such as
aerial bombardment, did not discriminate between combatants and non-
combatants, men and women; modern social practices, such as women's
participation in politics and a wide variety of paid work, had breached the
traditional divide between the sexes. Summerskill argued that there were
increasing numbers of women – and men – who had no time for the outdated prejudice against women's role in combat. She insisted on joining

the Parliamentary Home Guard and participating in rifle drill, one of many cases in which the rules were conspicuously flouted.[25]

Summerskill was particularly incensed by the contradiction between the Government's obdurate refusal of a place for women in the Home Guard, and the provisions of the National Service (No. 2) Act of December 1941. As we saw in Chapter 2, under the Act men aged 18–51 could be compelled to serve in the Home Guard in areas considered below strength: the context was that because of increased mobilisation and a decrease in volunteers, the number of men in the force had shrunk by 150,000 in the second half of 1941. The Act also made provision for the conscription of single women aged 19–30 to the ATS (as well as for other forms of war service). These policy decisions regarding the Home Guard and the ATS were linked. Both were designed to increase the personnel available to support the British Army; specifically, both male Home Guards and ATS women were deployed to replace regular soldiers on anti-aircraft batteries. Furthermore, in introducing the Bill to Parliament, Churchill and Margesson, Secretary of State of War from December 1940 to February 1942, announced the intention to encourage 16-year-old boys to volunteer for the Home Guard for duties with searchlight, anti-aircraft and coastal defence detachments.[26] Summerskill expressed outrage that men aged eighteen to fifty-one were conscripted and boys of 16 asked to volunteer, when there were plenty of 'mature' women volunteers asking to be recognised as members of the Home Guard. When a male colleague interjected 'What is a mature woman?' Summerskill coolly replied: 'I am sorry the Hon. Member has never met one' and offered to have a word with him later.[27] But such cheeky responses aside, the official rebuttal was that recruiting women to the Home Guard would drain the pool of female labour available for industry, civil defence and the women's auxiliary forces. This hardly made sense, given both the new provision for conscripting women for war service, and the rules governing Home Guard membership: Home Guard service need not exempt women, any more than men, from call up to the military or from the requirement to combine it with other types of war work. But the perceived threat to the female labour supply, in the context of intense wartime competition over 'manpower', remained a reason for the opposition of ministers who might otherwise have been expected to support the enrolment of women in the Home Guard.[28]

In December 1941, to emphasise the viability of women Home Guards, Summerskill reported on the development of the WHD to Parliament:

There is now in this country a Women's Home Defence Corps. It is not a small corps. The unit in Edinburgh is so strong that it cannot take any more women because there are not enough instructors. In Cambridge, Leamington, Pinner, Slough, Harrow and other districts all over the country women have come voluntarily together to learn how to use a rifle, and I wish the Minister, instead of frowning at them, would give them his blessing.[29]

A few months later, in March 1942, she estimated the WHD's London membership at 10,000, explaining in a letter to the War Office that the organisation co-operated with the Home Guard and the Civil Defence Services and that training included 'Musketry ... Bombing ... Tommy Gun ... Un-Armed Combat ... Field Craft ... Anti-Gas Drill ... Elementary First-Aid ... Sandbagging ... Trench-Digging ... Field Cooking ... Physical Exercises'. The WHD attracted members through announcements on cinema screens and in local newspapers and through its links with other women's organisations, including the Women's Voluntary Services (WVS).[30] The WHD's self concept was expressed by its badge. It was a deep red shield with gold edging, divided into four segments by crossed rifles. The letters WHD were positioned in three of the segments and the fourth was occupied by a revolver, emphatically associating women with lethal weapons. However, any War Office 'blessing' for such an organisation was to prove impossible to obtain, although not for want of trying.

One of the WHD's influential supporters was Dame Helen Gwynne-Vaughan, Professor of Botany at Birkbeck College, University of London, since 1909, and Director of the ATS from 1939 to 1941. Like Summerskill, she was well known for her equal rights views, which had made her unpopular in the War Office.[31] Her leadership of the ATS had ended in unhappy forced retirement in July 1941, largely because of her insistence on equal rights with male soldiers for ATS members, coupled with opposition to any integration of the force with the army that might reduce the authority of its women leaders.[32] Following her dismissal from the ATS in July 1941, Gwynne-Vaughan joined the WHD and became 'president' of the Holborn Defence Unit.[33] She was committed to cooperation between the WHD and the Home Guard, claiming that 14 per cent of the work done by men of the Home Guard could be done by women: she herself worked as a volunteer administrator for Lt.-Gen. Sir Douglas Brownrigg, commanding officer (CO) of one of the zones of the London Home Guard.[34] She also passed on her knowledge of the military to the WHD in a booklet which explained the structure of the Army and the Home Guard's place within it, as well as the conventions of military correspondence.[35] Gwynne-Vaughan was committed to the idea that the WHD might become 'the A.T.S. of the Home Guard'.[36]

In January 1942, in co-operation with Summerskill, Gwynne-Vaughan presented a 'memorial' (as she called it) to the War Office recommending 'the enrolment of women in the Home Guard ... for part-time, unpaid training and duty'. She was insistent on a uniform – 'a khaki cap, a brassard and possibly a khaki overall' – but she was not as committed as Summerskill to weapons training, which was not central to her vision of the WHD as an auxiliary force. In contrast, Summerskill felt that it was important to keep the possibility of armed involvement open. Gwynne-Vaughan's memorial stated that women should be enrolled 'for duties in case of invasion similar to those performed by women serving with the regular forces': Summerskill added the words 'and any others which may appear necessary in an emergency'.[37] The memorial was signed by twenty eminent figures, including members of the WVS,[38] the women's military auxiliaries,[39] the Home Guard,[40] heads of academic institutions,[41] politicians and military figures.[42] Discussion in the correspondence columns of *The Times* was largely favourable: women auxiliaries could perform 'secondary duties' like driving and could even volunteer for work on gunsites 'to set free ... trained men for actual fighting'.[43] But the discouraging official response was that the Secretary of State was 'not convinced that there is a need for the enrolment of women in the Home Guard at present'.[44] Thus at the beginning of 1942, the women campaigners appeared to be no closer to achieving their goal of women's membership of the Home Guard than they had been in the summer of 1940.

The War Office was consistently hostile towards the WHD. Both Gwynne-Vaughan and Summerskill were regarded unsympathetically as cranks who coveted men's part in war and would not be content with 'appropriate' wartime roles for women. An official record of a formal meeting between Summerskill and Sir James Grigg, then Secretary of State for War, on 27 February 1942, reads:

> Dr Summerskill made it quite clear that she is not in the least concerned with the question of fetchers and carriers. What she wants is the acceptance of the principle that women should be enlisted into the Home Guard as fully combatant members of it to man barricades, to go on reconnaissances etc after being trained in the use of the rifle and, if necessary, in automatic weapons ...The S.o.S. made it clear to her that he would not accept any such proposal.[45]

The minute continued by stating that the only arrangements acceptable to Grigg were informal ones between the Home Guard and the WVS.[46] Soon after this, Grigg said to Summerskill's face that he wanted to hear no more about 'your bloody women',[47] but she refused to give up, writing in March 1942 to request that Grigg 'consider raising the ban on the musketry instruction of women by the Home Guard',[48] and to Herbert Morrison, in April 1942, asking that 'all duties now allotted to the Home Guard which could be effectively performed by women should now be undertaken by them'.[49] The War Office regarded these proposals with deep suspicion as the thin end of a wedge: any scheme giving recognition to women who helped the Home Guard, as combatants or non-combatants, would 'burst its bonds in a very short time' and 'the road to a complete Women's Home Guard with uniform and compulsion and so on would [be] a short one'.[50] Following a WHD rally in London on 19 April 1942, which attracted press coverage,[51] the Permanent Under-Secretary, Sir Frederick Bovenschen, looked into the possibility of suppressing the WHD completely by means of a legal point:

> The training which is being given by Women's Home Defence appears prima facie to be contrary to the law which prohibits 'All meetings and assemblies of persons for the purpose of training or drilling themselves or being trained or drilled to the use of arms ... without any lawful authority from His Majesty or the Lieutenant, or two Justices of the Peace, of any county'.[52]

The implication was that the WHD was an illegal organisation. But the men from the War Office were inhibited in applying this law by two possibilities. Firstly, two JPs might, indeed, have 'given authority' for the formation of a WHD unit in their area;[53] and, secondly, a political head of steam had developed in support of recognition: 'If any steps are taken to stop the activities of the organisation there will no doubt be a mass of protest', wrote Bovenschen.[54] The War Office could not snuff out the WHD, nor could it ignore it. Yet any compromise on women's inclusion in the Home Guard threatened to 'burst its bonds' and lead to 'a complete Women's Home Guard'.

Women were suggesting that there were good reasons in wartime for breaching the conventional gender boundary that denied them equal membership of an armed organisation. Their temerity appears to have caused disproportionate offence at the top of the politico-military hierarchy. Lower down there was both support and opposition. Squadron-Leader Eric Errington, Conservative MP for Bootle, made the refusal to admit women to the Home Guard, and to arm them, a topic of his maiden speech in November 1941. He posed the question of what women were supposed to do if a German came to their door, responding to a fellow MP's interjection, 'Shoot him', with the objection:

> But they have nothing to shoot him with and the women are not to be trained and given information to enable them to protect themselves. I wish, and I am sure everyone wishes, that women and children could be kept completely out of this war, but I do not believe that to be possible. In Russia women are right in the war. Why should not our women be taught the use of hand grenades and revolvers with which they could protect themselves?[55]

Errington was not alone in referring to women's part in the 'Russian' war effort as a justification for recruiting women to the British Home Guard. Not only did other male MPs insist on it, but women themselves referred to 'the achievements of the Russian women' as a spur to joining.[56]

While Errington felt that the only possible response to total war was to arm women, echoing the proposals for a 'citizens' army' of the summer of 1940, at least other male MP expressed a clear distaste for such a step. In September 1942 David Robertson, Conservative MP for the Streatham division of Wandsworth, received a letter from Miss B. Gooch, 'organiser of the Streatham Unit of Women's Home Defence', explaining the purpose and character of her organisation and requesting 'that you will use your influence in Parliament to urge the Government to grant us official recognition'. Robertson replied that he certainly would not do so: 'A woman's duty is to give life and not to take it, and the training which your Movement gives in unarmed combat, signalling, fieldcraft and musketry, is abhorrent to me.' He saw no need for women to be members of the Home Guard: 'I am most anxious that women should go out into the world in all kinds of occupations which are congenial and useful to the community. But I am opposed to women fighting.' He advised Miss Gooch that her members should 'qualify in Home Nursing' or seek part-time work.[57] His 'abhorrence', based on an essentialist view of women's fundamentally maternal identity, may have given expression to the unarticulated beliefs of the political and military leadership.

Nevertheless, in the autumn of 1942 the Government conceded that some recognition of women who helped the Home Guard would have to be granted, envisaging an entirely non-combatant role for women and an arrangement that explicitly ruled out any links with Summerskill's organisation: 'it is not proposed to mention specifically the Women's Home Defence as one of the voluntary organisations through which this assistance should be afforded'.[58] In correspondence with Herbert Morrison, Minister of Home Security, in December 1942, Grigg dismissed

Summerskill as 'our Amazonian colleague', using the term to conjure up an aggressive and barbarous woman rather than the fearless fighters invoked by the Amazon Defence Corps. Morrison replied, snidely (with reference to current proposals that women should provide catering for the Home Guard): 'your critic referred to wants a gun, not a dish cloth. This proposal will appeal to her only if she sees in it a stepping-stone to manlier things.'[59] Even though this was a confidential exchange, Summerskill was evidently aware of the hostile use of the term 'Amazon'. In the same month she sought to distance WHD from its negative connotations by emphasising that the objectives of the movement were consistent with other ways in which women were participating in the war effort. At a meeting in Liverpool to inaugurate the Merseyside group of the WHD, in December 1942, she insisted that

> members were not Amazons, but determined, resolute women, who asked only that they should receive training in means of defence. Women were conscripted into the Services, directed to munition factories, put on gun sites and compelled to fire-watch. Why, in the name of common sense then, were they not given the right to defend themselves?[60]

The commonsensical case for including women in the Home Guard for combatant as well as non-combatant duties struck others as reasonable. In 1943, Vera Douie reported in her survey of wartime discrimination against women that there were now 250 WHD units, reflecting the demand of many British women for firearms training, 'so that their resistance to the enemy in case of invasion might be effective as well as determined'. She concluded, 'The discouragement of such eager volunteers seems a waste of very useful material.'[61] It was not, however, wasted everywhere.

Women's local participation

Edna Selwyn, at the time a secretary working for a Birmingham company director, remembered that in May 1940 Anthony Eden 'asked every sort of body' who wanted 'to defend the country if there was an invasion … to go to the nearest police station and sign on'. Accordingly, 'I went straight round there as soon as Anthony Eden finished'. She recalled that the police sergeant 'was quite horrified and said "I had no idea there'd be any women"', but gave her the job of helping male volunteers, many of whom were illiterate, to fill in their forms.[62] Her concurrent 'woman's work' ensured that she had the appropriate and much-needed clerical skills; subsequently she became secretary and telephonist to the West

Midlands Home Guard Zone Commander. In contrast, Ann Godden, a schoolgirl of 15 in Sunningdale, Berkshire, possessed skills unusual for a woman. Her father had taught her to shoot prior to May 1940 at the rifle club to which he belonged, and Ann recalled that, in response to Eden's message, 'he said, "Come on, get up, get your coat, we're going to enlist you know." So I got my coat and we went and enlisted just like that.' As in Edna's case, the response was not immediately welcoming: 'The police sergeant, he said "We don't want women." And Dad said, "Yes you do, she can shoot as well as any man", and so they took me, just like that.'[63] Pragmatism prompted the police to accept both Edna and Ann: clerical skills were useful in any organisation including an armed one; and, when invasion threatened, a woman who could fire a rifle was as valuable as a man who could not. As Ann said: 'It was obviously a time of great stress generally and things that people didn't normally do, they did, under those circumstances.'[64]

It was not only the case that women (and their fathers) insisted that the Home Guard should have female members: there were also Home Guard commanders who were keen to enlist them, before and after the publication of the War Office ban in November 1941. There were three – overlapping – reasons for this transgressive recruitment: shortage of male recruits; identification of 'feminine' roles that needed filling; and a more general conviction that women as well as men should be armed participants in home defence.

Brigadier H. P. Currey, Commander of the Sussex and Surrey Area Home Guard, emphasised the problem of shortages of male recruits in a letter to the War Office of 3 September 1941: 'there is a growing tendency to rely on the employment of women as the Home Guard loses men owing to call-ups for the services'. He said that women worked as clerical workers, drivers, store-keepers and cooks, and, citing the ATS as a model, argued: 'Official status or recognition should be given to the women who work for the Home Guard ... they should be recognised as members and allowed to wear uniform'.[65] At the end of September, Lt.-Gen. Sir Douglas Brownrigg, Commander of 'R Zone', London Home Guard, expressed a similar view. He said that the War Office should 'accept the principle that women should give voluntary, part time, unpaid service by allowing them to perform duties similar to those done by their male friends and relatives', although 'naturally these women would only be employed on non-combatant duties and would not therefore require arms and equipment'. He assumed they should have a uniform, and suggested (somewhat disingenuously since in July 1941 he had given Dame Helen Gwynne-

Vaughan 'entire control of the administrative side at Zone headquarters') that women might already be joining the Home Guard if they had names, 'like Evelyn', which were the same as men's: 'No-one would know except by the Size Roll for her clothes.'[66] The idea of a women's auxiliary service to the Home Guard was favoured on the Left as well. Tom Wintringham had written in September 1940 that the Home Guard 'needs a supply service and a medical service: it would be wise to entrust a very large amount of the work of these services to women'.[67] However, for all his praise of 'an armed people' and his evocation of typists bearing revolvers during the Spanish Civil War, Wintringham did not urge the inclusion of women in capacities other than 'auxiliary' ones.[68] He did not explain, but his colleague Hugh Slater said in a lecture at Osterley that he opposed women's membership, not because women lacked toughness, but because 'in Spain they had proved themselves quite appallingly foolhardy', although they could nevertheless play a useful role in home defence 'without actually fighting'.[69] Likewise, John Langdon-Davies, one of the signatories of Dame Helen Gwynne-Vaughan's memorial, argued in November 1940 that women should not be fully combatant members but could be trained to play 'the woman's part' in an invasion. His argument against women's membership was that male Home Guards who felt 'that their job is to protect their families' would not like it.[70]

Clerical work, driving, cooking and first aid were roles that numerous Home Guard COs entrusted to women. COs who sent information to Charles Graves in 1942, in response to his officially sanctioned request for accounts of 'incidents of interest' to do with the formation, training, equipping and activities of their units, were proud to claim pioneering status in the recruitment of women.[71] The CO of the 'A2 Shore Company' on the Upper Thames explained that he needed to use cars to link men scattered in small groups along the river: 'cars need drivers and I could not spare the men', but 'I had come across dozens of women who were anxious to do something beyond the rather colourless activities of the W.V.S.', so recruiting forty of them for this purpose had been easy. He also 'roped in' a woman as 'office second-in-command', 'a lady to whose efficiency the Company owed a great deal of its success'. He later discovered that 'no women were at that time allowed in the Home Guard', but at the time 'of all this I was blissfully ignorant'.[72] He was not the only CO who assumed that wartime conditions rendered obsolete the traditional boundary between women civilians and the male military.

The use of women in the Home Guard inevitably encroached on the combatant–non-combatant divide. Several COs were explicitly critical of the War Office prohibition, which made no sense 'since women are freely employed in all the armed forces and civil defence not only in non-combatant duties but in such directions as assisting the crews of anti-aircraft guns'.[73] The 'non-combatant duties' in which the BBC Home Guard's 100 women members were trained included first aid, telephony, signalling, cooking and intelligence, but they were also involved in 'handling ammunition'.[74] The 13th County of Durham Home Guard organised women in a canteen section serving tea, a comforts section providing scarves, socks and pullovers and a first aid section – conventionally feminine roles, though the latter was required to 'participate in all local exercises'.[75] In 51st Malden Home Guard the women auxiliaries' First-Aid Section 'take[s] a very active part in all forms of operational training', which included 'a week-end in camp doing field work and sharing fatigue duties along with the men'.[76] Women involved in military exercises worked in combat conditions (albeit simulated ones), even if they were not there to receive 'infantry training' themselves.[77]

Some COs were convinced that they should be allowed to deploy women in explicitly combatant roles, and, aware of Summerskill's views, contacted her for support. Major Gavin Jones, CO of Letchworth Home Guard, wrote to her in October 1941. For him, as for other commanders, the use of women on anti-aircraft batteries was a significant precedent:

> I want to raise a women's platoon in this town. My own Home Guard here are overwhelmingly in favour of the idea … I understand that recently you inspected women serving on the gun sites. Surely if women are capable of undertaking this work they can serve as guards for defence purposes … I do not expect the women to do heavy work like route marching or fighting in open warfare in the field. I want them for static guards in the town and if they will do this for me it will free my men to go out and meet the enemy outside the town.[78]

In short, Jones wanted to use women as *armed* auxiliaries who, by taking over guard duties, would release men for more active service. Summerskill copied the letter to the Prime Minister, explaining: 'I appeal to you because I have little hope of the War Office helping in this matter.' Churchill, who was enthusiastic about the use of women in anti-aircraft defence, wrote 'I favour the idea. WSC.'[79]

In spite of this high-level endorsement, Churchill's colleagues at the War Office were a long way from capitulating. On 5 December 1941 they turned down a request from Summerskill that Margesson should receive a deputation of ten Home Guard COs 'anxious to ask you to consider allowing women to join the Home Guard', some of whom 'wish the ban which prohibits men in the Home Guard instructing women in the use of rifles to be ended.'[80]

Women were joining in defiance of the ban, for armed as well as 'non-combatant' roles. The *Daily Mail* reported on 29 October 1941 that fifty women had been training with the Home Guard since July at a 'war factory' in Tolworth, Surrey. They had undertaken drill, marching and rifle drill, and had provided their own uniforms. The unit's Sergeant-Major said: 'Although the girls are not officially recognized as Home Guards, they go on manoeuvres and train the same as the men. Four nights a week they go on parade. Their keenness and spirit are magnificent.'[81] In response to urgent War Office enquiries, the works manager and the London District Home Guard CO qualified the picture: the women had been allowed to fire exclusively on the works' miniature rifle-range using .22 ammunition; they mixed with the men only when providing food for them.[82]

Nevertheless, as Chapter 8 shows, oral history confirms the existence of COs for whom no 'question of principle' obstructed the involvement of women in Home Guard activities, including combat training. Some of them may have agreed with Admiral Sir Reginald Bacon, who argued in the *Sunday Express*, in May 1942, that 'it is absurd not to arm the women' since experience in other countries showed that, if the Germans invaded, women would be indiscriminately raped and murdered.[83] Others may simply have felt that the women they recruited for 'auxiliary' functions should also take part in operational exercises and all types of drill as part of their Home Guard training. Many of these women recruits became nothing short of 'armed typists'. The most surprising evidence of such involvement, given the official prohibition, comes from women working in the offices of government ministries: 130 women at the Ministry of Food, which had been evacuated to Colwyn Bay in North Wales, formed a unit affiliated to the WHD in September 1942. They were accepted as a 'women's section', wearing the WHD badge, by the Ministry of Food's Home Guard. The women were organised in six sections (administration, catering, communications, guides, intelligence and transport) and took part in night exercises.[84] Miss A. G. Ascott joined the 58th County of London (Civil Service) Battalion Home Guard at the Ministry of Agriculture and Fisheries and received a special commendation in August 1944 for her shooting prowess: all the bullet holes on a target card dated 19 June 1944 are in the bullseye.[85] Oral history reveals that women clerks and typists at the Air Ministry and the Ministry of Aircraft Production joined the Home Guard units of those ministries, and that their COs flouted the dictates of their colleagues at the War Office by not only including the women as members but also training them in the use of weapons and providing them with uniforms.[86] This might suggest that the 'masculine' culture of the War Office was outdated compared with that of other ministries in which its prejudices were ignored. However, oral history reveals that the 'no armed women' rule was disobeyed at the heart of the War Office itself, albeit on an individual rather than collective basis. In May 1940 Joan Hardy took over a friend's job at the War Office as secretary to Colonel Meinertzhagen, who was running the War Office's own LDV.[87] Meinertzhagen taught her to shoot and to make Molotov cocktails. When he retired, she became secretary to Lt.-Col. Sir Edward Frederick, Commander in Chief of the London Home Guard, with whom she took part in 'operations' in London parks.[88]

The WHD was, as we have seen, committed to training women in armed defence. There is no national depository of documents relating to the organisation. However, the papers of Mrs Edith Roberts, organiser from 1942 to 1945 of Wallasey WHD, are available in a local library; they provide a unique insight into the life of one of the many branches of the organisation. Edith Roberts, a secretary and the wife of a merchant seaman, joined the Wallasey unit, one of six on Merseyside, after hearing Edith Summerskill speak in Liverpool.[89] She built it up from 12 to 145 women, by using the local press to publicise the unit's activities and to attract new recruits under headlines such as 'Girls Help to Defend! Join the Women's Home Defence Unit';[90] by fund-raising reciprocally with other local voluntary organisations, such as the Wallasey Drama Club and the New Brighton First-Aid Unit;[91] and by liaising with her local Independent MP, former Labour Councillor George Reakes, who helped in his capacity as a journalist as well as financially.[92] Roberts also secured the support of the CO of the 16th Battalion of the Cheshire Home Guard, Lt.-Col. Duncan Taylor.

The Wallasey WHD was a lively organisation of working women and housewives, probably of the lower and middle classes, aged approximately 20–50. About one-third were married and Roberts commented that many of them 'combined work and family with evening defence duties'.[93] They were required to make a weekly contribution of sixpence to WHD funds and to defray the cost of hiring premises; and they also incurred expenses associated with rifle drill, such as insurance and ammunition – none of which applied to male Home Guards.[94] The organisation focused on 'training [women] in means of defence' in a convivial social atmosphere. It announced its regular meetings in the press, offering an 'interesting programme followed by refreshments'. The 'programme' consisted of lectures by Home Guard personnel on various aspects of warfare, including signalling, gas attack, military intelligence, mines and hand-grenades.[95] Wallasey WHD persuaded Lt.-Col. Taylor to lend them a Home Guard Sergeant so that they could 'commence training', the idea being that trained women would be able, in turn, to instruct new recruits. The unit undertook squad drill and physical training at Elleray Park Senior School, and, according to the *Wallasey News* in February 1943: 'Their squad drill is particularly smart, the members being adept in taking and giving commands.'[96] Squad drill aimed 'to teach troops by exercise to obey orders', and it involved twenty minutes of falling-in, standing to attention, turning, marching and rifle exercises, from which the women learned to 'combine instruction in care of arms, names of parts of rifle, and aiming and firing'. In March 1943 the unit secured the services of a further Home Guard sergeant for rifle training, and made plans to hold a shooting contest on 5 May 1943. Hopes were high that Lt.-Col. Taylor would let them use the Home Guard rifle-range.[97]

Wallasey WHD's relationship with the Home Guard was, of course, in direct contravention of the War Office instruction of November 1941, 'that the training of women as unofficial Home Guard units has not been authorized', and that 'weapons and ammunition in the charge of the Army or of Home Guard units must not be used for the instruction of women'.[98] By lending the WHD his sergeants for any training, especially rifle training, Lt.-Col. Taylor made the same kind of transgression as the COs who recruited and trained women alongside men in their units. Yet Taylor was apparently content to work with the WHD, deeply questionable though that organisation was in the eyes of his masters in the War Office.

He was not alone. Even though the Secretary of State for War and his colleagues were particularly negative towards the 'Amazons' of the WHD, Home Guard COs availed themselves of their services locally. As we have seen, this was the case at the Ministry of Food in Colwyn Bay in the autumn of 1942. In Leeds in November 1942, Mrs Louie White, a factory worker, recorded in her wartime diary that she had joined a WHD unit: the subsequent entries describe links similar to those between Wallasey WHD and the 16th Cheshire Home Guard. Thus her entry for 3 December 1942 reads: 'A Corporal came and took us for musketry. It was grand. We handled the rifle and learned how to aim.' Rifle practice took place courtesy of the 9th West Riding Home Guard more than once a month from December 1942 until April 1943.[99] As Chapter 8 demonstrates, such contemporary evidence of involvement is supported by oral history interviews. Not surprisingly, in view of the co-operation and convergence between the WHD and the Home Guard, WHD members were confident that they would eventually receive official approval. At the Wallasey WHD unit's meeting in March 1943, 'the possibility of [the] organisation being recognised very shortly was discussed', and plans were eagerly anticipated.[100]

'Recognition'

As early as October 1941 there were signs that Lord Bridgeman, Director General of the Home Guard, was coming round to the idea that women helping the force would have to receive some sort of recognition, even though his public pronouncements were still negative. Bridgeman prepared three schemes, in October 1941, February 1942 and July 1942, the latter two being pared-down versions of their predecessor. All emphatically rejected the armed membership of women: the schemes had 'no connection with any proposal to give any women combatant status, or train them in the use of arms'.[101] But his initial plan was fairly extensive: he proposed to recruit up to 150,000 women as Home Guards, to use them on a wide range of duties, to provide them with uniforms, to pay them capitation grants and to treat them as (part-time) members of the ATS.[102] However, the implacable opposition of Sir James Grigg, fears that any such scheme represented the thin end of the wedge of women's full enrolment, and the objections of ministers with rival demands for women's labour led to extensive dilution of the first two plans. In July 1942 Bridgeman announced that 'it has been decided not to permit the enrolment of women into the Home Guard either for combatant or non-combatant duties' and he produced a new scheme in which women volunteers, drawn from 'recognised women's organisations' such as the WVS, would type, cook and drive for the Home Guard wearing Home Guard armlets, and without any War Office funding.[103] Even this modest plan was followed by a further nine months of wrangling.

During this period, reports appeared in the press under headlines such as 'Ban May Go', 'The Women's Home Guard Soon. But Women Will Not fight' and 'Women to Join Home Guard. Non-Combatant Duties Only', creating an expectation that women Home Guards would be recognised any day, and questions continued to be asked in Parliament.[104] As we have seen, the WHD was growing rapidly and numerous Home Guard officers were not only tolerating women's presence in the Home Guard but were actively encouraging it. The historian S. P. MacKenzie argues that Home

Guard leaders had so much influence on government policy that ministers, civil servants and army officers 'found themselves time and again
dancing to a tune set by influential members of the Home Guard'.[105] If
that was the case, it is reasonable to ask why those who had written to
the War Office asking for the enrolment of women, such as Brigadier
Currey, General Brownrigg and Major Gavin Jones, quoted above, were
not getting their way.

In practice, it appears that it was extremely difficult for Home Guard
commanders to exert influence on policy. The possibilities of doing so
were constrained by military procedure and hierarchy. To alter policy
they had to reach those in command of the Army (of which the Home
Guard was a branch) as well as those in charge at the War Office. Views
had to be expressed through the commanders of the seven army divisions
in Britain, to the Commander in Chief, Home Forces, who was, in 1942,
Bernard C. T. Paget. In the context of the public interest in the question
of women's role in the Home Guard, the War Office asked Paget to undertake an enquiry on the subject at the end of August 1942. Paget, however,
cast his questions in the most negative terms, informing the divisional
commanders that the Government was against 'enrolling women as
combatant members' and warning that their inclusion as non-combatants was likely to lead to 'a demand for full enrolment with everything
which it entails'. If the Home Guard required any help from women, that
of 'the W.V.S. and relations and friends' would suffice.[106]

Nevertheless, the responses of the seven army commanders, four of
whom stated that they had consulted Home Guard commanding officers,
expressed a range of views. The most negative was that of Sir Ralph
('Rusty') Eastwood, former Director General of the Home Guard, who
restated his earlier opinion that since the Home Guard was an arms-
bearing organisation, women, who could not bear arms, had no place in
it: non-combatant duties could be taken care of 'by the various women's
voluntary services, and by the Red Cross and St. John Ambulance'.[107] The
most positive comments came from the commanders of the eastern and
the south-eastern army divisions, based in the regions of Britain considered most vulnerable to attack and invasion. Major General K. J. Martin
(eastern division) wanted to increase the numbers of women to 5 per
cent of the strength of each unit, widen their functions, give them a
uniform, and pay them injury compensation and subsistence allowances.
Lt-General Sir John Swayne (south-eastern division) implied that women
working with the Home Guard should be exempt from evacuation in the
event of invasion, and said they should be paid allowances, issued with

badges and trained: 'Untrained women are no more use than untrained men.'[108] The other four army commanders supported the idea that women should continue to help the Home Guard and that they should be issued with a badge or brassard denoting their role.

The commanders thus did not present Paget with a consistently forceful demand for the regularisation of women's position in the Home Guard. Unlike many Home Guard members, they were not sympathisers of Summerskill: General Sir Arthur Smith, London District, divided the women helping the Home Guard into the 'good' who made no fuss and the 'bad' who, 'urged on by propaganda and Dr Edith Summerskill [were] asking for uniforms, compensation etc.'[109] But these army commanders had gleaned from their Home Guard underlings evidence of the extensive use of women in the force and, in spite of Paget's opposite steer, all but one expressed the view that women should receive some sort of recognition.

Meanwhile, Summerskill, aware of the watered-down proposal for the involvement of women, made every effort to insist that recognition should embrace the WHD's principles. At a meeting with Bridgeman in October 1942, she told him that women's duties should not be 'limited to those of the clerical and cooking type' but should include, at the least, 'signalling and other non-combatant duties' for which they were currently being trained by the Home Guard. She had plunged, however, into the swirling definitional waters of 'combatant' and 'non-combatant': Bridgeman replied that signalling *was* combatant, and 'if Home Guard were giving this training to women now, orders were being disobeyed and a breach of discipline committed'. Summerskill responded in the forthright language of the citizens' army: everyone should be 'trained to arms so that if a weapon came their way in battle they could pick it up and use it'. Bridgeman brushed this off. Weapons training for women was not government policy, which (as a soldier rather than a politician) he said he could not in any case discuss.[110] In spite of this unpropitious conversation, Summerskill was sent back to Bridgeman in January 1943 by Grigg, who refused to see her himself. She took with her a deputation of WHD members, who summarised for Bridgeman the training given under eight headings: cooking, driving, clerical work, first aid, musketry, drill, signalling and despatch-riding. Bridgeman acknowledged that the WHD's help 'seems welcome to Home Guard'.[111] But there was no question in his mind of capitulating to its demand that 'the War Office order that Home Guard Units must not give musketry instruction to women would be rescinded'.[112] In spite of Summerskill's pride in the deputation,[113] it appears to have made little difference to the shape which that recognition took. Bridgeman stood by his earlier view that the WHD should not be included in the list of voluntary organisations that might help the Home Guard.

On 20 April 1943 a scheme for 'nominated women' to assist the Home Guard was finally announced by Sir James Grigg in the House of Commons: 'It has been decided that a limited number of women, proportionate to the strength of the Home Guard, may be nominated for service as auxiliaries with the Home Guard to perform non-combatant duties such as clerical work, cooking and driving.' He went on to explain the 'nomination' procedure. Home Guard commanders were to 'make use of existing women's organisations' wherever possible, although individual women could be nominated by the commanding officer, who also made the selection. Numbers would be limited to 80,000 and preference would be given to women over 45 years of age. Women so nominated would 'wear a badge brooch' but would not have any other sort of uniform.[114] Briefing notes accompanying the announcement stated that the WHD was not to be identified as a source of recruits: 'it is in fact anticipated that the W.V.S. who are already rendering considerable assistance will provide the majority of women'. The notes also stated that 'no training in the use of arms will be given to women auxiliaries'.[115]

The WHD and its combatant values were thus allowed no legitimate place in the Home Guard, an exclusion represented visually in the contrast between the 'badge brooch' that the 'nominated women' would wear and the WHD badge. There were significant differences between them. The new brooch was round rather than shield-shaped, plastic not metal, very pale grey-gold rather than rich red and gold, and instead of

Figure 2 Membership badges: Women's Home Defence, Women's Home Guard Auxiliary and Women's Voluntary Services

displaying any sort of representative image of the functions of the wearer or an indication that she was a woman, it simply bore the letters H.G. surrounded by an indiscernible laurel-leaf moulding.

In spite of Bridgeman's acknowledgement that the WHD had been giving the Home Guard 'welcome' help for months, it was officially displaced by another wartime women's organisation, the WVS. There were two main reasons. Firstly, the formation of the WVS in the summer of 1938 had been government-sponsored. It was established in 1938 as the Women's Voluntary Services for Civil Defence, at the prompting of Sir Samuel Hoare, then Home Secretary, and was placed under the leadership of Lady Stella Reading, a well-connected establishment figure with experience of charitable work. Hoare had proposed it in the context of the threat of war and, specifically, of devastating air-raids, and conceived of it originally as the women's branch of Air Raid Precautions (ARP), formed in the same year (although that organisation rapidly became mixed-sex). The origins and leadership of the WVS ensured close co-operation with the Government: Lady Reading and her staff were accommodated in offices within the Home Office; branches could not be set up without approval from the local authorities under whose instruction and in whose premises they worked; and the Government gave the organisation a grant to offset expenses. The WVS insisted nevertheless on its 'voluntary' status, and claimed proudly (though not entirely accurately) that, in the words of its first historian, 'no voluntary organisation had ever before been used as part of the machinery of government'.[116] Secondly, although the role of the WVS in wartime expanded beyond ARP, the problems it addressed remained within what could be seen as the *feminine* sphere, relating particularly to social welfare. Its members organised the evacuation of schoolchildren from cities, established centres for people displaced by bombing, made comforts for the troops, ran salvage and recycling schemes and operated canteens to provide refreshments for groups who needed them, from travelling servicemen to fire-fighters in the Blitz. By the end of 1941 the WVS had one million members.[117]

Providing members of the Home Guard with mufflers and hot drinks after an evening's duty was not incompatible with such WVS functions, and in view of the close relationship of the organisation to national and local government it was not in a position to refuse to undertake them.[118] Such a service may well have been appreciated by members of the Home Guard. However, as we have seen, these kinds of functions by no means delineated the extent of women's participation in home defence to date. At least one Home Guard officer regarded them as 'colourless', and found it easy to attract women to the Home Guard for more vivid duties. A comparison of WVS activities with those of the Home Guard emphasises the different meanings of the terms 'civil' and 'home defence': civil defence was about assisting and sustaining local civilian populations under the duress of war; home defence concerned the military protection of such populations from invasion and bombardment. There was clearly a need in Britain in the Second World War for both types of defence. The proposal to link the WVS to the Home Guard, and to eschew the WHD, however, assumed that women could be involved only in civil defence. This was contradictory: the women's auxiliary services to the armed forces were increasingly involved in activities that came under the military defini-tion of defence; and, as we have seen, women were in practice involved in similar roles in relation to the Home Guard.

The official acceptability of the WVS to those in power was symbol-ised by its uniform and official badge – a silver rectangle on which the red embossed initials WVS and the words Civil Defence were framed by a red line and surmounted by the royal crown (see figure 2). This is not to say there was no controversy where the WVS was concerned. James Hinton, in a meticulous history of the organisation, traces the muscular influence exercised by WVS organisers in relation to the local authorities and its own membership. It was rarely at odds with government officials, although Hinton refers to Reading's fury when the Home Office 'put out civil defence posters depicting women as timid beings protected by their men folk'.[119] Like other wartime organisations, the WVS was caught up in the redefinition of femininity instigated by the destabilising conditions of war, which transformed women's conventional passive role of watching and waiting into active patriotic femininity. Even so, WVS activities could be encompassed within the enlarged understandings of womanliness to which its members themselves contributed in wartime. As Hinton puts it: 'During the war W.V.S. … served as a means of adapting traditions of middle-class female social leadership to the needs of the emergency'.[120] The meanings of feminine patriotism that the WHD aspired to enact, on the other hand, were considerably in excess of such adaptations and redefinitions.

Roles, uniforms and commemoration

After April 1943 there was some friction between the WHD and the WVS, owing to suspicions on either side that the other organisation was trying to monopolise the relationship with the Home Guard. In Liverpool it was alleged that 'the W.V.S. who were working for the Home Guard were rather hampering the Women's Home Defence ground', and WHD organisers reported to the organisation's newsletter, *The Eighth Pillar*, that 'the W.V.S. are insisting that women wishing to be nominated to the H.G. must first join the W.V.S.'[121] Likewise the WVS claimed that the WHD was trying to take 'control of existing arrangements made between H.G. and W.V.S.'[122] But there were also high-level attempts at diplomatic co-operation: after exchanging information about such attempts at gate-keeping, Summerskill and Reading agreed that 'no organisation ... can claim an exclusive right to work for the H.G.' and promised not to hinder each other's involvement.[123] A sympathetic Home Guard CO established a *modus vivendi* locally: the WVS provided canteens and the WHD gave other types of support, with 'members of W.V.S. and Women's Home Defence both wearing two badges'.[124] Aside from the relationship with the WVS, however, there were aspects of recognition that were unacceptable not only to the WHD but also in more conventional quarters.

The WHD's critique focused on two issues: the role of 'nominated women' and what they were to wear. The official scheme approved their involvement in clerical work, cooking and driving, but omitted more military functions in which they were already involved, such as 'signal-ling, intelligence, armoury, stores', ruled out field communications and first aid, and specifically banned weapons training: 'The employment of women will be restricted to non-combatant duties and no duties will be undertaken by them which necessitate training in weapons. Training of women in weapons by the Home Guard is, as hitherto, forbidden.'[125] The WHD contested this ruling: its objective was to provide a 'pool of trained women ready to fill any gaps in the H.G. at a moment's notice' and its members must therefore have 'training in musketry and any other subject deemed to be useful'. Its leaders urged local organisers to write letters of protest to their MPs and to persuade Home Guard commanding officers to write too. The WHD's spirit was confident: 'the whole organisation now runs on its own wheels' wrote the honorary secretary. Its newsletter was concurrently celebrating the success of another wartime campaign for women's rights: from April 1943 women would receive equal compen-sation for war injuries.[126]

Criticism of the constraints on 'recognition' did not come from the WHD alone. A leader in the *Daily Mail* on 21 April 1943, headed 'Haphazard Plan', argued that 'the casualness of the proposed system' had a negative impact on the men of the Home Guard. It 'encourage[s] the erroneous but rapidly spreading idea that the Home Guard is a body of amateur soldiers training for duties which they will never be called on to perform.' In fact, the Home Guard would have a 'vital part to play in the defence of these shores' when regular troops were engaged in the allied invasion of Europe (the Second Front), and it needed women's help. Thus there should be a proper plan for the allocation of women to the Home Guard under conditions as similar as possible to those of men.[127]

Even if the argument appealed to Home Guard COs, they were under clear instructions to conform to the terms on which 'recognition' was granted. The WHD was, however, determined to achieve creative compromises. In Wallasey, rifle practice, hitherto provided solely by the Home Guard, was postponed only until the organisers found an alternative organisation to provide instructors and the use of a range – the police.[128] Shooting competitions continued unabated, in May, August and October 1943: competing with the Home Guard (and sometimes beating them) was evidently considered legitimate, even if training with them was not.[129] As the months went by, Home Guard COs overlooked the rules, at least as they applied to the murky zone between 'combatant' and 'non-combatant' activities. Wallasey WHD organised 'Intelligence, Signals and Transport Sections' and 'put the excellent training received from the Home Guard into actual practice' in Home Guard exercises in 1943 and 1944.[130] In Leeds, weapons training for women resumed within a year of April 1943, and women participated in 'battle craft' exercises with the Home Guard regularly from September 1943 to September 1944.[131]

The WHD's other major concern after 'recognition' was with uniforms for 'nominated women'. These had been advocated from the start for their symbolic value and for reasons of practicality, discipline and protection, not only by the WHD but also by Home Guard members. In Autumn 1941, Brigadier Currey, General Brownrigg and even Lord Bridgeman suggested that women helping the Home Guard needed uniforms,[132] and sympathetic MPs such as Sir Thomas Moore, Conservative MP for the Ayr Burghs, suggested (against short-supplies arguments) that they should be given discarded ATS kit.[133] But cost was not the only consideration. In War Office discussions preceding recognition, every effort was made to keep the uniform of the 'nominated woman' to a minimum. Civil servants argued that the glamour of uniform in wartime encouraged pride in the service it denoted, and would create the illusion that women helping the Home Guard 'were members of the Armed Forces', which would deflect women's interest from other forms of service. Even armbands were too ostentatious; hence the eventual decision to issue no more than the 'badge brooch'.[134]

The badge was, according to one MP, 'one of the cheapest forms of plastic brooches, which breaks if you touch it'.[135] It was the object of numerous criticisms. Proper uniform, as opposed to a badge, would indicate the function and status of the wearer. It would 'prevent a woman being treated as a "franc tireur" by the enemy', that is as someone who could be refused prisoner-of-war status and summarily shot for engaging in military action when not a member of the regular forces.[136] The War Office eventually conceded the point in the months before D-Day: copies of a certificate dated 10 January 1944 were sent to Home Guard COs, to be issued to 'nominated women' if the Home Guard was mustered. They stated that the woman named 'is authorised to follow the Armed Forces of the Crown, and is entitled in the event of capture by the enemy to be treated as a prisoner of war'.[137] But women were still not granted the symbolic or practical protection of a uniform.

Summerskill and her parliamentary Home Guard ally Sir Thomas Moore stressed in the Commons the problem of inappropriately dressed 'nominated women'. Women were driving lorries and going on night exercises in cretonne frocks and high heels, protested Summerskill in August 1943.[138] Moore claimed in March 1944: 'These girls, supposing there was an invasion, would perhaps be driving lorries, taking ammunition to the front, while attired in flimsy chiffon frocks.'[139] The respective choice of fabric of the two MPs speaks to their different conceptualisations of wartime femininity. The chiffon of which Moore spoke was a luxury cloth, almost see-through, unlike Summerskill's patriotic cretonne, a heavy cotton print usually used for covering chairs but adapted for dressmaking as part of wartime 'make do and mend'. Chiffon's transparent romance was quite at odds with wartime austerity, but it conjured up the right image to reinforce both speakers' points about uniform, including its importance for discipline. The appearance of women in impractical, flimsy chiffon beside khaki-clad men accentuated gender differences: uniforms assimilated the two sexes.[140] Uniform also had a socially levelling effect central to the ideology of the people's war: it would 'eliminate class distinction' between women and 'put them on to a common basis.'[141] The War Office, however, was obdurate: no uniforms or protective clothing for 'nominated women'. They were to have neither steel hats and respirators (which any member might need) nor gloves and leather jerkins (required by drivers). In spite of sustained protest there was never an official uniform for women in the Home Guard.[142]

'Nominated women' themselves did not take the denial of uniform lying down. An angry letter to the editor of the journal *Defence*, dated

Figure 3 Jeanne Townend's Women's Home Guard Auxiliary unit, Goole, East Yorkshire c.1943. Jeanne is second from the left, back row; her father, the CO, is third from the left in the middle row

15 February 1944, was published under the heading 'Factory H.G. Girls Protest'. 'For one whole year' wrote Miss L. Lock of London,

> I and lots of other girls have belonged to a factory H.G., and not even a tin hat to show for it! … We are, mostly, hard-working girls of the working class, daughters of the men who fought in the last war. We want to help our men-folk in the Home Guard now, and we are willingly giving up our spare time to learn first aid and other things, and would use a rifle if given a chance. And yet they tell us, No uniforms. We reply, if others get them, how about us? We are all in this thing together.[143]

Miss Lock evoked several powerful wartime tropes in her letter: women in the Home Guard were 'hard-working' members of the community; they were the offspring of veterans of the First World War; they were prepared to use weapons; they were making willing sacrifices for the war effort; yet their treatment exposed the limitations of the ideology of national unity in wartime. While some women protested, others improvised.[144] Mr McEntee, Labour MP for Walthamstow, asked Grigg in March 1944: 'Is it against the law for women in the Home Guard to wear uniform, because, if so, many are doing it?' Grigg answered: 'The only prohibition is against wearing uniforms which simulate official uniforms. So long as they do not do that, I honestly think the best course is to turn the blind eye.'[145] Photographs of local women's units, however, suggest that their outfits did indeed 'simulate official uniforms'.

The awkward term 'nominated woman' was repeatedly queried: the reluctance to give women a name indicative of their role was symptomatic of their only-partial recognition. This, and the absence of an official uniform, had implications beyond the lifetime of the Home Guard. Women could not join in military parades in civilian dress: the Wallasey WHD unit was therefore refused a place in the town's 'Salute the Soldier' parade in June 1944;[146] likewise, women could not march in the Home Guard's national 'stand down' parade in London in December 1944, and so were not immortalised in newsreels of that event.[147] Consistent with the history of national prohibitions and local licence, however, women who had acquired uniforms did march in the parades in some towns.[148] As far as their name was concerned, even though Grigg upheld 'nominated woman' in April 1944, by June the more appropriate 'Woman Home Guard Auxiliary' had displaced it in official as well as other types of communication.[149] However, the public commemoration of women's participation in the Home Guard was never officially sanctioned.

If it had not been for Summerskill, individual Home Guard women would not have received any official record of their services, either. In October 1944 the War Office announced that all members of the Home Guard would be given a certificate, signed by the King, at the stand down in December. The certificate said: 'In the years when our Country was in mortal danger [name] who served [dates] gave generously of his time and powers to make himself ready for her defence by force of arms and with his life if need be. George R.I.'[150] Summerskill pressed Grigg to issue the same certificate to women, but he demurred, initially on the grounds that women were not members of the Home Guard,[151] and then because the men's certificate would not be 'appropriate' for women. Eventually he agreed that women would have a special certificate of their own.[152] Issued in the spring of 1945, it read: 'I have received The King's command to express His Majesty's appreciation of the loyal service given voluntarily to her country in a time of grievous danger by [name] as a Woman Home Guard Auxiliary. P. J. Grigg Secretary of State for War, The War Office, London.'[153] These certificates affirmed the identity of the Woman Home Guard Auxiliary, but they also differentiated crucially by gender: a *man's* country was feminine; a woman's country had *no* gender; a man guarded 'her' 'by force of arms and with his life'; a woman gave 'loyal service' but did not bear arms or risk her life; the danger of war for a man's country was 'mortal' but for woman's was only 'grievous'. The denial of women's combatant role in the Home Guard was inscribed in the certificate, and the linguistic differences suggest that posterity was fully intended to understand that the meaning of the Second World War for men and women was profoundly different.

Conclusion

In the contest between opposed views of women's contribution to home defence, Summerskill and Gwynne-Vaughan took a firm and clear position. In a modern democracy, the only possible response to the threat of invasion was universal participation in a volunteer defence force. Feminist rationality would overcome masculine prejudice: even the traditionalists in the War Office must recognise that women's membership of the Home Guard was consistent with women's expanding role in the wider war effort. To Summerskill there was no reason not to arm women Home Guard members: unarmed, they would be less effective either in an invasion or in relieving men for 'active service'. But nothing could have been further from the War Office's sense of propriety. Its officials gave reasons for the exclusion of women from the Home Guard based on shortages, expense and the rival demands for women's contribution to the war effort, all of which could have applied equally to male members. They also, but without ever articulating a coherent explanation, stated repeatedly that it was unacceptable for women to occupy combatant roles. For War Office officials, an all-male armed Home Guard evidently had such symbolic importance that it overrode rational argument.

It is possible that the fragile masculine status both of the military bureaucrats in charge and of the Home Guard as a military organisation contributed to the opposition. As we argued in Chapter 2 and will explore further in Chapter 4, the Home Guard was associated with impaired manhood, and uncertainties about its military role as well as its implied dispensability made its soldierly identity insecure. The inclusion of women in the force could have further destabilised the Home Guard's precarious military and masculine status. Against such an interpretation, however, is the evidence reviewed in this chapter of local acceptance and encouragement of women's membership. The reasons for recruiting women may have been mainly pragmatic: to ensure adequate numbers in Home Guard units and to secure services regarded as 'feminine'. But the line dividing combatant from non-combatant was blurred, and at least some Home Guard commanders trained the women whom they recruited to use weapons. Some of them may have believed that it was important for women to be able to protect themselves in the event of an invasion; others that combat skills were a necessary part of Home Guard membership. Although their reasons undoubtedly varied, these men had in common the view that the exigencies of total war overrode conventional gender divisions.

Whether combatant or non-combatant, the role of women in home defence was markedly different from that in civil defence. Yet when the Government was eventually prevailed on to recognise the Home Guard's need for women's help, the WVS was identified as the appropriate women's organisation to support it, rather than the WHD. The War Office evidently sought to displace the transgressive WHD with the more conformist WVS (rather than combining them) as part of a wider strategy of eclipse. Government policy was, as far as possible, to ignore women in the Home Guard. By not naming them, clothing them, paying them or thanking them appropriately, it also ensured that they would not be remembered. Subsequent chapters explore the effects of such silence on both popular and personal memory.

Notes

1 Hansard, vol. 362, col. 281, 25 June 1940, and col. 646, 2 July 1940.

2 Hansard, vol. 362, col. 281, 25 June 1940.

3 Hansard, vol. 362, col. 646, 2 July 1940.

4 Churchill, 'Wars Are Not Won by Evacuations', 4 June 1940, *Complete Speeches*, vol. 6, p. 6231.

5 P. Summerfield, '"Our Amazonian Colleague": Edith Summerskill's Problematic Reputation', in R. Toye and J. Gottlieb (eds), *Making Reputations: Power, Persuasion and the Individual in Modern British Politics* (London: I. B. Tauris, 2005), pp. 135–150; E. Summerskill, *A Woman's World* (London: Heinemann, 1967).

6 Hansard, vol. 365, cols 1887, 1897, 19 November 1940.

7 Hansard, vol. 365, col. 1928, 19 November 1940; and vol. 376, col. 2155, 18 December 1941.

8 Hansard, vol. 376, col. 2156, 18 December 1941.

9 Hansard, vol. 365, cols 1929–1932, 19 November 1940.

10 Hansard: vol. 365, col. 1356, 6 November 1940; vol. 376, col. 581, 25 November 1941; cols 2162 and 2187, 18 December 1941. NA, WO, 32/9423 'HG, use of women as auxiliaries, 1940–42', J. R. Eastwood, 27 December 1940; Brownrigg to Bridgeman, 29 September 1941; P. J. Grigg, 9 December 1941; Bridgeman, 10 April, 27 October 1942.

11 NA, WO, 32/9423, Bridgeman, 4 December 1941; P. J. Grigg, 9 December 1941; Oswald Allen, Ministry of Home Security, 16 February 1942; Mary Smieton, Ministry of Labour, 11 March 1942; Herbert Morrison, Ministry of Home Security, 10 October 1942; Minutes of Lord President's Committee, 1 February 1943.

12 Hansard, vol. 365, cols 1929–1930, 19 November 1940; and vol. 376. col. 2156, 18 December 1941.

13 Hansard, vol. 376, col. 2155, 18 December 1941; 'C3' and 'A1' refer to official assessments of fitness for military service.

14 NA, WO, 32/9423, J. R. Eastwood, 27 December 1940; D.G.H.G. (Major-General Lord Bridgeman) to Sir Douglas Brownrigg, 1 October 1941.

15 Women had formed a Home Service Corps with similar objectives in the First World War: K. Cowman, 'A Uniform Response? Militarism, Feminism and Home Service Corps, 1914–1918', unpublished paper presented at the International Seminar on Militarism and Gender, Leeds, November 1999.

16 The Annual Reports of the Small-Bore Miniature Rifle Club, noted the increasing popularity of such clubs for women: in 1931 there were'184 ladies' clubs, none with less than ten members'. Thanks to Brian Woodall, National Small-Bore Rifle Association.

17 Fawcett Library, 355.244.2:396.5.

18 NA, WO, 32/9423, Tate to Eden 10 December 1940.

19 Hansard, vol. 365, cols 1929–1931, 19 November 1940; Summerskill, *Woman's World*, p. 73. On WHD letterhead (1942), Summerskill was Chairman, Mrs V. A. M. Foster, Treasurer and Miss Y. Moss, Secretary, and twelve supporters were listed: see NA, WO, 32/9423, Summerskill to Grigg, 29 March 1942.

20 *The Times*, 12 November 1941; also *Manchester Guardian*, 12 November 1941.

21 Campbell, 'Women in Combat', pp. 250–269; Grigg's words quoted from p. 253.

22 DeGroot, 'Whose Finger on the Trigger?', pp. 434–453; Pile quoted on p. 453.

23 National Service (No. 2) Act, December 1941, stated that 'no woman should be liable to make use of a lethal weapon, unless she signifies in writing her willingness to undertake such service' but this did not mean that those who signed were allowed to use the lethal weapons to kill: DeGroot, 'Whose Finger on the Trigger?', p. 436. Exceptionally, in conditions of secrecy, British women were trained to kill: J. Pattinson, 'Passing Performances: The Gendering of Military Identity in the Special Operations Executive', unpublished PhD thesis, University of Lancaster, 2004, pp. 128–130.

24 Hansard, vol. 365, col. 1932, 19 November 1940; and vol. 376, col. 2158, 18 December 1941.

25 P. Brookes, *Women at Westminster: An Account of Women in the British Parliament 1918–1966* (London: Peter Davies, 1967), p. 139.

26 Hansard, vol. 376, col. 1033, Prime Minister, 2 December 1941; vol. 376, cols 2119–2120, SoS for War, 18 December 1941.

27 Hansard, vol. 376, cols 2158 and 2155, 18 December 1941.

28 Herbert Morrison, Minister of Home Security, was particularly sensitive about the effects on the supply of women to civil defence, especially if women Home Guards received uniforms: NA, WO, 32/9423, Oswald Allen, Ministry of Home Security, 16 and 18 February 1942; Herbert Morrison, Ministry of Home Security, 10 October 1942; Ministry of Home Security to Redman, 17 November 1942. Grigg thought he was right to worry: NA, WO, 32/9423, P. J. Grigg to VCIGS, 9 December 1941. There were fears at the Ministry of Labour that it would deplete the numbers of women available for full-time work, or force them to give up other voluntary work 'of national importance': NA, WO, 32/9423, Minute by Mary Smieton, 11 March 1942.

29 Hansard, vol. 376, col. 2157, 18 December 1941.

30 NA, WO, 32/9423, Summerskill to Grigg, 29 March 1942.

31 M. Izzard, *A Heroine in Her Time: A Life of Dame Helen Gwynne-Vaughan 1879–1967* (London: Macmillan 1969), pp. 324–334.

32 J. Rosenzweig, 'The Construction of Policy for Women in the British Armed Forces, 1938–1945', unpublished M.Lit dissertation, Oxford University, 1993, pp. 83–87, 90–99.

33 Izzard, *Heroine*, p. 344.

34 Izzard, *Heroine*, pp. 343–344.

35 H. C .I. Gwynne-Vaughan, *Military Correspondence for Volunteers helping the Home Guard in London* (London: M. A. Lawson, 1942).

36 The phrase sums up Gwynne-Vaughan's views. It was used by hostile War Office officials, as well as favourable members of WHD: NA, WO, 32 9423, W. G. Lambert to Lord Bridgeman, 4 July 1942; Birkenhead Central Library, Wirral Archives (henceforth BCL, WA), YPX/75, 1359/1, Wallasey Women's Home Defence, Merseyside Branch of WHD, letter to enquirer (n.d., but 1942).

37 NA, WO, 32/9423, Helen Gwynne-Vaughan to War Office, 21 January 1942.

38 Lady Apsley, also Chairman of the ATS Benevolent Fund, and Lady Helen Nutting, a leading member of the Married Women's Association, affiliations that may have been more important in determining their interest in the Home Guard than the WVS connection. Lady Nutting contributed a front page on the Home Guard to the Newsletter of the Hampstead Group of the Married Women's Association, August 1942. Thanks to James Hinton for this information.

39 Dame Rachel Cowdy-Thornhill, formerly Principal Commandant, Voluntary Aid Detachments, Mrs A. E. B. Johnston, General Secretary QMAAC and ATS Old Comrades' Association; Dame Helen Gwynne-Vaughan, formerly Chief Controller, ATS.

40 Sir Douglas Brownrigg, Home Guard Zone Commander; the Earl of Cork and Orrery, retired Admiral of the Fleet and second-in-command to Brownrigg; General Sir Hubert Gough, Home Guard Zone Commander; John Langdon-Davies, Commandant, Home Guard School of Fieldcraft; Lt-Col. H. A. H. Newington, JP, Home Guard; G. H. S. Williamson, Battalion Commander, Home Guard.

41 Miss J. R. Bacon, Principal, Royal Holloway College; A. M. Carr-Saunders, Director, London School of Economics; Professor H. G. Jackson, Acting Master, Birkbeck College; Major-General Sir Frederick Maurice, Principal, Queen Mary College; Sir Allen Mawer, Provost, University College London.

42 Vernon Bartlett, MP; Dr Edith Summerskill, MP; Sir John Salmond, Marshal of the Royal Air Force; the other signature was that of Lady Bingham, of the governing body of the Royal Free Hospital.

43 'Service in the Home Guard. Reserve Units Suggested: A Women's Auxiliary?' *The Times*, 14 January 1942.

44 NA, WO, 32/9423, 27 January 1942.

45 NA, WO, 32/9423, 27 February 1942.

46 Such arrangements had been cautiously foreshadowed: NA, WO, 199/3238, Item 813, 8 September 1941.

47 Summerskill, *Woman's World*, p. 74.

48 WO, 32/9423, Summerskill to Grigg, 29 March 1942.

49 WO, 32/9423, Summerskill to Morrison, 28 April 1942.

50 WO, 32/9423, Minute by Frederick Bovenschen, 1 April 1942; Memo by DGHG, 10 April 1942. Grigg and others at the War Office were particularly incensed by Summerskill's desire for combat training for women: NA, WO, 32/9423, Grigg to Summerskill, 1 May 1942.

51 Brownrigg suggested at the rally that 'there is nothing to prevent Home Guards from teaching their wives how to use their rifles': 'Home Guard Teach Wives to Fight', *Daily Herald*, 20 April 1942; 'Women's Part in Defence: General's Hint', *Daily Telegraph*, 20 April 1942.

52 NA, WO, 32/9423, Minute by Frederick Bovenschen, 22 April 1942.

53 That this was a possibility is borne out by the fact that one of Dame Helen's memorialists, H. A. H. Newington, was a JP, and by the evidence of an oral history interviewee who remembered that the initiator of her WHD unit was a JP: Project interview (PI), Vida Staples (pseud.), 26 May 2000 (110–112).

54 WO, 32/9423, Minute by Frederick Bovenschen, 22 April 1942; Grigg agreed, 1 May 1942.

55 Hansard, vol. 376, cols 108–109, 13 November 1941.

56 See Hansard, vol. 376: cols 2128–2129, Major Marlowe, MP; col. 2141, Mr McEntee, MP, both 18 December 1941. A Miss Bridgman wrote that in 'September, 1942, when the achievements of the Russian Women were making headlines', she and other women at the Ministry of Food formed 'a Women's Home Guard': H. Smith, *Bureaucrats in Battledress: A History of the Ministry of Food Home Guard* (Conway: R. E. Jones, 1945), p. 122.

57 NA, WO, 32/9423, Miss B. Gooch to Mr Robertson, MP, and Robertson to Gooch, 2 October 1942. The Ministry of Labour in fact rebutted his suggestions. NA, WO, 32/9423, Ernest Bevin to Robertson, 6 November 1942.

58 NA, WO, 32/9423, DGHG, 1 October 1942.

59 NA, WO, 32/9423, Morrison to Grigg, 19 December 1942; Grigg to Morrison, marked 'Secret', 22 December 1942; Morrison to Grigg 6 January 1943.

60 BCL, WA, YPX/75, 1359/1, 'Women's Home Defence Training: Appeal in Liverpool', unidentified newscutting, November 1942.

61 Douie, *Lesser Half*, p. 44.

62 IWM, SA 11228, Edna Selwyn.

63 (PI), Ann Godden, 30 March 2000 (11).

64 (PI), Godden (425).

65 NA, WO, 32/9423, Brigadier H. P. Currey to War Office, 3 September 1941.

66 NA, WO, 32/9423, 'Brownie' (Lt. Gen. Sir Douglas Brownrigg) to Major General the Viscount Bridgeman, 29 September 1941.

67 *Picture Post*, 21 September 1940, p. 14.

68 For 'an armed people' see *Picture Post*, 15 June 1940, p. 12. Wintringham's brother John, CO of the Lindsey Home Guard, sent him the leaflet 'Some Plain Words to the Men and Women of Lindsey', 24 October 1941, which urged the women of Lindsey to persuade their menfolk to join the Home Guard by taking over their spare-time activities and cooking for their units. Wintringham responded: 'Very good leaflets. Kitty [Wintringham's wife] gives me hell because she says you put in more of the right mixture of things about women than I ever do': KCLA, T. H. Wintringham Archive, 1/34, Wintringham to John, 18 November 1941.

69 Panter-Downes, *Letter*, pp. 233–4. In spite of these negative attitudes on the Left towards women and combat, there is evidence that some left-wing women in London were trained to shoot by veterans of the Spanish Civil War: see D. Weinbren, *Generating Socialism: Recollections of Life in the Labour Party* (Stroud: Sutton Publishing, 1997), p. 142.

70 NA, WO, 32/9423, Helen Gwynne-Vaughan to War Office, 21 January 1942; also Langdon-Davies, 'Home Guard Parade', *Sunday Pictorial*, 24 November 1940.

71 E.g. Lt-Col. A. H. Austin of the 34th Warwickshire (Birmingham) Battalion Home Guard wrote of his 'Women's Auxiliary ... which staffs Signals Office, Intelligence Office and provides the necessary clerical and other assistance': Graves, *Home Guard*, p. 345.

72 Graves, *Home Guard*, pp. 342–343.

73 Graves, *Home Guard*, p. 352. Major General H. Martelli, 8th Battalion Wiltshire Home Guard, wrote of his frustration at trying to organise a Home Guard unit and criticised 'the determined ban against allowing the enrolment of women in the Home Guard even in clerical and first-aid capacities'.

74 Graves, *Home Guard*, p. 186.

75 Graves, *Home Guard*, p. 94.

76 Graves, *Home Guard*, p. 325; he commented: 'There is never a grumble or a grouse – they just get on with the job.'

77 The provision of medical services for Home Guards was only slowly thought out, and Graves commented that there was strong feeling in 1941–42 that first-aid personnel, 'particularly women', should be given official recognition: Graves, *Home Guard*, p. 145.

78 NA, WO, 32/9423, Summerskill to W. S.Churchill, 31 October 1941.

79 NA, WO, 32/9423, note from W. S.Churchill, 31 October 1941.

80 NA, WO, 32/9423, Summerskill to Rt Hon. Captain Margesson, MP, 5 December 1941.

81 *Daily Mail*, 29 October 1941.

82 NA, WO, 32/9423, Letters from Works Director, Mollart Engineering Co. Ltd, 6 November 1941, and London District Commander Home Guard, 11 November 1941.

83 *Sunday Express*, 17 May 1942.

84 Smith, *Bureaucrats*, pp. 122–124.

85 IWM, DD, Misc 126, Item 1956, Miss A. G. Ascott.

86 (PIs): Lois Baker, 490, 534, 576, 602, 686; Marion Bourne, 74, 629, 641, 703, 735, 790, 869, 877, 987; IWM, SA, 16762, Mary Warschauer, letter and recording, reel 3.

87 (PI), Joan Hardy, 181, 149, 157, 152.

88 (PI), Hardy, 6–10, 200–4.

89 BCL, WA, YPX/75, 1359/1, Report on Wallasey Women's Home Defence, July 1943.

90 BCL, WA, YPX/75, 1359/1, 'Girls Help to Defend!', *Wallasey News* (n.d.); YPX/75, 1359/6, Edith Roberts to G. L. Reakes, MP, 30 January 1945.

91 BCL, WA, YPX/75, 1359/1, *Wallasey News* (n.d., but February 1943); Concert Programme, 19 February 1943; Minutes, Wallasey WHD, 8 March 1943.

92 BCL, WA, YPX/75, 1359/1, Report on Wallasey WHD, July 1943. Reakes, a former Labour Party member, contested and won a bye-election at Wallasey, in April 1942, as an Independent candidate with Common Wealth sympathies, against the local Conservative: P. Addison, *The Road to 1945: British Politics and the Second World War* (London: Jonathan Cape, 1975), pp. 157–158.

93 BCL, WA, YPX/75, 1359/7, *Wallasey News*, 5 January 1994.

94 BCL, WA, YPX/75, 1359/1, undated leaflet (1942–43).

95 BCL, WA, YPX/75, 1359/1, Report on Wallasey WHD, July 1943; Notes for Speech to Liverpool Business and Professional Women, 27 Jan. 1945; *Wallasey News*, 18 Dec. 43, WHD Unit; Report on Monthly Meeting (n.d., but Jan.–Feb. 1944).

96 BCL, WA, YPX/75, 1359/1, *Wallasey News* (n.d., but Feb. 1943).

97 BCL, WA, YPX/75, 1359/1, Minutes, 8 March 1943.

98 *The Times*, 12 November 1941.

99 IWM, DD, 86/54/1, Mrs Louie White, Diary; entries referring to 'musketry' or rifle drill include 3 December 1942; 7, 14, 28 January 1943; 4, 6 February 1943; 13, 26 March 1943.

100 BCL, WA, YPX/75, 1359/1, Minutes, 8 March 1943.

101 WO, 32/9423, Bridgeman to Vice-Chief of the Imperial General Staff (VCIGS), 23 October 1941; and Note for ECAC (Executive Committee of the Army Council) on the employment of women to assist the Home Guard by DGHG, submitted by VCIGS.

102 NA, WO, 32/9423, Bridgeman to VCIGS, 23 October 1941. The proposal stated that women were required 'as clerks, orderlies, telephone operators, despatch riders; cooks and canteen helpers; car, lorry and ambulance drivers; nursing orderlies; and as gun [altered to instrument] numbers of anti-aircraft and coast defence guns'. The proposed uniform was to consist of hat, shoes, overalls, badge, scarf and greatcoat.

103 NA, WO, 32/9423, Draft ACI (Army Council Instruction), Women's Services in Connexion with the Home Guard, 2 July 1942.

104 *Daily Telegraph*, 21 July 1942; *Daily Express*, 14 December 1942; *Daily Telegraph*, 14 December 1942; Hansard, vol. 385, cols 1413–1414, 8 December 1942.

105 MacKenzie, *Home Guard*, p. 3

106 NA, WO, 32/9423, Commander-in-Chief Home Forces, General Sir Bernard C. T. Paget to Army Commanders (less Canadian) and GOC, London District, 30 August 1942.

107 NA, WO, 32/9423, Rusty Eastwood, Northern Command, York, to Paget, 17 September 1942.

108 NA, WO, 32/9423, Maj.-Gen. K. J. Martin, DSO, Eastern Command, Home Forces, to Paget, 4 September 1942; Lt-Col. Jack Swayne, South Eastern Command, Home Forces, to Paget, 21 September 1942.

109 NA, WO, 32/9423, Arthur Smith, Home Guard Branch, London District, to Paget, 8 September 1942.

110 NA, WO, 32/9423, DGHG, Note of discussion with Edith Summerskill, 27 October 1942.

111 NA, WO, 32/9423, DGHG to SoS, 30 January 1943.

112 *Evening Standard*, 27 January 1943.

113 BCL, WA, YPX/75, 1359/1, Edith Summerskill, Stand-down speech (n.d., but Dec. 1944).

114 Hansard, vol.388, col.1532, 20 April 1943.

115 NA, WO, 32/9423, 'Suggested Answer'; 'Note for S. of S.'; 'Employment of Women to Assist the Home Guard', April 1943.

116 C. Graves, *Women in Green: The Story of the Women's Voluntary Service* (London: Heinemann, 1948), p. 7; see also pp. 1, 23, 12.

117 L. Westwood, 'More than Tea and Sympathy', *History Today*, 48:6 (June 1998), p. 3.

118 Lady Reading nevertheless chided Grigg for lack of clarity about the relationship between the WVS and the Home Guard: NA, WO, 32/9423, Reading to Grigg, 14 December 1942.

119 J. Hinton, *Women, Social Leadership and the Second World War: Continuities of Class* (Oxford: Oxford University Press, 2002), p. 94.

120 Hinton, *Women, Social Leadership*, p. 239.

121 BCL, WA, YPX/75, 1359/1, WHD, Minutes (Liverpool), 17 May 1943; YPX/75, 1359/5, *The Eighth Pillar* (n.d., but 1943).

122 Reading to Summerskill, printed in *The Eighth Pillar*.

123 *The Eighth Pillar.*

124 BCL, WA, YPX/75, 1359/1, Response of WHD Unit, Wallasey, Cheshire, to Summerskill's questions, 30 April 1943. Graves, *Women in Green*, p. 55, refers to the provision of canteens for the Home Guard by the WVS but gives an otherwise confusing account, suggesting that 'up to 80,000 women' were nominated for clerical and telephone work. This is far higher than the recorded figure of 32,000 women Home Guards after 'recognition', many of whom are likely to have been WHD members. (Summerskill claimed a W.H.D. membership of 30,000 in April 1943: 'Women May Join Home Guard as Auxiliaries', *Manchester Guardian*, 21 April 1943.) Hinton, *Women, Social Leadership*, does not discuss WVS–HG involvement because it did not figure as a major issue in the minutes of the main national committees. However, WVS, *Report on Twenty-five Years' Work 1938–1963*, states 'approximately 20,000 WVS members enrolled as Home Guard Auxiliaries' and that 'W.V.S. members were given clear instructions that on no account were they to carry arms or take part in any fighting'. Thanks to James Hinton for this information and for permission to quote it.

125 WO, 32/9423, Draft 'Employment of Women to Assist the Home Guard', April 1943; BCL, WA,YPX/75, 1359/1, copy of Army Council Instruction, April 1943, Summerskill to Unit Organisers, 21 April 1943.

126 BCL, WA, YPX/75, 1359/ 5, Hon. Sec. Women's Home Defence, to Organisers, signed Y.M. Moss, (n.d., but May 1943); *The Eighth Pillar.*

127 BCL, WA, YPX/75, 1359/1, *Daily Mail*, 21 April 1943.

128 Shooting competitions were resumed, May 1943, with Mr O'Flaherty 'of the Liverpool Police Range' as coach: BCL, WA YPX/75, 1359/1, Minutes (Liverpool), 17 May 1943; Report on Wallasey WHD, July 1943; Minutes (Liverpool), 6 December 1943.

129 BCL, WA,YPX/75, 1359/1, Minutes, 8 March 1943; *Wallasey News*, 7 August 1943 and 23 October 1943; Minutes (Liverpool), 6 December 1943.

130 BCL, WA,YPX/75, 1359/1, Draft report for *Wallasey News*, 6 May 1944.

131 IWM, DD, 86/54/1, Mrs Louie White, Diary: entries referring to 'musketry' or rifle drill after April 1943 include: 18 April 1944; 23 May 1944; entries concerning exercises include: 12 September 1943; 5 December 1943; 23 January 1944; 19 March 1944; 24 September 1944.

132 WO, 32/9423, Communications from Brigadier H. P. Currey, 3 September 1941; General Brownrigg, 29 September 1941; Lord Bridgeman, 23 October 1941.

133 Hansard, vol. 376, col. 2162, 9 December 1941. The response was circular: Captain Margesson said: 'I do not think it would be right that Home Guard uniforms should be worn by persons not enrolled in the Home Guard' (vol. 376, col. 1373, 9 December 1941).

134 NA, WO, 32/9423, PJG to VCIGS, 9 December 1941; Note of a Meeting in FM's room, 25 September 1942; G.W.Lambert, DUS to Bridgeman, 4 July 1942.

135 Hansard, vol. 397, cols 1662–3, 2 March 1944, Sir Thomas Moore.

136 Hansard, 3 August 1943, vol. 391, col. 2117–8. There had been concerns along these lines before the men of the Home Guard were issued with proper Army uniforms, in 1940.

137 NA, WO, 32/9423. The certificate, signed by Sector Commander, was '[n]ot to be issued until the Home Guard is mustered' (e.i.o.), and stated that the woman named 'is authorised to follow the Armed Forces of the Crown, and is entitled in the event of capture by the enemy to be treated as a prisoner of war under the provisions of Article 81 of the International Convention relative to the treatment of Prisoners of War … her status is equivalent to that of an Other Rank in the British Army with the rank of Private'. Some commentators argued that a *franc-tireur* could not exist till after an armistice or surrender: 'Before that happens any civilian is in duty bound to assist in repelling the invader': Marquess of Donegall, *Sunday Dispatch*, 16 May 1943.

138 Hansard, vol. 391, cols 2117–2118, 3 August 1943.

139 Hansard, vol 397, cols 1662–1663, Debate on supply, army estimates, 2 March 1944. On chiffon, see C. McDowell, *Forties Fashion and the New Look* (London: Bloomsbury, 1997), p. 150, caption to illustration.

140 A correspondent to the journal *Defence* made this point, though in relation to function rather than sexual attraction: BCL, WA, YPX/75, 1359/1, Letter to the editor of *Defence*, 15 February 1944.

141 Hansard, vol. 391, cols 2117–2118, 3 August 1943, for Summerskill; vol 397, cols 1662–1663, Debate on supply, army estimates, 2 March 1944, for Moore.

142 Hansard, vol. 398, cols 1223–1224, 28 March 1944; vol. 399, col. 1702, 9 May 1944; vol. 400, col. 3, 16 May 1944, and col. 751, 24 May 1944. The Inter-Parliamentary Home Guard Committee took up the issue fruitlessly: NA, WO, 32/9423, 'Memorandum with regard to wearing of uniform by Nominated Women in the H.G.', November 1943. The WHD continued 'the fight': BCL, WA, YPX/75, 1359/1, Letter from Hon. Secretary, WHD to organisers, February 1944.

143 BCL, WA, YPX/75, 1359/1, Letter to *Defence*, 15 February 1944.

144 *Daily Mail*, 29 October 1941; 'Women H.G.s Set Riddle', *Daily Express*, 30 October 1941; Smith, *Bureaucrats*, p. 125. Oral history provides further evidence which is reviewed in Chapter 8.

145 Hansard, vol. 398, col. 1223, 28 March 1944.

146 BCL, WA, YPX/75, 1359/1, *Wallasey News*, 17 June 1944.

147 'Last Parade of Home Guard', *The Times*, 4 December 1944, explained that the London parade was composed of 3 men from each unit in the UK, 'together with some 3,500 from the London district'.

148 IWM, DD, 86/54/1, Diary of Mrs Louie White, 3 December 1944; Smith, *Bureaucrats in Battledress*, p. 125.

149 NA, WO, 32/9423, 22 February 1944; Hansard, vol. 398, col. 1814, 4 April 1944. For use of 'Woman Home Guard Auxiliary' in official correspondence

see, e.g., NA, WO, 32/9423, Sussex Territorial Army Association to War Office, 26 June 1944.

150 Longmate, *The Real Dad's Army*, illustration, p. 127.

151 This denial was echoed in official literature issued to the armed forces. The army publication *War* stated: 'There are no women H.G. properly so described': Army Bureau of Current Affairs, *War*, No. 70, 13 May 1944, 'The Other Army', p. 14.

152 Hansard, vol. 404, col. 605, 31 October 1944, and col. 1231, 7 November 1944.

153 See B. Anderson, *We Just Got on With It: British Women in World War II* (Chippenham: Picton, 1994) illustration, p. 43. The women's certificate was surmounted by the War Office crest, the men's by the royal crest.

~
PART II
~

Representations

4

The Home Guard in wartime popular culture

The Home Guard was powerfully evoked by politicians during the Second World War as a symbol of British 'unity and brotherhood' that was propelled by 'surging anger' at the thought of invasion and was 'unfailing' in its defence of 'the light of freedom' in 'our island home'. In political rhetoric the Home Guard was, in short, 'Britain incarnate'.[1] These selectively constructed images were taken up and elaborated on, as well as subjected to critical scrutiny, in numerous cultural products during the war. Three themes recur. In one, the Home Guard was addressed as a site of geographical and social inclusivity, and hence as a symbol of national unity. Another concerned the position of the Home Guard within the national war effort as an anti-invasion force guarding the home and nation. A third engaged with the issues of the military functions of the force and the masculinity of its members.

Wartime portrayals of the Home Guard were offered in a wide variety of media, including films, poems, adult murder mysteries, children's adventure stories, joke books, comics, newspaper cartoons, art exhibitions and theatrical productions. Some, but by no means all, were officially commissioned. The Ministry of Information (MoI) had responsibility for maintaining morale in the face of the German threat, and for informing the population in general and wartime military and civilian organisations in particular about how to support the war effort. It issued posters, radio broadcasts, booklets and short films about the Home Guard that were intended to educate the public as well as to recruit and train members of the force.[2] Although the MoI did not directly control other types of cultural production, it monitored and influenced them.[3] The press was kept under observation by the MoI's Scrutiny Division, and newspaper editors and broadcasters were provided with topics to cover as well as to avoid. But the ways in which the Home Guard was represented were not all determined by government instruction or censorship. Although authors and artists were relatively rarely officially commissioned to work on the Home Guard, they often chose to use it as a subject, and even though not everything they produced had to be approved by the MoI, they frequently included messages about the Home Guard, the nation and the war effort. The divide between official propaganda and other types of cultural representation in Britain in the Second World War was blurred and the outcomes were largely dependent on self-regulation rather than government control.

Many representations of the Home Guard, non-official as well as official, were serious. But there was also a strong current of humour concerning the Home Guard in the popular culture of the Second World War. Humour in wartime has multiple roles, some of which can be seen as aiding the war effort, such as the capacity to define and belittle the enemy, to reassure a population disturbed by destruction and upheaval, and to release tension and defuse internal antagonism. Others appear more transgressive, such as exposing the folly of authority or highlighting the fragility of social identities.[4] Later in this chapter we ask whether the use of humour in representations of the Home Guard supported or challenged both the force's own legitimacy and that of the wider project of which it was a part.

As we saw in Chapters 2 and 3, ideas about the Home Guard's composition and purpose were contested and they, as well as the functions of the force, changed over time. If the meanings and understandings of the Home Guard that appeared in the public media were to circulate through society – that is to say, if a 'cultural circuit' was to operate – the representations offered could not be completely foreign to people's experience. Official posters would not be heeded, films would not attract audiences, cartoons would not help to sell the newspapers in which they were printed if the representations they offered did not have at least an element of familiarity for their audiences. Moreover, Home Guards were members of both the force and the public at the same time, in a way that even the 'citizen soldiers' of the British Army of the Second World War were not.

Representations of the Home Guard were framed in terms of common cultural references: we interrogate their contribution to the construction of the British national character at war and hence to the imagined community of the wartime nation. We explore the extent to which popular culture, official and unofficial, comic and serious, was responsive to changes in the force over time; and we assess how far popular culture identified the Home Guard with the greater endeavour of which it was part, and how far it expressed scepticism about the competence of the force to fulfil its roles within national defence.[5]

The nation at war

In cultural representations, the Home Guard played a central part in the concept of the 'People's War', that is 'the idea of ordinary people pulling together to defeat a common foe'.[6] The official version stressed the notion that national territory and traditions defined and delimited a diverse but united British population. Thus, as we have seen, speeches about the Home Guard by political leaders evoked a history of successful collective British endeavour against external threats, in which volunteer organisations played a crucial role. The trope was widely taken up: *Home Guard*, an MoI short film released in 1941, refers to 'local defence volunteers' at the time of both the Armada and Napoleon,[7] and a history of British home defence published in 1945 claimed the Saxon *Fyrd* as the original Home Guard.[8] But such officially approved accounts conceived of the People's War and the Home Guard very differently from more radical versions. Tom Wintringham's 1942 account *People's War* defined such a war as one in which guerrilla 'home guards', supported by local populations, would rise up against fascism not just in Britain but all over Europe, fired by a commitment to liberation and the establishment of democratic socialist societies.[9] The official versions of the invented tradition did not include Wintringham's lineage of radical civilian soldiers, nor did they encompass any of the female militants, such as Boadicea, whom Summerskill evoked as precedents for women Home Guards.

The wartime community which the Home Guard represented in officially approved accounts was located in territory encompassing the nations and regions of Great Britain. This was part of a deliberate project to encompass British disparity within an image of a unified nation.[10] There were, however, obvious difficulties with representing unity in diversity, especially where visual representations of 'Britain' were concerned: a solution was to collapse locational differences into a single iconic – and, hence, by elision – generic British landscape. The rolling green hills of southern England became just such an icon.[11] But inevitably such a strategy involved the deselection of other landscapes, not just the hills of north-west England, Snowdonia or the Scottish Highlands, but especially the industrial powerhouses of the war, such as Clydeside, the Black Country or Belfast.[12] Pastoral imagery was intended 'as a stay against the horrors of industrialized warfare and a representation of all that is threatened by such warfare', but its use as a symbol of an industrialised nation was contradictory.[13]

As far as the Home Guard was concerned, the greatest concentrations of 'homes' to guard were in urban and suburban locations: nevertheless, representations of the homeland that it was to defend were predominantly rural. The poet Cecil Day Lewis, who joined the Home Guard in Devon and who was keen to write 'vigorous patriotic verse',[14] powerfully established the rural identity of the Home Guard in his poem *Watching Post*, depicting night-time guard duties:

> A hill flank overlooking the Axe valley.
> Among the stubble a farmer and I keep watch
> For whatever may come to injure our countryside –
> Light-signals, parachutes, bombs, or sea-invaders.
> The moon looks over the hill's shoulder, and hope
> Mans the old ramparts of an English night.[15]

The poem moves from topographical realism (the 'hill', the 'Axe valley' and the 'stubble') to abstraction: England's nocturnal 'ramparts' are manned by 'hope', in this context a metaphor for the Home Guard. The English countryside is represented as a body (the hill has both a 'flank' and a 'shoulder') that may be injured by a catalogue of wartime dangers. But it is also imbued with the timelessness evoked in the lyrical final lines: the countryside, England, the moon and the night itself will survive any enemy incursions. The unchanging landscape, in such depictions, endowed the Home Guard with security and reliability as well as standing for enduring values worth fighting for. This literary representation of a Home Guard centred in rural southern England, however, strained against complex and potentially divisive visions of other – urban and industrial, regional and national – Britains. As Simon Featherstone comments: 'the distinguishing feature of the pastoral is not an established code of signifiers recalling and recreating "the English nation" ... but a rhetoric of persuasion that the nation does exist as a whole'.[16]

A contrasting way of representing a nation unified by war was to depict a Home Guard made up of numerous regional *types*, recognisable by distinctive differences in their physiognomy, but united by the cause which brought them together. John Brophy's celebration of the Home Guard, published in 1945, was illustrated with pastel portraits by Eric Kennington which were intended to represent both urban and rural Home Guards and to show differences of region, rank and age. The text claimed that each face expressed both individuality and membership of a community: 'Look at them one by one, and each man – English from north or south, east or west, Scots or Welsh – is himself, unmistakable, self-reliant, distinctive. Look at them in quick succession and you get the impression of a team; a co-operation of effort. That is why they represent the Home Guard so faithfully and well.'[17] However, as in the case of historical precedents, so in that of social and geographical inclusivity, politically sensitive areas and social groups were omitted: the citizens of Northern Ireland and of Eire had no place in Kennington's gallery.

The stylistic device of *listing* was used by poets and writers to convey the diverse social composition of the Home Guard. Lists of Home Guard members, in which the men's names, attributes and/or professions were recited, drew attention both to each individual and to the collective of which they were a part. Listing used words to achieve the effect that Brophy claimed when he recommended that the portraits in his book should be viewed together: it was a team-building technique that enabled authors to suggest that the Home Guard as a whole was greater than the sum of its parts. A combination of visual and verbal listing was not uncommon. In the catalogue accompanying an exhibition of paintings by the artist Gilbert Spencer, for instance, his representations of the Home Guard are described as including 'all characters of the English countryside', including 'farmer and labourer, blacksmith and village ancient, poacher and gamekeeper, the local squire, the old officer and the retired business man'.[18] This list of civilian occupational identities indicates both the range of skills upon which the Home Guard draws, and the social diversity of the force. It also contributes to the construction of the Home Guard as a site of social reconciliation. The pairing of 'poacher and gamekeeper' was a popular trope in Home Guard literature, not only because both were assumed to have expert knowledge of local topography, camouflage and the use of rifles, but also because putting them together underlined the wartime co-operation between members of social groups whose habitual antagonism had allegedly been dissolved by the common cause.[19] In such representations, the Home Guard figures as a wartime site in which social mixing produces change: the war in general and the Home Guard in particular provide experiences that lead to the review and rejection of prejudices. Bairstowe, the main character in Belton Cobb's crime novel *Home Guard Mystery* finds himself serving in the Home Guard with a cockney, a blasphemer, a spiv and a 'side-street draper', men with whom he would not have associated before the war: 'But when those same men appeared in the Home Guard, those were not the characteristics that one noticed ... These were good fellows, every one of them ... they gave one faith in human nature'.[20] Wartime national unity is thus achieved through the transformation of socially divisive attitudes and values.

The use of pastoral England and the rural Home Guard as metaphors for Britain and the British at war presented attractive images of rural peace and social harmony, in spite of the tensions with the experience of the British people, most of whom were living in towns where many had suffered social deprivation in the inter-war years as well as bombing during the war. The need to ensure that such people were not alienated from the war effort, as well as that communities barely touched by the war made a full contribution, concerned the Government throughout the war. An MoI memorandum of 1940 required its official film-makers to address 'what Britain was fighting for, how Britain was fighting, and the need for sacrifice':[21] representations of the Home Guard were included in this mission. In an MoI film of 1941, *The Dawn Guard*, two Home Guards, one (Bernard Miles) younger than the other (Percy Walsh), debate what Britain is fighting for as the sun rises on their guard duty on a hill overlooking rolling English countryside. Walsh expresses a nostalgic view of Britain, essentially rural and frozen in time, which must be defended against invasion. Miles draws attention to the ills of pre-war urban Britain, and sketches a vision of the better world to be built after the war, a project which will be possible only if the Nazi menace is repulsed.[22] Walsh comes to accept Miles's argument that the war must lead to change, and not to a return to pre-war standards.

The film went further in its understanding of 'what Britain was fighting for' than many MoI productions. It was made by twin brothers Roy and John Boulting, who 'were committed to the idea of the war as a stepping stone towards a new, better and more equitable society'.[23] They self-consciously attempted to reconcile the conservative rural Home Guard iconography, reviewed above, with a view of a radically changed future. The tone of outrage about the neglect of Britain's industrial areas before the war, the focus on the need for a programme of reconstruction, and the identification of the incompatibility of Nazism with social justice, parallel the work of Abram Games, who contributed posters to the 'Your BRITAIN – fight for it now' series. Games depicted the ill-health and poverty of urban dwellers and indicated the modern solutions that could be achieved by the extension of wartime collectivism into the peace-time polity. Such ideas became central to Labour Party policy during the war: they were fed from outside the Labour Party by publications such as William Beveridge's proposals for the reform of social insurance in 1942.[24] *The Dawn Guard* located the discussion of such politicised programmes of change in the Home Guard, with two effects: to suggest a modern as well as a traditional identity and outlook for the Home Guard; and to evoke the engaged citizen whose involvement in the war stimulated a sense of social responsibility. Here were the anti-fascist, socially concerned Home Guards of whom George Orwell wrote, and the 'armies of freemen', postulated by Wintringham, who debated the ideological meanings of the war they were fighting.

The Dawn Guard was unusual in depicting the Home Guard as a site of radical philosophical debate. Although some reviewers were enthusiastic and claimed that audience reactions were positive,[25] other reports of the film's reception suggest that it was resisted by viewers suspicious of 'the idea that someone is trying to put something over on them'.[26] These responses were indicative of British ambivalence towards idealistic propaganda during the war.[27] Other authors and artists who featured in the ideological project of the 'people's war' in fiction and film put explicit statements about it into the mouths of vicars, as in *Mrs Miniver* (1942), or of other social leaders, rather than 'ordinary people'. For the most part, they did not use the Home Guard as a vehicle. An exception was the novelist Ruth Adam, who published a crime novel focused on the Home Guard which engaged with issues concerning the objectives and morality of the British war effort.

The plot of *Murder in the Home Guard* (1942) is as follows. A young Home Guard, Philip Spencer, is shot dead while on patrol near his home of Longmarket, a southern English country town. On the same night, lights are observed flashing from the vicinity of the cottage hospital, as if to attract an approaching German bomber – which shortly afterwards deposits its bomb load on the town. Hitherto untouched by bombing, and affected mainly by shortages of consumables rather than by the productive or military war effort, the inhabitants of Longmarket are self-centred. Instead of helping a German–Jewish woman refugee they exploit her as a domestic servant, and a bed-wetting Cockney girl evacuee is rejected by one household after another. Adam's sympathetic presentation of these characters leads the reader to understand the generosity of spirit that is so evidently lacking in the Longmarket populace.

The Home Guard leader Colonel Markover, who has lost his only son, a fighter pilot, in the Battle of Britain, is eventually identified as both the murderer and a 'fifth columnist'. Spencer, patrolling the wood alone, discovers him signalling to the German bomber, and Markover shoots him so that Spencer cannot prevent him accomplishing his mission.

Markover's motives are spelt out didactically near the end of the novel: the Blitz must be brought home to the inhabitants of Longmarket so that they understand the sacrifices that have been made on their behalf by pilots like his son, and realise that a spirit of unity and co-operation, not their mean-mindedness, is necessary to win the war. Having explained this in a speech to Sally, a young nurse whom we discuss further in Chapter 5, and in a letter to the local newspaper, the Colonel takes his own life.

The novel is effectively a polemic against the wartime failings of members of English communities such as Longmarket: it contests the strong association of such 'heartlands' with the 'England' that must be defended against enemy attack. As far as home defence is concerned, it initially suggests that the Home Guard may provide opportunities for fifth-column activities; the conclusion, however, overwrites this unsettling possibility. The Home Guard turns out to be not a nest of Nazi sympathizers or conscientious objectors but the site of patriotic activity. In contrast to the inward-looking middle-class community of Longmarket, members of the Home Guard perform their patriotic duty earnestly, if, in the case of Markover, disastrously, not only for Philip Spencer but also for those bombed on the night in question, and for himself.[28]

The Boulting brothers were controversial figures[29] and Ruth Adam was unconventional.[30] Other authors and artists avoided such radical critiques of wartime society or such idealistic visions of postwar reconstruction in work depicting the Home Guard.[31] On the other hand, numerous representations, especially humorous ones, were unsparing in their exposure of the contradictions of national unity in the Home Guard context. Tapping into a strong British tradition of irony, scepticism and satire, they used the Home Guard to emphasise the difficulties of achieving a united war effort, given Britain's national and regional divisions and the resilience of the British class structure.

Comic representations of fissures in national unity in the Home Guard drew on long-standing satirical treatments of tensions between town and country and between the various sub-nations of the 'United Kingdom'. The iconic status of countryfolk as representatives of the best aspects of British character was contrasted in satirical treatments of the Home Guard with the long-standing urban view of the slow-witted countryman,[32] and the fictional names of Home Guard localities often evoked the less attractive aspects of rural life: Mudleigh, Mudthorpe, Mudford.[33] Anglo-Irish relations and the problem of the Home Guard of Northern Ireland do not appear to have been taken up by humorists, whether because they were too sensitive or as part of the habitual neglect of Northern Ireland in British culture.[34] But the quasi-colonial dynamics between England and Wales, and England and Scotland, were probed. 'These Furriners' is a comic sketch of 1942, in which a Home Guard is captured on an exercise. Believing that he is hearing German, he assumes he has been caught by the genuine enemy and manages to knock out two of them before he is restrained, only to discover that 'his captors were Welshmen'.[35] The joke is multifaceted. It is about the stupidity of that Home Guard for mis-recognising the Welsh language, and it is about the dominance of the English-speaking population of Britain: the nation's Celtic minorities are incomprehensible to them, but can nevertheless be assumed, like colonial subjects, to be loyal participants in the war. The joke also expresses a theme within Home Guard humour to which we return: an acknowledgement of the bravery and accomplishment of Home Guard members, coupled with the suggestion that the valour they displayed was misplaced.

In the comic treatment of the fragility of wartime unity, tensions arising from national differences were paralleled by those resulting from local rivalries, transposed in cultural representations on to competing Home Guard units. Such accounts exposed weaknesses in the polity yet were supportive of the rhetoric of the war effort: these divisions were part of British life but could be overcome by the necessity of fighting a common enemy. The plot of the 1943 comedy film *Get Cracking*, starring the comic actor, singer and ukulele-player George Formby,[36] is driven by the competition between two localities and, specifically, two men who are rivals in love and business. The Home Guard units of the villages of Minor and Major Wallop are vying for a Vickers gun which will help them win a Home Guard exercise. Minor Wallop and George eventually vanquish their opponents, only to be told that the authorities have merged the two units, whereupon they agree to share weapons, and start planning joint-action against the neighbouring village of Midgeley.

Compton Mackenzie, who was himself Commander of the Eriskay Home Guard,[37] combined national difference and local rivalry in his comic novel *Keep the Home Guard Turning* (1943). Its narrative, like that of *Get Cracking*, is powered by the mutual loathing of neighbouring Home Guard units, in this case those of the Hebridean islands of 'Great' and 'Little Todday'. The islanders explicitly subvert wartime rhetoric:

> 'Surely at a time like this we should all pull together?'
> 'Och, we'll all pull together right enough,' Roderick declared. 'But we'll each keep to our own side of the rope.'[38]

Although the islanders do not intend to co-operate, their rivalry ensures that they take Home Guard exercises seriously and practice defending their localities with stubborn passion. Furthermore, they demonstrate their capacity for combined action when the authorities, based on the mainland and associated with England, insist bureaucratically that the islanders have permits to cross the sea. The colonial English are 'the enemy' who unites the islanders. The English are personified by the Home Guard captain who is endeavouring to control the island units. Captain Waggett, former chartered accountant and an English middle-class stuffed shirt, is pompous and ineffectual: his attempts to exert authority over the wily Scots are always frustrated.

The exposure of enduring class relations in wartime Britain involved the satirical treatment of misplaced authority and a critique of precarious social identities, both characteristics of Captain Waggett. The pretensions of inexperienced men who were given military authority, and who tried to use it to enhance their social standing, were mercilessly dealt with by some authors. In Belton Cobb's *Home Guard Mystery*, Cunningham is a subservient grocer by day, but a pompous and aggressive Home Guard sergeant at night.[39] 'He was ... convinced that he was the only real soldier in the Section (if not the Platoon), that the men – even old Davis, who wore a D.C.M. ribbon from the last war – were congenital nit-wits, and that everything depended on himself.'[40] Cunningham's misplaced sense of superiority ensures that the reader will have little sympathy for him, and makes him a suitable murder victim. He has not undergone the change of consciousness vital for building a united war effort: unlike Bairstowe in the same novel, he is unable to recognise that his Home Guard comrades 'were good fellows, every one of them'.[41] Authors' treatments, whether humorous or serious, of Home Guard characters such as Waggett and Cunningham constitute the moral censure of behaviour that is defined as inappropriate in the collective endeavour of fighting a 'people's war': these characters are punished for their individualism and selfishness.

More gently, cartoonists drew attention to the difficulties for the 'democratic' Home Guard of exerting its authority in a society in which class-based patterns of deference were well-entrenched. One of the Home Guard's roles was checking the identities of passers-by at roadblocks, part of their task of controlling population movements and detecting delib-erate or inadvertent subversion. Identity checks were unpopular on the grounds that they were both time-consuming and, as far as local people already known to the Home Guard were concerned, unnecessary.[42] The cartoonist 'Sillince' depicted the problems the Home Guard might experi-ence when required to examine the credentials of their social superiors (see figure 4). The cartoon achieves a carnivalesque reversal: the two

Figure 4 '… and 'ere's me Identity Card, Lady' by Sillince, *Punch*, 23 July 1941

Home Guards should have authority over their aristocratic superior, but in the face of the traditional class-based power that she exudes, they abase themselves. Such humour depends on its audience's recognition that, in spite of the wartime rhetoric of national unity which proclaimed the dissolution of class barriers, the British class structure stood firm.

Counter-invasion

The Home Guard was created to defend the nation against invasion, and as we saw in Chapter 2, its conception as a counter-invasion force in political discourse was sustained well beyond the period in which that role was likely to be fulfilled. Projections of the Home Guard, whether emanating from the political establishment or from the Left, rarely referred to its less glamorous functions of substitute for the regular forces and supplement to civil defence. The emphasis on anti-invasion was also strong within popular culture.

Take-up of the idea of the Home Guard as Britain's 'first line of defence' was prompted by the MoI, as part of its endeavour to sustain morale as well as its responsibility to inform the population about what to do in the event of invasion. In the summer of 1940 the MoI made a public instruction film, *Miss Grant Goes to the Door*, that tells a gripping story of the arrival of the invasion, personified by a German parachutist followed by a German spy, at the door of two spinster sisters, Edith and Caroline Grant, living in a picturesque country cottage. The film informs viewers that the ringing of church bells would herald the invasion; that people should stay at home rather than try to run away; that they should disable vehicles that might be used by the enemy; and that they should lock up maps and not give away locational information to strangers. The depiction of the LDV is encouraging: its members are young, alert and virile; they are referred to as 'parashots', defining their anti-invasion role; their training is focused and evidently effective. An LDV lecture about the weapons and supplies contained in the capsules that the Germans drop with their paratroops, and how to deal with them, is interrupted by a telephone call from the ARP warden: Miss Edith Grant has arrived at his post reporting that there is a German in the sisters' house. The unit takes immediate action, passing and blowing up a capsule as members speed to the cottage in two cars. The LDV do not dominate the film (in which the sisters take centre stage; see Chapter 5) but they constitute its discursive context as a locally available and effective military presence, able to articulate what is going on and decide what to do about it. The LDV captain spells out the message of the film, at once supportive and inspirational, to the two women – and to the wider population: 'You kept your heads. The front line's in every home these days.'[43] That final statement encapsulates the justification for the creation of the Home Guard.

From the summer of 1940 through to 1944, popular representations of the threat of invasion were, like *Miss Grant*, designed to reassure. Church towers featured frequently, their inclusion adding a specifically Christian dimension to the imagined community of wartime Britain. Long-standing symbols of safety and sanctity, churches now had special significance as invasion beacons.[44] The ringing of church bells would mean not only that the invasion had begun but that the Home Guard could fulfill its role, and cartoonists suggested that this was something Home Guards were keen to do. Joseph Lee, whose cartoons in a wartime series entitled 'Smiling Through' were published daily in the London *Evening News*, depicted a sergeant instructing three Home Guard members outside a bell tower in May 1941. 'Now you understand your duties, lads. You're here to play the signature tune for the invasion.'[45] They were evidently preparing for a long-awaited performance which they expected to enjoy.

More generally, comic accounts in 1940 and 1941 implied that British civilians in general, and LDVs and Home Guards in particular, were not only calmly and courageously prepared for invasion, but were eagerly anticipating it.[46] Leslie Illingworth, who contributed regularly to the *Daily Mail*, as well as to numerous other publications,[47] combined these two themes in his cartoon 'Alarms and Excursions', published in February 1941. It shows a large, manly, well-armed Home Guard on sentry duty beside a fortification of sand-bags and barbed wire, talking to a well-dressed elderly lady, against a rural backdrop of cottages, woods and a church. To her enquiry 'Is it true that Hitler's going to invade us with five million men?' he replies: 'I hope so, Missus. If he doesn't I think I shall have to pop over and fetch him.'[48] The size of the potential invasion force has been exaggerated, to emphasise both the old lady's 'alarm' and the confident bravado of the Home Guard, whose soldierly appearance and physical stature prevent the message from being read ironically. The proffered reassurance works in a number of dimensions. The image counters anxieties about Britain's military unpreparedness by depicting the Home Guard as a well-equipped, fully uniformed force which could be relied on to combat invasion, even though in February 1941 there were still not enough weapons for every Home Guard to be armed.[49] It also addresses the popular view of invasion early in 1941: according to the Government's Home Intelligence Division's reports on public morale in January 1941, invasion had not been greatly feared since July 1940, although it was still expected; there was even disappointment that it had not happened, based on the belief that if the Nazis invaded they would be defeated, bringing the war to a welcome conclusion.[50] Finally, Illingworth's cartoon proclaims the *raison d'être* of the Home Guard: if there were no invasion the front line would not be in every home and the Home Guard would have been formed in vain.

In spite of the diminution of the Home Guard's counter-invasion role in 1942 to '43, official representations kept it to the fore. This was in part because the MoI needed not only to inform and reassure the population about invasion; it had also to ensure that public complacency did not set in and endanger national security, and that morale did not plummet should there be an unexpected invasion scare. The feature film *Went the Day Well?* addressed those concerns. It was made in the context of events in February 1942 when three German warships passed uncontested through the English Channel on their way back to base, and Singapore fell to the Japanese. Its making was informed by Home Intelligence reports that indicated renewed public anxiety about both the likelihood of invasion and the capacity of the British, including the Home Guard, to strike back. Production began in March 1942 and the film was released in November.[51]

Went the Day Well? was directed by Alberto Cavalcanti, previously a documentary film-maker, and was based on a short story by Graham Greene, *The Lieutenant Died Last,* in which a nondescript, unsuspecting village is the target of German invaders intent on sabotaging the main railway line. In Greene's story the invaders are thwarted by a poacher, whose military service in the Boer War, coupled with his efficiency at shooting rabbits, enables him to despatch all the Germans, their 'Lieutenant' dying last.[52] The film develops and elaborates this story almost beyond recognition. In terms of the meanings communicated, there are two fundamental differences. One is the emphasis in the story on individual agency – Purves, the poacher, is not a member of the Home Guard and acts alone – compared to the film's collective solution to the problem of home defence. The other is the interpretation of violence. In the story, killing is posed as an unpleasant necessity that leaves disturbed even a morally liminal member of local society like Purves: he feels remorse over the photograph of a baby that he has taken from the dead Lieutenant. In contrast the film asserts that where defence against brutal German invaders is concerned, ordinary British people need have no qualms.

Went the Day Well? deploys a number of the symbols of wartime national identity reviewed earlier in this chapter. The setting is, like that of *Miss Grant Goes to the Door,* a picturesque southern English village; the events occur over a Whitsun weekend, a significant date in the Christian calendar; and crucial parts of the action take place in the village church and its graveyard.[53] The Home Guard, which, as we have seen, was associated with such symbolism, has a small but nevertheless integral part in the plot. Our reading here focuses on its role.

When the 'Royal Engineers' arrive in the village they are greeted without suspicion. But the soldiers are in fact German troops who have been parachuted into Britain to prepare for a full-scale invasion in the next forty-eight hours. They are working in collaboration with Oliver Wilsford (Leslie Banks), Home Guard captain and apparent pillar of the community, but in fact a fifth columnist. The plot develops around the villagers' discovery of the subterfuge, their imprisonment, escape attempts and ultimate heroic counter-attack, leading to the defeat of the enemy. The Home Guard features in the film as an accepted part of the village's system of home defence. Its members take their duties seriously, but in spite of their official role of detecting fifth columnists, they are as fully duped as the rest of the villagers by both Wilsford and the visiting 'English' troops, to whom they reveal their defence plans. When the villagers' mounting suspicions lead them to challenge the visitors, and the Germans imprison them in the village church, the Home Guard are on manoeuvres in the surrounding countryside (without Wilsford, who has feigned a sprained wrist so that he can assist the Germans). The vicar is shot trying to ring the church bells. Although a young Home Guard hears the bells, his companions dismiss their significance: the men are engaged in a military exercise, and the idea that the bell-ringing is not part of the same simulation of war seems too far-fetched. They pay the price for their insouciance: all of them are shot dead as they cycle back to Bramley End. Not only have they played no part in defending the village, but they have increased its vulnerability by sharing their local knowledge with the Germans.

The brutality of *Went the Day Well?*, including the killing of the four Home Guards, was controversial but intentional. It was designed to disabuse its audience of the view that a Nazi occupation would make little difference to British lives, to stimulate anger against the enemy and to encourage civilians to engage, when necessary, in 'robust self defence'.[54] The dramatic role given to women in this respect is explored in the next chapter. As far as home defence is concerned, the Bramley End Home Guard is clearly culpable for its lack of alertness, but Britain is not defence-less. Once news of the invasion has reached the outside world, British troops (including the neighbouring Home Guard) mobilise quickly and effectively, and the Germans are defeated in a final and decisive 'Battle of Bramley End'.

By the time the film was released, in November 1942, the invasion scare of that spring was over. The film was nevertheless on the whole well received, because, as Aldgate and Richards argue, it depicted a population capable of fighting back at a time when successes in North Africa were encouraging greater optimism about the ability of Britain and the allies to defeat the axis powers. However, it did nothing to alter the association of the Home Guard with an invasion threat that never materialised.

The emphasis on counter-invasion continued throughout the war, even in representations of the Home Guard to themselves. One of the concerns of the period after the introduction of conscription in 1942, was with declining enthusiasm for the Home Guard and persistently high absentee rates. A home defence training broadcast of 1943–44 addressed this problem in terms of the danger to national security of complacency as to the improbability of invasion. *Descent at Dawn* includes factual information and speeches from Home Guard dignitaries, as well as a fast-paced fictional account of a German invasion. It tells the story of Lieutenant Rourke, a 'subaltern in X company in a battalion of the Home Guard', who was a 'good fellow', but who did not take his training, and that of the men under his command, seriously:

> He didn't concentrate his energies on making himself and his platoon a fighting team, ready to meet and beat the Boche. He wasn't 100 per cent Home Guard. He wasn't really trying to achieve 100 per cent efficiency. And then, one day, it happened, as it happened in France in 1940, as it happened to civil defence all over England during the months of the Blitz. And Rourke was not ready.[55]

In the German attack on Rourke's area, 20 Home Guards are killed and 7 wounded. As one of the only survivors and a guilty man, Rourke commits suicide. Officers and non-commissioned officers are asked bluntly in the broadcast whether they are similarly indifferent or ignorant.

Military competence

Neither *Went the Day Well?* nor *Descent at Dawn* suggested that the Home Guard was incompetent. On the contrary, in these accounts its members were as capable of defending Britain as were any other troops, provided that they took their roles seriously, trained for them and did not become complacent. Numerous accounts suggested that by 1942 the Home Guard had been successfully transformed from the 'ragtag' army of the summer of 1940 to a reliable defence force. The BBC included a feature on the Home Guard in 'Army Week', 28 February–6 March 1943, which concluded: 'while our armies are fighting and beating the Huns all over the world, Britain's Home Guard stands fast defending Britain … We won't let you down.'[56] This was also the official message of the third anniversary celebrations of May 1943.[57] It linked the idea of the individual member's daily transition from civilian to soldier and back again with that of the evolution of the force over time from an improvised amateur organisation lacking uniforms and equipment into an efficient military body, trained, disciplined and well equipped. The official account created the impression of smooth transitions at both individual and collective levels. Thus the official short *One Man, Two Jobs* (1943) made the most of the possibilities offered by film to fade individual civilians into Home Guard soldiers: a factory worker taking off his overall becomes a uniformed Home Guard putting on his greatcoat; a postman dismounting from his bicycle is transformed into a Home Guard with a rifle; a gardener tying his shoe on the edge of his wheelbarrow becomes a Home Guard doing up his army boots. The commentary underlines the visual message, embellishing it with Churchill's exhortation of May 1943:

> [T]he Home Guard has become used to doing two jobs. After knocking off civilian war work, he goes home and turns out for evening parade. It has all become part of his everyday existence … [I]n factories, in shipyards, in offices, on the land, work the men who by night, on holidays and at the weekends change into uniform and carry out the Prime Minister's charge to guard well the light of freedom in their native land.[58]

At the collective level, *One Man, Two Jobs* asserts that Home Guards are 'well versed in the use of modern weapons', and that the training they were receiving 'would have severely tested a regular soldier of the same age', over footage of Home Guard troops, almost indistinguishable from regular soldiers, efficiently taking over home defence responsibilities.

This official narrative implied that the force had originally been different, without drawing conclusions about its earlier military competence: as we have seen, propaganda of 1940–41 presented the Home Guard as a reassuring defence presence. But the idea that the Home Guard was ever an effective military force was contested in popular culture throughout the war. Sceptical representations, especially comic ones, were variously critical of government policies and military leadership, and suggested that members of the Home Guard themselves had serious shortcomings not only as soldiers but also as men.

A joke representative of the genre of sketches and cartoons, contradicting the numerous reassurances that the Home Guard had been capable of defending the nation against invasion in 1940, went as follows:

> In the early days of the Home Guard, a sentry outside Platoon H.Q. challenged a person approaching his post and received the answer, 'Enemy'. Completely non-plussed, he repeated his challenge, only to receive the same answer. After cogitating a bit, he strolled over to the H.Q. and shouted to the Officer in Charge, 'Hey, Bill, there's a bloke here wot says he's an enemy. What shall I do with him?' 'I dunno,' came the reply, 'Tell 'im to come back when we're better organised.'[59]

The joke was about the early lack of clarity concerning the Home Guard's role, and the absurdity of the idea that an invader would obey the instruction to go away and come back later. But its implications were also wider: it suggested both that Britain had not been ready for war in 1940 and that the humane British would not simply shoot a self-declared 'enemy', as the Germans would have done.

While the initial unpreparedness of the Home Guard could be attributed to its enthusiastic but hasty formation, the failure to equip the force
was blamed on the Government. Noel Coward turned his satirical attention to the issue when soliciting support for the British war effort in
the United States in 1940. In a letter in the form of song from 'Colonel
Montmorency' of the Home Guard to the Ministry of Supply, Coward's
(rather camp) colonel points out that his unit is armed with little more
than an arquebus and damp ammunition. He describes how 'Last night
we found the cutest/ Little German parachutist/ Who looked at our kit/
And giggled a bit,/ Then laughed until he cried', and concludes, 'So if
you can't oblige us with a Bren gun –/ The Home Guard might as well
go home.'[60] The Government's attempts to arm Home Guards with
inappropriate weapons were as vigorously contested as was its failure to
arm them at all. As we saw in Chapter 2, the decision to issue pikes to
the Home Guard in 1942 was angrily challenged in Parliament and the
press. Cartoonists represented it as symptomatic of a military command
dominated by leaders with anachronistic ideas: Orwell's colonels with
pre-machine-gun mentalities. One of the pike's virtues was said to be
its silence, so Illingworth, whose cartoons combined support for the
Home Guard with criticism of some of the policies applied to it, offered
three further suggestions (see figure 5). This was one of the most direct
of numerous critical representations which satirised the Government's
inadequate provision.[61] If the Home Guard was not properly equipped,
not only was the force subject to ridicule but the nation was rendered
vulnerable.

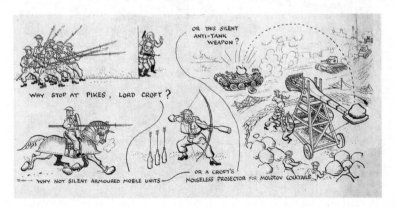

Figure 5 'Why stop at pikes, Lord Croft?' by Leslie Illingworth, *Daily Mail*, 6
February 1942

In spite of the genuine urgency of the demand for adequate equipment, however, the ingenuity with which the Home Guard met the problem of supply in the first months of its existence was applauded in popular culture. Wintringham published instructions in *New Ways of War* in July 1940 for the manufacture of home-made grenades, and the training at both Osterley Park and official Home Guard schools encouraged the Home Guard to make a lot of a little, whether it was using cheesewire to garrotte sentries, stringing 'necklaces' of grenades in the path of tanks

Figure 6(a) 'Portrait of a Soldier' by E. H. Shepard, *Punch*, 12 May 1943; *6(b) over*, 'Standdown' by Leslie Illingworth, *Daily Mail*, 4 December 1944

or engaging in entirely unarmed combat.[62] The anniversary of May 1943 was the occasion not only for celebration, but also for nostalgia for the early improvisational days, expressed in reconstructions that looked back to a time when local defence was free of the 'red tape' consequent on its assimilation to the army and, although under-equipped, was proudly self-reliant.[63] The *Punch* cartoonist E. H. Shepard questioned the value of the evolution of the Home Guard in a cartoon of 12 May 1943, in which a Home Guard in full battle gear wistfully regards a portrait of himself

as an LDV over the caption '"*Who is the happy warrior, who is he?*" How different from what he used to be!'[64] (figure 6a). In contrast, other cartoonists followed official representations in seeking to validate the change that Shepard questioned, especially towards the end of the war. At the stand down of the Home Guard in December 1944, Leslie Illingworth used Shepard's idea of contrasting the same man at different stages in the history of home defence, but with a message supportive, rather than critical, of the changes (figure 6b).[65] The image maintains the positive tone of the official account of the transformation of the force, and seeks to secure for the Home Guard an honourable place in the memory of the British war effort. It evokes the heroism of the early LDV rather than drawing attention to the weaknesses that its lack of equipment implied, and focuses on the convincing militarism of the latterday Home Guard.

Although they drew different conclusions about the effects of militarisation on the Home Guard, both Shepard and Illingworth endowed their ill-equipped LDVs with the valour of patriotic volunteers ready to use any weapon, from the pitchfork to the spade handle, against the enemy. However, the capacity of the LDV and the Home Guard to improvise was also portrayed more sceptically, as a wartime development of the tradition of the English amateur inventor whose creations might or might not be effective. F. R. Emett, a cartoonist who delighted in outlandish contraptions, contributed such a cartoon to *Punch* in May 1942, depicting home defence in action against incursion in the idyllic setting of rural England (figure 7): thanks to the Home Guard's improvisational talents, Germans

Figure 7 'Englysh Pastorale' by Emett, *Punch*, 18 May 1942

are being rounded up and the invasion is being averted. But although Emett's image is comforting and consoling, it is suggestive of grown-up play: it may inspire affection, but it belittles the serious purpose of the Home Guard. In similar vein, George, a motor mechanic, in George Formby's film *Get Cracking* (1943), transforms an old car into a versatile tank which, by becoming amphibious at crucial moments, enables George not only to defeat the competing Home Guard unit but also to survive the live ammunition of the regular army. Emett and Formby's celebrations of the almost magical triumph of home-made armaments over the real thing were not, of course, to be taken literally. But while endowing the Home Guard with enormous entertainment value, they placed it in the realms of fantasy.

The Home Guard made a variety of appearances in children's fiction, the traditional home of fantasy. Addressed to younger audiences such stories (obviously) did not have the intention of influencing their readers' views of government policy. Nevertheless, they communicated messages about the nature of the Home Guard and what could be expected from it. Richmal Crompton's schoolboy character William encounters the Home Guard in a number of his home-front adventures published between 1940 and 1945.[66] The Home Guards he meets are tough, rugged, patriotic and courageous: role models of military masculinity in a home environment. They become part of a world of boyhood games and fantasies by virtue of the fascination they hold for William rather than any childishness of their own.[67]

However in other representations for children, the elision that Emett and Formby made between the Home Guard's improvisational imagination and fantasy play is stronger. A case in point is Alison Uttley's *Hare Joins the Home Guard* (1941). In this story for young children, the worthy animals of Little Grey Rabbit's picturesque southern-English village community defend their homeland against an army of wicked weasels. Hare is instructed to 'defend Grey Rabbit's house, and all our homes with your life'.[68] But although he takes his role seriously, he is not a good soldier. His bombastic posturing before the arrival of the weasels is matched by cowardice when he thinks they are approaching, and when he finally advances into battle, he is more preoccupied with his improvised armour, consisting of a saucepan and a dish cover, than with military strategy. In the end he does no more to see the weasels off than wave his saucepan at their retreating backs. In the person of Hare, the 'Home Guard' is ridiculous. Uttley's purpose, however, was evidently not to imply to her young readers that their own homes were vulnerable in 1941. The village army as a whole is a home defence force, and under Moldy Warp's leadership it is well organised, uses improvised weapons to good effect, and fights bravely and well. Local defence is a serious and reassuringly successful venture. Nevertheless the only animal labelled 'Home Guard' is the pompous, pathetic and comical Hare. [69]

The figure of Hare was an extreme expression of the view that Home Guards were not 'proper soldiers'.[70] Uttley's affectionate but nevertheless critical depiction in a story for young children was a long way from a high-profile attack on the political and military design of the force. But wartime popular culture bristled with the scepticism of other observers concerning the official claims that the Home Guard had been transformed into an efficient fighting force by 1942. These critical constructions reversed various aspects of the official narrative. Thus Home Guards' constant oscillation between civilian and military status was read as both interfering with their occupational efficiency and undermining their Home Guard military status. The civilian occupational habits and the Home Guard service of commuters, barbers, plumbers and greengrocers left indelible comic marks on each other in cartoons of 1942–44.[71] And the idea that they had been trained to fire accurately was challenged in jokes in which Home Guard sentries hit cars which failed to stop, and even their occupants, and ended in punchlines such as 'It's a d— good job you stopped; I wouldn't have fired in the air a third time.'[72] Such representations perpetuated the image of the Home Guard that Tom Wintringham had attacked in May 1941: namely that its members could not be trusted not to shoot themselves and were incapable of learning how to fight a modern war.[73] In this sceptical brand of humour, the force's officially vaunted military identity was a pretension.

Within popular culture, Home Guard participation in military exercises contributed to the idea that the Home Guard was playing at soldiering. Home Guard involvement in such manoeuvres was, as we saw in Chapter 2, stepped up after the introduction of conscription at the beginning of 1942, particularly in the run up to D-Day in 1943–44, the period during which the idea of transformation was vigorously projected. In exercises, combat was simulated and umpires decided on the outcome of military engagements (as in whether participants were alive, dead, injured or prisoners): however seriously the exercises were taken, the appearance of play-acting was strong. This was, of course, the case whether the British Army or the Home Guard was involved, and army activities were not exempt from being depicted as futile. Indeed, there was some continuity between humorous treatments of the Home Guard and the army. Samuel

Figure 8 'Did I understand you to say *you've* killed *me?*' by Giles, in S. E. Thomas, *Laughs with the Home Guard* (London: Harrap, 1942), p. 47

Evelyn Thomas edited numerous collections of jokes and cartoons in the *Laughs With ...* series, including 'laughs with' all three armed forces as well as the Home Guard. In the most satirical contributions all the services were alleged to be inadequately trained, tied up in bureaucratic red tape, led by men with outdated ideas and full of 'browned-off' and 'bolshy' civilian servicemen.[74] The other forces, however, were sent to the numerous 'theatres of war' across the globe. The Home Guard was not. The military exercise was known to be as near as most of its members ever came to military combat.

Cartoonists repeatedly used military exercises to portray the Home Guard's war as a make-believe one. In one of Giles's military exercises a burly Home Guard responds to his diminutive challenger with profound incredulity (figure 8). For David Langdon Home Guard members are earnest to the point of absurdity: convinced he has made a 'kill' in an exercise, one Home Guard shouts at another: 'Hey, you're dead!' but is greeted with the defiant response: 'No, I'm not. I'm just sort of staggering forward, weak with loss of blood and exhaustion, to recapture our position ....'[75] Home Guard play is excessive: it leaps the boundaries of the exercise in representations of city workers commuting, commando-style, across rivers and through trees (figure 9).[76] In such depictions the Home Guard

Figure 9 'Play the game, Perks. You know that bridge was "totally destroyed" in Sunday's exercise!' by Lee, *Evening News*, 5 July 1943

offers mild-mannered suburban dwellers novel opportunities for danger and excitement: the free play of ingenious strategy and imagined battle unfetters the tempered masculinity of these patriotic and sincere Britons. Yet their valour is overstated, and their ever-to-be-frustrated military aspirations are, ultimately, pathetic.

The story that the Home Guard had become an efficient fighting force by 1942 received a serious blow from *The Life and Death of Colonel Blimp*. The film, produced and directed by Michael Powell and Emeric Pressburger, brought to life David Low's cartoon character Colonel Blimp, who made regular appearances in the London *Evening Standard* between 1934 and 1949. In Low's cartoon, Blimp represents the stupidity and political ignorance of the British upper classes. Rotund and red-faced, with a walrus moustache, he is frequently depicted sounding-off about current affairs in a Turkish bath. His views are conventional and conservative: he expresses them in a muddle-headed way that emphasises the prejudices of those who hold them, as in his statement 'To preserve British liberty, Sir, we must lock up the entire Labour Party.'[77]

The name 'Colonel Blimp' is used in the title of the film and is closely identified with the film's main character, General Clive Wynne-Candy (Roger Livesey); but it is not used in the script. Candy looks exactly like Blimp, but Powell and Pressburger depart from Low's pithy satire in their exegesis of the character. Their project was to develop Blimp as a 'symbol of British procrastination and British regard for tradition and all the things ... which were losing the war'.[78] They stress the benign upper-class myopia of their retired general, rather than the prejudice and hypocrisy of Low's politically reactionary Blimp. They show that, despite his best intentions, Candy did little for the British in the Boer War, the First World War or the first months of the Second World War: they make him, after he has been withdrawn from active service, a zone commander in the London Home Guard.[79]

The film is largely composed of flashbacks to Candy's earlier experiences of war. The connecting theme is the attempt of his German opponent, turned friend, Theo Kretschmar-Schuldorff (Anton Walbrook), to educate him in the ruthless realities of twentieth-century warfare and persuade him to drop the traditional English upper-class values of gentlemanly sportsmanship, in the interests of winning the war. The army is shown to have successfully shed such values and to have adopted more cunning ways of waging war. The Home Guard, under Candy's leadership, has not. The climax of the film, encapsulating this message, is a military exercise between the British Army and the Home Guard. Under the rules of the manoeuvres, 'war begins at midnight'. In anticipation, Candy and his Home Guard colleagues plan to spend the evening lounging in a Turkish bath in Piccadilly. But the young Lieutenant leading the army battalion, 'Spud' Wilson (James McKechnie), decides to 'make it like the real thing' by pre-empting the 'declaration of war'. Bursting in on Candy in the steamroom, the Lieutenant asserts that war is not run according to 'National Sporting Club rules' and the 'toughs' of the army, versed in unorthodox methods, trounce the Home Guard.

The film was set and made in 1942, widely acknowledged to have been the lowest point of the war for the British. The MoI was unenthusiastic but tolerant; the War Office, on the other hand, was hotly opposed.[80] Sir James Grigg, as Secretary of State for War, and Churchill tried to have it banned. Overlooking its actual depiction of the army, and making no distinction between General Wynne-Candy's role in the army and the Home Guard, they focused their anxieties on the film's message about army leadership.[81] Candy (though depicted sympathetically) personi-fied the targets of Wintringham's criticisms in 1940–42: the self-deluded appeasers of the 1930s, who had underestimated the Nazis, and the anach-ronistic colonels, who refused to train the army or the Home Guard in modern methods. Churchill announced, before the film was finished, that it expressed 'propaganda detrimental to the morale of the Army'.[82] But, as Brendan Bracken, Minster of Information, pointed out, to suppress it the British Government would have to assume powers of censorship far beyond those consistent with its status as a guardian of democracy. Grigg and, eventually, Churchill, backed down.[83] All this, of course, helped to make the film a box-office success and reinforced its contribution to the leftward swing of public opinion during the war when it was finally released in June 1943. The Home Guard was not the main focus of either the film or the controversy; however, the references to it did nothing to support the idea that it was a modern fighting force.

Masculinity

Whatever the political nuances, *The Life and Death of Colonel Blimp* belongs to a strand of wartime popular culture in which the Home Guard was represented as a home defence force that never had to defend the nation against the expected invasion, and hence ended up playing at soldiering. Such representations diminished the masculinity of the Home Guard's members. Humorists played on three themes to that end: the Home Guard's physical appearance; its relationship to domestic space; and its position in 'the local'.

The rule that the Home Guard could recruit only men who were not eligible for the armed forces identified as its potential members those outside the military age-limits, those who did not meet the medical requirements and those who were in reserved occupations. Ignoring the last category, which in practice included many physically fit men between 18 and (after December 1941) 51, humorists impugned the military capacity, and the masculinity, of the Home Guard. Large stomachs and bottoms were frequently used to signify the difficulties of its members in fulfilling a military role. In *Blimp*, Candy's ageing obesity contrasts with Lieutenant Wilson's youthful and streamlined virility; Home Guards in jokes were reminded that the 'generous portions' of their anatomies were in danger of drawing enemy fire and causing the line to straggle on manoeuvres.[84] Thin, weak and bespectacled men were also depicted as sub-standard soldiers, especially in comparison to 'the real thing'.[85] Such physical deficiencies deprived culturally constructed Home Guards of the sex appeal which was conventionally signified by military uniform.[86] At the same time, members of the force were shown to be desperately aspiring to the uniforms which were so slow to arrive, for the military status, including the masculine allure, it was hoped they would bestow. Thus in Basil Boothroyd's 'Home Guard Goings On', a humorous account of his experiences serialised in *Punch*, the men believe that the great coats with which they are issued transform them into glamorous 'swashbuck-lers', but their hopes of attracting female admiration are dashed by the odd sizes in which the other parts of the uniform are at first available: Boothroyd's section leader 'found it impossible to keep his rifle sloped and his trousers up simultaneously'.[87] The theme of the endangered trousers of the Home Guard reinforced its comic identity. Loss of trousers was undignified and ridiculous, and made masculinity vulnerable.

Another way of casting doubt on the military status of the force was to take the 'home' in its title literally, rather than as a metaphor for the nation. Depicting the Home Guard in domestic settings, where fighting was unlikely to occur in the absence of an invasion, cast doubt on the seriousness of the enterprise. Gardens, bedrooms and bathrooms were among the incongruous locations for depictions of Home Guards in action.[88] A cartoon of August 1941, by Joseph Lee, showed two Home Guards charging through a man's bathroom, to the surprise of the owner in his tub: 'Don't worry about us, Sir. Just a bit of Home Guard house-to-house fighting.' Their military uniforms and demeanour distinguish them from the naked civilian, but the implication is that the Home Guards' field of operations will go no further than the 'Bathroom Front', Lee's title for the cartoon.[89] Moreover, the connotations of play were reinforced by such treatments: the Home Guard was not protecting these domestic locales, nor was it fighting military battles in them; it was rehearsing for roles it would never be called on to fill. (On the other hand, the home *was* the site of a different sort of battle. The next chapter explores the gender wars, especially the marital strife, in which the Home Guard was deemed to be involved.)

The domesticity of the Home Guard was also evoked in representa-tions of its relationship to the WVS, which, as we saw in the previous chapter, was at the head of the list of women's organisations, announced on 20 April 1943, permitted to assist the Home Guard. In a cartoon by

Joseph Lee in the *Evening Standard* on 28 April 1943 one WVS member is saying to another inside a mobile canteen: 'You can always tell when they're Home Guards. They like their own table napkins.'[90] The uniformed appearance of the Home Guard made them all but indistinguishable from regular soldiers: it took a knowledgeable observer to detect the difference. The clue (the request for personal table linen) sums up the homeliness and also the stasis of the Home Guard. It made comic sense for the WVS to store table napkins for the regular use of these respectably middle-class Home Guards because, unlike regular soldiers, they were not going to be sent away on *active* service.

A third way of destabilising the Home Guard's military identity was to suggest that members spent their time not on guard duty or military manoeuvres, but in the pub. The theme was closely linked to that of gender relations and marital strife, but there was also a strong cultural association between drinking and masculinity that was used ironically in depictions of the Home Guard. The pub, also known as 'the local', was a natural environment for men involved in local defence, and was used as a suitable setting for the Home Guard in official films.[91] It was also a homo-social environment in which men's personal and collective priorities – drinking and sociability – were pursued. It constituted a space in which men clubbed together to resist external interference, whether that of women (especially wives) or of 'the authorities'. The pub featured in Home Guard humour not only as an alternative to home, but also as a rival attraction to Home Guard activities, and featured as such in numerous knowing jokes. Home Guards are skilled at moving 'unseen and unheard (sometimes through the back entrance of the local)'; they camouflage themselves so well in long wet grass that army officers do not suspect that they have in fact disappeared into the nearby pub; they are always ready, when enemy attack threatens, to guard the local pub; they compete fiercely with both civilians and regulars over limited supplies of beer.[92] The frontispiece of a collection of *Home Guard Rhymes* depicts two Home Guards heading for 'The Lion and the Lamb' over the caption 'Warriors brave, go gaily forth … to fight!': the inference is that these warriors are in fact going forth to drink.[93] Of course, the high profile of the pub in Home Guard culture is paralleled in representations of the military more widely, where convivial drinking is one of the expressions of much-valued male camaraderie. Indeed the men of the Home Guard are the subjects of songs, as bawdy as any army ballad, that celebrate their masculine capacity to sustain a drinking culture: 'Drunk last night, drunk the night before./ We're off to get drunk tonight, if we never get drunk no more./ The more we are, the merrier we shall be,/ We are the lads of the L.D.V.'[94] But a major difference is that members of the army are popularly supposed to combine drinking and fighting, whereas the suspicion in this brand of humour is that in the Home Guard – or the 'Foam Guard' as it was dubbed in *Get Cracking* – the one supplants the other.

Conclusion

Images of the Home Guard pervaded wartime popular culture. Brand new in 1940, it was an evolving phenomenon, highly visible in the everyday life of the home front, that attracted a great deal of attention. The rhetoric of national leaders and the discourse of productions approved by the MoI emphasised the reassurance that it offered: Britain was not defenceless even when the regular forces were a long way off or depleted, and all sorts of men could participate in this democratic form of home defence, which would have been impossible in a dictatorship. The Home Guard was associated with the war effort and with established signifiers of national identity: a historical tradition of British self-sufficiency; territorial integrity focused on the rural landscape; social cohesion built on the natural order and enhanced by the exigencies of war. The Home Guard's primary purpose in such representations, whether official or not, was to repel invasion. The public was assured that the Home Guard could do so effectively because it had undergone a transformation since its rapid and amateurish, if heroic, formation in 1940: by 1942 it was as competent as the army to perform its defensive function.

This confident narrative was, however, contested in popular culture. The conservative imagery of the Home Guard's place within a pastoral vision of the nation was in tension with the idea that the Home Guard was a site in which a radically changed future, centred on the city as much as on the countryside, was envisioned. Authors and artists who were sceptical about the united war effort pointed out the persistence of social and regional divisions within the Home Guard, as within the nation. The failure of the Government to equip and train the Home Guard for its much-vaunted anti-invasion role was exposed, and the idea that the Home Guard had become an efficient fighting force by 1942 was rejected by some, while others regretted its assimilation to the army. The official story about the Home Guard's key place in national defence, in which it represented all that was best in the British at war, was challenged by an alternative version. In this account, the Home Guard was a fantasy force, at best motivated to play earnestly at soldiers by the spectre of an invasion that would never happen, and at worst led by those who did not understand the meaning of modern war. Either way, Home Guards were not proper soldiers and their masculinity was in deficit: their lack of true military identity was written on their childish, aged or physically inadequate bodies, which were in any case to be found in homes and pubs, rather than on the battlefield.

How are such critical and satirical representations of the Home Guard to be understood? They can appear subversive. As popular and humorous versions of the critiques advanced by commentators such as Wintringham and Orwell, they seem to cast doubt on the leadership and training of the force, and hence to undermine the official attempts to invest reassurance in the Home Guard. But they have also been interpreted in quite the opposite way. As manifestations of another facet of the British national character, they can be viewed as supportive of the war effort. The British love of self-deprecating humour was construed during the war and afterwards as 'a precious gift', 'the very life-blood of democracy',[95] and this ability of the British to laugh at themselves was contrasted with the alleged humourlessness of the Germans. In this account, far from subverting the war effort, Home Guard humour did nothing less than help to win the war.

Notes

1 Hansard, vol. 365, cols 1897–8, 19 November 1940; Brophy, *Britain's Home Guard*, p. 5; Churchill, *Complete Speeches*, vol. 7, p. 6772.

2 J. Chapman, *The British at War: Cinema, State and Propaganda, 1939–1945* (London: I. B.Tauris, 1998), Chapter 4.

3 I. Mclaine, *Ministry of Morale: Home Front Morale and the Ministry of Information in World War II* (London: Allen & Unwin, 1979), pp. 3–11; A. Calder, *The People's War, Britain 1939–45* (London: Panther Books, 1971), pp. 583–584.

4 V. Holman and D. Kelly, 'Introduction. War in the Twentieth Century: The Functioning of Humour in Cultural Representation', *Journal of European Studies*, 31:3–4 (2001), especially pp. 252–253 and 262.

5 See also C. Peniston-Bird and P. Summerfield, '"Hey, You're Dead": The Multiple Uses of Humour in Representations of British National Defence in the Second World War', *Journal of European Studies*, 31:3–4 (2001), pp. 413–435.

6 A. Aldgate and J. Richards, *Best of British: Cinema and Society from 1930 to the Present* (London: I. B. Tauris, 1998), p. 58.

7 *Home Guard* (Donald Taylor, 1941, GB, Strand for MoI).

8 Radnor, *It All Happened Before*.

9 T. Wintringham, *People's War* (Harmondsworth: Penguin, 1942).

10 For the BBC's efforts see S. Nicholas, *The Echo of War: Home Front Propaganda and the Wartime BBC, 1939–1945* (Manchester: Manchester University Press, 1996), p. 228.

11 A. Howkins, 'The Discovery of Rural England', in R. Colls and P. Dodd (eds), *Englishness: Politics and Culture 1880–1920* (London: Croom Helm, 1986), pp. 62–88; Rose, *Which People's War?*, pp. 198–218.

12 A leading exponent of the use of the southern rural landscape as a national symbol in wartime was Frank Newbould: see J. Darracott and B. Loftus (eds), *Second World War Posters* (London: IWM, 1985), p. 46.

13 S. Featherstone, 'The Nation as Pastoral in British Literature of the Second World War', *Journal of European Studies*, 16 (1986), p. 158; Featherstone is referring to Fussell's ideas in *The Great War and Modern Memory* (Oxford: Oxford University Press, 1975), Chapter 7.

14 Featherstone, 'The Nation as Pastoral', p. 159, quoting Day Lewis's biographer.

15 C. Day Lewis, *Watching Post*, in *Collected Poems of C. Day Lewis* (London: Jonathan Cape with the Hogarth Press, 1954), p. 226.

16 Featherstone, 'The Nation as Pastoral', p. 160; Featherstone analyses Day Lewis's *The Stand-To* in these terms, but they apply as well to this poem.

17 J. Brophy, *Britain's Home Guard: A Character Study* (London: Harrap, 1945), p. 12.

18 G. Spencer, *John Bull's Home Guard* (London: Artists' International Association, 1944).

19 On this theme see 'Dawn Patrol', *Picture Post*, 22:10, 4 March 1944, p. 21; and '… Funny you being in a Bank, chum! Once I got three years for brekin' inter one …', in S. E. Thomas, *Laughs with the Home Guard* (London: Harrap, 1942), p. 14.

20 G. Belton Cobb, *Home Guard Mystery* (London: Longmans, 1941), pp. 18–19.

21 Aldgate and Richards, *Best of British*, p. 57.

22 *The Dawn Guard* (Roy Boulting, 1941, GB, Charter, UKY 268).

23 M. Paris, 'El Alamein: The People's Battle', *History Today*, 52:10 (October 2002), p. 23.

24 Addison, *Road to 1945*, pp. 217–219.

25 Chapman, *British at War*, p. 102, quoting *Documentary News Letter*, February 1941.

26 Ministry of Information projectionist, July 1941, quoted in Chapman, *British at War*, p. 102; also MOA, TC17 Films, Box 8, 17/8/a, MoI Reports and Memos 1940–1943, AT, 25 January 1941.

27 R. Mackay, *Half the Battle: Civilian Morale in Britain during the Second World War* (Manchester: Manchester University Press, 2002), p. 181.

28 The Home Guard was also used as a setting for criminal activities motivated by patriotic intentions in Powell and Pressburger's film *A Canterbury Tale* (1944, GB).

29 See N. Pronay and D. W. Spring, *Propaganda, Politics and Film, 1918–45* (London: Macmillan, 1982), p. 242.

30 Adam wrote novels, children's literature, autobiography, biography and women's history from the 1930s to the 1970s, as well as experimenting with communal living in the 1950s.

31 This comment does not apply to the documentary accounts of, e.g., J. Langdon-Davies, George Orwell, Molly Panter-Downes, A. G. Street and Tom Wintringham, referred to in the previous chapter.

32 For example, J.G., 'Yokel Defence' *Punch*, 24 July 1940, p. 105.

33 Joseph Lee, 'Smiling Through: Road Defences', *Evening News*, 1 March 1941; Joseph Lee, 'Smiling Through: Expert Warrior', *Evening News*, 23 October 1942; Philip Millar, '… then, under cover of darkness, we attacked the Mudthorpe Home Guard …', *Punch*, 3 February 1943.

34 Nicholas, *Echo of War*, p. 232.

35 Thomas, *Laughs with the Home Guard*, p. 13

36 Formby in fact played a banjulele, a hybrid between a ukulele and a banjo: D. Bret, *George Formby: A Troubled Genius* (London: Robson Books, 2001), pp. 286–287.

37 A. Linklater, *Compton Mackenzie: A Life* (London: Chatto & Windus, 1987), Chapter 16.

38 C. Mackenzie, *Keep the Home Guard Turning* (London, Chatto & Windus, 1943), p. 8.

39 Cobb, *Home Guard Mystery*, p. 16.

40 Cobb, *Home Guard Mystery*, p. 25.

41 Cobb, *Home Guard Mystery*, pp. 18–19.

42 Street, *From Dusk Till Dawn*, pp. 31–41.

43 *Miss Grant Goes to the Door* (Brian Desmond Hurst, 1940, GB, Denham and Pinewood Studios, COI 455).

44 Collier, *Defence*, p. 105.

45 *Evening News*, 21 May 1941.

46 Pont (cartoon), 'It seems a pity to discourage them too much – they mightn't come', *Punch*, 23 October 1940; 'Last Lay of the L.D.V.', *Punch*, 31 July 1940.

47 See M. Bryant, 'Crusader, White Rabbit or Organ-Grinder's Monkey? Leslie Illingworth and the British Political Cartoon in World War II', *Journal of European Studies*, 31:3–4 (2001), pp. 345–366.

48 Leslie Illingworth, 'Alarms and Excursions', *Punch*, 5 February 1941.

49 MacKenzie, *Home Guard*, p. 91.

50 MoI, Home Intelligence Reports on Opinion and Morale, 1940–1944, Home Intelligence Division, 'Weekly Report', 8–15 January 1941, reel 2.

51 Aldgate and Richards, *Britain Can Take It*, p. 127; other films that warned of ongoing fifth-column activity in Britain included *The Next of Kin* (1942).

52 Graham Greene, 'The Lieutenant Died Last', *Colliers Weekly*, 29 June 1940.

53 *Went the Day Well?* (Alberto Cavalcanti, 1942, GB, Ealing Studios).

54 Aldgate and Richards, *Britain Can Take It*, p. 133, quoting Charles Barr.

55 *Descent at Dawn* Broadcast 'restricted for use of HM forces only' (n.d., but 1943–44) IWM, SA, Various 7386.

56 BBC, WAC, R19/509, Entertainment Home Guard 1940–43, 25 February 1943; R9/9/7 Audience Research Special Reports, indicate the programme was well received.

57 *War Pictorial News*, 1943.

58 *One Man, Two Jobs* (Gerald Sanger, 1944, GB, British Movietone News).

59 Thomas, *Laughs with the Home Guard*, p. 28.

60 *Could You Please Oblige Us with a Bren Gun?*, words and music by Noel Coward (London: Chapel, 1941).

61 Also Giles (cartoon), 'Good Evening, Sir Launcelot', in Thomas, *Laughs with the Home Guard*, p. 9.

62 As did an official training film, *Unarmed Combat* (1941, GB, British Foundation Pictures), showing a confrontation with the enemy with and without the use of such techniques.

63 The bureaucratic practices and inappropriate demands that the Army inflicted on the Home Guard are lampooned in an unpublished collection of cartoons by Captain F. C. Saxon, *Trials of the Home Guard*, discussed in the next chapter. See also B. Boothroyd, *Home Guard Goings On, from "Punch" or the London Charivari 1940–41* (London: George Allen & Unwin Ltd., 1941), p. 49.

64 *Punch*, 12 May 1943. Italics in original, borrowing from Wordsworth's 'Character of the Happy Warrior', 1807: 'Who is the happy warrior, who is he?/Whom every man in arms should wish to be'. On the same theme, see 'The Tragic Mystery of Corporal Plum', Cilias (pseud), *Home Guard Rhymes* (London: no publisher, 1942), p. 7.

65 For an official photograph making a similar contrast see IWM, Photograph Archive (PA), HU 18501.

66 R. Crompton, *William at War: A Collection of Just William's Wartime Adventures* (London, Macmillan Children's Books, 1995).

67 This was also the case in other schoolboy fiction: for instance, R. Browne, 'The Schoolboy Home Guard', in *Schoolboys' 4d Pocket Library*, No 2 (London: Gerald G. Swann, 1941), pp. 1–35. Children's joke books, on the other hand, indulged wholeheartedly in fantasy representations: for examples, see D. Girrod, *Run, Adolf, Run: The World War Two Fun Book* (London: Corgi, 1975).

68 A. Uttley, *Hare Joins the Home Guard* (London: Collins, 1941; 2nd impression February 1942), p. 25. The book underwent at least seven impressions.

69 Uttley saw the war as one against tyranny; she feared invasion and regarded her home 'as a stronghold, ready to fight to the end'. *Hare* was 'one of her few books for children to reflect the contemporary scene'. In spite of Hare's evident inadequacies the message of reassurance worked for at least one child, who wrote to the publisher: 'Goebbels won't let the Nazis come now because Hare will stop them': D. Judd, *Alison Uttley: Creator of Little Grey Rabbit* (Stroud: Sutton Publishing, 2001), pp. 165, 167, 184.

70 The theme song of Formby's *Get Cracking* was 'When the lads of the village get crackin' and the whole platoon turns out,/ Off we go, rain or snow, just like proper soldiers all in a row', but the film casts doubt on whether 'the lads' were really 'proper soldiers'. George Formby and Eddie Latta, *When the Lads of the Village get Crackin*, in D. Gifford (ed.) *'Bless 'Em All!' The World War Two Songbook* (Exeter: Hebb & Bower, 1989), p. 81.

71 David Langdon, *Punch*, 30 September 1942; Neb, *Daily Mail*, 9 December 1943; Lee, *Evening News*, 20 January 1944; T. C. Gamble, in Thomas, *Laughs with the Home Guard*, p. 19.

72 Thomas, *Laughs with the Home Guard*, p. 27.

73 *Picture Post*, 11:7, 17 May 1941, pp. 24–28.

74 Thomas's 'forces' collections included *Laughs with the R.A.F.* (London: Harrap, 1942); *Laughs with the Forces* (St Albans: J. W. Vernon, 1943); *Laughs with the Navy* (St Albans: J. W. Vernon, 1944).

75 David Langdon, 'Lilliput', in Thomas, *Laughs with the Home Guard*, p. 46.

76 Also 'He always comes home by the trees. It's his guerrilla training,' by Joseph Lee, *Evening News*, 26 February 1942.

77 C. Seymour-Ure, 'Introduction', in M. Bryant (ed.), *The Complete Colonel Blimp* (London: Bellew Publishing, 1991), p. 26.

78 Michael Powell, quoted by Aldgate and Richards, *Best of British*, p. 79.

79 The military adviser was Lt-Gen. Sir Douglas Brownrigg, whose own career was not dissimilar to that of the fictional Wynne-Candy.

80 Aldgate and Richards, *Best of British*, p. 83; also J. Chapman, 'The Life and Death of Colonel Blimp Reconsidered', *Historical Journal of Film, Radio and Television*, 15:1 (1995), pp. 19–36.

81 Grigg thought it would revive criticism of the 'imaginary type of Army officer' that it ridiculed: Aldgate and Richards, *Best of British*, p. 90.

82 Aldgate and Richards, *Best of British*, p. 90.

83 Aldgate and Richards, *Best of British*, p. 91.

84 Thomas, *Laughs with the Home Guard*, p. 42; Cobb, *Home Guard Mystery*, pp. 38–39; Neb, 'Of course the idea is to lie perfectly flat', *Daily Mail*, 8 May 1941.

85 Unflattering contrasts between Home Guard and army include: Neb, *Daily Mail*, 21 October 1941; Millar, *Punch*, 3 February 1943.

86 Romantic fiction in women's wartime magazines was dominated by heroes in uniform, but Home Guard members occupied roles as fathers rather than lovers: e.g. 'Food for Romance', *My Home*, April 1943, p. 5.

87 Boothroyd, *Home Guard Goings On*, pp. 33, 29. Also Robb Wilton, 'The Day War Broke Out', IWM, SA, 13921; IWM, DD, 75/35/1 T, Captain F. C. Saxon, *Trials of the Home Guard*, 'Sir, may I wear my Home Guard trousers to go home?'

88 Giles, 'I'll give you 'Ome Guard' (Home Guards charging across a garden, dodging washing and an irate housewife), in Thomas, *Laughs with the Home Guard*, p. 43; in *Get Cracking*, George hides under Mary's bed, having broken in to out-manoeuvre his Home Guard rival who piles in looking for him.

89 Joseph Lee, 'Smiling Through: Bathroom Front', *Evening News*, 30 August 1941. The radical version of Home Guard warfare took such house-to-house fighting seriously: M. Panter-Downes, *Letter from England* (Boston: Little, Brown & Co., 1940), p. 233, records the the startled response of those training at Osterley to a lecture about using a tommy-gun in a bathroom.

90 Joseph Lee, 'Smiling Through: Gentlemen Bakers', *Evening News*, 28 April 1943. Lee also used the relationship of the Home Guard to the WVS to carica-ture Home Guard pride in its voluntary status, already eroded by compulsion, in the summer of 1943, in 'Smiling Through. Home Guard. Gents v. Players': 'I trust this tea and bun issue in no way impairs our amateur status', *Evening News*, 10 June 1943.

91 As in *Citizen Army* (Ivan Moffat, 1940, GB, Strand for MoI, UKY 304) and *Home Guard* (Donald Taylor, 1941, GB, Strand for MoI, COI 1090).

92 IWM, DD, Misc 167, Item 2565, Bubear, 'Humorous Description of the Duties of the Home Guard'; Boothroyd, *Home Guard Goings On*, p. 130; Wyndham Lewis (ed.), *I Couldn't Help Laughing! An Anthology of Wartime Humour* (London: Lindsay Drummond, 1941), p. 76; Neb, *Daily Mail*, 26 April 1944.

93 A. H. Watkins, *Home Guard Rhymes* (London: Practical Press, 1943).

94 *The Home Guard Song*, in M. Page (ed.), *For Gawdsake Don't Take Me! The Songs, Ballads, Verses, Monologues, etc of the Call Up Years, 1939–1963* (London: Hart-Davis MacGibbon, 1976), p. 183.

95 Artists' International Association, *John Bull's Home Guard. Fifteen Water Colour Drawings by Gilbert Spencer and Caricatures of the French Wars* (London: AIA, 1944), p. 2.

5

Representations of women
and home defence

In official discourse the Home Guard stood for patriotism, national
unity and military dependability: in the most general sense it symbolised
Britain at war. As we have seen, much popular culture questioned such
representations: the Home Guard might be patriotic but its valour was
misplaced; it was fractured by rivalries and social differences; it played at
war rather than fulfilling a genuine military role; the masculinity of its
members was, in various ways, impaired. This chapter explores the place
of women in popular representations of the Home Guard, official and
unofficial, serious and comic. Women frequently commented on men's
membership of the Home Guard, particularly in comic representations.
However, and in contrast to this role on the margins, women were also
surprisingly prominent figures in a number of serious representations of
home defence outside the institutional context of the Home Guard. This
chapter discusses both types of representation, but it starts by probing
the position of the women whose campaign to join the Home Guard
we reviewed in Chapter 3: what place did they have in wartime popular
culture?

Women in the Home Guard

In spite of their substantial history of participation, women were rarely
represented as Home Guard members in their own right, even after their
partial official recognition in 1943. In principle, women's roles could quite
well have been depicted by authors, cartoonists or film-makers in their
explorations of the character of the Home Guard and Britain at war, had
they chosen to devote attention specifically to the 'feminine' side of the

force. As we have seen, women engaged in or with Home Guard activities through their 'accidental' recruitment as LDVs in May 1940 and their formation of the WHD in 1941, via the official recognition of 'nominated women' in April 1943 (belatedly renamed Women Home Guard Auxiliaries, in 1944), and as a result of the rifle-training versus tea-making tensions between WHD and WVS in 1943–44. However, our searches of films, plays, comic verse and prose, children's stories, adult fiction and women's magazines suggest that wartime popular culture avoided the topic of women's involvement with the Home Guard. The exceptions were the newspaper commentaries referred to in Chapter 3 and a tiny number of cartoons.

One was by Joseph Lee and two were by Ronald Niebour ('Neb'). Lee's cartoon, published in the *Evening News* on 6 November 1941, referred obliquely to Summerskill's campaign for women to be instructed in the use of weapons, around the time of the official ban on the Home Guard's involvement in such training.[1] A husband is rushing through his front gate, while his grim-faced wife observes him through the front window, and one astonished male onlooker says to another: 'He hasn't been a minute late home for dinner since the "Arm the Women" talk started.'[2] The reference is clearly topical, but the cartoon engages only superficially with Summerskill's campaign: the wife is situated indoors, and the reference to the struggle concerns its possible impact on the husband only. The depiction belongs to a genre of jokes and cartoons about marital strife that we discuss shortly, and is a long way from engaging with women at war or in the Home Guard.

The two cartoons by 'Neb' come closer to addressing women's participation. In the autumn of 1942 discussions in Parliament suggested that it would not be long before women could become auxiliaries. In response to a question about the role of WHD in releasing Home Guards 'for combatant service' on 13 October 1942, Sir James Grigg responded: 'I am aware that there are many useful services of a non-combatant character that women can render in connection with the Home Guard, and arrangements for placing assistance of this kind on an official footing are at present under discussion.'[3] In a cartoon of 15 October 1942, Neb featured a 'non-combatant' but belligerent wife in a Home Guard armband and cap, challenging the 'combat' affecting her husband that was going on before her (figure 10). Neb's cartoon, like Lee's, draws on the well-established theme of marital relations: it evokes the big, bossy wives and the pathetic, little husbands of Donald McGill's postcards.[4] It also adds a new dimension to jokes about Home Guard exercises: with women

Figure 10 'Nonsense, Madam! For the purpose of this exercise,
I have every right to attack your husband' by Neb, *Daily Mail*,
15 October 1942

involved, the force would become a site not only of male play but also of
female interference.

The other cartoon by Neb that related to women's involvement in the
Home Guard was published in the *Daily Mail* on 22 April 1943. It followed
the announcement in Parliament on 20 April 1943 that 'a limited number
of women', preferably over 45 years of age, were to assist the Home Guard
and that 'the women nominated will wear a badge brooch'.[5] This was
criticised in the *Daily Mail* on 21 April 1943 in a leading article that
attacked the plan for its casualness, on the grounds that it was damaging
to the reputation of the Home Guard as a whole. The leader reported
that women 'will have no uniform – only a brooch' and argued that if
they were needed in the Home Guard 'their conditions should approxi-

mate as closely as possible to those of the men'.[6] Neb's cartoon places two respectable middle-aged women in civilian outdoor attire (hats, coats, skirts, umbrellas, seamed stockings, sensible shoes and handbags), in front of 'H.G. Company Notices', looking at each other aghast. The caption is 'Brooch inspection by the CO on Sunday at 10.00 hrs'.[7] The cartoon exploits the comic incongruity of military examination of the contents of these ladies' jewellery boxes and plays on presumptions that the habits of civilian women in general were incompatible with military practices. At the same time it expresses sympathy for the women: they are well-meaning participants in an alien enterprise for which they have been ill-equipped.

The absence of other published representations with which to compare these three cartoons focuses attention on why Lee and Neb – and the newspapers for which they worked – included *any* topical references to the issue of women's admission to the Home Guard when others were ignoring it. Lee specialised in 'non-political topical cartoons': his 'hugely popular' series 'London Laughs', which began in the *Evening News* in 1934, was renamed 'Smiling Through' in the Second World War.[8] Ronald Niebour joined the *Daily Mail* in 1938 as an illustrator for various features including the Women's Page; he thus had a professional concern with women's affairs.[9] Both cartoonists worked within the frame of 'pocket cartoons': they exploited their small size to deliver pithy commentary on both passing events and familiar social behaviours. Home, family and marital relations, as well as, in wartime, the Home Guard, were strong themes in the thousands of cartoons they produced.[10]

The only other wartime representations of women in the Home Guard to have come to light are in the unpublished pages of a logbook kept by Captain F. C. Saxon, Commanding Officer of the Sixth Battalion of the Cheshire Home Guard. His logbook was in itself part joke and part protest, aimed at the Home Guard authorities who, in Saxon's view, sought to tie up the force in the red tape of unnecessary and often incomprehensible regulations. His predecessor had kept a diary; instead, Saxon kept a folder of sketches. When asked to submit a report on his battalion, he submitted his 'Sketch Book on Home Guard Regulations', sub-titled 'Trials of the Home Guard'. He explained: 'These amateur cartoons exposed the ambiguity of many of the regulations as well as the difficulties that a part-time military force had in observing them.'[11] Three of the cartoons (all undated) address regulations concerning women.

The first, referring to the absence of any uniform beyond the 'badge brooch', adopted a more sexually suggestive slant than Neb's in the *Daily*

Mail. Three women are gathered round a notice headed 'Home Guard Regulations', which states: 'Nominated women will wear a badge only, and will not be issued with uniform.' One, eyeing with a smile the badge on the table, is apparently completely naked, another has a blanket round her, and the third, fully dressed with the badge pinned to her sweater, is saying: 'I can't help wondering whether it really means "only".'[12] The women look as though they are enjoying the possibility that they will really wear no more than the badge. At the same time they are in league with their commanding officer (through whose eyes they are represented) to ridicule this regulation.

'Only' is also the keynote of the next of Saxon's cartoons to address women, which engages with the recommendation that Nominated Women should be over forty-five. A large crowd of women of all ages is gathered round a soldierly male Home Guard holding a sheet of what are no doubt 'regulations'. A notice pinned behind them refers to 'nominated women'. It is partially obscured, but the words 'duties', 'assist', '45', 'officer' and 'concentrate' are clear. The women look concerned and one of them is asking 'Do the Regulations say that *only* the C.O. is to concentrate on women over 45?'[13] The point is not so much that only older women are wanted. It is more that the women will have the benefit only of the CO's 'concentration' upon them. It is a joke at the same time against unclear regulations and against Saxon himself as CO.

The third cartoon refers to the controversial issue of training women Home Guards in the use of weapons (figure 11). To the confusion of the women depicted, a notice headed 'W.D. [War Department] Shooting Competition, rules for H.G. Women Auxiliaries' is posted next to 'Home Guard Regulations' that state 'Shooting is not allowed for nominated women (*crossed out*) H.G. Women Auxiliaries (*inserted*)'.[14] The cartoon, which offers an interpretation of women's participation in the Home Guard, also provides evidence for the recovery of that history. Firstly, it is dated by the substitution of the terms in the notice, since the replacement of 'nominated women' by 'Women's Home Guard Auxiliaries' occurred well after April 1943, possibly (as we saw in Chapter Three) as late as June 1944. Secondly, it reveals the enduring practice of women's involvement with the Home Guard in armed activities (training, exercises and competitions). Thirdly, the regulation at the heart of the cartoon, 'shooting is not allowed for women', adds to the evidence that this ban, originally issued in 1941, was constantly reiterated because of recurrent refusals to observe it. Finally, the caption expresses the determination of women to continue with this activity: whatever the answer to the question about the

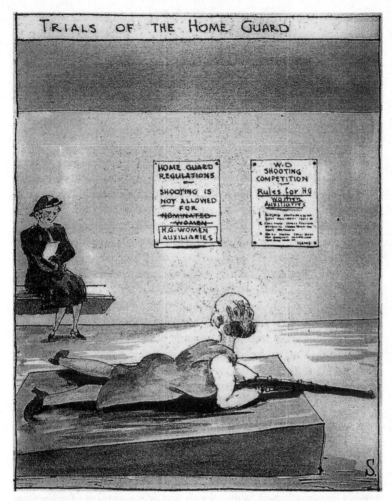

Figure 11 'Do I shoot and resign – or – resign and shoot?' by Captain F. C. Saxon, Imperial War Museum, Documents Department (75/35/1 T), Papers of Captain F. C. Saxon

timing of her resignation, this woman is going to shoot.

The 'shoot and resign' cartoon encapsulates Saxon's two-sided approach to women members. He uses some familiar features of femininity seen through the 'male gaze' (nudity, age and dress), as vehicles in his critique of Home Guard regulations. But at the same time as emphasising feminine physical, sexual and cultural differences, all three cartoons and the accompanying written memoir suggest that he regarded women as having a legitimate combatant place in his Home Guard Battalion. In other words, Saxon's cartoons of women in the Home Guard express visually the attitudes of those COs keen to recruit and train women who we encountered in Chapter 3.

The inclusion of nominated women and Women Home Guard Auxiliaries in Captain Saxon's 'log' sharpens questions about their absence elsewhere. Saxon was an amateur artist producing work for private and local enjoyment: his collection never rounded the curve of the cultural circuit to enter mainstream popular culture, and there is no evidence that he wanted it to. But by his own account his cheeky submission of the cartoons had meaning for its audience of military personnel. He described in his memoir his superior officers' excited absorption in the 'log': they evidently did not punish him for this unorthodox record of his battalion's activities.[15] His work, although distinctive and original, drew stylistically on the kinds of visual humour reviewed in Chapter 4, and his cartoons about men in the Home Guard bear many similarities to the treatments in, for example, *Laughs with the Home Guard*, with one major difference. He evidently regarded women's experience in the Home Guard as an appropriate subject: he attributed to women the same grievances as those of men about the discouraging complexities of Home Guard red tape. But, apart from the isolated examples of Lee and Neb, national professional cartoonists did not make use of this subject.

Supporters, sceptics and subversives

Even though authors and artists did not, it seems, depict women as members of the Home Guard, wartime films, fiction, plays, prose, cartoons and comic verse about the force featured female characters. Women and girls appear in all these genres (with the one exception of schoolboy fiction, which was resolutely single sex). They had a variety of relationships with male members of the force, but in terms of disposition they adopted three main stances: support, scepticism and subversion. Depictions of each offered distinctive interpretations of the Home Guard's place within the configuration of gender relations and identities.

Women in popular culture contributed supportively but passively to the idea that the Home Guard was a serious enterprise in depictions in which they were the objects of its protection: official images include photographs of a Home Guard in a doorway, shielding his wife and child with his rifle, then seen through a window, waving goodbye to them.[16] Women played more active supportive roles only in the background of serious films in which the Home Guard itself occupied a background role. Thus, for example, in *Went the Day Well?*, discussed in the previous chapter, a Home Guard wife presses a packet of sandwiches lovingly into her husband's hands as he leaves Bramley End to take part in an exercise on the morning of the German occupation. Her wifely act is matched by her panic and distress as she realises that he has been killed. In the film *Mrs Miniver* (1942), Kay provides sandwiches for her LDV husband Clem: she gets up to make them at 2 a.m. before his departure with the 'River Patrol' for Dunkirk. Feeding a husband is presented as a normal aspect of wifely care. His part in wartime national defence simply complicates the woman's role: a wife may have to do it at extraordinary hours; what is more, she may never see him alive again.

But sandwich sustenance and the provision of tea, cocoa and other wifely services, such as sewing and knitting, for the Home Guard are frequently treated humorously. The same is true in a few instances of WVS support, as we saw in Chapter 4,[17] but depictions of wives' contributions to the Home Guard enterprise are more thoroughly interwoven with popular accounts of the Home Guard than are depictions of institutional arrangements. One of the principles underlying government policy, reviewed in Chapter 3, was that the Home Guard had no need of a women's auxiliary because its members were sustained by their womenfolk at home: culturally construed, this implicated Home Guard men in the gender tensions of the home and became a key feature of Home Guard identity. Thus in May 1944 Neb depicted a Home Guard in his underpants waiting by the ironing board as his wife crossly presses his trousers in readiness for a 'special parade' (figure 12).[18] *Real* soldiers did not have such options: even though sustenance and 'comforts' were provided by the WVS and the NAAFI (the Navy, Army and Air Force Institute), these services were not equivalent to the wifely care from which the Home Guard was presumed to profit.

On the other hand, the qualifications of the Home Guard to benefit from the knitting of their patriotic womenfolk were popularly perceived to be less sound than those of the other forces.[19] Women's role in knitting, sewing and cooking for the military was a well-established social practice, but when related to the Home Guard it became an integral part of the construction of the comic, quasi-military, identity of the force.[20] The association was used by Alison Uttley in *Hare Joins the Home Guard* (1941), discussed in Chapter 4. The animals are given gendered roles:

Squirrel is ordered 'to knit socks and stockings and mittens and scarves for all our fighters' and Grey Rabbit 'must be a nurse, and take care of the wounded', a role in which she dispenses healing, comfort and courage to all the animals, as well as providing Hare with sandwiches.[21] The two female characters are thus given recognised status as feminine auxiliaries to the masculine army, and perform their support roles successfully. Hare the 'Home Guard', in contrast, as we have seen, although full of bravado and good intentions, is both deeply dysfunctional, in any military sense, and dependent on the more resourceful females.

Rendered ironically, the theme of wives' support of Home Guard husbands was part of the demilitarising, and even emasculating, representation of the domestic embeddedness of the Home Guard. There

Figure 12 'Always some last minute job before these blessed Special Parades' by Neb, *Daily Mail*, 13 May 1944

were three main variants. In one, wives benefit domestically from their husbands' membership of the Home Guard: in a dramatic example that is also an ironic inflection on the issue of combatant women, wives bearing their husbands' Home Guard weapons obtain priority service in shops.[22] A second group of cartoons caricatures wives' expectations that a husband's military rank, acquired from Home Guard membership, would enhance both his (and her) social status and his civilian career prospects. In a *Punch* cartoon by 'Snaffles' Payne, a short, tubby, balding bank manager admires himself in the mirror in his Home Guard uniform, while his adoring wife says, without irony: 'Oh, Henry! If only Head Office could see you now!'[23]

A third set of representations acknowledges the disturbance to the domestic order created by men's Home Guard membership but, by relating it to home and family, diminishes it to comic effect. On 2 December 1944, the eve of the 'stand-down' parade of the Home Guard, the *Evening News* published a Joseph Lee cartoon entitled 'Tomorrow's Big Parade if Mrs Home Guard Had Her Way'.[24] In this fantasy of the form that the parade might take, 'Mrs Home Guard' imagines her husband marching apart from the other Home Guards, his tin hat at a rakish angle and a big grin on his face as he gives her a cheerful wave. Thought-balloons surround her. She is remembering 'those spoiled Sunday dinners', 'those aches and pains' and 'those holey socks', all of which demanded work from her. The cartoon does not suggest that the policy of having a Home Guard in wartime was mistaken: Mr Home Guard is marching between well-disciplined ranks of Home Guards indistinguishable from rugged soldiers, and Mrs Home Guard's patriotism is assured by the Union Jack over which she leans to cheer him. Nor does it criticise the gendered division of labour: his place is in the Home Guard and hers is on the sidelines cheering enthusiastically. Indeed, the cartoon's recognition of her contribution to his Home Guard service (accepting his absence from meals, nursing his minor injuries and mending his clothes) represents a comic celebration, rather than a criticism, of the couple's differentiated gender roles. The cartoon nevertheless caricatures the domestic and familial side of the Home Guard: the proud wife imagines her husband being singled out from the collective endeavour for special recognition that does not take a conventional military form and that acknowledges her own contribution. Separated by white space from the other marching men, Mr Home Guard carries a placard declaring 'Dad. Bless him!' If his place in the parade positions him in relation to the nation, his placard signifies the equal importance of his place in the family.

The ostensible appreciation in 'Tomorrow's Big Parade' for the 'dads' who turned out regularly to defend home and country was echoed in numerous accounts which also diminished it by comparing it with the impact of real military service. Lee in particular contributed cartoons on this theme: the Home Guard father and husband is a stranger in his own home; he has not yet seen the latest addition to the family; he is unrecognisable to his own children.[25] These were known to be common wartime experiences for regular army fathers, but they were not meant to affect the Home Guard, who lived at home and whose duties, however time-consuming and dinner-spoiling, were not supposed to occupy more than forty-eight hours a month. Read sympathetically, such jokes offer a critical commentary on the demands imposed on men by the war effort. Read ironically, they suggest that there may have been other reasons than military service for Home Guard husbands' absence from home.

More explicitly sceptical accounts focused on the strain placed on marital relations by husbands' participation in the Home Guard, and implicitly cast doubt on the idea that the role of Home Guard husbands was to protect their wives and children. They built on long-standing constructions in popular culture of the 'trouble and strife' inherent in marriage. Late-nineteenth and early twentieth-century music hall, for example, staged numerous songs and sketches that depicted the power struggle between husband and wife. Spouses sought to outwit each other in vigorous verbal exchanges and with subterfuges which, for husbands, frequently involved disappearance from the scene of battle to the public house and more congenial company.[26] The advent of the Second World War provided new grist to this mill, and Home Guard membership in particular became endowed with specific meanings. They were summed up by a minor character in a wartime murder mystery: 'they say that the Force is only recruited from men who can't afford a Club subscription but want to be sure of one evening a week away from their wives'.[27] Home Guard history, in this interpretation, was more important for its part in the war of the sexes than in the war between nations.

The comedian Robb Wilton, who broadcast regular comic sketches on wartime themes, was a doyen of this type of representation. In an account that begins 'The day war broke out', the narrator tells of his wife's scepticism about his contribution to the war effort: 'The day war broke out my missus looked at me and she said "what good are you?"' He cannot serve in any of the armed forces because he is too old, and owing to the blackout he cannot go back to work (even had he wanted to) because he had previously been a lamp-lighter. Fed up with his wife's nagging about how he proposes to support her during the war ('Oh, she's got a cruel tongue'), the narrator goes to the pub: 'The times that woman's driven me into the local.' There he meets two men filling out application forms for the Home Guard, and decides to join the force with them. When his uniform finally arrives, he shows it off to his wife: 'The missus looked at me and she said, "What are you supposed to be?" I said, "supposed to be? I'm one of the Home Guards." She said "One of the Home...?" She said, "What are the others like?"' She then quizzes him on what the Home Guard is supposed to do and establishes that he and seven others will be 'guarding' in a hut behind the Dog and Pullet:

> 'What are you supposed to be guarding?' I said, 'Oh don't start all that again, we're guarding the British Isles.' I said, 'We're guarding all the millions of men, women and children. Millions of them. And you.' She said, 'Oh, then you're on our side?' I said, 'Well of course I'm on our side.' 'Well,' she said, 'I think we'd be a darn sight better off if you were on the other side.'[28]

This wife doubts her husband's capacity to act as a man should, either at home (he is out of work and cannot provide for the family) or in war (he is too old for the military). His irresponsibility is symbolised by his preferences – for the pub rather than his home and for male company rather than his wife's constant interrogation. He keeps saying that she 'asks daft questions' and 'doesn't seem to concentrate', while the listener hears her puncturing his pretensions and exposing his maladroit logic. She is the astute, nagging wife and he is the lovable rogue. The audience sympathises with both of them, but the suspicions cast on the husband reinforce the doubts about the Home Guard's military capacity that we reviewed in the last chapter. Service in the Home Guard is no different from disappearance to 'the local', and this 'Mrs Home Guard' derisively points out the consequences: it would be better for 'us' (the family, the nation) if Home Guards like him were on 'the other side', ineptly fighting against Britain rather than for it.

Wives' suspicion that Home Guard membership was about drinking rather than fighting was frequently portrayed. It effectively reinforced and legitimised the cultural association between the two, in spite of the often explicit suggestion that drinking undermined the military credibility of the Home Guard. Thus the full dedication of the two collections of humorous sketches and poems by 'Cilias' (Lieutenant A. H. Watkins), published in 1942 and 1943, was 'To those poor Home-Guard "Widows"/ Who sit alone at night/ And wait, while we, their warriors bold/ Go gaily forth to ... fight'.[29] Not only were these Home Guards going to drink rather than fight, as we observed in Chapter 4, but in so doing they were neglecting their waiting wives.

The theme of wives' suspicions was complemented by that of Home Guard husbands' cunning in pursuit of opportunities for drinking in the company of other men. For example, in 'Careless Talk', one of Cilias's story–sketches, a wife called Florrie does not know that 'wallop' is a euphemism for beer. When her husband lets slip that his Home Guard platoon goes to the pub for 'wallop' after duty he pretends it is a top secret term, fearing that all the wives will thwart the Home Guards' indulgence in this post-parade practice if they find out the truth. However, once the less-naïve wives have enlightened Florrie about the meaning of 'wallop', they collectively decide that '[t]hey'll all come straight home in future, the beauties'. The moral of the tale for Home Guard members is stated: 'Avoid Careless Talk. Be Like Father, Keep Mum.' It gives a twist to the pun in the famous wartime security slogan 'Be Like Dad, Keep Mum' (to which Edith Summerskill objected in Parliament) in which 'father', setting a patriarchal and patriotic example to others, both supports mother and keeps quiet about wartime information.[30] In Cilias's rendering, the meaning is returned from the national to the familial, and 'keeping mum' means not just keeping quiet but also keeping mother in ignorance. The male space is defended, by means of silence and deception, against the enemy at home.[31]

More direct forms of female subversion of the Home Guard enterprise were also depicted in popular culture. The representation of women as unreliable and unpatriotic, whether through ignorance, indifference or malice, has a history that is as long as the often misogynistic accounts of marital strife referred to above. The *femme fatale* achieved her sexual and material desires through ruthless exploitation of her charms, and in contravention of the moral imperatives invested in marriage, community or nation. Her wartime variant was the female spy, the Mata Hari who slept with her enemy in order to extract secrets that she could trade, or the female fifth columnist who betrayed a position of trust for personal gain. Accounts of the Home Guard, both serious and humorous, drew on this stereotype in their portrayal of women.

Barmaids offered appropriate personae. They occupied roles in which they were privy to the exchanges of Home Guard members in the otherwise all-male environment of the pub. They were in a position to pass on secret plans from one Home Guard platoon to another, a potent means of intervention in view of the rivalries between units. In the stage comedy *According to Plan* by Lawrence du Garde Peach (1943), Alice, the barmaid at the Bull's Head, behaves in just this way, betraying to the Home Guard battalion's CO, Major Manley, the plans of 'B Company' to seize some ammunition from the railway station so that none of the other companies in Manley's command can get it. Lieutenant Eliot of 'B Company' hopes to use Alice as a decoy, unaware that she is, in effect, acting as a double agent, since she is feeding the plans to Major Manley. Eliot plans to send Alice to the railway station with a conspicuous handbag which she is supposed to drop in the river in order to distract the attention of the station master, while B Company's men help themselves to the ammunition. The dialogue sends up the 'Mata Hari' role: Alice is preoccupied with glamour, whether or not she looks like Greta Garbo and 'how far she will have to go' in her role as decoy.[32]

Alice's subversive character is developed further, although in a less playful and more unsavoury direction, in George Formby's film *Get Cracking* (1943), which was based on Peach's play. The Alice of the film is devious and underhand. She gives away Minor Wallop Home Guard's secret plans to seize a Vickers machine-gun, left at the railway station, to Everitt Manley, leader of the Major Wallop Home Guard, in the hope of winning his affection. But the Manley of the film is a cad, and reneges on the deal that Alice thought she had made with him by telling her, after she has imparted the information, that he'll give her money for a cinema ticket and that she can 'hold her own hand'. This Alice is eventually caught in the act of imparting secrets to Manley over the pub telephone, and is sacked from her job, having failed to achieve her personal objectives. She is a sordid 'fifth columnist' rather than even a comically glamorous spy, and she is punished for her lack of community solidarity and loyalty. Her role as a sneak is part of the construction of Home Guard rivalry, so intense that betrayal really matters, and it serves to cement the loyalty of the audience towards the unit that is threatened. The Home Guard in this cultural construction constitutes a local entity, like a football team, that inspires intense partisan passion: women are not members of the team.

Women also appeared in potentially subversive roles in a quite different genre. As we saw in Chapter 4, the Home Guard lent itself to crime fiction. The force offered opportunities for foul play, in that armed men performed solitary patrol duties late at night, and its circumstances were productive of motives: it was officially charged with the task of detecting neighbourhood fifth-columnist activities, which might even be taking place within the force itself; it brought together a socially mixed collection of community members, but civilian social divisions and patterns of authority might well be reproduced its own ranks. Furthermore, it operated in a society in which (despite the continuities under discussion) gender relations had been destabilised by mobilisation. Crime fiction of the 1930s and 1940s has been seen as conservative: the solution of a socially disruptive mystery typically restores conventional class and gender norms.[33] But recent discussion by Kristine Miller suggests that women's wartime crime fiction 'is socially and politically ambivalent ... because it both upholds the British establishment and condemns it for refusing to allow social change'.[34]

Two wartime crime novels featuring the Home Guard illustrate these points. In Belton Cobb's *Home Guard Mystery* (1941) the Home Guard is the site of a crime of passion. Both the victim and the main protagonists are male members of the force – and although the murderer turns out to be a woman, she is a background figure until the solution of the mystery. Home Guard activities (patrols, guard duties and the successful capture of a parachutist) are central to the action. Class issues have underpinned the crime: the implied message is that class prejudices need to disappear from Britain so that such tragedies are not repeated. But the conclusion restores conventional gender relations.

In *Murder in the Home Guard* by Ruth Adam (1942), issues of social class are again at stake, but so are those of gender, and women are central to the action. As we saw in Chapter 4, solitary Home Guard patrol duties provide the opportunity for the murder, which is not premeditated and is perpetrated by one Home Guard member, Colonel Markover, on another, Philip Spencer. Women feature as suspects, both of signalling to a German bomber and of the murder. A German–Jewish woman refugee who has been employed as a domestic in several of Longmarket's middle-class households is an obvious potential fifth columnist, but is not guilty. Betty, a deeply unhappy, working-class, evacuee who has been rejected by many similar Longmarket households, does in fact 'show a light' in the hope that it would attract the plane, because she has heard that if a 'reception area' were bombed, its evacuees would be returned home on the grounds that the area was not as safe as had been supposed. But hers is not the crucial signal; and she has not committed the murder. Sally Dawson, a nurse who was supposed to be on duty, but who has gone to a dance, returns alone through the wood where Spencer was shot. She could have committed the murder, but has no motive.

Sally is neither subversive, as the other female characters in the novel might have been, nor is she sceptical about the Home Guard's role. She figures as a metaphor for the local community. Sally undergoes a personal and social transformation due to her wartime encounters with Tom, an RAF pilot with whom she falls in love but who must return to his squadron, and with Colonel Markover, who confesses his crime to her and explains the reason for it. Sally thus comes to understand the sacrifices and the spirit of unity and generosity that are necessary to win the war and that have been so sadly lacking in the community: as a result she gains an adult sense of citizenship. The transformation of Sally stands for the process of change required in the town: this crime story goes further than those discussed by Kristine Miller in critiquing complacent British middle-class society as well as insisting that it change. But while Sally's development evokes the emergence of a new wartime female subjectivity, Ruth Adam does not depict roles for women alternative to those of nurses and evacuee hostesses. In spite of her unconventional approach to gender and sexuality,[35] and her decision to use the Home Guard as the hook on which to hang her story, Adam does not suggest that women should play any role in their own right in organised home defence.

Women as combatants

Women Home Guards were almost non-existent in wartime popular culture. But there was not, in fact, a complete absence of representations of female agency in home defence. Three wartime films addressed civilian women's role in the expected invasion which the LDV and the Home Guard were formed to repel, and in all three, at a moment of crisis for national defence, a weapon is placed in the hands of a woman.

The three films are *Miss Grant Goes to the Door* (1940), *Went the Day Well?* (1942) and *Mrs Miniver* (1942). The latter was one of the most popular representations of the British war effort. Made by an American production company, it was designed to maintain US sympathy for the British war effort following the US entry to the war at the end of 1941, as well as to appeal to the British viewer.[36] We have already commented on representations of the Home Guard in *Miss Grant* and *Went the Day Well?* in Chapter 4. Other authors' discussions of these films and of *Mrs Miniver* have focused, variously, on their representations of the British class structure, national identity, the British response to enemy violence and brutality, and feminine heroism.[37] Our concern here, however, is with their depictions of women's agency in home defence.

In *Miss Grant Goes to the Door*, sisters Caroline and Edith Grant (Mary Clare and Martita Hunt) act with pluck and good sense when two German soldiers come, one after the other, to their front door. The first, an injured parachutist, dies on their sofa, whereupon Caroline Grant

Figure 13 Still of Miss Grant from *Miss Grant Goes to the Door*, 1940

presciently removes his revolver. The other, disguised as an English army officer but in reality a Nazi intent on sabotage, tries to trick Caroline Grant into giving him a map, but she detects his nationality when he mispronounces a place name.[38] At this she turns the confiscated revolver on him and sends Edith off to get the LDV, robustly dismissing her sister's qualms about leaving her alone with the Germans: 'One of them's dead and the other one will be if he moves.' The high point of the short film follows. As Miss Grant gives all her attention to the German at her mercy, the audience sees her briefly from his perspective: we look up past the barrel of the gun into the eyes of an astonishingly fearless and determined middle-aged woman in a dressing gown. Miss Grant's control of the situation is, however, shortlived. The German tricks her into giving him a cigarette and at the moment when her concentration is broken, he knocks her to the floor and the gun out of her hand. Thereafter the LDV, alerted by Edith Grant, takes over the action, blowing up the enemy's supplies and rounding up the spy as he attempts to get away.

This depiction of 'the active service of a country lady who is called on by a Nazi parachutist'[39] was controversial. Members of the War Office regarded the film as 'too frightening', presumably because of the displacement of armed confrontation from the battlefield to a domestic setting where it involved women. Reviewers pointed out that the film did not offer realistic advice about what to do in an invasion: 'most of us have no revolvers', and could not rely on the availability of dead Germans to supply them.[40] These points related to the question, posed in Parliament in November 1941 by Squadron-Leader Errington, referred to in Chapter 3. When he asked what women 'should do if a German came to their door' a fellow MP quipped 'Shoot him', to which Errington replied: 'But they have nothing to shoot him with' and deplored the fact that the War Office refused to recognise the all-encompassing reality of modern warfare and to train British women (like their Russian counterparts) to protect themselves.[41] As we have seen, anything that had been done in this respect since the release of *Miss Grant* in the summer of 1940 was in defiance of War Office policy. *Miss Grant* was deeply contradictory: implicitly the film made the case for armed women's defence, yet its explicit message was that women must rely on the protection of the male home defence force.

A woman's use of a revolver is also significant in the plot of the full-length feature film *Went the Day Well?* discussed in Chapter 4. There are three key women in the film: the imperious lady of the manor, Mrs Frazer (Marie Lohr); the sociable and absent-minded postmistress, Mrs Collins (Muriel George); and the vicar's unmarried daughter, Nora (Valerie Taylor). All three, as well as two Land Girls, become combatants when the villagers strike back against the German invaders. Mrs Collins disables her Nazi guard at the post office by throwing pepper in his eyes, and then kills him with an axe, only to be bayonetted by another German. Mrs Frazer dies with a grenade in her hand, having snatched it from the feet of the evacuee children in her manor house. The Land Girls snipe at the enemy from an upstairs' window: newly trained in the use of a rifle, once they have overcome their initial qualms they vie for success in killing. Nora's role as a combatant woman is, however, even more transgressive.

Nora is a dutiful daughter, caring and supportive. She is the first villager to open her front door to the soldiers when they arrive, with the result that the German commandant (Basil Sydney) is billeted at the vicarage. She is on more than neighbourly terms with Oliver Wilsford (Leslie Banks), the local squire: even though the couple never get beyond hand-patting affection, the audience knows that they are an obvious match, at least in Nora's eyes. Nora is also perspicacious: she plays a leading part in the detection of the subterfuge. It is she who notices the 'elongated fives' and the number 7 crossed 'in the continental way' on the back of a telegram left accidentally in the church hall by Mrs Collins and used by the soldiers for scoring a game; she ponders the harsh treatment by one of the soldiers of an inquisitive evacuee, George; her doubts about the authenticity of these 'British' soldiers are confirmed when George finds Viennese chocolate in the commandant's pack, and she springs into action. Her confidant, however, is the perfidious Wilsford, who instantly alerts the invaders.

Nora gradually comes to suspect Wilsford, even though it means that she must (painfully) overcome her emotional proclivity towards him. Her suspicions are confirmed in the manor house, which the Germans are preparing to storm: Wilsford has announced that he will help to barricade the drawing room. Nora realises the implications and prepares to deal with him. In a powerful sequence, we see her picking up a revolver and asking if it is loaded. 'Yes, think you can handle it?' she is asked. 'Well enough' is the reply, echoing the title of the film.[42] As if in a trance, Nora descends the grand staircase holding the gun at her side and enters the drawing room where Wilsford is perched on the barricade, hurling chairs away from the window. The camera, viewing him from Nora's angle, focuses on him as she mounts her challenge:

W: Hello, Nora.
N: What are you doing?
W: Barricading the window.
N: It was barricaded already.
W: The latch was undone. I was bolting it.
N: Unbolting it.
W: Nora!

In a series of rapid cuts we see Wilsford's shock and fear as we hear the report from Nora's weapon. She is framed very briefly behind the gun, determined if wide-eyed, then the sequence cuts to Wilsford as he falls towards her. Returning to Nora, the camera reveals that the composure she has sustained throughout the dialogue is gone: she trains the gun on Wilsford and shoots twice more to make sure he is dead, her usually neat hair in disarray and her normally controlled limbs suddenly loosened as she wipes a hand across her forehead. In the final image she looks shocked and horrified by what she has had to do.

Nora's role is in several respects a development of that of Miss Caroline Grant. Nora is younger than Caroline, but just as responsible. Both detect the attempted subterfuge with which they are confronted because they are well-informed and quick-witted: they recognise the German pronunciation of the letter 'J' and the written form of the German '7'. Caroline demonstrates her awareness of wartime government regulations,

Figure 14 Still of Nora from *Went the Day Well?*, 1942

concerning taking shelter in an air-raid, maintaining the blackout and disabling vehicles. Nora is politically aware: she argues, at dinner on the eve of the action, that the French have let the British down because they did not stand up to the invasion of their country, and 'deserve to suffer for it'. As the film historian Christine Geraghty points out, Nora's statement helps to justify the brutal engagement of the villagers in the fight that follows.[43] Similarly, Caroline Grant succinctly enunciates the moral justification for threatening a German soldier with a revolver, 'I wouldn't trust one of you an inch', and assures her sister that she is prepared to kill him, even though she does not do so. The justification for Nora's killing of Wilsford is more complicated. In a discussion of fifth columnists at dinner, Nora professes to be unable to understand what they can 'hope to gain in the long run'. Wilsford diverts attention from himself to Mrs Frazer, in an attempted joke that at the same time offers an explanation for his own motives: 'You're just the type. You love exercising power.' But the power that Mrs Frazer wields is innocent compared with the Nazi immorality, brutality and tyranny exposed in the film. Wilsford deserves to die because of his association with these traits, and Nora is the right person to despatch him: the German lieutenant has murdered her father, the vicar, in cold blood in the church. In addition to these justifications, the audience is also aware of the personal betrayal which Nora is avenging: this was the man she thought she loved. The scene of his killing is shocking: Nora, a woman with a gun, is not killing in self-defence but is performing the premeditated execution of an apparently unarmed man; she is, however, acting both patriotically as an English woman and individually as a woman whose trust has been abused.

This reading differs from that of the film historian Sue Harper, who analyses the women in both films as propaganda vehicles. Harper suggests that the ideological reliability of the female protagonists derives from the lack of sexual desirability signified by their age and single status.[44] She sees Caroline and Edith Grant, Mrs Collins, Mrs Frazer and Nora as embodiments of the MoI's puritan, middle-class values. Harper contrasts them with the heroines of Hollywood's *Lady Hamilton* (1941) and of Gainsborough historical melodramas such as *The Wicked Lady* (1945), whose popularity at the box office she attributes to the appeal to the female viewer of their feminine subjectivity and especially their active sexuality.[45] This is a powerful interpretation. But it underestimates Caroline and Nora. Both dramatically challenge a key dimension of wartime patriarchy – the refusal to arm women – and neither is punished for her combative actions. Both films, nevertheless, limit and contain their transgressions.

Caroline Grant is hurt physically by her German captive, but is compensated by the congratulations she receives from the LDV captain for her actions. Yet those very congratulations, and the manner of their delivery, enact patriarchal containment more emphatically than in the case of

Nora. The presence of the young, virile LDV in the sisters' small sitting room underlines their domestic confinement in contrast to his dynamic role in the outside world. And delivering the propaganda message of the film, he enunciates women's marginal role in repelling invasion. Remarkably, he says nothing about Caroline's use of the revolver. If a potential Nazi comes to your door you should keep your head, as Miss Grant did, and keep him talking: he will soon give himself away, whereupon you can send for the LDV.

Went the Day Well? makes no such awkward attempt to reverse the transgression of gender roles that the film depicts and that Summerskill and others believed was required by the threat of invasion. The film's message is more emphatically about social unity: men, women and children work together to repel the invader. Nevertheless there is some normalisation of fighting roles. Nora performs her key act for national defence alone, on the edge of the collective war effort that is being galvanised in the rooms above her. Meanwhile the armed Land Girls, after their rapid training, fight for only so long as they have to. When the immediate emergency is over, and when the men's superior weapons run out of ammunition, the women readily relinquish their rifles to them. The female characters in *Went the Day Well?* act heroically – like men – at the height of the invasion crisis, and Mrs Frazer and Mrs Collins die like men. But the film hints that as the crisis subsides, normality will return, and with it the restabilisation of gender relations. We see no more of Nora after the shooting: there is no indication that, like Sally in *Murder in the Home Guard*, she has been transformed by her experiences of war.

The third film to explore women and home defence, *Mrs Miniver* (1942), offers a very different perspective. Unlike *Miss Grant Goes to the Door* and *Went the Day Well?*, it is not focused on invasion, even though the high point is a confrontation between Mrs Miniver and a German pilot. Its concerns are primarily with the effects of the war on the Miniver family and on the internal social structure of their village, Belham, situated in yet another picturesque corner of one of the southern counties of England. Although the film places the experiences of female protagonists at its centre, the plot focuses on crucial readjustments between the social-class positions they occupy,[46] rather than on changes in gender relations, apart from the addition of a modicum of modernity. Kay Miniver (Greer Garson), a self-declared member of the middle class, has been described as 'the prototype for a range of specifically British and class-bound femininities'.[47] The war brings out the best of her maternal and wifely characteristics: she cares for her children's emotional as well as physical well-being during air-raids, and champions the youthful wartime marriage between her son Vin (Richard Ney) and Carol Beldon (Teresa Wright), against the opposition of Carol's aunt, Lady Beldon (Dame May Whitty). The relationship between Kay and her husband Clem (Walter Pidgeon) evokes the companionable marriages advocated in the USA in the interwar years, in which husband and wife shared family concerns as well as a good sex life, while preserving most aspects of differentiated gender roles.[48] But Kay Miniver is on the sidelines of military action. That is what her husband and son do, while she provides them with sandwiches and support, and watches and waits.

Mrs Miniver's discovery of a German airman in the garden, during one of her anxious dawn vigils, is thus unexpected and alarming. But it does not herald the transformation of her subjectivity, as does Nora's discovery of Wilsford's treachery. Kay's attempt to assert herself is both timid and thwarted: she tries to take the fallen pilot's gun from his hand (paralleling Miss Grant's disarming of the parachutist who came to her door); but, having woken him in the process, she runs away and the German chases her at gunpoint into the kitchen. Far from the transgressions of Caroline Grant and Nora, who placed men at their mercy at the other end of a gun, Mrs Miniver is in the traditional position of a woman subjected to the power of a man. Indeed Mrs Miniver, Carol Beldon and the children in this film stand for innocence. They do not slough it off in order to mobilise to kill the enemy as Mrs Collins, Mrs Frazer, the Land Girls and Nora do in *Went the Day Well?* When Mrs Miniver's German pilot collapses after eating her bread and ham and drinking her milk, she finally succeeds in removing the gun from his hand, taking it from him as a mother might take a dangerous toy from a child. She keeps it with her while she calls the police and then, far from using the gun herself, she conceals it amid the domestic clutter on a kitchen surface, confident that the police will soon come to take the German away and thus restore her security. They do not arrive, however, until the pilot has delivered a savage message about the Blitz to come, in which 'innocent people … women and children' will rightly die. Rather than shooting him for this, Mrs Miniver expresses her outrage by slapping his face. It is an act of assertion, but it makes no impact on him and he does not retaliate: the slap is that of a mother chastising a teenager who has gone too far, not an act of national defence. It is certainly not equivalent to Caroline Grant's gunpoint hold-up or Nora's shooting of Wilsford. As the police take the pilot away, Kay Miniver fishes out the gun and hands it to the last policeman to leave. The village doctor, who has come with them, asks her if she is all right, and, straightening her spine, she asserts that she is. The achievement of the upright back, 'a metaphor for moral rectitude and fortitude',[49] is the public face of her response to war. But after everyone has gone Kay's feminine demeanour returns and she sinks weakly into a chair. When her younger son, Toby, comes in asking 'Who was here?' all she can do is to cuddle him, the protective mother of the innocent child.

This dramatic episode is immediately followed by the return of Clem from Dunkirk, an unharmed hero at the helm of his bullet-riddled boat. He does not need to tell her of his horrific experiences because the newspapers have covered the retreat, and he does not suspect that there is anything for her to tell him. Thus the story of Kay's confrontation is revealed with a mild irony that serves to confirm the natural order. As Clem rests in bed after his ordeal, he announces: 'I'm almost sorry for you having such a nice quiet peaceful time when things were really happening, but that's what men are for, isn't it, to go out and do things, while you womenfolk are looking after the house?' The audience, however, is aware from what has gone before that women's role in 'looking after the house' elides in wartime with national defence and that Clem is about to discover this. When Clem awakes, Kay nonchalantly confesses that she had a German pilot in 'for ham and eggs this morning' and, quizzed on whether he had a gun, says demurely: 'I just took it away from him and called the police.' 'And then I suppose you gave him tea?' 'Milk', says Kay, turning to tidy the bed. Clem walks away and then swings round and spanks her as she bends over, saying 'Milk, eh?' This jocular horseplay embarasses the cook, who enters at that moment, but we understand it to be of a piece with the Minivers's relationship. Following a spate of good-humoured banter, Clem has delivered a mild – and sexualised – reprimand for Kay's mild – and maternalised – transgression.

The confrontation between a woman and the enemy in *Mrs Miniver*, the position of the pistol within it, and the subsequent account of the event, serve to maintain male power. Even though the episode focuses on a woman's sensibility and sexuality within the domestic sphere, it is dominated by the external war in two ways: it occurs under the shadow of Dunkirk, the scale and seriousness of which are indicated by shots of ships massing and a megaphone announcement from a battleship to the crews of the small boats about the dangers they will face; and it is overshadowed, too, by the German pilot's prophetic threat of the devastation to come. The bombing of the village, including the Minivers's house, follows soon afterwards. A raid disrupts the annual flower show and makes victims of Carol, a choirboy and the station master. In the final scene, in the shored-up church, the vicar echoes Bramley End's vicar in his principled opposition to all that the Nazis stand for. But the vicar of Belham emphasises the sacrifice of the innocent rather than the immorality of the enemy: 'Children, old people, a young girl at the height of her loveliness. Why these? Are these our soldiers, and are these our fighters – why should they be sacrificed?' In Churchillian rhetoric he gives the answer:

> This is not only a war of soldiers in uniform. It is a war of the people, of all the people. And it must be fought not only on the battlefield but in the cities and in the villages, in the factories and on the farms, in the home and in the heart of every man, woman and child who loves freedom … This is the people's war. It is our war. We are the fighters. Fight it then. Fight it with all that is in us. And may God defend the right.

The meaning of the 'people's war' for quiet corners of England such as Belham, then, was the united participation of the nation in a war effort characterised by endurance, sacrifice and unflinching morale. The film, made in Hollywood rather than at Ealing (where *Went the Day Well?* was made), was intended to present a version of the war in England that would encourage American commitment.[50] There are constant reminders of the film's US provenance, particularly the accents of the lead characters as well as the domestic interiors of the Minivers' home, 'Starlings', which are more suggestive of Massachusetts than of Kent. Nevertheless, *Mrs Miniver* was extremely popular with British audiences.[51] The patriotic sentimentality of the film and the correction of old injustices perpetrated by class divisions,[52] as well as the modern marriage of the good-looking lead couple and the active (if well-behaved) sexuality of Kay, contributed to its success. Additionally, in view of the extensive Blitz and other bombing campaigns, and in the absence of an invasion on Bramley End (or other) lines, the film's presentation of the impact of the war was arguably more realistic, from the perspective of 1942, than the 'citizen army' messages of the other two national-defence films discussed here. Even though *Mrs Miniver* was, as all commentators agree, highly romanticised, it spoke to a socially pervasive British experience of war. The film was, however, contradictory: its final message was that women and children as well as men must fight the people's war, but, unlike *Went the Day Well?*, it did nothing to demonstrate how the necessary transformation of innocent victims into 'freedom-fighters' might take place. Even when she gains a gun and has the opportunity, Mrs Miniver does not shoot the enemy.

Conclusion

We have seen that in their roles as Women Home Guard Auxiliaries and members of the WHD, women were almost entirely absent from wartime film, fiction and drama featuring the Home Guard. Why were they so overlooked? The answer suggested here is that their presence in the Home Guard disturbed entrenched gender norms: for a home defence force to make sense, it needed to be armed, and armed women could not be comfortably included in the catalogue of British characteristics for which the war was being fought. In other words, the presence of women in the Home Guard breached a gender boundary that was also a frontier between two gendered types of citizenship. Women could appear as WVS members, dishing out tea and comforts, but not as comrades of men on the home front in their daily activities of pursuing parachutists, detecting fifth columnists or participating in military manoeuvres.

The Home Guard was represented as an all-male outfit with which women had a variety of relationships. Some sustained the men of the Home Guard in conventionally womanly ways in representations that contributed to the theme of a domesticated Home Guard whose home-based, part-time and familial nature implied a fundamental lack of militarism. Many other women in popular culture were overtly sceptical: they expressed derogatory perceptions of the age, the competence and the priorities of Home Guard members for whom, they suggested, alcohol and male company were more important than either fighting or the home. The coupling of Home Guard membership with the pub and drinking culture positioned Home Guard members in the space that errant husbands had occupied in popular culture for centuries. Yet the criticisms expressed by the carping wives created by male cartoonists, journalists and script-writers were not necessarily those the audience was supposed to share. Robb Wilton's character could be allowed to escape to the Dog and Pullet. The community understood where the 'warriors bold' of the 'Home Guard "widows"' were going. Rather than disapproving, the audience was invited to join in the music-hall fun of conflictual marital relations in which women and men wanted something very different from each other. Furthermore, the construction of the Home Guard and male drinking culture as closely associated activities that must be defended against feminine intrusion and control made it unthinkable that women could have a place within the Home Guard. It set the seal on women's exclusion from organised home defence.

The representation of women as subversives in comedies featuring the Home Guard ironically underscored the seriousness of the Home

Guard enterprise: the Home Guard was worth betraying; it generated a group loyalty sufficiently powerful to define such activity as treachery. Crime fiction, in contrast, used the cultural link between femininity and subversion in different ways. The women in *Murder in the Home Guard* were directly suspected of fifth-columnism, and could convincingly be presented in this way because of the cultural connotations linking women and subversion. But none of the adult women in fact acted subversively, and, far from undermining the war effort, the key female character attained a new maturity and social awareness as a result of her experiences of love, war and death: the murderer, captain of the local Home Guard, had been one of her teachers. The novel made clear that the Home Guard was genuinely committed to home defence (as opposed to the pub). It did not, however, suggest that there was a place for women in the Home Guard.

The three films explored here, on the other hand, questioned the norms outlined above by depicting women performing armed roles in home defence: Miss Grant held the enemy at pistol-point; Nora shot dead a fifth columnist; Mrs Miniver disarmed a German pilot. These films suggest that the logic of total war made these activities real possibilities rather than celluloid fantasies: they were presented as encounters that might be thrust on any 'ordinary' woman in wartime. But in each case the focus on the individual emphasised the exceptionality of such confrontations. All three women were fortuitously armed and found themselves almost accidentally in the 'front line' facing the enemy. They were not there as a result of collective decision and organisation; nor were they trained for their roles. These representations alone acknowledged the issues that underpinned the formation of the WHD and the Women's Home Guard Auxiliary: the threat of invasion, the merging of the front line with the home front, and the destabilisation of the gendered boundary between military mobilisation and domestic support for the war effort. But they stopped well short of any commitment to the inclusion of women in organised home defence: indeed the nuances of these depictions served to emphasise how profoundly problematic that would have been. Cultural representations could envisage change in the British class structure, but not in the gender order, for all that it was rocked by war.

Notes

1 See Chapter 3; the ban was printed in *The Times* on 12 November 1941, and Summerskill argued against it in Parliament the same week: Hansard, vol. 365, col.1932, 19 November 1940, and vol. 376, col. 2158, 18 December 1941.

2 Joseph Lee, 'Smiling Through: Danger Near', *Evening News*, 6 November 1941.

3 Hansard, vol. 383, col. 1467, 13 October 1942.

4 Donald McGill designed seaside postcards 1904–62.

5 Hansard, vol. 388, col. 1532, 20 April 1943; see Chapter 3.

6 *Daily Mail*, 21 April 1943.

7 Neb, 'Brooch Inspection by the C.O. on Sunday at 10.00 hrs', *Daily Mail*, 22 April 1943.

8 M. Bryant, *Dictionary of Twentieth-Century British Cartoonists and Caricaturists* (Aldershot: Ashgate, 2000), p. 138.

9 Bryant, *Dictionary*, p. 164.

10 Lee had 9,000 cartoons published between 1934 and 1966: Bryant, *Dictionary*, p. 138.

11 IWM, DD, 75/35/1 T, Captain F. C. Saxon, unpublished memoir (henceforth Saxon memoir), p. 77.

12 IWM, DD, 75/35/1 T, Captain F. C. Saxon, 'Trials of the Home Guard' (henceforth Saxon cartoons), 6.

13 Saxon cartoons, 11.

14 Saxon cartoons, 23.

15 Saxon memoir, p. 77.

16 IWM, PA, The Home Guard 1939–1945, H5869; H5870; H5871.

17 See Chapter 4, note 90.

18 The 'special parade' to which the cartoon refers marked the fourth anniversary of the Home Guard.

19 Boothroyd commented that Home Guards confronted their wives with 'powerful propaganda' to the effect that they were equally deserving: Boothroyd, *Home Guard Goings-On*, p. 57.

20 Official knitting patterns included the Home Guard, suggesting that in official thinking there was no reason that Home Guards should not benefit: e.g., *All Services Knitwear for the Navy, Army, Air Force, Mercantile Marine, Home Guard: Clear Instructions for Knitting All Comforts Required by Servicemen* (London: John Bale & Staples, 1941).

21 A. Uttley, *Hare Joins the Home Guard* (London: Collins, 1941), p. 35.

22 Lee, 'Smiling Through: Persuasive Customers', *Evening News*, 19 November 1942; also Neb, 'I bet that one of those on last night has a missus making jam', *Daily Mail*, 23 June 1943; Lee, 'Smiling Through: Camouflage', captioned: 'He learned how to do it [hat-trimming] at the Home Guard', *Evening News*, 3 April 1944.

23 Charles Johnson 'Snaffles' Payne, 'Oh, Henry!', *Punch*, 30 December 1942;

also Lee, 'Smiling Through: Officer Commanding', *Evening News*, 2 February 1942 ('the wife' has instructed her Home Guard husband to 'put up' sergeant's stripes).

24 *Evening News*, 2 December 1944.

25 A small boy asks 'Mummy, who is that strange man who keeps rushing in and out and appears to know us?': Lee, *Evening News*, 3 January 1942; another child asks '... and when the war is over, will Daddy come back from Home Guard?': Lee, *Evening News*, 10 August 1942; a mother says to a friend over the head of her baby, 'No, his father hasn't seen him yet. He's in the Home Guard': Lee, *Evening News*, 4 December 1942.

26 Failings as husbands and fathers tended to be 'subtly exculpated' by the hostile portrayal of the womenfolk: Lois Rutherford, ' "Harmless Nonsense": The Comic Sketch and the Development of Music-Hall Entertainment', in J. S. Bratton (ed.), *Music Hall: Performance and Style* (Milton Keynes: Open University Press, 1986), pp. 147–149. Marital strife was depicted more critically by female artists: J. S. Bratton, 'Jenny Hill: Sex and Sexism in Victorian Music hall', in Bratton (ed.), *Music Hall*, p. 105.

27 Cobb, *Home Guard Mystery*, p. 35.

28 IWM, SA, 13921, 'The Day War Broke Out', Robb Wilton's Home Guard monologues (n.d.).

29 'Cilias', *Home Guard Rhymes* (London: no publisher, 1942); Lieut. A. H. Watkins, *Home Guard Rhymes: The Home Guard in 'Di-Verse' Moods* (London: Practical Press, 1943).

30 Summerskill objected because she thought the slogan had offensive implications for women: Brookes, *Women at Westminster*, p. 139.

31 'Cilias', *Home Guard Rhymes*, pp. 11–12. A short story by Basil Boothroyd, 'Loss of Public Confidence', involves the public exposure of such Home Guard subterfuges: Boothroyd, *Home Guard Goings-On*. Mothers, such as Mrs Campbell, in Mackenzie's *Keep the Home Guard Turning*, occasionally tried to prevent sons both drinking and joining the Home Guard.

32 Greta Garbo played the lead role in *Mata Hari* (1932), the film about the legendary First World War spy.

33 See, e.g., J. Symons, *Bloody Murder: From the Detective to the Crime Novel* (London: Faber & Faber, 1992 [1972]), pp. 10, 104.

34 K. Miller, 'Case Closed: Scapegoating in British Women's Wartime Detective Fiction', in S. Gillis and P. Gates (eds), *The Devil Himself: Villainy in Detective Fiction and Film* (Westport, CT: Greenwood Press, 2002), p. 93.

35 Adam depicts Sally as a vocationally inspired nurse who casts off her nun-like persona and discovers her own vibrant sexuality in the course of the novel. Energised by the blossoming of love, Sally dances naked and alone in the wood and sleeps in a woodland shelter used by the Home Guard; it is there that she and Markover meet and he confesses his crime to her.

36 Aldgate and Richards, *Britain Can Take It*, p. 292.

37 See Aldgate and Richards, *Britain Can Take It*; Chapman, *The British at War*;

C. Gledhill and G. Swanson (eds), *Nationalising Femininity: Culture, Sexuality and British Cinema in the Second World War* (Manchester: Manchester University Press, 1996).

38 He says 'Yarvis Cross' for Jarvis Cross.

39 Basil Wright, in the *Spectator*, 16 August 1940, quoted by Chapman, *British at War*, pp. 96–97.

40 *Documentary News Letter* (September 1940), quoted by Chapman, *British at War*, p. 96.

41 Hansard, vol. 376, cols 108–109, 13 November 1941.

42 The title refers to an unattributed poem that appears at the start of the film, evoking the numerous sacrifices that the villagers will make: 'Went the day well?/ We died and never knew./ But, well or ill,/ Freedom we died for you.'

43 C. Geraghty, 'Disguises and betrayals: Negotiating Nationality and Femininity in Three Wartime Films', in Gledhill and Swanson (eds) *Nationalising Femininity*, p. 233.

44 S. Harper, 'The Years of Total War: Propaganda and Entertainment', in Gledhill and Swanson (eds) *Nationalising Femininity*, p. 202.

45 Harper, 'The Years of Total War', pp. 196–197.

46 See Janet Thumim, 'The Female Audience', in Gledhill and Swanson (eds), *Nationalising Femininity*, p. 250.

47 'Introduction', in Gledhill and Swanson (eds), *Nationalising Femininity*, p. 10.

48 During and after the Second World War a range of social policy pronouncements helped to establish this type of modern marriage as a model for British couples: see J. Finch and P. Summerfield, 'Social Reconstruction and the Emergence of Companionate Marriage, 1945–59', in D. Clark (ed.), *Marriage, Domestic Life and Social Change: Essays for Jacqueline Burgoyne* (London: Routledge, 1991), pp. 7–32.

49 P. Kirkham, 'Fashioning the Feminine: Dress, Appearance and Femininity in Wartime Britain', in Gledhill and Swanson (eds), *Nationalising Femininity*, p. 155, n. 7.

50 Aldgate and Richards, *Britain Can Take It*, p. 292.

51 It was the top box-office attraction in Britain in 1942: Aldgate and Richards, *Britain Can Take It*, pp. 16, 338; Thumim, 'The Female Audience', p. 248.

52 Aldgate and Richards, *Britain Can Take It*, p. 341.

6

Dad's Army and Home Guard history

In the summer of 1968, BBC Television broadcast the first series of a situation comedy about a seaside Home Guard unit. *Dad's Army* became enormously popular: 80 episodes were transmitted in 9 series from 1968 to 1977. Viewing figures exceeded 13 million in 1969, after which the show attracted an average of over 12 million viewers per week from 1969 to 1975, with a peak of 18 million in 1972. These were remarkably high viewing figures compared both with other BBC comedies and with broadcasts on rival channels.[1] The popularity of *Dad's Army* ensured considerable 'commercial intertextuality' – that is, the marketing of related products, ranging from other media productions, including a full-length feature film in 1971, to commodities like games and models.[2] Since 1977 there have been numerous re-runs of episodes on British television and the right to transmit the series has been sold to broadcasting agencies in over thirty countries.[3]

Dad's Army is about the Home Guard unit of a fictional coastal town, Walmington-on-Sea, in the part of southern England closest to the Nazi threat from across the Channel. The unit is led by Captain George Mainwaring (Arthur Lowe), self-important and status-conscious bank manager, whose well-bred chief clerk at the bank, Arthur Wilson (John Le Mesurier), becomes his sergeant and second-in-command of the platoon. This Home Guard unit features five other key characters: Frazer (John Laurie), a Scots undertaker; Godfrey (Arnold Ridley), an elderly, retired, gentleman's outfitter; Jones (Clive Dunn), an ageing butcher; Pike (Ian Lavender), a very junior bank clerk; and Walker (Jimmy Beck), a 'spiv' – the word for the distinctive wartime flashy opportunist who made money from the black market.[4] These seven members of the Walmington-on-Sea

Home Guard play their parts against a background of uniformed and mostly silent men who make up the platoon to the correct strength. Other characters, in particular the vicar, the verger, the local Air Raid Warden, and Mavis Pike, 'friend' of Sergeant Wilson and mother of the youngest member of the platoon, pass in and out of the programme as required. Each episode is a self-contained story, drawing on features of Home Guard life, such as the arrival of uniforms and weapons, the presence of suspected fifth columnists, training exercises, competition over rank, and rivalry with other Home Guard units as well as with the army and civil defence organisations. The humour is generated by a combination of farce, slapstick, wordplay and innuendo, but is derived above all from the strong characterisation of the seven key members and their relationships with one another and with those outside the unit.

This chapter explores the meaning for Home Guard history of the *Dad's Army* representation. The first section builds on earlier chapters by seeking to identify the wartime and post-war representations of the Home Guard available to the creators of *Dad's Army*, Jimmy Perry and David Croft, in the 1960s. It discusses the genre in which Perry and Croft worked, the cultural influences they acknowledged (as well as those which they did not), and the congruence between *Dad's Army* and wartime representations of the Home Guard. The second part discusses the historical interpretation of the Home Guard offered in the series, focusing in particular on the characterisation of Walmington-on-Sea's commanding officer, Captain Mainwaring. The third section addresses the contribution to the comedy of personal memories of the Home Guard and initiates an exploration of the 'cultural circuit' between personal and public memory, which we take further in Chapters 7 and 8. Overall, the intention of the chapter is to analyse the interpretations of the Home Guard and the Second World War generated by *Dad's Army*, and to understand both their resonance and their durability.

Dad's Army and the cultural heritage

Jimmy Perry, who had the idea for the programme in 1967 and, with David Croft, wrote the scripts, declared that two elements were crucial for its creation: his own experience as a youthful member of the Home Guard from 1941 to 1944, aged 17–20;[5] and the dearth of available cultural representations of the Home Guard in the mid-1960s. Perry said that he went to the public library in search of books about it and found nothing: 'The Home Guard had never been discussed for twenty years before I got the idea of *Dad's Army*.[6] He explained that he followed the visit to the library with one to the Imperial War Museum, where he found wartime Home Guard instruction manuals 'and, strangely enough, a book of Home Guard cartoons', which stimulated his own memories.[7] Perry did not refer to any other Second World War representations, although, as we have seen, there were plenty: even if Perry and Croft were not aware of them, they form part of the cultural heritage from which *Dad's Army* emerged.

When the war ended, the two accounts of the Home Guard explored in Chapters 4 and 5 were still in tension: the confident narrative of an efficient defence force marked by the best aspects of British wartime identity; and the sceptical story that stressed the Home Guard's social tensions and military failings. Some of the wartime representations discussed in Chapter 4 had more lasting afterlives than others. Among the best-known of them is the film *The Life and Death of Colonel Blimp* (1943). Its enduring popularity is indicated by its presence in a Centenary Poll conducted in 1995 of the 'one hundred best films'.[8] As we have seen, the film establishes Candy–Blimp and with him the Home Guard as a symbol of outdated (if honourable and sincere) approaches to war. But it is arguable whether the film was really *about* the Home Guard: it does not explore the Home Guard's membership and inner workings in a way which lodges the force firmly in popular memory. Another survivor, the George Formby film *Get Cracking*, does so to a greater extent. Embedded in a drinking culture centred on the local pub, the Minor Wallop Home Guard is inspired by local and internal rivalries and is threatened by unreliable colleagues, girlfriends and by the Major Wallop Home Guard, though not by the enemy. The precarious value of the Home Guard's contribution to the war effort is the central motif of *Get Cracking*: at the same time Home Guard improvisation and inefficiency are undoubtedly combined with patriotic good intentions.[9]

The Home Guard was not completely absent from new cultural products in the immediate post-war years. It had a role in the film *Whisky Galore*, released in 1949 and based on Compton Mackenzie's comic novel of the same name, published in 1947, itself in effect a sequel to Mackenzie's wartime novel *Keep the Home Guard Turning* (1943), which we met in Chapter 4. Made by Alexander Mackendrick and Monja Danischewsky, of Ealing Studios, *Whisky Galore* became, like *Blimp*, an enduringly popular film. It features the efforts of a Hebridean island community to lay claim to a cargo of whisky lying in the hold of a ship wrecked off its shores, before the authorities can confiscate it. The adult men on the island are

members of the Home Guard, which provides the organisational structure for their efforts at the same time as requiring that they outwit their
English captain, Waggett, who is of course on the side of the Revenue.
The film thus evokes an association of the Home Guard with drinking
culture, parochial patriotism, ingenious improvisation and masculine
camaraderie similar to that of *Get Cracking*. Like the two novels on which
it drew, *Whisky Galore* adds specifically Hebridean elements, including
the social practices of sabbatarianism and *rèiteach*,[10] and it augments
Home Guard solidarity with traditional islander suspicion of outsiders
in general and the colonising English in particular. The film does not
focus specifically on the Home Guard, however. It is possible for viewers
to overlook the Home-Guard membership of the characters, so strong is
their Hebridean identity: several synopses either omit any reference to the
Home Guard or mention it only in relation to the pompous English Home
Guard Commander, Waggett.[11] The primary theme, a topical one in 1949,
concerns bureaucratically-imposed austerity and how to combat it. The
drama lies in the islanders' collective efforts to thwart official shortages,
imposed by an alien officialdom, of the commodities that make life worth
living, rather than the Home Guard's contribution to the war effort.

Whisky Galore in 1949 was the last new representation of the Home
Guard on the cinema screen until *Dad's Army: the Movie* in 1971. The
Home Guard had also been vanishing from the printed page, although
it had a surprising but brief afterlife in the 1950s. Between 1950 and
1954 successive governments pursued a policy of re-mustering the force
to defend Britain against the threats of communism and nuclear war.[12]
This initiative was represented satirically by cartoonists Lee and Niebour,
who, in a reprise of their wartime Home Guard interpretations, discussed
in Chapters 4 and 5, depicted ageing men whose portly proportions
indicated their unsuitability for military roles enthusiastically resuming
Home Guard manoeuvres behind deckchairs and among cows.[13] The pub
was, as before, a vital component. A 'Neb' wife commented in July 1950,
'and if this means that Sunday dinner time Home Guard pub lark all over
again, my old man will have plenty of atomic explosions to deal with when
he gets home'.[14] But the cold war justification for the revival was uncon-
vincing. The 1950s' Home Guard never gained widespread support and in
1954 the magazine *Picture Post* sounded its death knell in a serious feature
emphasising its unpopularity and lack of purpose.[15] Thereafter until the
first series of *Dad's Army* in 1968, references to the Home Guard in the
press were extremely sparse.[16] Perry's claim that the Home Guard had not
been discussed for twenty years before he had the idea for *Dad's Army* was

an exaggeration, but few public representations had broken the silence since the early 1950s. In particular, the Home Guard had not been used in television comedy, the medium and genre in which Perry chose to work.

This was important, not only for the element of originality in Perry's creation, but also for the impact of his interpretation. The absence of alternatives meant that the *Dad's Army* account had the opportunity to dominate understandings of what the Home Guard was like, provided that anyone was, by the late 1960s, interested. Perry's attempt to ensure that his show attracted attention was based on two key elements: his use of television and his manipulation of history.

Perry stated that he chose to write in the genre of the television situation comedy, or 'sitcom', as part of an attempted career move.[17] In 1967 he was working as an actor at Joan Littlewood's Theatre Workshop in the East End of London.[18] In addition he occasionally found small parts in television shows with the help of his agent, Ann Callender. She was married to the television producer David Croft, with whom, eventually, Perry wrote the *Dad's Army* scripts, and who became producer and director of the show. Perry wanted to write himself a part in a production and so achieve a more secure career in television.[19] His choice of situation comedy as the specific television genre in which to work served his purpose well. Sitcoms requires the same set of characters to appear in a number of relatively short episodes in a variety of situations – hence the genre had the advantage for Perry's career plan of enabling him to develop a particular character within a series of programmes over time. The comedy in sitcoms is usually generated by gags, jokes and slapstick humour which are structured by a plot that fits the *situation* in which they take place. The challenges for Perry were to decide on the situation, the funny stories and the characters who would people them.

While Perry did not refer to the influence of earlier representations of the Home Guard, he did acknowledge the effect on his creation of successful television comedy shows that featured military service, notably *The Army Game*. This half-hour comedy show broadcast on Independent Television (ITV) ran for 154 episodes over 5 series between 1957 and 1961, and spawned a number of subsequent productions.[20] It featured a group of young men conscripted to the army under the post-war National Service regulations and kept more or less in order by a bellowing sergeant-major. It presented a variety of British character types, such as Corporal Springer, a 'wide-boy' from London's East End, and Major Upshot-Bagley, an upper-class dimwit.[21] While not directly referring to wartime Home Guard humour, *The Army Game* echoed it: the base where the conscripts served was at 'Nether Wallop', surely not far from Minor Wallop of *Get Cracking* fame.[22] National servicemen and Home Guards suffered from similar quasi-military status. From 1949 to 1960, in the context of the Korean War, the cold war and anti-imperial independence movements, men between the ages of 18 and 28 were required to undertake 18 months of military training, extended to 2 years in 1950, and to be members of a reserve force for up to 4 years thereafter.[23] But after the Korean War of 1950–53 it became increasingly clear that those conscripts were unlikely ever to have to fight. National servicemen, like Home Guardsmen, appeared superfluous to military requirements, a point underscored by setting *The Army Game* in a 'surplus ordnance depot' and by the use of the term 'game' in the title of the show. The humour of *The Army Game*, like much wartime humour concerning the Home Guard, was generated by attempts to knock into military shape men who were not cut out to be soldiers, in the context of social-class hierarchies and bureaucratic red tape. Perry was convinced that 'a good service comedy series never failed' in the 1950s and 1960s.[24] The recent experience of military conscription by 2.5 million national servicemen, as well as over 5 million men during the war (the eldest of whom would have been 75 in 1964), helps to explain this popularity.

Perry also acknowledged the influence of a pre-war film with a non-military theme, starring the actor Will Hay. *Oh! Mr Porter* (1937) was shown on television in 1967 at the time Perry was thinking about his sitcom.[25] In *Oh! Mr Porter* Hay played a garrulous, officious and incompetent station master of a remote railway station in Eire who tries to modernise the almost defunct service but becomes entangled with gunrunners. The importance of the film for Perry lay in the characterisation: 'One of the movie's strengths was the wonderful balance of characters: a pompous man, a boy and an old man. The combination made for perfect comedy.' [26] Perry used just such a balance of characters in *Dad's Army*, giving the lead role to Captain Mainwaring, played by Arthur Lowe, the actor whom Perry sought out for the part.[27] Although the two men's physical characteristics and mannerisms were very different, a description of Hay's screen persona also fits Lowe's as Mainwaring: he was 'sometimes clever, sometimes ludicrous. He displayed all the human weaknesses of vanity and pomposity, yet he remained warm and likeable'.[28]

Crucially for the strength of *Dad's Army*, Perry positioned Mainwaring in a nexus of other well-developed characters. Two were clearly inspired by the boy and the old man in *Oh! Mr Porter*: young Frank Pike, a particularly naïve and callow recruit of 17, and old Jack Jones, the Walmington-

Figure 15 Photograph of the cast of *Dad's Army*

on-Sea butcher and veteran of campaigns in the Sudan, the North-West Frontier, the Anglo-Boer War and the First World War. Perry elaborated Mainwaring's relationships, adding most significantly Sergeant Arthur Wilson as his second-in-command. Wilson is the pompous leader's principal foil. The relationship of the captain and the sergeant enables Perry to foreground Mainwaring's aspirations to be an effective military leader. Wilson's casual and amateurish performance of his role as sergeant ('Pay attention you chaps, would you *mind* just falling in, in three ranks, quick as you can?') allows Mainwaring frequent opportunities to assert his (precarious) military professionalism ('Just get on with it, Wilson … You're supposed to be a sergeant, not the headmistress of a girls' school. Platoon, SHUN!').[29] The relationship also brings out one of Mainwaring's major weaknesses, acute class consciousness. Wilson occupies a higher position than Mainwaring on the social ladder: he has been to public school and has aristocratic relatives; but this is in tension with his position of inferiority to Mainwaring both at the bank and in the platoon. This situation provides numerous opportunities for the exposure of Mainwaring's snobbish resentment of the upper classes and simultaneous differentiation of himself from the lower classes, as well as from radical social change. In the episode 'Wake Up Walmington' Mainwaring and Wilson are discussing the consequences of the war:

M: You privileged classes all stick together. Things will be very different after the war, you mark my words. The common man will come into his own. This country will be run by professionals, doctors, lawyers – bank managers.
W: People like you.
M: All right, people like me.
W: You mean common.
M: Now watch it, Wilson.
W: I didn't know you were a socialist, Sir.
M: How dare you! You take that back.[30]

The rival authority of not only the socially elevated Arthur Wilson but also the 'common' Mr Hodges, greengrocer and ARW, who moves in and out of episodes impugning the effectiveness of the Home Guard, are almost unbearable to Mainwaring: he strives constantly to deny his inferiority to one and prove his superiority to the other.

Three other leading characters complete the web of relationships. Private Charles Godfrey represents a different sort of ageing veteran from Jones. Gentle and sweet, Godfrey is a doddering old man plagued by incontinence and reliant on the priorities, mores and upside-down-cakes of the two spinster sisters with whom he lives. Private James Frazer, the undertaker, of about the same antiquity as Jones and Godfrey, represents the Scot who, according to Perry, inhabited every southern English town, much revered by the locals but disdainful of his neighbours.[31] Finally, Perry created Joe Walker, the spiv, commenting: 'Everybody did a spiv, it was a common wartime character.' Walker is a man of call-up age not known to be in a reserved occupation, who can obtain, at a price, scant wartime resources of almost any description, but who, in spite of his sharp practices and avoidance of military service,[32] is loyal to the platoon and warm-hearted. This was the part Perry intended to play himself.

Perry's agent, Ann Callender, encouraged him to show David Croft the first script, entitled 'The Fighting Tigers', while Perry was playing a minor part in one of Croft's productions.[33] Croft liked it and persuaded Michael Mills, Head of Comedy at BBC Television, to back it. Mills not only did so, but improved on the title, renaming the show *Dad's Army*. 'Dad' was a familiar way of addressing any older man, not just one's father, in 1940s Britain. It was used in wartime in the 'Be Like Dad, Keep Mum' security poster, as well as, occasionally, with specific reference to the Home Guard: in Lee's cartoon 'Tomorrow's Big Parade if Mrs Home Guard Had Her

Way', discussed in Chapter 5, 'Mr Home Guard' carries a placard identifying him as 'Dad'. It is not the case, though, that the Home Guard was
known as 'Dad's Army' during the war: Mills's title was in tune with the
sitcom's representation of the force as, predominantly, a group of affec-
tionately-regarded older men, but was a creative distortion, a matter to
which we return. Croft and Perry developed and co-wrote the show, but
as producer and director Croft would not give Perry a regular part, ostensibly because he felt it more useful for a scriptwriter to help to direct than
to act in his own show.[34] As a result Perry wrote rather than acted his
way into a secure place in television. He and Croft went on to create at
least three more highly successful sitcoms together, *It Ain't Half Hot Mum*
(1974–81), *Hi-De-Hi!* (1980–88) and *You Rang, M'Lord?* (1988–93).[35]

The rich vein of Home Guard humour that Perry, apparently unwit-
tingly, inherited contained four themes, as we saw in Chapters 4 and 5.
These were scepticism about the achievement of national unity in the
Home Guard in view of local, regional, rural–urban and class tensions;
acknowledgement of the Home Guard's enthusiasm for the task of
defending Britain against invasion coupled with doubts about its capacity
in this role; celebration of the improvisational initiative of the force that
simultaneously suggested that the Home Guard was playing at soldiering;
and incredulity about the military masculinity of members depicted as
physically unsuitable types who inhabited the home and the pub rather
than the battlefield. Women had almost no place within these representations except as commentators, sometimes supportive, often sceptical and
occasionally subversive.

These themes were all inscribed in *Dad's Army*. Its episodes indicate
the importance of wartime unity while at the same time delineating
and emphasising the difficulty of achieving it. The Walmington-on-Sea
platoon mixes men of different ages and social origins, and they operate
within a community that (mostly) supports them and that they support.
But Mainwaring's acute status consciousness, Frazer's Scottish nationalism, the tensions between the Home Guard and the ARWs led by Bill
Hodges, the platoon's precarious relationship with the church represented by the Reverend Timothy Farthing and Yeatman, his loyal verger,
and the rivalry between the Walmington-on-Sea and the neighbouring
Eastgate platoons all suggest the implausibility of the ideal of national
unity. Co-operation is frequently jeopardised; nevertheless, the cracks in
Walmington's unity usually result from rivalry over who is doing most in
the war effort, rather than any disagreement about the rectitude of the
effort itself.

There is no doubt that Mainwaring is keen to go into action against the German invader. In 'Something Nasty in the Vault' he is visited by a bank inspector:

BI: Do you always interview people with a revolver on your desk?
M: Oh yes, especially in spring.
BI: What's spring got to do with it?
M: Well surely you realise, Mr West, that Hitler is only waiting for the spring to invade.
BI: And I suppose you think you're going to stop him with that pop gun.
M: Not only me. I mean there's the rest of my platoon. We're all fully armed and trained to kill.[36]

In the 1940s, comic treatments of the Home Guard had criticised the outdated approaches to warfare that the force was expected to adopt, as well as its military pretensions. The Walmington-on Sea platoon makes determined, if incompetent, efforts to be modern. Mainwaring is always keen to receive new weaponry although he rarely knows how to use it, and he enthusiastically attempts to implement the latest techniques. These include, for example, getting the platoon fit, giving them guerrilla training, dressing them up in a variety of disguises to outwit the enemy, inspiring them with pep talks and taking them on river patrols. ('Half-a-dozen determined men, armed to the teeth, with a boat. They could play havoc with the Nazis!').[37] Improvisational imagination is allowed free rein: Jones's butcher's van is given gas propulsion, onions are substituted for ammunition in the platoon's Smith gun, and nooses dangling from trees are used to capture the enemy in an exercise with the Highland Regiment.[38] The platoon's precarious competence is emphasised by the fortuitous quality of its victories over its local rivals and the army – as well as over the real enemy on the rare occasions when it confronts Germans.[39] As in wartime cartoons, so in *Dad's Army*, the Home Guard is frequently misunderstood by the army and oppressed by military regulations. Mainwaring is uncomfortable in the presence of 'professional soldiers' and is, on occasion, humiliated by them, while striving to fulfil to the letter (usually ineffectually) the army instructions that he receives.[40]

Representations of the 1940s had emphasised the local, all-male characteristics of the force. The Walmington-on-Sea platoon is firmly embedded in a small town and rural community. The world beyond is a shadowy one in which only nearby Eastgate has any salience. There are occasional references to London, whence Walker came, but Jones's reminiscences position Omdurman and the Somme more firmly in the platoon's imaginative geography than any current British, let alone French, German,

Russian or North African location. The local community is represented mainly via the various rivalries referred to above, supplemented by other reminders of the presence of a world outside the platoon such as periodic intrusions, into the platoon-on-parade, of outsiders with little time for military form, such as the vicar, the verger, the ARW and Mrs Pike, arriving to check on Frank. Like the women depicted by Lee, Neb and other wartime cartoonists, Mrs Pike contributes an implicitly critical commentary and occasionally humiliates Mainwaring and his men with her greater competence, for example in the tasks of unblocking a rifle and putting out an incendiary bomb.[41] Members of the platoon occasionally appear in their daytime roles, for example Jones in his striped apron serving in his butcher's shop, Mainwaring and Wilson in their formal business suits working in the bank, and Frazer in his dour undertaker's garb. As in wartime satire, such images of the proximity of the Home Guard to normal civilian society emphasise the pretensions of the so-called military force. They also help to delineate its all-male club culture. Intrusions are predicated on exclusions: the expulsion of women, squabbles with air raid wardens and the ejection of clerics serve to emphasise the closed membership of the platoon.

Perry and Croft were working with, rather than against, the grain of wartime Home Guard humour, even if it was not as apparent to them as the television sitcoms that suggested the civilian–military theme of *Dad's Army*, and the pre-war film that inspired its nexus of pompous-young–old characters. But there were two significant departures from wartime renderings. Firstly, the members of the Walmington-on-Sea Home Guard are not united by drinking culture. The platoon does not meet in the back room of a pub, as the Home Guard did in *Get Cracking*, in the Basil Boothroyd stories and in *Laughs with the Home Guard*: its parades take place in the more respectable setting of the church hall. Pubs and drink are evidently liked by the Walmington-on-Sea Home Guard, but their appearance in an episode is disruptive, involving a range of comic interactions during which Mainwaring's authority typically suffers, in spite of his endeavours to restrain consumption.[42] In 'Fallen Idol', for example, the platoon attends a weekend course under canvas. The men are allowed two pints of beer each, which suits Mainwaring well. However Captain Square, CO of the rival Eastgate platoon, persuades him to join the other Home Guard officers, who decide to play a mess game involving a recitation. The penalties for making a mistake are to drink a tot of whisky and to repeat the recitation from the beginning. The result is that the normally sober Mainwaring ends up reeling into the tent where his men are sleeping, extremely drunk and with his reputation in tatters.[43] As this and other episodes suggest, the evils of drink are many and varied, a message possibly favoured by the lingering Calvinism in the BBC. From time to time, drink serves to develop the characters, their relationships and the humour of the series, but, in contrast to wartime representations, a drinking culture is not the main factor that unites the men in *Dad's Army*.

Secondly, whereas women members of the Home Guard were almost completely absent from wartime representations of the force, *Dad's Army* devoted one (though only one) episode to the theme. 'Mum's Army' confronts gender issues through the surprising device of involving Mainwaring in an extra-marital romance.[44] Mainwaring decides that it is time to enrol some women. The first four female candidates for the Walmington-on-Sea platoon are actual or would-be girlfriends, brought by Pike, Frazer, Walker and Jones for their own strategic reasons. In contrast, a fifth woman, Mrs Gray, volunteers independently, her motives apparently purely patriotic. Mainwaring, Walmington-on-Sea's bank manager and Home Guard CO, faithfully married and a pillar of respectability and propriety, is instantly and completely smitten by her. In a spoof of the well-known film *Brief Encounter* (1945) Mainwaring is prepared to risk his carefully nurtured social status for an (unconsummated) affair with Mrs Gray.

The development of Mainwaring's character in the series makes his sudden capitulation understandable, if unexpected. It is clear from hints in numerous episodes that his is a loveless marriage in which his masculine authority is deeply undermined, itself a comic trope well established in popular culture. The audience never sees his wife, Elizabeth, but is aware of a formidable physical presence (signified by a bulge in a bunk and heavy footfalls) and of an intimidating personality (indicated by Mainwaring's dealings with her on the telephone).[45] 'Mum's Army' presents Mainwaring as a figure seeking not only social affirmation, but also, almost poignantly, affection. Nevertheless, his pursuit of Mrs Gray is comic. Mainwaring, pompous, balding and overweight, is the inverse of a masculine romantic hero, and his efforts to appear youthful and attractive, by, for example, taking off his spectacles, lead to plenty of slapstick. Yet it is just plausible that Mrs Gray and he would be mutually attracted. A respectable widow evacuated to the south-coast town, she too is lonely, as well as serious about the war effort. She embodies a restrained yet dynamic version of middle-class femininity, expressed in her trim figure, grooming, social graces and accomplishments, markedly superior to those of the other women recruits, which would naturally appeal to the snobbish Mainwaring. In the end, however, morality and patriotism triumph over love: when faced with the alternatives of destroying Mainwaring's position in the community and resigning from the Home Guard, Mrs Gray prepares to leave Walmington-on-Sea. At the station a distraught Captain Mainwaring pleads with her to stay, but the train carries her away. Her departure marks the end of the experiment with a women's section of the Walmington-on-Sea Home Guard; women never again become members.

It is remarkable, in view of the cultural veil over women's presence in the Home Guard explored in Chapter 5, that Perry and Croft included anything at all about women's involvement. Two clues as to why they did so are, firstly, an undated photograph in the Imperial War Museum Photographic Archive of women learning to shoot with the Watford Home Guard, which Perry had joined in 1941,[46] and, secondly, letters from some of the earliest viewers of the series suggesting women's involvement as a theme.[47] In any case, although the choice of the theme was strikingly out-of-keeping with published 1940s representations, the outcome of the episode was not inconsistent with them. 'Mum's Army' is not about the struggles of Summerskill and the WHD for women to play an equal part in the Home Guard. Its main purpose is to develop the character of Mainwaring as an emotional man who has a romantic and susceptible side, and who, though normally prudent, is capable of recklessness. It also makes explicit the conservative interpretation of gender offered implicitly in the series as a whole. The short-lived and unsuccessful attempt to include women in the Home Guard suggests that women constitute a danger to male cohesion and a distraction from masculine military endeavour. The denouement of the episode restores gender boundaries to the Walmington-on-Sea Home Guard and to the series: the dynamic of gender relations henceforth operates, as it did with very few exceptions in 1940s humour, between the Home Guard and the local community rather than within the unit, which is thus marked as unassailably, if comically, masculine.

Dad's Army and historical interpretation

Perry and Croft embraced the past wholeheartedly in *Dad's Army*. They recreated a wartime atmosphere through the care they took to make as authentic as possible every setting within which the action took place, be it the church hall, Jones's shop, Godfrey's cottage, Pike's bedroom or street and field scenes in and around 'Walmington-on-Sea'. Wartime posters and products were carefully selected and positioned; uniforms and medals, dress and hairstyles, were rendered accurately; appropriate weaponry was chosen and use was made of genuine wartime vehicles. The action was interspersed with snatches of wartime songs and allusions to wartime films.[48] The emphasis on historical authenticity endowed the series with considerable authority.

Nevertheless there were significant departures from the historical 'truth'. The title song *Who Do You Think You Are Kidding, Mr Hitler?* sounded like a wartime production, but was in fact composed in 1968 by Perry, who persuaded Bud Flanagan, responsible with Chesney Allen for numerous wartime hits, to record the song to the suitably military accompaniment of the Band of the Coldstream Guards.[49] Another major departure from historical authenticity concerned the ages of the members of the Walmington-on-Sea platoon. Perry admitted that the depiction of the Home Guard as a bumbling group of mainly *elderly* men was unrepresentative. In a radio programme, he described to his young male interviewer his own experience of the development and composition of the Watford Home Guard unit: 'We became a very efficient guerilla force ... the idea [that it was] full of old men is totally wrong. There *were* older men in it, there were men in their mid-60s, but most of it were boys and chaps about your age waiting to be called up, and middle-aged men. So it was quite an efficient fighting unit.'[50] There was scope in the humour for the inclusion of one youth, the dysfunctional Pike, and one man of call-up age, Walker, but the other five 'front-line' characters are all ageing: Jones, Frazer and Godfrey are supposed to be in their seventies, and Mainwaring and Wilson are approaching 60. The representation of the force as a group dominated by incompetent old men, expressed succinctly in Michael Mills's title *Dad's Army*, was vital to fulfill the requirements of the sitcom.

Perry and Croft departed from other television sitcom treatments of the military by choosing to locate their series in a specific historical context that was essentially serious, rather than the 'never-never land' of *The Army Game*. The Second World War setting for the action indicated the existence, and importance, of a real enemy, and Perry asserted repeatedly, in print and in interviews, that he did not regard British involvement in the Second World War as a joke. For example, he declared in a publication of 1998: 'Make no mistake, it was our finest hour. We stood alone against the most evil tyranny the world had ever seen. To be alive at that time was to experience the British people at their best and at perhaps the greatest moment in their history.'[51]

Nevertheless, combining a loyal representation of Britain's part in the Second World War with a comedy about a wartime organisation was not easy to achieve. Perry's Home Guard characters were not only ineffectual soldiers, but some (Private Walker and even Sergeant Wilson) were not averse to shirking. 'Make no mistake, it was our finest hour …' could be read ironically, especially in view of jokey references in early reviews to the thirty-minute show as 'comedy's finest half hour'.[52] There was unease about it within the BBC. Tom Sloan, Head of Light Entertainment and the man above Michael Mills in the hierarchy, was known for his 'old-fashioned BBC standards' which were encouraged in the mid-1960s by the reactionary National Viewers' and Listeners' Association led by Mary Whitehouse. In a BBC lecture in December 1969 Sloan reported that he had considered whether the script was 'making mock of Britain's Finest Hour', but he decided that, while 'it was funny', it redeemed itself because it was also 'true':[53] characters like Perry's did exist 'in those marvellous days'; the techniques of home defence that the Walmington-on-Sea platoon practised were those that were officially recommended; and, according to Sloan, 'the possibility of defeat did not enter our minds!'[54]

Perry certainly did not allow his characters to express defeatism, or, to be more precise, if there was even a hint of lack of confidence in a British victory (apart from Frazer's gloomy reiteration of 'We're all doomed' when things got rough), Perry had Mainwaring pounce on it. For example, in the episode 'Sons of the Sea' Mainwaring and his men find themselves adrift at sea in a rowing boat that Mainwaring has acquired for river patrols. Towards the end of a long night, Mainwaring perks up:

M: Pay attention, men. It will be light soon. We shall be spotted by a boat.
W: Suppose it's a German boat, sir?
M: I don't want any of that sort of talk here. There are no German boats in the English Channel.[55]

While such sentiments were sincere and even laudable, they were, as in this example, exaggerated to the point of absurdity.

The obvious incompetence of the unit unmistakably told the audience that the Walmington-on-Sea platoon, and by implication the British Home Guard as a whole, could not have defended Britain effectively against invasion. The tension between the comic incompetence of the platoon and the seriousness of the situation in which it was placed, came to a head over the opening credits. A figure even more senior than Mills and Sloan, Paul Fox, the Controller of BBC1, expressed anxiety that the programme mocked the war effort. The original opening titles showed scenes of refugees fleeing the German Army in France and Belgium and the closing credits featured 'shots of Nazi troops with the captions and the artists super-imposed'.[56] Paul Fox was adamant, and Tom Sloan in the end supported him, that this was unacceptable. There were, as Fox put it, plenty of people alive in 1968 who knew that the threat of invasion was not funny. However, the programme as a whole was not under threat: Fox, like Sloan, agreed implicitly if not explicitly that the Home Guard could be represented humorously. The *real-life* opening sequences were replaced by an animation showing arrows representing British and Nazi forces, symbolised by the Union Flag and the Swastika respectively, chasing each other first one way then the other across the Continent and, following the withdrawal of the British arrow to the south coast, confronting each other across the Channel. The authentic war footage in the closing credits was replaced by film of the key members of the cast lurching through the English countryside with arms at the ready.

Michael Mills was deeply offended by the required removal of the planned scenes. Departmental rivalries and a desire to put Fox to the test as the new controller may have energised him,[57] but Mills also argued angrily that Fox had misunderstood the sitcom's message:

> The whole object of this comedy series is to contrast the pathetic, comic but valorous nature of the Home Guard, who believed at the time that this (the Nazi hordes) was what they were up against. It seems to me to be not only right but essential that this fact is brought home to the viewers – and it is, surely, our justification for doing a comedy programme on this subject.[58]

What exactly did Mills mean? The series did not in fact systematically 'contrast' the Home Guard with the enemy – there are very few episodes in which the Walmington-on-Sea platoon confronts German forces. The best-known is the episode 'The Deadly Attachment', in which the platoon is made to guard overnight a captured German submarine crew awaiting an armed escort.[59] Mainwaring uses the occasion to emphasise the difference between his British troops and the German 'automatons', but the submarine crew's brisk generation of a wide variety of orders for fish and chips suggest good teamwork rather than subjugation. Furthermore, the Germans, led by their undoubtedly ruthless captain (Philip Madoc), rapidly turn the tables on the Walmington-on-Sea platoon: as he draws up a list of those Home Guards who are to be 'brought to account' when the Germans win the war, Mainwaring famously demonstrates his incompetence by blurting out 'Don't tell him, Pike' when the captain demands the name of the platoon's youngest member.[60] Finally, the crew manage to place a hand-grenade down Jones's trousers, arranging for Mainwaring's men to march them to the docks to make their escape, with the submarine captain holding the detonator: if the platoon does not let the Germans go, the grenade will be set off. In the event it proves to have been primed with a dummy detonator,[61] and Jones and the rest of the platoon live to see another episode, while the Germans are taken under the wing of the army. But the message of the confrontation is clear: the Home Guard is no match for the German forces and its triumph is more a matter of luck than good management.

Mills described the Walmington-on-Sea Home Guard in his defence of the programme as 'pathetic, comic, but valorous'. All the characters are indeed 'comic'. Some are particularly 'pathetic': for example, the incontinent Charles Godfrey, who punctuates every episode with requests to 'be excused', usually at inopportune moments; the one-step-behind Corporal Jack Jones, inclined to run around in small circles shouting 'Don't panic!' whenever anything goes wrong; and Pike, the 'stupid boy'. Some are more 'valorous' than others: in spite of his weak nerves in a crisis, Jones is always ready to volunteer, whatever the risks;[62] and James Frazer, motivated by his rivalry with the equally aged Jones, whose lance-corporal's stripe he covets, and by his determination to demonstrate the superiority of the Scots to the Sassenachs can be relied on to be tough and brave, if pessimistic. In contrast, Sergeant Wilson and Privates Walker, Godfrey and Pike have little appetite for strenuous military duties: Wilson is ever-sceptical about Mainwaring's enthusiastic determination to try out new methods of defence, often repeating 'Is this really necessary, Sir?'; Walker finds ways of avoiding the most arduous duties, or at least of combining them with a quick smoke or a speedy deal; Godfrey doubts whether his sisters would really like him to do what is required; and Pike usually has a note from his mother prohibiting him from participating in cold, wet and nocturnal activities, which he draws to Mainwaring's attention when orders are issued, even if Mainwaring rarely takes any notice. Only one character combines all three of Mills's attributes: Captain George Mainwaring.

Mainwaring is comic in his vanity. For example, he dons a toupée to make himself look younger when the platoon receives an order stating that older members of the Home Guard will be transferred to ARP, and consults Wilson about his 'best side' after hearing that the platoon is going to be in an army training film.[63] He is pathetic in his routine insistence on his superiority as a military leader to his rivals (principally the vicar and verger, and the ARW), even though his military ineffectuality is repeatedly demonstrated.[64] But Mainwaring's valour is equally evident: it is composed of patriotic fervour coupled with complete confidence in the vital role of the Home Guard in the war effort and the sincere belief that the Walmington-on-Sea Home Guard is the first line of defence against the invader.[65] At the beginning of 'Turkey Dinner' he lectures Wilson on the best preparation of men for battle, whereupon Wilson asks in surprise: 'We're not going into battle, are we?' Mainwaring's response – 'We are in the front line every minute of our lives here'[66] – conveys his outrage at the suggestion that the members of the Home Guard are anything less than 'real soldiers'.[67] Even though Mainwaring's courage and determination are often punctured, usually by Wilson, there is no doubt that he is ready to die for his country. In 'The Battle of Godfrey's Cottage', for example, he thinks the invasion has started while, apart from himself, Jones and Frazer, the entire platoon is at the cinema. ('We've waited six months for this and now that Hitler's at our throats my platoon's at the pictures.') He plans to go with his two men to Godfrey's cottage:

> M: If we can hold out for long enough there, it will give our regular troops time to regroup before they counter attack, y'see. Mind you, it will probably be the end of us. But we're ready for that, aren't we men?'
> Men: 'Course (*looking rather doubtful*).
> M: Good show.[68]

Mainwaring's valour, coupled with the way everything always turns out for the best, make it plausible that *Dad's Army* was about the British people united behind a successful war effort. Yet Mainwaring is also the chief butt of the comedy, the Will Hay figure whose pompous behaviour is constantly undermined by slapstick or by the repartee of the other characters. Leading characters in farce, it has been suggested, are ironically similar to tragic heroes in that their greatest strengths and passions are also the site of their undoing. [69] In Mainwaring's case patriotism, social ambition and desire to command respect are his key characteristics. He constantly fails to achieve the authority he craves, even though his men obey him and are loyal despite their sardonic comments,[70] and social advancement always seems to accrue, unearned, to Wilson rather than to Mainwaring who works so hard for it.[71] His patriotism, although unswerving and sincere, is absurdly overstated, leaving open the possibility that he was indeed a caricature of inept British military leadership, unequal to the German forces depicted in the censored closing credits.

Perry and Croft's creation in 1968 of a patriotic but ineffectual military leader who was also a source of humour paralleled the creation by Powell and Pressburger of Colonel Wynne Candy in 1943; and the fears of Sloan and Fox that *Dad's Army* would be understood to ridicule the British war effort was in the same register as the reaction of Grigg and Churchill to *The Life and Death of Colonel Blimp*. Perry and Croft protested that they were not mocking Britain's 'finest hour', just as Powell and Pressburger had insisted that they were not caricaturing wartime army leadership. But was this the whole truth or could *Dad's Army* also be viewed as satirical?

One of the influences on his creative development that Perry acknowledged was an innovative and outspoken experiment in theatrical satire: Joan Littlewood's Theatre Workshop. He did not dwell on its significance for *Dad's Army*, although in his autobiography he referred to Littlewood as his 'inspiration and mentor' and stated that it was while working with her that he started to write.[72] The Theatre Workshop was a left-wing venture that produced political satire critical of 'the establishment', often scripted by actors working with a playwright. Notably, in 1963, the Theatre Workshop created *Oh! What a Lovely War*, written, in conjunction with the cast, by Joan Littlewood and Charles Chilton. The play had a long run, transferred to the West End, and was made into a film in 1969.[73] *Oh! What a Lovely War* was a rollicking satire about the First World War, told from the angle of vision of the common soldier. It indicted the myopic generals who sent millions of men to untimely and unprofitable deaths in a war that lacked any purpose. The military historian Brian Bond has argued that the play contributed to a radical rethinking of the First World War in the 1960s which transformed popular views of that conflict.[74]

Even though the target of *Oh! What a Lovely War* was the military leadership of the First World War, it belonged within a critique of political, economic and military leadership that also embraced other wars. Humorous and satirical work of the 1950s and 1960s, including the British *Goon Show* and Spike Milligan's autobiographies, as well as the American novel and film *Catch 22*, questioned the military logic, capacity and leadership of the allies in the Second World War.[75] The scepticism expressed in such work was augmented by mounting criticism of the use of military force in global disputes in the late 1960s and early 1970s, including opposition to the Vietnam War and to the invasion by Soviet forces of Czechoslovakia in 1968 (which, in a nice example of BBC proportionality, forced Episode 4 of *Dad's Army* to be postponed for a week). The period was marked by a growing disrespect for institutionalised authority and discipline, expressed in the social protests, the lifestyle changes and the popular culture of the time. These developments created a permissive atmosphere in which scepticism about any major wartime institution could flourish.

Dad's Army was not ostensibly a radical anti-war production. But it owed to *Oh! What a Lovely War* its treatment of patriotic military leadership in the person of Mainwaring. There were of course differences. These included Mainwaring's heartfelt engagement in the war effort, his relatively lowly social origins, his attempts, unlike the First World War generals, to adopt modern methods of leadership and his involvement with his men in all their military (and unmilitary) manoeuvres. Mainwaring may have bossed his men about and made them do things they did not wish to do, but rather than lounging in a deck-chair far from the action he participated in everything with them. Nevertheless, in creating him, Perry and Croft sailed close to the wind of satire. Mainwaring was, at the same time, the bearer of a serious patriotic message about the Second World War and the place of the Home Guard within it, and the object of humour based on his own military incompetence. Could Mainwaring, as medium, be separated from the message that the Second World War was a just war, that brought out the best in the British?

The fact that those within the BBC hierarchy who could have vetoed *Dad's Army*, such as Sloan and Fox, merely insisted on changes at the margin suggests that they accepted the separation which Perry and Croft had contrived.[76] The success of the series may have depended, as Michael Mills implied, on its combination of humour with a complete acceptance of the necessity and justice of the Second World War, enabling *Dad's Army* to make people laugh without offending them. Many early reviewers, however, understood *Dad's Army* to caricature the Home Guard, albeit with varying degrees of approbation. In August 1968 the television critic of the *Bath & Wiltshire Evening Chronicle* described it as 'a non-malicious lampoon mixing satire and slapstick',[77] and Michael Billington in *The Times* also thought it satirical, but argued that it did not go far enough: the attitude to the Home Guard was equivocal, 'as if afraid of making too much fun of a hallowed wartime institution'.[78] In February 1969 Henry Raynor wrote that *Dad's Army* suggested that the Home Guard's 'mere existence is such a joke that its activities don't really matter' and that it 'would be more enjoyable if it did not believe the notion of a Home Guard to be so ludicrous that only the quaint or the pompous would ever join it'.[79] *Dad's Army* became a metaphor for valiant but self-important leadership and incompetent soldiering that was applied critically to numerous political and military developments from the late 1960s onwards.[80]

The changes of this period, however, also stimulated a nostalgia for an age of greater confidence in established social and political structures, which focused a different kind of attention on the Second World War. From 1970 to 1974 Edward Heath's Conservative Government was rocked by a series of bitter industrial disputes marked by transport paralysis, food shortages and power cuts, which led to the introduction of a 'three-day week' in

December 1973, to save fuel and power. In this context memories of the
Blitz and D-Day were evoked, as Heath appealed for national unity,[81] and
apparently coincidentally numerous depictions of aspects of British life
in 1939–45 appeared on the small screen. They included *A Family at War*
(Granada, 1970–72), *Colditz* (BBC, 1972–74), *Carrie's War* (BBC, 1974),
The World at War (BBC 1973–74) and, of course, *Dad's Army*. In a review
of *Carrie's War* in *The Times* in January 1974, Leonard Buckley wrote:
'Television is obsessed with the Second World War.'[82] The explanation,
to which correspondents and reviewers subscribed with varying degrees
of criticism, was that the Second World War appeared, from the vantage
point of the early 1970s, to have been the last period when Britain was
united against a serious threat over which it was, ultimately, victorious.[83]
Dad's Army fed this wave of Second World War nostalgia, and Mainwaring's earnest ineptitude and the comic triumphs of his platoon were not
read as satire by all of *Dad's Army*'s huge audience: however implausibly,
the Walmington-on-Sea Home Guard was viewed by some as nothing
short of a symbol of British heroism.[84]

The perception that *Dad's Army* is nostalgic rather than satirical has
become dominant. In 1997 the cinema historian Jeffrey Richards argued
that *Dad's Army* inspired 'a nostalgia not so much for the war as a time of
shortage, destruction and loss but as a period of shared effort and sacrifice, common purpose and good neighbourliness and justified struggle
against a wicked enemy'. He goes on to argue that nostalgia has positive
social consequences: far from being passive, nostalgia 'is a vital force,
passionate, active, committed to the ideal of reviving and preserving
the best of the past, not just because it is the past but because it works,
it is needed and it is right'. To Richards, *Dad's Army* expresses 'shared
memories and shared values' and 'an ideal of national identity rooted in
tradition, community, tolerance and good nature'.[85] However, although he
points to various changes that can be attributed to nostalgia as a political
force, such as the preservation of old railway lines and the redesign of city
centres, Richards does not give examples of the re-creation in the present
of the aspects of the past he attributes specifically to *Dad's Army*: shared
sacrifice, common purpose, just causes. Other commentators have been
equally confident about, but more critical of, *Dad's Army* nostalgia. Television critic Stuart Jeffries wrote in 2001: 'We are encouraged to want to live
in the past where society was more homogeneous and people were more
strongly, even sentimentally linked, or rather a past that is all the better
for never having really existed. Hence some of *Dad's Army*'s enduring
appeal … Thus, Britain recycles its history, remakes it better without the

taint of blood and violence, leaving it mythical and thus safe for us to live there for the first time.'[86] Mark Connelly, writing in 2004, agrees: '*Dad's Army* touches us because it is the way we like to think of Britain in 1940 … The show acts as an anaesthetic, dulling the drift of Britain into obscurity and disunity.'[87] Richards, on the one hand, and Jeffries and Connelly, on the other, take different positions on the effects of nostalgia, but they nevertheless agree that *Dad's Army* works by stimulating a longing for the past. This consensus, however, means that the possibility that *Dad's Army* ever had any satirical intention has been largely forgotten.[88]

Personal histories

Critics and other commentators may have taken time to settle on nostalgia as the defining characterstic of *Dad's Army*, but delight in the series' evocation of the Second World War characterised audience responses from the first broadcast.[89] Letters of appreciation sent to Perry and Croft in 1968–69 frequently referred to feelings of nostalgia that the show provoked, often linked to the correspondent's sense of the Second World War as a finer time to be alive than the late 1960s. Mr L. E. Tindall referred to the way the show brought back so vividly 'those grand, pulsating brave years of us, the "British People"'. Miss K. Carruthers contrasted her exciting wartime experiences with those of 'the overfed, bored youngsters these days'. And Mr J. W. Camp wrote even more gloomily: 'in view of what has happened since 1946, I often wonder whether it was all worth it'.[90] Others stressed, more simply, the pleasure they took in the show's accurate rendering of life in the Second World War. Mr J. Board's comment stands for many: 'I would like to congratulate you for the true to life picture you have produced.'[91]

Few viewers regarded the presentation as satirical. Only one ex-Home Guard wrote to say that he thought the show caused offence. This was J. W. Camp, quoted above, who complained 'I do not think that most hard-working officers and N.C.O.'s of the Home Guard like to be shown as a rather inept crowd, quite useless against the German Paratroopers they were expected to tackle.' But even Mr Camp evidently found it 'difficult not to laugh at some of the characters', and he went on to reflect on some of the 'curious' men in his platoon whom he had had 'to mould into shape'.[92] Several correspondents pointed out that although the Home Guard started as an ill-trained and ill-equipped assortment of men, it was quite rapidly turned into a well-organised military force.[93] Otherwise, viewers went no further than seeking to correct what they perceived as inaccuracies. According to one woman, wartime butchers were not as nice as Corporal Jones: 'If I have one criticism, it is the open and kindly way that the old corporal brings extra meat for the bank manager and sergeant. Butchers during the war became secretive, mean, close fisted, close mouthed. They had to be men of steel, because all the housewives were very nice to them.'[94] J. W. Camp also complained that, until conscription was introduced, it would not have been possible for a Home Guard captain to instruct his sergeant to 'take that man's name'; as Mainwaring did when confronted with Pike's refusal to remove the brush from the end of his improvised weapon (a broomstick), since army discipline did not apply. Croft and Perry took note of such observations: it was clear that these letter-writers wanted them to improve the accuracy of the programme, and hence to enhance their enjoyment of it, rather than to put an end to the show.[95] Thus while Jones continued to curry favour with his officers by providing them with extras, we see him ruthlessly manipulating the queue of housewives in his shop through his control of the meat ration, and after the first episodes Mainwaring usually says to any miscreant, headmaster-style: 'I'll see you in my office afterwards.' However, the alleged transformation of the force into an efficient adjunct of the British Army was one aspect of historical authenticity that Perry and Croft chose not to incorporate. Far more comedy was to be gained from fixing the Walmington-on-Sea platoon forever in a time-warp of improvisation and partial militarisation.

In spite of such a selective use of history, viewers responded appreciatively, sometimes in kind – Perry and Croft were sent drawings of the principal Home Guard weapons as well as details of training in, for example, guerrilla warfare and camouflage. They also received offers of Home Guard greatcoats, battle-dress, vehicles and buttonhole badges. While their polite replies usually indicated that they had enough of whatever was offered for now, they accepted the badges and distributed them to the cast.[96] Such things contributed to the verisimilitude for which they were striving.

So, too, did the interweaving of personal experience. Perry explained that he drew on his own memories as well as his investigations: 'quite a few episodes were actually based on truth, not actually what happened to me all the time, but quite a few of them were based on research I had done'.[97] He cited, for example, attacking a tank with a burning blanket, an exercise that the newly recruited men attempted in the first episode[98] as well as being issued with pepper to throw at the enemy. In addition Perry and Croft were offered a wealth of personal testimony by members of their first audiences, who wrote in with reminiscences and suggestions for episodes, and even in some cases their own dramatisations. However, little distinction was made in those letters between Home Guard and army experience, suggesting that in viewers' memories the follies as well as the relationships and procedures encountered in one were similar to those met in the other.[99]

Some of these personal accounts and suggestions contained ideas that were incorporated into *Dad's Army* plots, albeit usually considerably adapted. For example, L. E. Tindall wrote of his Home Guard officer's attempts to discharge an unexploded bomb with rifle fire. Such were the officer's difficulties in hitting it that the men standing around started to take bets, the odds lengthening as his misses grew in number, until, humiliated, the officer gave up and handed the rifle to Tindall. There was a similar scene in 'Wake Up Walmington'. During a practice at a rifle range owned by a local grandee, Mainwaring endeavours to demonstrate the correct way to shoot, but, distracted by the landowner's snooty butler, he cannot hit the target. The men start a book, involving Mainwaring in the bets, with the result that he ends up owing Frazer ten shillings for his own shortcomings.[100] In another example, Mrs Barbara Summers recalled that men from her father's Home Guard unit were posted at night to a shepherd's hut on a hillside. If they saw anything suspicious they were supposed to run down the hill, armed with pennies kept in the hut, to the public telephone-box to inform her father and the police. A minor incident revealed that none of them knew how to use a pay-phone, so her father instituted telephone-box drill, that is, instruction in inserting the pennies and pushing buttons A and B. The men of Walmington-on-Sea platoon reveal a similar ignorance, leading to telephone drill in 'The Lion Has Phones'.[101]

Perry and Croft did not acknowledge their use of such accounts directly. They usually replied to viewers along the following lines: 'Many thanks for your letter. I am so glad you are enjoying the series. Your reminiscences and those of the many members of the public who have written to us, are a great encouragement to us, and I hope you will continue to watch the series.'[102] Croft frequently stated that he and Perry had already written or were planning an episode along the lines indicated, for example in relation to suggestions involving a home-made armoured car ('The Armoured Might of Lance Corporal Jones') and women and the Home Guard ('Mum's Army').[103] Presumably these responses were intended to protect the BBC from claims of appropriation of intellectual property and fee liability, at the same time as enabling Perry and Croft to select freely from this rich store of personal memories. Viewers' responses suggested that *Dad's Army*'s articulation of public with personal memories was successful. The process exemplifies the theory of the cultural circuit: individuals' particular experiences were given generalised rendition in the public narrative of the television show. Mainwaring, Wilson and 'wide-boy' Walker were all 'recognised' by viewers recalling either the Home Guard specifically or the Second World War context more generally. For example Mr J. J. Burton wrote: 'We had a Captain "Mainwaring" remarkably like the character in the show but he managed the local co-op not a bank'; and Miss Reed, referring to her experiences at an ARP post, said: 'Mr John le Mesurier was my first aid instructor – in every way – appearance and voice and manner.'[104]

Perry and Croft deliberately – and selectively – cultivated the credibility of their characters. Perry identified the originals of at least three of them in his own wartime encounters. His first CO in the Watford Home Guard had been 'the manager of a Watford bulding society and was short and round, rather like Captain Mainwaring. He was always fussing and inspecting things.' He was also vain and status-conscious, but 'if it had come to the push, he'd have been as brave as anyone else'. This man was succeeded by a Major Strong, whose enthusiasm 'verged on the fanatical': he had served in the International Brigade in the Spanish Civil War, 'had no time for "Blimp tactics"', 'was a seasoned guerilla fighter' who 'hated Fascism' and gave the men lectures on the fairer and more equal society to be achieved after the war. While this character may have lent something to Mainwaring's commitment to the cause and willingness to try guerilla methods, Perry de-selected his radicalism: Mainwaring's patriotism and approach to social class are deeply conservative.[105] Perry built the character of Frank Pike on his own persona in the Home Guard: young, obsessed with cars and guns, and fussed over by a protective mother.[106] The model for Jones was a former regular soldier who repeatedly regaled the Watford Home Guard with old-soldier yarns, notably his memories of the Battle of Omdurman in 1898. Perry also endowed Jones with the sayings of a First World War veteran at the training camp to which he was sent when he was finally called up to the army. This man accompanied his instruction in bayonet drill with the words 'They don't like it up 'em', which Perry made Jones's catch-phrase.[107]

The casting augmented personal connections with the past. All the key actors had had military experience in the First and/or the Second Wars, apart from Ian Lavender (Pike) and James Beck (Walker) who were too young (although Beck had done National Service). John Laurie (Frazer) had, like Perry, been in the Home Guard, where he said nothing ever happened. Clive Dunn (at 48 in 1967 much younger than Corporal Jones, the 70-year-old character he played) had been a prisoner of war in an Austrian labour camp from 1941 to 1945 and spoke of acting in *Dad's Army* as a form of revenge, although it is not clear whether he meant revenge on the Germans or on incompetent military figures like Jones. John le Mesurier (Sergeant Wilson) was a captain in the Royal Armoured Corps on the North West Frontier in the Second World War and decided to play his part in the same casual and apologetic manner he had adopted as an army officer. Arnold Ridley (Private Godfrey) had been an army major, involved in both the Battle of the Somme in 1917 and the evacuation of Dunkirk in 1940. Arthur Lowe (Mainwaring) had served in the Middle East as an army sergeant major in the Second World War. Perry and Croft were conscious of the abundant military experience possessed by the cast and, so they said, regarded the distinction between the Home Guard and the army as less important than the re-creation of authentic military relationships, styles and attitudes: they encouraged the actors 'to draw on any memories which might help them to add the odd distinguishing detail'.[108]

This high level of personal involvement in the production, between the authors, the actors and the viewers, owed something to the democratic methods of the Theatre Workshop, even though Perry and Croft did not encourage improvisation or involve the actors in scriptwriting. The result was a recognisable version of a past presented in a way that was satisfying to recall whether it was read satirically or sentimentally. Over time the series itself became a source of nostalgia: its familiarity meant that audiences could anticipate where it would take them but nevertheless enjoy the journey. In November 1974 Stanley Reynolds wrote that it was 'as comfortable as an old shoe ... but still it retains its comic edge'.[109]

Conclusion

In *Dad's Army*, representations of the Home Guard, in particular, and of the Second World War, in general, resonated with personal memories, both those of Perry and his cast, and of their early viewers. Locally told accounts of personal experience became, through Perry and Croft's creative processes, public accounts, embodied in easily-recognised characters who were, nevertheless, more than stereotypes. Each episode expressed a cluster of specific and general meanings about the British and about the Second World War. The cultural traffic was busy.

The genre, television comedy, shaped the generation of meanings about the Home Guard by concentrating characterisation and interaction within the tight frame of the thirty-minute episode on the small screen. It was distinct from the films, cartoons and comic sketches of wartime, yet the interpretation of the Home Guard that *Dad's Army* offered was largely consistent with the earlier sceptical and satirical treatments: unity was menaced by rivalries and class tensions; the Home Guard's task was to protect Britain against invasion but there were doubts about its ability to do so; the force may have been game, but was also playing at soldiering, as women occasionally pointed out. Perry and Croft gave their unmilitary characters origins, current circumstances and adventures, worked up from various sources of personal testimony, that made them live for their audiences.

Historical 'accuracy' was closely observed, yet *Dad's Army* represented, as we have seen, a selective version of Home-Guard history. Most notably it omitted the Home Guard's achievement of military efficiency, preferring for the purposes of comedy to render it an armed and uniformed but forever aged and incompetent force. Women members were included in only one of the eighty episodes, and the interpretation underlined the inappropriateness of the Woman Home Guard Auxiliary: she represented nothing less than a threat to male cohesion. *Dad's Army* thus offered an account of the Home Guard in the Second World War that was at the same time radical and conservative. It owed to *Oh! What a Lovely War* a deep scepticism about military authority and competence, expressed in the treatment of Mainwaring's comic and pathetic leadership, and extended through him to the Home Guard as a whole; yet it also celebrated Mainwaring's valour and patriotism. Its 'feel-good' message was that national unity was not torn apart by local rivalries, just as British victory was never seriously threatened by the enemy, in spite of the Home Guard's hopelessness.

The most remarkable aspect of the production was its success in combining the diametrically opposed ways in which the Home Guard had been represented in wartime: that is, as a key part of an heroic war effort and as a dubious contributor to an insecure project. The result was that *Dad's Army* appealed both to national pride in the Second World War as a period of British greatness and unity and to scepticism of war, military endeavour and authority. *Dad's Army* could work in the dual registers of nostalgia and satire, firstly, because it was not about the 'pathetic, comic yet valorous' RAF, Army or Navy, but about the Home Guard which audiences knew was never called on to defend Britain against invasion, and, secondly, because Britain and the allies were not defeated. It represents the humour of the victors rather than the vanquished, within a culture that (still) enjoys laughing at itself: it is hard to imagine it as a cultural possibility in a society that had been defeated in war. Yet *Dad's Army* does not offer a strong interpretation of the British war effort as such. Although it depicts the wartime environment with great specificity, occurrences such as air-raids, evacuation, rationing and the call-up constitute the background rather than the focus of the action. The meanings attributed to them are, as a result, much the same as those with which the Home Guard is endowed. The Second World War is, by implication, a just war against a real (though mostly unseen) enemy. It is waged by well-meaning but not very competent people, who muddle through and triumph in the end, not because they are well organised or more efficient than the enemy, but because they are (somehow) intrinsically better. As with the Home Guard, so with the British at war, the *Dad's Army* interpretation could be read either as criticism or as celebration. It was this feat of cultural mastery that enabled *Dad's Army* to make an indelible mark not only on the history of the Home Guard but on representations of home defence across time, and to have a profound influence on understandings of the British war effort.

Notes

1 See G. McCann, *Dad's Army: The Story of a Classic Television Show* (London: Fourth Estate, 2001), p. 120 (for peak-viewing figure), and pp. 111, 112, 194, 196, 199 (for averages and comparisons).

2 J. Storey, *Cultural Theory and Popular Culture* (Harlow: Pearson, 2001), p. 165. *Dad's Army* was adapted for radio and stage, and recorded on vinyl records, audio and video tapes, and DVDs. *Dad's Army* books, annuals, guides, histories, scripts and extensions of the story have been published. Games, puzzles and models extend the fantasy. There are websites and appreciation societies and a *Dad's Army* museum at Diss in Norfolk, where the on-location filming of the show was done: McCann, *Dad's Army*, pp. 222–223.

3 IWM, SA, 11225, interview with Jimmy Perry, 15 May 1990. Repeats were shown on television throughout the 1980s and 1990s. The thirtieth anniversary of the first series, in 1998, increased media references both to the programme and to the Home Guard. See C. Peniston-Bird, 'Will the Real Captain Mainwaring Please Stand Up: *Dad's Army* between Media and Memory', unpublished paper presented at the conference 'Media History and History in the Media', Gregynog, west Wales, April 2005.

4 See D. Thomas, *An Underworld at War: Spivs, Deserters, Racketeers and Civilians in the Second World War* (London: John Murray, 2003); D. Hughes,

'The Spivs', in M. Sissons and P. French (eds), *The Age of Austerity 1945–51* (Harmondsworth: Penguin, 1964).

5 Jimmy Perry, *A Stupid Boy: The Autobiography of the Creator of Dad's Army* (London: 2002), pp. 90–113; Perry interview.

6 Perry interview; also R. Webber, *Dad's Army: A Celebration* (London: Virgin, 1999), p. 12.

7 Perry, *Stupid Boy*, p. 101; the cartoons were not those of Captain F. Saxon which were deposited in February 1975.

8 John Pym (ed.), *Time Out Film Guide*, 8th edition (London: Time Out, 1999), pp. x and 596; *Blimp* was twenty-third.

9 Other films with a post-war life, such as *Went the Day Well?* and *A Canterbury Tale*, presented the Home Guard as part of the wartime scene, but their focus lay elsewhere. There is no evidence that wartime historical accounts, e.g. Graves's *The Home Guard of Britain* and Radnor's *It All Happened Before*, continued to sell after their initial publication. The after-life of the crime fiction discussed in Chapters 4 and 5 was probably also the shadowy one of the library shelves (even if Perry did not find those books there).

10 According to Mackenzie, *rèiteach* was Gaelic for a betrothal celebration in which whisky is an essential component.

11 This is true of the Screenonline and Britmovie summaries: www.screenonline. org.uk/film/id/441458; www.britmovie.co.uk/studios/ealing/filmography/53. html (both accessed 5 December 2003). The account of the film in Pym (ed.), *Time Out Film Guide*, p. 1160, omits any reference to the Home Guard.

12 MacKenzie, *Home Guard*, pp. 157–173.

13 Neb, *Daily Mail*, 19 July 1950, 31 July 1950; Joseph Lee, *Evening News*, 21 July 1950, 8, 22, 26 November 1951.

14 Neb, *Daily Mail*, 27 July 1950.

15 *Picture Post*, 2 October 1954 'Do We need a Home Guard?' by Kenneth Allsop.

16 For a rare reference see *Daily Herald*, 9 August 1962.

17 J. Perry and D. Croft, *Dad's Army: The Lost Episodes* (London: Virgin 1998), p. 7; Webber, *Dad's Army*, p. 11; McCann, *Dad's Army*, p. 36; Perry interview.

18 Joan Littlewood, born in 1914, pioneered political and community theatre involving improvisation and the use of working-class language through her Theatre Workshop, based from 1953 in east London: John Ezard and Michael Billington, 'Joan Littlewood: Obituary', *Guardian*, 23 September 2002.

19 Webber, *Dad's Army*, p. 11.

20 These included the film *I Only Arsked* (1958) and two more television series, *Bootsie and Snudge* (1960–63) and *Foreign Affairs* (1964); *The Army Game* was also said to have influenced the *Carry On …* films of the 1950s and 1960s.

21 See www.phill.co.uk/comedy/armygame (accessed 10 October 2003); ITV may have been inspired to sponsor *The Army Game* in part because of the success of the American *Phil Silvers Show*, broadcast by CBS in the USA from 1955 to 1959, and shown in Britain in the 1950s and 1960s: Martin Wainwright, 'Bilko Named Best Ever Comedy', *Guardian*, 30 September 2003; also see:

www.cbsnews.com/stories/2003/09/29/entertainment/printable575634.shtml (accessed 10 October 2003).

22 Use of 'wallop' (soldiers' slang for beer) was also related to the Home Guard in 'Cilias's' comic verse *Careless Talk*, reproduced in *Home Guard Rhymes* (1942), p. 11.

23 The final conscript left in 1963. As in the case of compulsory recruitment to the Home Guard, men in Northern Ireland were exempt, as also were Black and Asian men living in Britain: T. Royle, *The Best years of Their Lives: The National Service Experience 1945–63* (London: Michael Joseph, 1986); D. H. J. Morgan, 'It Will Make a Man of You: Notes on National Service, Masculinity and Autobiography', *Studies in Sexual Politics*, No. 17 (Manchester: Department of Sociology, University of Manchester, 1987).

24 Webber, *Dad's Army*, p. 11. Other 'service comedies' included *The Navy Lark*, a spoof of life in the Royal Navy set sometime after the war, BBC Radio,1959–1977, and *Get Some In*, ITV 1975–1978, about national servicemen in the R.A.F.

25 McCann, *Dad's Army*, p. 38. Hay was the star of nineteen films between 1934 and 1943. 'He was always the figure of total incompetence, engulfed in all the trappings of authority, surrounded by sidekicks who were full of high spirits and stupidity': http://homepage.ntlworld.com/trevor.buckingham/willhay1.htm (accessed 10 October 2003).

26 Webber, *Dad's Army*, p. 13.

27 Perry decided on Lowe early on, but the BBC was reluctant because he had worked mainly for ITV, notably as Leonard Swindley, in *Coronation Street*: see McCann, *Dad's Army*, p. 130; Webber, *Dad's Army*, pp. 19–20.

28 See http://homepage.ntlworld.com/trevor.buckingham/willhay1.htm (accessed 10 October 2003).

29 Lines from *Dad's Army*, Episode 20, 'The Day the Balloon Went Up', 30 October 1969, reiterated with variations in many episodes.

30 Episode 75, 'Wake Up Walmington', 2 October 1977.

31 Perry, *Stupid Boy*, p. 105.

32 In Episode 9, 'The Loneliness of the Long Distance Walker', 15 March 1969, when Walker is finally called up he is rejected because he has an allergy to the staple of the army's diet, corned beef.

33 McCann, *Dad's Army*, pp. 39–40.

34 Perry appeared only once, in Episode Six, 'Shooting Pains', 1 September 1968.

35 McCann, *Dad's Army*, pp. 204, 216, 222.

36 Episode 17, 'Something Nasty in the Vault', 9 October 1969.

37 Examples include Episode 29, 'Boots, Boots, Boots', 9 October 1970; Episode 14, 'Battle School', 18 September 1969; Episode 50, 'Brain Versus Brawn', 8 December 1972; Episode 66, 'Turkey Dinner', 23 December 1974; Episode 26, 'Sons of the Sea', 11 December 1969.

38 Episode 57, 'We Know Our Onions', 21 November 1973; Episode 13, 'The Armoured Might of Lance Corporal Jones', 11 September 1969; Episode 7, 'Operation Kilt', 1 March 1969.

39 Episodes involving confrontations with Germans include: 15, 'The Lion Has Phones' 25 September 1969; 24, 'Man Hunt' 27 November 1969; 53, 'Time On My Hands' 29 December 1972; 54, 'The Deadly Attachment', 31 October 1973; 70, 'Come In, Your Time Is Up', 26 September 1975. In the film *Dad's Army: The Movie* (dir. N. Cohen; prod. J. R. Sloan, Columbia, UK, 1971) a group of German soldiers imprisons the townspeople in the church until the platoon, dressed as choristers, comes to the rescue.

40 E.g. Episode 7, 'Operation Kilt', 1 March 1969, and in Episode 52, 'Round and Round Went the Great Big Wheel', 22 December 1972.

41 Episode 16, 'The Bullet Is Not For Firing', 2 October 1969; Episode 12, 'Under Fire', 5 April 1969.

42 Drink also exposes the upright Mainwaring's feet of clay: along with the treacle and other home comforts, obtained for him by Walker, is whisky. When provoked, Walker reminds him publicly that whisky does not fall off the back of a lorry; it has to be pushed: Episode 17, 'Something Nasty in the Vault', 9 October 1969.

43 Episode 39, 'Fallen Idol', 18 December 1970, and at least two other examples: Episode 66, 'Turkey Dinner', 23 December 1974; and Episode 55, 'My British Buddy', 7 November 1973.

44 Episode 35, 'Mum's Army', 20 November 1970.

45 E.g. in Episode 75, 'Wake Up Walmington', 2 October 1977, Mainwaring capitulates to Elizabeth on receiving a stentorian phone call; her bulk is indicated by a bulge in a bunk in Episode 43, 'A Soldier's Farewell', 20 October 1972, and by her heavy footfalls in Episode 47, 'The King Was in His Counting House', 17 November 1972.

46 IWM, PA, HU 36 277, 'A member of the local Home Guard gives rifle instruction to a member of the Watford Woman's Home Defence Unit': see this book's cover.

47 BBC, WAC, T12/880/1, Dad's Army, General, Letters from: Miss A. J. Reed, August 9 1968; Mr R. A. Fletcher, 15 July 1970; Mrs D. M. Kleyn, 5 September 1968.

48 McCann, *Dad's Army*, pp. 70, 161. E.g. in Episode 8 the platoon has been ordered to go to see *Next of Kin*, an official film of 1942; the title of Episode 15, 'The Lion Has Phones', 25 September 1969, is a skit on the 1939 propaganda feature film *The Lion Has Wings*; and that of Episode 31, 'Don't Fence Me In', 23 October 1970, borrows from the well-known Cole Porter song recorded by the Andrews Sisters in July 1944.

49 Perry, *Stupid Boy*, pp. 66–67.

50 Perry interview.

51 Perry and Croft, *Dad's Army*, p. 9, repeated in *A Stupid Boy*, p. 100, and in radio and television interviews.

52 E.g. Ron Boyle, 'Give it a Week or Two and I'll Tell You Whether This Is Really Comedy's Finest Half-Hour', *Daily Express*, 1 August 1968; quoted in McCann, *Dad's Army*, p. 88.

53 McCann, *Dad's Army*, pp. 43–46.

54 Tom Sloan, 'Television Light Entertainment' (London: BBC, 1969), a publication arising from a BBC lunch-time lecture delivered on 11 December 1969; quoted in McCann, *Dad's Army*, pp. 46–47.

55 Episode 26, 'Sons of the Sea', 11 December 1969.

56 BBC, WAC, T12/880/1, Michael Mills, Head of Comic Light Entertainment, to Controller, BBC1, 23 May 1968.

57 This was what Fox himself believed. See McCann, *Dad's Army*, p. 79.

58 BBC, WAC, T12/880/1, 23 May 1968, Michael Mills, Head of Comic Light Entertainment, to Controller, BBC1.

59 Episode 54, 'The Deadly Attachment', 31 October 1973.

60 This scene came first in a poll of television's 'favourite comedy moments' conducted by *Classic Television Magazine*, 22 June 1999, and topped a BBC internet poll of 1,000 people in February 2002 as 'the funniest TV line of all time': http://www.chortle.co.uk/news/feb02/pike.html (4 March 2002).

61 By Wilson, who earlier disobeyed Mainwaring's command to make the grenades 'live' in order to avoid accidents.

62 There is hardly an episode out of the eighty in which Jones does not volunteer for something daring, usually with dire consequences. Thus, in Episode 7, 'Operation Kilt', 1 March 1969, he offers to be a decoy and ends up dangling upside down from a rope.

63 Episode 42, 'Keep Young and Beautiful', 6 October 1972 (Mainwaring to Wilson, 'I too have taken some steps to look a little more – a little more virile.'); Episode 67, 'Ring Dem Bells', 5 September 1975.

64 The main object of rivalry is the church hall, used by home defence, civil defence and of course the church, e.g. Episode 38, 'Uninvited Guests', 11 December 1970. The three groups are frequently in competition over which should take precedence at civic events: e.g. the visit of a Russian statesman in Episode 58, 'The Honourable Man', 28 November 1973; and the honouring of a Free French General in Episode 65, 'The Captain's Car', 13 December 1974.

65 Paul Waggett, Laird of Snorvig on Great Todday and Home Guard Captain, in Compton Mackenzie's novels *Keep the Home Guard Turning* and *Whisky Galore*, expresses similar sentiments with parallel comic pomposity.

66 Episode 66, 'Turkey Dinner', 23 December 1974.

67 E.g. Episode 55, 'My British Buddy', 7 November 1973, when a contingent of US troops arrives and Wilson says: 'Of course, you see, we're not real soldiers'; and Episode 75, 'Wake Up Walmington', 2 October 1977, when Mainwaring and his men are told: 'This firing range is for real soldiers not Home Guard.'

68 Episode 8, 'The Battle of Godfrey's Cottage', 8 March 1969. Mainwaring's heroism is in the event shortlived: the German forces they think they have encountered turn out to be Wilson, Walker and Pike, who had not gone to the cinema either, and the church bells had, of course, sounded a false alarm.

69 Alfred Hicklin, 'Ooh-La-La, There Go My Trousers', *Guardian*, 24 September 2003.

70 When Mainwaring allows Frazer to replace him as the head of the platoon rather than put up with his grumbling any longer, the men eventually rally round their original leader: Episode 46, 'If the Cap Fits …', 10 November 1972.

71 Notably in Episode 37, 'A. Wilson (Manager)?', 4 December 1970; Episode 58, 'The Honorable Man', 28 November 1973; Episode 65, 'The Captain's Car', 13 December 1974.

72 Perry, *Stupid Boy*, p. 259, caption to photograph of Littlewood. In fact Perry claimed not to have understood Joan's left-wing approach even though there is 'no doubt that she was my mentor, as it was during my time with her that I started writing': Perry, *Stupid Boy*, p. 260.

73 *Oh! What a Lovely War* (dir. Richard Attenborough, prod. Brian Duffy, Accord Productions, UK, 1969).

74 B. Bond, *The Unquiet Western Front: Britain's Role in Literature and History* (Cambridge: Cambridge University Press, 2002), p. 65.

75 *The Goon Show*, BBC Radio, 1951–60; J. Heller, *Catch-22* (London: Jonathan Cape, 1962); S. Milligan, *Adolf Hitler: My Part in His Downfall* (London: Michael Joseph, 1971).

76 *Dad's Army*, Episode 1, 'The Man and the Hour', 13 July 1968, begins with a prologue, in which Mainwaring and the men meet at a dinner in the present day (1968) to support the 'I'm Backing Britain' campaign, 'to reassure the viewers that the show wasn't going to be sending up our finest hour': Croft quoted in McCann, *Dad's Army*, p. 81.

77 BBC, WAC, T12/880/1, *Bath & Wiltshire Evening Chronicle*, 15 August 1968.

78 *The Times*, 1 August 1968, col. E, p. 7, Michael Billington, 'Honest Frontier Drama'.

79 *The Times*, 8 February 1969, col. B, p. 19, Henry Raynor, 'What Are You Laughing At?' and 'Jokes and People'

80 *The Times*, 15 November 1969, col. E, p. vi, Leonard Buckley, 'Politics Are No Joke'; 17 March 1971, col. B, p. 10, 'Tripartite Arrangement'; 7 April 1971, col. A, p. 4, Henry Stanhope, 'TAVR Recruits 2,000 in Less Than a Week' ('with none of the *Dad's Army* image'), 7 April 1971, col. A, p. 4.

81 R. Weight, *Patriots: National Identity in Britain 1940–2000* (London: Macmillan, 2002), pp. 520–523.

82 *The Times*, 29 January 1974, col. E, p. 11, Leonard Buckley, 'Carrie's War'.

83 For example, *The Times*, 1 November 1973, col. F, p. 13, Alan Coren, 'Dad's Army'; 4 February 1974, col. G, p. 13, Letters to the editor, John Mander: 'we are obsessed with a good fight we once fought and, thankfully, won'; 19 February 1974, col. E, p. 15, Stanley Reynolds, '*Dad's Army* is nostalgia done properly.'

84 For example, *The Times*, 15 September 1971, col. G, p. 15, Letters to the editor, 'The Sorrow and the Pity': Mr R. A. Clegg asserted that the British would not have 'acted the same way as the French if there had been an invasion of Britain' because 'there was a difference – "Dad's Army"'; see also *The Times*, 31 January 1974, col. E, p. 2, 'Ex-Officer Rallies Aides for "Dad's Army"'.

85 J. Richards, '"Dad's Army" and the Politics of Nostalgia', in J. Richards, *Films and British National Identity: From Dickens to Dad's Army* (Manchester: Manchester University Press, 1997), pp. 360, 365, 366.

86 S. Jeffries, *Mrs Slocombe's Pussy: Growing Up in Front of the Telly* (London: Flamingo, 2001), p. 37.

87 M. Connelly, *We Can Take It: Britain and the Memory of the Second World War* (Harlow: Pearson Education, 2004), pp. 78–79. Connelly's analysis is mainly of *Dad's Army The Movie*, rather than the television episodes, hence his focus on 1940 and also on the 'potent use of landscape', which does not feature strongly in the series.

88 Connelly recognises the 'debunking' that also characterises *Dad's Army*, but argues that it 'actually buttressed the myth': Connelly, *We Can Take It*, p. 82.

89 The three test audiences on which the Audience Research Department piloted the show, however, *disliked* the emphasis on the war: Croft admitted that he 'suppressed the evidence' of their unfavourable reactions: McCann, *Dad's Army*, pp. 81–82.

90 BBC, WAC, T12/880/1, Letters from L. E. Tindall, 20 January 196[9]; Miss K Carruthers, 4 September 1968; J. W. Camp Esq. (.n.d., but after 3 September 1968).

91 BBC, WAC, T12/880/1, Letter from Mr J. Board, 7 September 1968.

92 BBC, WAC, T12/880/1, Correspondence with J. W. Camp Esq., 3 August and 3 September 1968.

93 BBC, WAC, T12/880/1, Letters from Barbara Summers, 19 August 1968; Mrs Isobel Pickering, 27 August 1968.

94 BBC, WAC, T12/880/1, Letter from Miss K. Carruthers, 5 September 1968.

95 BBC, WAC, T12/880/1, Correspondence with J. W. Camp Esq., 3 August and 3 September 1968.

96 BBC, WAC, T12/880/1, Letters from: Sonia Thurley, 8 August 1968; R. Fortescue-Foulkes, 9 August 1968; J. Board, 7 September 1968; Robert Huntley (n.d.); W. Perry, 18 June 1970.

97 Perry interview, 15 May 1990.

98 Webber, *Dad's Army*, p. 13; Episode 1, 'The Man and the Hour, 13 July 1968.

99 E.g., L. E. Tindall sent in details of seven funny incidents in which he was involved in the LDV and Home Guard, plus a memory of an incident during his pre-war service in the Army, in which a shot fired accidentally by a batman hit the latrine in which an officer was seated, written in script form: BBC, WAC, T12/880/1, *Dad's Army*, Letter from L. E. Tindall, dated 20 January 196[9].

100 BBC, WAC, T12/880/1, Letter from L. E.Tindall, dated 20 January 196[9]; *Dad's Army*, Episode 75, 'Wake Up Walmington', 2 October 1977.

101 BBC, WAC, T12/880/1, Letter from Mrs Barbara Summers, 19 August 1968; Episode 15, 'The Lion Has Phones', 25 September 1969.

102 BBC, WAC, T12/880/1, David Croft to Robert Huntley, 3 September 1968.

103 BBC, WAC, T12/880/1, Armoured car: correspondence with J. J.Burton, 16

August 1968. 'Mum's Army': correspondence with Mr R.A.Fletcher 15 July 1970. See Episode 13, 'The Armoured Might of Lance Corporal Jones', 11 September 1969; Episode 35, 'Mum's Army', 20 November 1970.

104 BBC, WAC, T12/880/1, Letters from J. J. Burton, 16 August 1968; Miss A. J. Reed, 9 August 1968; there were many other cases of 'recognition'.

105 Perry, *Stupid Boy*, pp. 93 and 98–99.

106 Perry interview, 15 May 1990: 'I was the boy Pike'; Perry and Croft, *Dad's Army*, p. 9.

107 Perry, *Stupid Boy*, pp. 94–96 and 128.

108 McCann, *Dad's Army*, pp. 75, 71, 58, 126, 59.

109 *The Times*, 16 November 1974, p. 9.

PART III

Personal testimony

7

Men's memories of the Home Guard

Wartime political rhetoric proclaimed confidently that the Home Guard was formed in an upsurge of patriotic passion to defend Britain against invasion, and that within two years it had become an effective military force. As we have seen, political leaders depicted it as a symbol of national unity and a key component of the British war effort, expressive of the wartime ethos of being 'all in it together' and providing opportunities for civilian men to 'do their bit'. Such representations were widely disseminated in wartime films, poetry, non-fiction and visual culture and were part of a rhetoric of persuasion according to which British traditions were worth fighting for and that British solidarity was sufficient to ensure victory.

However, this coherent account was challenged on many fronts. In Chapters 2 and 3 we discussed the social and political discrimination in recruitment that contradicted the Home Guard's much-vaunted inclusiveness. We also explored the profound differences in views of the Home Guard's military role and political purpose that cut across its standing as a metaphor for the united war effort. In Chapter 4 we encountered a satirical strand in wartime popular culture that expressed scepticism about the achievement of unity in the Home Guard and the nation, criticism of the inadequacies of the Government's efforts to equip and train the Home Guard as a counter-invasion force, and doubts about the capacity of its members to fight. Doubts about military effectiveness, which in a war context also concerned the manliness of Home Guards, were triggered by the slow advent of weapons and uniforms for them, their deployment on static guard duties, and the condition that only those who were ineligible for the armed forces could join. Wartime humorists exploited the notion that, however patriotic, Home Guards were not 'proper soldiers'. More than two decades later *Dad's Army* built its success on the elaboration of this idea. Women's struggles to participate fully in organised home defence had been, as we saw in Chapter 5, almost entirely ignored in popular culture, for all that individual women were permitted exceptional roles on a temporary basis in some high-profile films. *Dad's Army*, like wartime representations of the Home Guard, placed women on the margins of the force as critics and commentators rather than comrades-in-arms.

In this chapter and the next we ask how men and women who had themselves served in the Home Guard recall their service. Our sources consist of various types of personal testimony drawn from 69 men and 32 women. Most of this material takes the form of oral-history interviews, either archived in the Imperial War Museum or conducted by ourselves, and of letters responding to our enquiries.[1] Since oral history is, thus, an important part of our evidence, it needs a brief introduction. There are two distinct approaches: in one, oral history is seen primarily as a means of retrieving hidden histories, and in the other it is regarded as occupying a position at the interface of memory and social and cultural change.

The first approach has placed oral history at the centre of 'recovery history'.[2] Oral history provides evidence of experiences of which little or no trace exists in more conventional historical archives (such as collections of ministerial and parliamentary records) and demonstrates that such sources often give partial accounts that ignore or misrepresent developments that ran counter to official policy. This is the case with the history of women's membership of the WHD and the Home Guard, an issue to which we return in the next chapter.

The other intellectual vantage point from which oral history is viewed is that of studies of social and cultural memory. This expanding field challenges the tendency to read personal testimony as a transparent window on the past, insisting that the analysis of the cultural mediation of remembered experiences is an important aspect of historical enquiry.[3] It assumes that memory is interpretative and creative. Personal-memory stories inform and are informed by history in the sense that they draw on and contribute to the collectively generated account or accounts of the past that are available within a society or community. They are narratives shaped by social conventions of story-telling and verbal expression. At the same time, they are deeply personal and individual, involving both conscious and unconscious processes of sifting, accepting and rejecting aspects of a self formed by its past.[4] The cultural-memory approach therefore focuses attention on the complex and multiple ways in which people recall and tell their personal histories, identifying for analysis, rather than rejection, a number of aspects that have been seen by critics as invalidating oral history as a source: omission and inaccuracy; accounts that serve the ends of the teller; the influence on the narrator of the interviewer; and the interactions of popular culture with personal memory. It highlights a number of themes, including the interplay of memory with representations of the past that are popularly available; the choice of narrative forms; the personal satisfaction or discomfort that narrators get from telling their stories; the dynamics of the relationship of narrators to their audiences; and the personal re-evaluation that can accompany an individual's reconstruction of his or her past. Concepts that are used to describe these underlying processes of oral history include the cultural circuit, composure, intersubjectivity and life review.[5]

We met the idea of the cultural circuit in Chapter 6, when discussing the contribution of personal memories to the representation of the Home Guard and the Second World War in *Dad's Army*. As we saw, *Dad's Army* was inevitably selective, studded with omissions and emphases dictated by the nature of the cultural product, and by ideological and artistic choices. We traced the inclusion, through a process of translation, of locally told personal stories in *Dad's Army*'s public version of the past. But theorists of popular memory suggest that the circuit also works the other way round: individuals borrow from the versions of the past that circulate in the public domain, when making sense of and expressing their personal pasts. Graham Dawson argues that public accounts tend to impose constraints on recall: they 'limit imaginative possibilities' for recalling past subjectivities and composing narratives about them.[6] Al Thomson illustrates this idea with interviews of of Australian First World War veterans, conducted in the 1980s, who described episodes from the film *Gallipoli*, released in 1981, as if they had personally experienced them.[7] But the process is complicated: public discourses are never unified and free from contradiction: unconscious selection and conscious preferences interact in the composition of life stories. Furthermore, there are more than two points on the cultural circuit: it is also linked with the reception of what is told. Audiences for memory stories may be small and casual, as well as larger and more formal; in either case they are likely to affirm recognisable accounts that match what they *know* of the past, but to be less receptive to those that are not consistent with such representations.

In this chapter we explore the use by, and the usefulness to, men recalling their own Home Guard service, of the wartime construction of the Home Guard as a symbol of the British war effort. In particular, we examine men's take up of serious and sceptical treatments of the Home Guard as an anti-invasion force and as a site of masculine solidarity. And we end by discussing the role of *Dad's Army* in the composition of personal memories of Home Guard service.

Recalling unity

The idea of a nation united by war and of the Home Guard as a specific site of wartime togetherness and of commitment to the war effort, was, as we have seen, a major component of official rhetoric and popular culture. The take up of such ideas by men recalling their Home Guard experiences was pronounced, on the part both of those who accepted them and of others who challenged them.

Men who reconstructed their wartime subjectivities using the language of national unity and the war effort included several who joined the Home Guard under-age as well as others for whom alternative forms of military service were not an option. They described their motivation in terms of their desire as very young men to be involved in the military war effort. Ray Atkins, who was working in the publicity department of the Co-operative Wholesale Society in Manchester, was one of several interviewees who was accepted under-age by the Home Guard: Atkins joined in 1941, aged 16, before his call up to the army in 1943, prompted by the news that the war was going badly:

> And it's simply that you felt that you'd got to do your bit, you'd definitely got to do something, you know. I mean it's all right as a child but if you were growing up and you knew you'd got two years to wait before you went in the army, you see, so you felt you had to do something, to be honest.[8]

Men who were unable to serve in the military for reasons other than age used similar language. Victor Waterhouse, a building apprentice in Burwash, Sussex, contracted meningitis in 1941, when he was 17, and so was rejected on medical grounds by the army. He wrote: 'I felt I was doing "my bit" in the Home Guard as I was unfit for National Service.'[9] On the other hand, to be excluded from the army for failing its medical tests, and also to be discharged from the Home Guard on health grounds, was deeply humiliating. Nigel Grey, who joined the Home Guard in Hounslow, Middlesex, in 1940, when he was a 16-year-old trainee tailor, was found to have a heart condition when he was called up two years later:

> I was reject material, likewise for National Service (factories, mines, etc.) and even the canteen services wouldn't touch a heart case ... the HG doctor

tracked it all down, then recommended me for discharge from the HG. It was devastating to feel so unwanted in a time of national crisis.[10]

The evaluation of membership of the Home Guard in such accounts was positive. Grey called it 'a most worthwhile experience', and Tex Laws, who joined the Home Guard as a 17–year-old Post Office messenger-boy in Battersea in 1941, wrote: 'The experience of comradeship and joint effort by fellow workers was well worthwhile; we were in this together and doubtless would have done our bit if required.'[11] The reiteration of phrases such as 'doing your bit' and 'all in it together' suggests that in these cases the dominant historical discourse supplied 'the very terms by which a private history is thought through'.[12]

Such recall produced a strong sense of satisfaction: it contributed to the 'composure' of the interviewee. This concept is used by cultural oral historians to indicate the dual process at work in an interview: the composition of a life story and the achievement of psychic comfort, or personal composure, by the narrator. Public discourse provides the necessary cultural context for such 'composure'. Ray Atkins, from Manchester, was explicit about the personal equanimity that he achieved through recalling his Home Guard service in terms of the discourse of wartime national unity:

> Thinking about it now always takes me straight back to the feeling of how things once were in this country ... All of the British population had this feeling of being in it together and backs to the wall and all that. So that if I do think about the Home Guard I think of that feeling I had about, you know, all pulling together, all working together, you know. And from that point of view – it's not that bad a feeling, you know.[13]

Those who framed their memories in such terms tended to underline the warm glow by contrasting the war years with a present that had lost those qualities. Atkins's reference to 'how things once were' evokes a clear sense of loss: past cohesion and youthful camaraderie contrast with a more fractured present and the relative isolation of old age. He was not alone. Bill Trueman joined the Home Guard in 1941 just before he became 17, while in a reserved occupation as an apprenticed wagon-builder at the Great Western Railway in Swindon. He wrote:

> Being involved with the Home Guard gave me a lot of respect and confidence, while appreciating the friendship created and having more trust in other people, unfortunately now we seem to be missing this, and the whole amount of comradeship created then is getting to be something of the past.[14]

Such assessments of 'then' and 'now' were an integral part of the life review these men were undertaking when recalling the Home Guard. In evaluating their Home Guard service and its place in their lives as a whole, they drew with no apparent reservations on the idea that the Second World War was Britain's 'finest hour' in which the Home Guard played a significant part.

Several men substantiated the notion of 'all pulling together' with details of the social mix they had found in the Home Guard. Echoing the 'lists' used in wartime representations of its social diversity, Christopher Redmond, an apprentice draftsman living in Wootton, near Oxford, described his unit as comprised of 'all sorts, there were butchers, there were bakers, there were labourers, there were bookies, there were all sorts of people, doctors'.[15] Fred Whitlow, an apprentice draftsman at the Mersey Power Company, in Liverpool, emphasised the Home Guard's role in breaking down class barriers. Prior to the war,

> there was a sort of class distinction business, and because I worked in the drawing office, I was on the staff, whereas the lads who were electricians working on the tools were on what they call the 'pay-roll'. And there was a line drawn between the two, you see. ... So when we joined the Home Guard the lads who were on the pay-roll we didn't know very well because we'd never mixed with them. We knew all the blokes in the office who ran the staff. So one good thing that came out of it was [that] you got to know them, you know, and make friends with them, you see. And a lot of this class distinction business went overboard, and that was one of the good things that came out of the war really.[16]

But memories of wartime collaboration across class also evoked occasions when unity was not achieved. Whitlow may have remembered that 'a lot of this class distinction business went overboard' but he also confessed that he and a colleague were promoted in the Home Guard purely because they were 'on the staff', and he recalled that the platoon commander was also the boss of the Mersey Power Company.[17] However, rank and its coincidence with class was sometimes cast as unproblematic on the grounds that in the Home Guard everyone 'mucked in, there was no class distinction';[18] and the embeddedness of the force in the local community was felt to foster this solidarity. Cyril Hall, who was working at a bakery in Gainsborough, Lincolnshire, during the first years of the war and joined the Home Guard in 1942, at the age of 29, contrasted it with his later experience in the army of what he saw as individualism:

> There is a difference, in as much as in the Home Guard you were all men. You hadn't been called up, as a soldier. You were giving your time to the

Home Guard, you see. And you even knew your officer ... Your own officer could be, would be, perhaps, one of your customers. So, I mean, there was a lot of friendliness in the Home Guard, but in the army, well, everybody was there to look after himself.[19]

However, Whitlow was not the only interviewee to note the persistence of class effects in the Home Guard. Contrasting with the rosy and nostalgic picture painted by those who regarded the Second World War (for all its horrors) as a better time to be alive than the present, were those accounts thoroughly sceptical of claims of wartime national unity. They focused on a set of social tensions.

James Kendall, a skilled fitter working on admiralty commissions at Rose Brothers' machine factory in Gainsborough, joined the Home Guard in August 1940 at the age of 30. His criticisms of the link between class and rank in the Home Guard echo the wartime public allegations of social preference that we encountered in Chapter 2. Although Kendall enjoyed his time in the Home Guard, 'I didn't like the commander, you see. He, they called him Captain Shaw, he was from Thatchby. He was a, I think he was a solicitor. He'd pots of money, [or] appeared to have ... To me he was ... not very efficient and ... he seemed to run the job ... for his own pleasure kind of thing.'[20] Kendall believed that Shaw had been 'asked by the Government' to form a River Patrol, because of his wealth and social standing, and because he owned a river launch. He went on to give some horrific examples of this man's lack of leadership skills: while on the water, he commanded the men to throw a coiled rope to another boat, seriously endangering the unsuspecting crew; then a man was killed under his command in an incident involving a Lewis gun:

We got this Lewis gun, and he gave it to a chap who wasn't proficient at all in ... handling machinery. We were mechanics, and we was hoping that one of us would get this machine-gun. We didn't. He gave it to a chap who hadn't a clue.[21]

The man got a live bullet stuck in the breech and, in his efforts to dislodge it, shot and killed another officer who was coming to help him. Kendall's disgust at such tragic incompetence, as well as his dislike of the high-handed attitude towards him of a young lieutenant, led him to leave Shaw's unit and join a Home Guard Signals company attached to his workplace. His account of this experience was more positive, mainly because the officers, who had served in the First World War, earned his respect, and because he was mixing with fellow-workers: this was a meaningful and democratic (if also sometimes comic) Home Guard unit, as opposed to the ineffectual and badly led River Patrol.[22]

Men remembered other unresolved social tensions which suggested that the unity rhetoric was at best an oversimplification. In 1941 Arthur Brown enrolled, aged 16 (and therefore, like Atkins and Grey, underage), in the Home Guard in central London, while he was working as a trainee chef. Then, when he quit cooking and became a storekeeper at a Royal Ordnance Factory in Donnington, Shropshire, he joined a unit there. He perceived a huge difference between the smartly turned-out and well-trained London Area Home Guard and the Shropshire force. Brown described himself as a 'city-slicker down amongst the hicks!'[23] The Shropshire unit was made up mainly of 'yokels, locals',[24] among whom were men he described as 'old sweats' who had learned to keep their heads down in the First World War: far from seeking promotion from the ranks themselves, 'they never accepted a stripe' because 'you don't get any money for being a lance-corporal, but you get a lot of abuse' – with the result that, ironically, the 17-year-old Brown 'was more or less fêted' for his 'self-sacrifice' when he was made a corporal.[25] His popularity may have been for taking on unwanted responsibility, but in general there were tensions between the Shropshire men and the outsiders that were not overcome by joint service. 'Londoners were not popular down there. "They take over our buses" and all this sort of thing.'[26]

Alfred Claxton, who joined the Home Guard in 1941 in the East End of London when he was a 16-year-old messenger-boy, had memories of racial difference. He said 'we only had one coloured chap, but there were no problems'. Speaking in 2000 after five decades of tension over the growing racial diversity of British society, he evidently felt the need to remark on potential 'problems' and explain their absence. He did so in terms of other kinds of social divisions: 'When you have accountants and different types and that, and not the labouring classes, no, they got on very well. I never found any bother, no sort of racial discrimination or anything like that.'[27]

Such recollections put the discourse of wartime unity into critical perspective: its achievement was patchy, given the social distinctions built into the Home Guard hierarchy, and in view of longstanding rural–urban tensions. The most thoroughgoing rebuttal in our sample of the celebratory language of the war effort was the account of agricultural labourer Leslie Revill, who worked on his father's farm in Lincolnshire throughout the war. He used wartime terminology to explain his voluntary enlistment in the Home Guard: 'It seemed to be your duty to do a bit, a bit more really than just your daily work', because 'the country was fighting for its life'.[28] But he emphasised from the beginning of the interview that he regretted having joined the Home Guard: 'I shouldn't do it again'.[29] We saw in Chapter 2 that compulsory Home Guard service was particularly disliked by agricultural labourers, and Revill's main declared reason for his disaffection was his job: 'we were having to work so hard on the land all hours'.[30] He remembered perpetual fatigue: 'Friday, I was absolutely done for. You'd ... a job to drag yourself out of bed the next morning.'.[31] He had no holidays throughout the war and he resented the sacrifice of his few opportunities for non-work activities to the Home Guard. In particular he hated Sunday morning Home Guard duties, because they interfered with his church attendance as a regular worshipper: he regarded church parades as the one good aspect of Home Guard service because they at least enabled him to attend a place of worship.[32] The men had to do night exercises and attend training camps periodically: 'If it were a wet weekend we were all wet through and all that sort of thing ... you tried to get out of that if you could.'[33] Although he conscientiously trained to use a rifle, he hated the idea of killing anyone,[34] and he remembered the unit's acquisition of a machine-gun simply in terms of the unwelcome extra labour it entailed:

> That thing was a great heavy thing ... [It] went in ... a webbing bag on your back, [you were] biking everywhere with it. And ... if you had firing practice with live ammunition on the Sunday morning, that was bike three miles with that thing on your back, and then all Sunday afternoon [to] strip it down and clean it and oil it again and get it ready for inspection next time you went on. I mean, what sort of life is it? Who would do it today? ... I seem to think it had about twenty-two parts.[35]

Home Guard service extended the hard work he did all week, to no good purpose: something which the army personnel who instructed his unit did not understand:

> Well, when you're working all those hours like that, and then being treated like the regular Army, I mean the regular army, they had the one job. They weren't ... working in agriculture, were they? They had that one job, the army.[36]

More generally, Revill remembered the wartime 'all in it together' spirit as oppressive: 'Everybody thought if you ... were doing something of national importance, that was as it should be',[37] whereas 'all we really wanted was to get the war over and get free, get free'.[38] He regarded the Home Guard as coercive: he did not resign (although some of his friends did), because he believed that 'they'd have fetched me back anyway. Once they've got you there and got you in uniform, then you're half-trained and you haven't a leg to stand on'.[39]

In contrast to the delight that Ray Atkins took in his memories, Revill insisted that recalling the war gave him little pleasure: 'Basically they're days you want to forget.'[40] He was exceptional among those who were prepared to reminisce, most of whom manifestly achieved 'composure' in the dual sense of putting together a coherent story of their personal experience and deriving satisfaction from telling it. Nonetheless, the national narrative of the 'people's war' was pervasive: that story shaped and facilitated all the accounts, whether supportive or, like Revill's, deeply sceptical.

Invasion and militarism

The Home Guard, as we saw in Chapters 2 and 5, was constructed in political discourse and wartime propaganda as primarily an anti-invasion force. But since it was never put to the test in this respect, its effectiveness was never established. Both Sir James Grigg, Secretary of State for War, and King George VI sought to counter the resulting uncertainty: 'there can be no doubt that the existence of the Home Guard was one of the main reasons why the threat was not carried into an actual invasion', asserted Grigg in October 1944.[41]

Men recalling the Home Guard wrestled with the problem of the absence of an invasion, the question of 'what might have been' and the issues of the Home Guard's merit and effectiveness. A number of them were emphatic that the force had been important. John Lewis, who joined the Home Guard in 1942, on leaving school at 16 in rural Gloucestershire, echoed Grigg: 'I think its value was as a morale booster and the fact that the Germans never invaded, so you could argue that they were of deterrent value.'[42] Fred Lusted, who joined as an 18-year-old errand-boy in Burwash, Sussex, wrote more subjectively of his personal feelings, stressing that, although it took time, the Home Guard did develop a military capacity which, looking back after his subsequent experiences in the army, he believed would have been strategically significant:

> I felt proud in being in the Home Guard and eventually once trained and fully armed felt ready to defend England and my village against the invaders. Today, through overseas experience, I feel knowing every inch of the Burwash countryside, as well as defending the village, we could have acted as guides and led the more experienced troops to numerous advantage and ambush positions.[43]

Christopher Redmond also maintained that Home Guard members believed at the time that it was worthwhile: 'we all felt that we were all doing our bit and if that bugger comes over here, he's got to deal with us'.[44]

However, he was also conscious that the Home Guard could be viewed differently from the perspective of the year 2000, even if he distanced himself from that viewpoint:

> We … felt that we were doing some good at that time, certainly. Looking back, if you think, well, the whole thing was a bit of a waste of time. But at that time, you see, we were all very conscientious, we all believed in the country, we were all sort of, you know, 'We are going to beat Hitler' and all that sort of thing. And so we weren't cynical. Today I think so many people are so cynical about everything. We weren't in those days. We were very naïve. We just felt that this was something we were doing to help the war effort.[45]

As Redmond hinted, there were plenty of reasons to think that the Home Guard had been a waste of time, many of which (its lack of equipment and training, and the age of its members, for instance) were articulated, as we have seen, in wartime and post-war humour. Some of the men who acknowledged these ways of understanding the Home Guard struggled, like Redmond, to recuperate the value of the force.

Then and now, the possession of weaponry was a key indicator of authentic military identity and effectiveness. The initial need to improvise, as well as the policy of providing pikes, had fed an image of under-resourcing, but many respondents stressed that this did not last for long. Ray Atkins said that when he first joined, in 1941,

> it was very true, we only had pikes … a metre-long metal tube and it had a First War, 17-inch bayonet welded into it, and that was what you had. But of course, after about two months, I think it was, we got a great delivery of the First World War Lee Enfield rifle, you know, the 300, and from then on we started getting really well armed, you know.[46]

John Best, who joined the LDV as an 18-year-old printer in Manchester, explained that the knives, walking-sticks, .22 rifles and shotguns with which the men first trained were initially supplemented by bizarre weapons such as 'four army rifles dated 1857 from Belle View Zoo'. However, 'this was soon upgraded to standard army rifles and hand grenades, a single Browning automatic rifle and two or three Tommy Guns'.[47] Bill Trueman, who joined the Home Guard in Swindon a few months before his seventeenth birthday in 1941, put it succinctly: 'as time advanced, so did our equipment', and he went on to supply a long and detailed list of items.[48] Martin Maunder joined in Devon aged 17. He recalled the emotion that the acquisition of weapons provoked: 'We were always jubilant to see more weapons', and drew sketches of key items such as the Northover Projector; like Trueman and many others, he supplied a list.[49]

However, some respondents suggested that it was no bad thing that the Home Guard was not issued with real weapons and live ammunition. James Kendall, a Gainsborough fitter who had joined aged 30, said that his unit was never issued with live grenades, but practised with stones of the same weight:

> Some of the old boys, you know, they used to throw straight up in the air and God knows what … They used to fling them all over the place. Good job they weren't live, they fell down the back of them, some of them … It was fun really. I thoroughly, really did enjoy all that sort of activity.[50]

He and others told numerous anecdotes of the dangers of training, in which humour was mixed with a recognition of the gravity of using lethal weapons. Apart from stories critical of incompetent officers (as above), the message was not that the Home Guard could not be trusted not to shoot itself (the view to which Wintringham objected); rather, these were mostly accounts of dramatic and memorable incidents indicative of the Home Guard's integration into genuine military service. Norman Griffin, who joined the LDV in Blackpool at the age of 15 while at technical college, described an exercise in which a colleague primed his hand-grenade and endeavoured to throw it, on the word of command, at a target 25 yards away,

> but that [hand-grenade] unfortunately went up in the air and landed back in the pit where we were; we had a seven second fuse on it, mind you, so we moved out of there very rapidly! And that was the first experience I had I think in warfare.[51]

In these men's memories, potentially lethal accidents were a natural concomitant of training. They were to be expected in a man's world; and, underlining the separateness of this new world, such accidents had to be concealed from civilians. In particular, men who had been youthful Home Guards stressed the need to keep quiet about them at home. Ray Atkins said: 'There was always a bit of this. So you hadn't to speak to your mother about this when you got back, you know.'[52]

Memories of equal competition with and, still better, victory over the only 'enemy' which the Home Guard actually fought – other platoons or the army – were treasured. Fred Cardy was in the Railway Home Guard in Colchester. During an exercise, the army 'captured the downside general waiting room', so two Home Guards with the requisite skills formulated a plan to outwit them. They commandeered a tank engine, obtained clearance from the signalman to 'go down into the siding … stopped outside the … waiting room … dashed across the platform to the door which

Figure 16 Ray Atkins as a 16-year-old recruit. Ray commented, with a laugh: 'Good job Hitler didn't see that picture. He'd have packed the war in!'

was open, "Come on you lot, hands up!" ... "Yes, they were captured themselves!"'.[53] Such stories evoked the kind of Home Guard that Orwell and Wintringham favoured: one that did not wait for orders, but improvised and exploited its local knowledge and civilian skills to military advantage.

Some of the men recalled training on Osterley's lines. Nigel Grey, for example, recalled that in late 1940 we spent one Sunday being instructed in unarmed combat by three of the most villainous-looking desperadoes I've ever seen. They were veterans of the Spanish Civil War, or so we were told. It all came as a shock to discover that the humble army boot wasn't just designed for marching, but was also a lethal weapon. We were also encouraged to equip ourselves with 6-inch hat pins (from our grandmothers) and shown how to kill without leaving a mark.[54]

For many of those interviewed, exercises had been enjoyable, but they were also serious.[55] Ray Atkins rejected the notion that the Home Guard was *playing* at war: for young men like himself this was valuable training for 'the real thing' when they were called up into the regular forces.[56] Indeed, a narrative of gaining a maturity in the Home Guard through military training that subsequently paid off in the army, navy or RAF was commonplace. Norman Griffin, the Blackpool Home Guard quoted earlier, explained:

> We had in our Home Guard company two Sergeant-Majors from the Regular Army who were there to teach us weapons – weapon drill, weapon usage, range firing, grenade-throwing, and they were absolutely excellent in the field they specialised in, so that really by the time that I joined the army as a volunteer at seventeen-and-a-half at the end of 1942, and I joined the Royal Welsh Fusiliers, I was in actual fact a proficient soldier in many respects. I could certainly use every weapon, from pistols right the way through to Browning automatics, and this stood me in good stead of course when – even as a young soldier – when I joined, I was in my preparatory training, in the regiment in south Wales.[57]

In such accounts the Home Guard was integrated into a larger story of masculine development, and of fully living up to the expectations that a young man would join the military in wartime.[58] Young Home Guards learned not only proficiency with weapons, but also a knowledge of military culture more generally – including subterfuges for evading unpleasant duties.

But this kind of positive, if sometimes humorous, account of Home Guard experiences was not the only one that men articulated. Respondents also expressed scepticism about the value of training and other activities: these accounts were redolent of the genre of wartime satire we reviewed in Chapter Four, that lampooned the Home Guard's out-of-date methods and inadequate equipment. Some men recalled traditional procedures they had found ridiculous, such as the practice of issuing challenges when on sentry duty. Ron Smith, for example, who worked in the building trade and joined the Home Guard in rural Leicestershire in 1940 or '41, at the age of about eighteen, said:

The proper procedure used to be standing there menacingly with a rifle and a bayonet, 'Halt who goes there?' in the dark ... And they're supposed to say 'Friend' or 'Foe' (*laughs*). Imagine a German saying 'I'm a foe.' (*Laughs*) Laid down procedures that were ridiculous really. And at the end you say 'Halt, or I'll fire' but you haven't got a bullet ... (*laughs*). You could run after him with a bayonet.[59]

Smith's account was in general sceptical and sardonic – 'had to hand the rifle in every night, in case I shot meself with no bullets!'[60] – but he also remembered his fears: he felt menaced by the threat of invasion by German soldiers who, he believed, were efficient and well equipped, at a time when Home Guards were issued with little more than 'pick-axe handles':[61]

At that time our biggest fear was that the Germans would land paratroopers ... Now, they're the elite of any army. And old men with bits of— (*laughs*). They're armed to the teeth, they've got grenades and bayonets and semi-automatic rifles, they've got the lot.[62]

Smith referred disparagingly to the age-profile of the Home Guard as 'old men'. Looking back from the vantage point of their own advancing age, he and others interviewed doubted whether the Home Guard would ever have been capable of combat. Alfred Claxton, aged 76 at the time of the interview, reflected:

I don't think, be fair, like me now, at this age. A number of those old folk were in the Home Guard, I don't think they would have stood a chance, they couldn't run even, half of them, could they? Looking at it in its right light, I don't think they could have done an awful lot. Yeah, they would have had a go, yes, but not a lot.[63]

The life review occasioned by the interviews complicated matters. Claxton assumed that the older men in the Home Guard were in the age-group to which he *now* belonged, but several interviewees were conscious that many of the men they had seen as 'old' during the war were in fact younger than they were at the time of their interview. Ray Atkins said: 'As I say, there were a lot of ... what they called 'old sweats' from the First War with plenty of medals. But they weren't really old when you think back. They were only in their forties, weren't they? So no way were they old.'[64]

Political discourse during the war stressed the value to the Home Guard of experienced veterans of the First World War (Atkins's 'old sweats'), even though critics were suggesting that such men were responsible for perpetuating outdated and inappropriate methods. Those interviewed on the whole remembered the 'old sweats' with respect: John

Graham, who came from a military family and joined the Home Guard at 17 as a lance corporal on the strength of his successful training in the Cheltenham College Officer Training Corps (he later became a Major-General in the army), said that a veteran of the Boer War 'was the best shot of the lot of us'.[65] Alfred Claxton greatly admired 'Old Gus', as his sergeant was known, who had served in the First World War: he was fond of alcohol and colourful language and Claxton regarded him as 'a warrior, you might say, really, in lots of ways you know'.[66] 'Old sweats' were hard-bitten and independent-minded: Claxton thought that Gus was never promoted beyond the rank of sergeant by his own choice: 'he did not want them coming here telling me [sic] what to do'[67] while Arthur Brown, as we have seen, remembered ex-servicemen in the Shropshire Home Guard single-mindedly avoiding unwelcome responsibility or (in their view) unnecessary exertion.[68] Young and inexperienced NCOs might not be able to exert authority over ex-servicemen, but in at least one case they found they could rely on their loyalty. Len Hill, a corporal in the Leicester Home Guard at the age of 28, told such a story. While he was drilling his men, they asked to stop for a smoke, which he permitted: they were promptly caught by the Home Guard Lieutenant on his rounds. Hill defended himself for allowing the men a break, but the Lieutenant insisted on putting their drill to the test:

> They all got up and I've never seen anybody present arms and all that so perfect, everything was perfect, I think the Lieutenant was astounded because one old gentleman, Bill Cook I think his name was, he couldn't care less about anything, never, but he did that morning. And when they'd gone, he said, 'There you are, you knew we wouldn't let you down, didn't you?' And they all sat down and had another smoke.[69]

Masculinity

Alessandro Portelli has observed that 'war myths and war narratives are one way of shaping ideas of manhood and identity'.[70] Respondents' stories of their Home Guard experiences served to evoke both their passage into and their membership of a wartime masculine community. One aspect was the solidarity of the unit, described by Len Hill, that inspired collusion against authority. Official rhetoric depicted the force as a symbol of male comradeship – 'an outward and visible sign of an inward unity and brotherhood, without distinction of class or calling', as Sir James Grigg put it.[71] Popular culture also stressed Home Guard camaraderie, albeit in representations that focused primarily on drinking rather than military activity. Memories of sociability in the Home Guard were closely associated with the pub, and those interviewed often recalled their membership in the same way as it had been depicted by wartime comedians such as Robb Wilton and crime novelists like Belton Cobb: as a low-subscription men's club. Ron Smith, identifying with his older comrades in the Home Guard from the vantage point of his interview, at the age of 76, commented:

> I think the men in the Home Guard enjoyed it. It got them out the house once again and [they could] mix with other men. After all, when you are retired you are only too grateful for other men's company. That's what I miss most of all now, isn't it?[72]

This stress on the benefits of male company was echoed in other accounts. John Shuttleworth, who joined the Home Guard while working in munitions in Birmingham in 1940, suggested that the force appealed particularly to ex-servicemen because it evoked positive memories of regimental life in the First World War.[73] The pub played a vital role in facilitating this sense of community.[74] Shuttleworth said that his unit at Great Barr

> used to go and train on the field opposite the pub. And of course, their greatest delight when they'd finished was to go into the pub (*laughs*), all pals together, like, you know. Had a good time, like, you know. Yeah, I think it brought a lot of er, camaraderie, is it, comrade-erie?[75]

In searching for the correct pronunciation, Shuttleworth illustrated the links between the terms 'camaraderie' and 'comrade'. The latter word has associations that are both military (comrade-in-arms) and political: it was widely used by respondents, frequently in association with alcohol-based sociability. Arthur Ambler, a trainee draughtsman who joined the Home Guard with his father in Littleborough, Lancashire, at the age of 21 in 1941, said: 'They were great people to be with. Great companions, great comrades, and they all liked a pint, which is where we usually finished up after a parade.'[76] Arthur Brown recalled that in his Shropshire unit, 'half an hour's square bashing' was regularly followed by decampment to the pub.[77] Men negotiated pub time with their COs, agreed that training would finish before the pub closed and colluded to ensure that by opening time they would be 'taken prisoner' in exercises.[78] For the younger members of the Home Guard, pub time was part of being admitted into the world of men.[79] Alfred Claxton, who joined the Home Guard at 16, and George Nicholson, who joined at 17, learned to drink (in both cases under-age) with the Home Guard, as did Christopher Redmond, despite the fact that he had signed 'the pledge' aged 11.[80] For most of our male respondents, Home Guard duties, drinking activities and comradeship were interlocked in wartime memories that were pleasant to recall; men who still had access to such a masculine drinking culture indicated that it provided them with an enduringly supportive audience for their reminiscences. Ray Atkins spoke warmly of 'swinging the lamp', a term he used to describe men vying with each other to tell the best story over a drink:

> To be honest, there's nothing like it. If you've had a few drinks, and some of these funny stories come out and you are all trying to outdo each other and make your story funnier than the last chap, and you feel very comfortable about that, very comfortable, you know. But it can only be with that generation, really, you know. People would wonder what the hell you're talking about, you know.[81]

Such male bonding was predicated on the exclusion of women. Ron Smith joined the Territorial Army just before the outbreak of war because his fellow construction workers already belonged to it: 'not because they were patriotic and wanted to fight for their country in time of war, [but] because they got a free holiday every year':

> You had a fortnight's camp, away from the wife and the kids, what could be better? Drinking and boozing and chasing women with your mates, and your wife didn't know. They had a whale of a time once a year. And of course they were on full pay. Firms were forced to pay you full pay but they were then reimbursed for it. So they didn't lose anything. And the men got a darn good holiday.[82]

Ron described how he thought 'Ooh, I'll have some of that' and joined the TA under-age, but did not stay long enough to acquire a uniform, for the humiliating reason that his mother put a stop to it. 'Oh, the indignity of it! There I was enjoying myself among men, then mum came and took me home (*laughs*).'[83] The quest for similar opportunities in a homo-social world later prompted Ron to join the Home Guard.

However, as we have seen, women were recruited to some Home Guard units, both before and after the official recognition of 'nominated women' (later Women Home Guard Auxiliaries) in April 1943. When asked whether they remembered women members, most male interviewees were adamant that there were none. Only James Kendall recalled any women: four joined his unit as signals clerks, and he had nothing but praise for them, 'They were damn good, those women were.'[84] Although wartime women featured in other men's narratives as members of the ATS, the Land Army and the WVS, most of the men expressed surprise at the question about women Home Guards, and even thought it anachronistic.[85] Some found it funny. George Nicholson joined his village's Home Guard with his father, James ('our Jamie'), at 17 in 1941, when he was an apprentice bricklayer at Rowntree's in York, before enlisting in the navy the following year. When asked whether there were any women in the unit, he said: 'No, no, just men. I don't think such as me Dad would have said much about it (*laughs*) ... if they'd had women in. No, mind you, they'd have spoiled their enjoyment (*laughs*).'[86] One of George's anecdotes explained the nature of this 'enjoyment':

> Before I joined up I used to go fishing. Mind, I had all the tackle, two or three rods and what not. And I come home one Saturday morning, said to me mother, 'Where's father?' 'Fishing.' I said, 'He's what?' – he never went fishing in his life. She says, 'Well, him and Bill Smith', that's the other one on that photograph, 'have borrowed your gear, the rods and what not, and they have gone to the Home Guard, fishing.' Now of course it was near the end of the war, this. So anyway I had a chat to me mother, cup of tea, and what not. I got the bus to Stamford Bridge where the battle was (*laughs*). I could hear them singing before I got there, and I went along the river bank and I pulled one or two rods up No bait on them. Anyway I walked in the pub, that was it – our Jamie (*laughs*). He would never have caught 'owt there.[87]

Nicholson had included this story in his original letter to us, in which he added that the men (most of whom, like his father, were ex-servicemen) were singing First World War songs, and he provided an alternative punchline: 'When I got home, my mother asked if they had caught anything. I thought to myself, only you and a few more wives.'[88] Such was the stuff of wartime representations of a Home Guard comically oriented to the pub, rather than to the military or domestic battlefields: thus was the culture of Home Guard 'unity and brotherhood' remembered.

Even though popular culture questioned the authenticity of its militarism, the Home Guard's uniform was remembered as a prize possession. It was not only a marker of membership of a military organisation, but its differences from army uniform could be detected only by cognoscenti: in most respects it was 'just like an Army uniform'.[89] Fred Lusted recalled that the arrival of full battledress and rifles meant that 'we at last looked like soldiers'.[90] The satisfaction of passing as servicemen was great. Tex Laws remembered:

> We attended a weekend assault course in North London ... I'd been given a lift to Balham underground station by a motorist who'd mistaken me for a soldier, which was flattering, but only natural as we'd the same uniform.[91]

This had particular significance for men too young for the armed forces or unable to join because of their occupations.

One of the latter was Christopher Redmond, who, as an 18-year-old engineering draughtsman living in the village of Wootton near Oxford, found to his dismay that he was in a reserved occupation, meaning that his applications to join the armed forces were rejected. He recalled his concern that he might be mistaken for a conscientious objector: 'We heard lots of rumours about people receiving white feathers and so on. And that was the most ghastly thing to us.'[92] Joining the local Home Guard was a temporary solution: 'I joined the Home Guard there, and then of course I was issued with a proper uniform and I looked like a soldier, you know, I mean, I really did.'[93] But even so, a Home Guard was known not to be 'a proper soldier': in Redmond's small community the difference between part-time Home Guards and full-time servicemen posted away from home was well known. So Redmond found a way of simulating a life of military service, in which his Home Guard uniform played a crucial part. He successfully applied for a place on an engineering training course in Wolverhampton, some way from home. The course aimed to create a pool of men qualified in specific trades for the armed forces: throughout its two-year duration the students remained civilians, but they were required to join the local South Staffordshire Home Guard.[94] Redmond took care to ensure that his departure from home and periodic return 'on leave' would be understood in the village to indicate that he had indeed joined up. He came and went in uniform, and his fellow students initiated him into a method of enhancing the pretence:

> On here (*indicates shoulder*) we had 'Home Guard', we had a little strip which said 'Home Guard' ... sewn or printed, or what, and you were issued ... these and you had to sew them on here. Well, what some of the lads started to do, and I soon cottoned on to this, was when we went home for our holidays, our break, our leave, [we] went home in uniform, you see ... What we did was to take our 'Home Guard' off, the night before we were going ... get a razor blade and take it off ... off our overcoats, you see. And then off we'd go.[95]

Redmond mimed arriving home with a kit-bag on his shoulder, walking down the street greeting people – to make sure he had been seen – and then, 'once we'd got that over with, everybody knew we were home on leave and you know, sort of thing, then you'd take off [your uniform] and put on your ordinary gear and that was OK.'[96] The appearance he gave of being in the military was so vital to his sense of self in wartime that he undertook this subterfuge repeatedly. He acknowledged with hindsight that this was 'ridiculous' but explained: 'We sort of pretended an awful lot, I think, we were sort of masquerading as something that we weren't quite, because it

Figure 17 Home Guard shoulder patch

was terribly important to us to, you know, [to be] recognise[d] as one of them, we were fighting for our country, and so on and so forth.'[97]

Redmond did not stress the sex appeal of uniform, but it was in the background of his description of himself –'a big chap' who looked 'much older than my age', and it was particularly implied by his detailed account of the smart appearance it was possible to achieve in the naval uniform he eventually acquired, after graduating from his course.[98] Most respondents however, were sceptical about the attractiveness of the Home Guard uniform to the opposite sex. John Shuttleworth commented that wearing a uniform 'was great (*laughs*). I mean, it's just, it's a young bloke's dream, sometimes, to be in uniform. It was, God, you pulled the girls anyway (*laughs*).'[99] But on closer questioning Shuttleworth decided that his success with girls was 'not particularly in the Home Guard. It was in the RAF. No, I don't think the Home Guard did much for the, the, ladies (*laughs*).'[100]

Dad's Army and the memory of the Home Guard

Dad's Army generated a powerful image of the Home Guard. As we argued in Chapter 6, the programme straddled both wartime modes of representation, celebrating the force for its earnest commitment to the defence of Britain as well as lampooning it for its incompetence and ineffectuality. *Dad's Army* exercised enormous power over reminiscence: it was an inescapable reference point for men recalling their Home Guard experiences – as well as for women, as we shall see in the next chapter. There was even some elision of terminology: Ted Petty, who enlisted as a 21-year-old munitions worker in Weybridge, said: 'It really was fun when we joined the L.D.V., latterly known as the Home Guard, or Dad's Army',[101] and others referred to the sitcom as *The Home Guard* rather than *Dad's Army*, as in 'I've a soft spot for *The Home Guard* you know, and, I mean that *Dad's Army*, to me, it's absolutely marvellous you know, that programme.'[102] In about half of the interviews used in this study men referred to the programme before being asked, and all of those who responded had heard of it.[103]

In contrast to the viewers who wrote to the BBC between 1968 and 1970, men recalling their personal experiences in the 1990s and 2000s were inclined to regard *Dad's Army* as satire rather than celebration, although Tex Laws, who, as we have seen, joined aged 17 in 1941 as a Post Office messenger in Battersea, wrote that 'the best show was the last, wherein Mainwaring said we'd given a good account of ourselves and a highly appropriate toast was drunk'.[104] The 'good account' is in fact ambiguous. At the end of the episode, which features Jones's marriage to Mrs Fox, Warden Hodges disparagingly suggests that 'real soldiers' would 'walk straight through' the Walmington platoon. Offended, Mainwaring tries to rebut the allegation: 'We'll all stick together. If anybody tries to take away our homes or our freedom they'll find out what we can do. There are thousands of us all over England —'. Frazer (*interrupting*): 'And Scotland.' Mainwaring agrees to the inclusion of Scotland, and concludes the last episode of the last series with a toast (wedding champagne in tin mugs), 'To Britain's Home Guard!'[105]

Many respondents believed that the show alone had perpetuated the memory of the Home Guard, making comments such as 'But for the TV series *Dad's Army* I doubt the H.G. would be remembered at all'; and 'I doubt if many people born during the past forty years have heard of the Home Guard – apart from watching *Dad's Army*.'[106] A few men expressed ambivalent or contradictory views, but otherwise their responses were of two main types: they either suggested that the show's comic rendering of the Home Guard was accurate; or they challenged this depiction.

One respondent spontaneously recalled one of the wartime interpretations of the Home Guard and related it to the *Dad's Army* version. Bill Trueman wrote:

> I think today the Home Guard is remembered by most people in England who were not involved with them the same as they did at the time, which was, I quote, 'A lot of old men and boys playing at soldiers'. But nowadays I'm sure the TV series of *Dad's Army* sums it up well.[107]

Those, like Trueman, who felt that the series was authentic, acknowledged the constraints of the sitcom genre while still regarding *Dad's Army* as a true-to-life representation. Nigel Grey wrote:

> One feels the authors of the series must have had first hand experience, or at least have done much in-depth research into the subject. There was so much I could relate to, even allowing for comedy having to be larger than life to project itself from the small screen.[108]

The pleasure of recognition was intense. Thus Bill Trueman commented that 'the researchers of that TV programme certainly depicted the events and characters. I enjoy them every time, as memories flow back and can laugh at events that you experienced and was associated with.'[109] He substantiated his statement that the *Dad's Army* characters were 'typical of the Home Guard as I knew it' by relating them to members of his own platoon:

> We had the officer who was the one who thought he knew best, the young one who had mother behind him looking after his well being. Then the 'spiv' always able to get the unobtainable item from the Black Market. The jittery sergeant. I can put names to most of them.[110]

He was by no means alone. Christopher Redmond also took pleasure in fitting *Dad's Army* characters to men he remembered, albeit possibly drawing on the 'silent army' as well as the seven front-row characters for his analogies:

> You've got the spiv, you've got the youngster, which was probably me, you know, Pike. I mean, that would be me, wouldn't it? You've got somebody like the Scotsman, I can remember a chap, I can't remember his name, but yeah I can remember him well enough and so on. My father would have been one of the more, he wouldn't be the larger than life one, my father would just be a soldier there you know, he'd just be one of the sort of steadier, he wasn't the buffoon, he wasn't a fool, he wasn't like the corporal, you know, sort of getting all panicking and all that sort of thing. He was just an ordinary sort of soldier. But they were all there, yes, I've seen all of them.[111]

Incidents as well as characterisation rang true. They were echoed not only in content but also in form: the *Dad's Army* delivery of a comic plot in each episode, with numerous funny sub-plots, paralleled the anecdotal style that dominated the men's oral accounts. The anecdote has conventionally been condemned by historians as an often-told tale more likely to be an inaccurate elaboration than a reliable account of events. In social research more widely, 'anecdotal evidence' is regarded as interesting and colourful, but unrepresentative and therefore not, ultimately, valid. Cultural historians have, however, sought to recuperate the anecdote for what it is in everyday life, a widely-used and well-understood narrative form,[112] a snapshot that can be shared, provided the audience recognises the subject matter that is encapsulated. The men's testimony was filled with anecdotes: in some of them the subject matter was explicitly linked to *Dad's Army*.

James Kendall told a story about an exercise involving one of the older members of his platoon, 'Old Bill':

> There was an old fella called Bill, Bill Smith … and he always smoked a pipe, and then this particular occasion, it was beautiful weather, this summer. We was up [Funnett], we was doing exercises, and we was in a long line, and we was told when the whistle went we had to run, advance, and as soon as the whistle went again, down, you see. And we did that several times. And this particular time, old Bill was again' me, he was only about three or four yards away from me, we had to go down and Bill, he used to carry his tobacco, his pipe, in his side pocket, and his matches, and he fell on his matches and they went up. There was such a cloud of blue smoke, you know. And old Bill looked, and he run like the devil. I did laugh. We all did. Old Bill. A real old man he was, old enough to have been my dad then. Old Bill he took off. And of course we run after him like. He says, he says, 'What's up? What's up?' he says. I says 'Let's have a look at you Bill.' And (*laughs*) he hadn't burnt himself but he'd burnt his coat and that. Oh it was funny that. Talk about *Dad's Army*, you know, it was one of those sort of things, incidents. We had one or two of those sort of incidents.[113]

Kendall related several more anecdotes: in one a guard accidentally shot a bullet through the ceiling; in another an incompetent rifleman fired into the ground; in a third a log rolled out of the fire the men had made in the guardroom, nearly burning their hut down while they were all fast asleep. He punctuated these accounts with remarks such as 'when they started showing *Dad's Army* we used to think that's us all right'; 'it's typical *Dad's Army* this'; and 'again, *Dad's Army*'.[114] These stories shared with *Dad's Army* an emphasis on comic incompetence, near-misses and comradeship: they supported Kendall's view that in as far as the Home Guard was united, the rank-and-file made it so.

Other men linked *Dad's Army* with memories of inflated military authority. Nigel Grey remembered (albeit sympathetically) a sergeant's attempts to fill his role adequately:

> On one occasion our CSM [Company Sergeant Major] was endeavouring to emulate an RSM [Regimental Sergeant Major] of the Guards Brigade, and as I recall doing a very good job of it. However, the raucous barking got too much for the poor man's dentures, which suddenly ended up on the road. I always expected this incident to be repeated in *Dad's Army*, as there was so much I could identify with in that excellent show.[115]

Grey, like Christopher Redmond quoted above, and several other men who joined up in their teens, identified with the youngest member of the Walmington-on-Sea platoon, Frank Pike. Grey described his performance at a shooting competition:

> Looking along the sights my immediate vision was of steam rising ... while beyond that the rain pelted downward. I let off my 5 rounds hopefully but nothing was recorded on the target. However, the chap on my left ended up with 10 holes in his target. I can hear Captain Mainwaring saying 'Stupid boy' every time I think of it.[116]

Grey signed his subsequent letter with his name, followed by 'Alias Stupid Boy'.[117] He had had to leave the Home Guard, as we have seen, when, to his dismay, he was pronounced unfit for any kind of war service because of a weak heart. His fluent letters reminiscing about his service, with their numerous references to *Dad's Army*, suggest that, for him, the show facilitated composure.

. That was not, however, always the case. A number of men enjoyed *Dad's Army* and appreciated its 'authenticity', yet emphasised that it distorted the memory of the Home Guard. Christopher Redmond who, as we have seen, felt that the characters in the show were true to life, nevertheless pointed out that regional differences (and, by implication, changes over time) meant that *Dad's Army* represented some Home Guard units more accurately than others. He contrasted the village unit at Wootton, which he had joined in 1941, with his experiences of a Wolverhampton unit in 1943. The latter

> was of course a much bigger, a much more organised than our little one down at Wootton ... I mean, there, I suppose, it really was a good illustration of *Dad's Army*, you know. But it wasn't when we got to Wolverhampton, now that was much more organised, we were sort of in the army, it was much more like being in the army.[118]

D. E. Brundrett, who joined the Home Guard in Surrey at the age of 16 in 1941, while working for the Croydon Gas Company, said simply that 'in many ways [it] was partly true to form but not quite like I remember it!'; and John Best wrote: 'I think it was trivialised by Capt. Mannering [*sic*] and his Dad's Army, but I must admit his show was enjoyable.'[119] These men agreed that there were comic aspects to their own experiences, and that *Dad's Army* expressed them well, but they were conscious of the programme's exaggerations and selectivity. John Shuttleworth said, 'I think it's very funny. I don't think it was as funny as they depict but there was funny things in the Home Guard without a doubt really. I mean,

Sevenoaks Dad's Army boys create a poser

● On parade: Sevenoaks Home Guard. But who, when and on what occasion?

Figure 18 'Sevenoaks Dad's Army boys create a poser', *Sevenoaks Chronicle*, 23 September 1999

there's got to be, hasn't there? But not so bad to that extent you know. Actually really it was serious stuff really in the Home Guard'.[120] Fred Bailey, who joined the force while working for the Colne Valley Water Company in 1940, wrote that 'the Home Guard is remembered good-naturedly, as a joke (Dad's Army). The serious side of its work is rarely, if ever, referred to.'[121] John Lewis commented:

> I have to say *Dad's Army* is one of my favourite programmes, but of course it is a gross caricature of the real thing. Towards the end of the war I would almost equate the Home Guard with the standard of training of the peace-time TA, with the exception of the senior officers.[122]

To Shuttleworth, Bailey and Lewis the Home Guard had its funny aspects, but by stressing them at the expense of its meaningful military role and its development over time, *Dad's Army* misrepresented the force. Some men were even more critical of *Dad's Army*'s neglect of the Home Guard's essential seriousness. Frederick Johnes, who was born before the First World War and was working as an engineering draughtsman in Sydenham in the Second, 'strongly objected' to *Dad's Army* because of its disregard of the real dangers Home Guard personnel had faced, substantiating his point with an account of a night on which nine Home Guards lost their lives manning an anti-aircraft site in a bombing raid.[123] Arthur Brown was critical of an item in his local newspaper in September 1999, requesting information about a photograph of the Sevenoaks Home Guard on parade in wartime. Brown objected to the characterisation of the unit in the headline 'Sevenoaks Dad's Army boys create a poser' because

> you can see there's nothing *Dad's Army* about them ... very smart turnout ... A lot of them are ex-First World War soldiers, and they've obviously been well drilled and well trained and they look smart and I reckon they would have given a good account of themselves, but this *Dad's Army* stuff, it's very funny and all the rest of it, but it doesn't represent the truth at all.[124]

Dad's Army's satirical representation of the Home Guard dominated these men's perception of the programme: the Walmington-on-Sea platoon was a travesty because of its unmitigated incompetence; the patriotism and valour in the interpretation was not enough to counter the de-selection from *Dad's Army* of the serious and well-trained Home Guard they remembered. For some men this cramped the possibilities of reminiscence. Dennis Smith, who had joined near Canterbury as a tall fourteen-and-a-half year old, and who consistently emphasised the seriousness of the force, said mournfully, in response to the question 'How do other people react when you talk about being in the Home Guard?': 'They tend to laugh.'[125] David Jones, who joined as a 16-year-old coal miner in Nantyffyllon, Glamorgan, wrote: 'The Home Guard is hardly remembered at all except as a lot of buffoons as presented in *Dad's Army* ... but perhaps that's how they were. Certainly we, in our unit, were surely unprepared.' He concluded with a statement that echoed the 'comic, pathetic yet valorous' representation in *Dad's Army*: 'It is very difficult to realise now, how close we were to being a part of a Nazi Empire, but I am sure if they had come the Home Guard would have gone down fighting.'[126]

Whether they regarded *Dad's Army* as an accurate representation, were critical of its omissions, or, like David Jones, rather unwillingly accepted its judgements, men remembering their own Home Guard experiences could not escape *Dad's Army*. As the dominant representation of the Home Guard from the 1970s into at least the early years of the twenty-first century, it influenced the imaginative possibilities of their own recall and shaped their personal memories.

Conclusion

Men's oral testimony revealed many aspects of Home Guard experience unrecorded elsewhere not least that sixteen-year-olds were routinely enrolled even after the crack-down on age in 1941.[127] Evidently COs keen to recruit members overlooked the 17-year-old minimum age-limit, just as they overlooked the upper age-limit and the gender qualification, a subject to which we return in the next chapter.

Men recalling their Home Guard experiences made use of the rhetoric of the 'people's war': accounts were framed in terms of 'doing your bit' and being 'all in it together'; the Home Guard was remembered as an important wartime institution requiring and facilitating the war effort. But the sceptical account of the Home Guard also made sense to many men: they recalled the impossibility of 'unity', the persistence of class-based appointments and incompetent officers, regional tensions, and unrealistic expectations that a civilian force could comply with the standards of the regular army. The dual mode in which the Home Guard was represented during and after the war meant that both ways of remembering it were conducive to 'composure', although in at least one case memories of the coercive pressures of the 'people's war' were uncomfortable, and, on the other hand, some men resisted and resented the critical–satirical account.

The idea that the Home Guard was primarily a counter-invasion force made it difficult for men to evaluate its effectiveness, even though doing so was an important part of life review. The Home Guard was never put to the test, but assertions that it was a deterrent, as political leaders claimed, co-existed with almost apologetic explanations that it was at least believed to be one. Some men echoed official discourse in stressing the change over time – even though things sometimes went wrong, the Home Guard became efficient and was a valuable experience, especially for young men on their way into the armed forces 'proper'.

But scepticism was also prevalent: out of date procedures, lack of firepower, the advanced age of many members and the negative attitudes of some of them, suggested ineffectualness. Yet 'old sweats' were also repositories of skills, knowledge and cherished values, including a culture of anti-authoritarianism and comradeship. Memories of Home Guard solidarity were informed not only by the rhetoric of wartime unity, but also by memories of the camaraderie of the pub. Nostalgia for that lost community was strong: any possibilities for its re-creation in the present were diminishing as the men aged and the opportunities it might have offered for 'composure' declined. The Home Guard was remembered as a homo-social culture. Women, if wives or mothers, were to be evaded; if not, they were to be attracted (or not) by the military uniforms that were essential signifiers of wartime masculinity; either way, the Home Guard was remembered, with few exceptions, as aiding and abetting the maintenance of women's 'otherness'.

Dad's Army played a major role in recall. Its mixture of satire and celebration facilitated composure for men who 'recognised' its characters and incidents, and whose anecdotal narrative style was stimulated by *Dad's Army*'s plot structures, built on the themes of comic incompetence, military pretension and solidarity. But for others, the show, even if it was enjoyable, did not provide a comfortable framework for recall. It did violence to memories of the serious and sometimes tragic business of war in which the Home Guard was involved; it ignored the development of the Home Guard as an effective military force. *Dad's Army* may have kept the memory of the Home Guard alive, but its strong viewpoint meant that some experiences were omitted from public memory. If this was the case for men, it was even more so for women.

Notes

1 The personal testimony on which we drew included the following: *men*, total 69: 12 oral history interviews conducted for the project; correspondence with 19 men, including responses to a brief questionnaire (the same set of questions used as prompts in the interviews); 38 oral history interviews held in the Imperial War Museum's Sound Archive (IWM, SA classmark); *women*, total 32: 17 oral history interviews conducted for the project; correspondence with 9 other women former Home Guards, including questionnaire responses; 5 interviews archived in the IWM, SA; one diary (by one of our correspondents) in the IMW, DD; one memoir in a local history newsletter. Project interviews (PIs), correspondence and questionnaires were transcribed and transcript paragraph numbers are included in brackets. In references, respondents' full names and dates of interviews and correspondence are given for the first citation and, thereafter are abbreviated. For brief biographical details, see appendices 1 and 2.
2 See P. Thompson, *The Voice of the Past: Oral History*, 3rd edition (Oxford: Oxford University Press, 2000 [1978]); T. Lummis, *Listening to History: The Authenticity of Oral Evidence* (London: Hutchinson, 1987); A. Thomson, 'Unreliable Memories: The Use and Abuse of Oral History', in W. Lamont (ed.), *Historical Controversies* (London: University College London Press, 1998).
3 See Popular Memory Group, 'Popular Memory: Theory, Politics, Method', in R. Jones, G. McLennan, B. Schwartz and D. Sutton (eds), *Making Histories: Studies in History-Writing and Politics* (London: Hutchinson, 1982).

4 See A. Portelli, *The Death of Luigi Trastulli and Other Stories: Form and Meaning in Oral History* (Albany, NY: SUNY Press, 1991); Thomson, *Anzac Memories*; Summerfield, *Reconstructing*.

5 For a discussion of these concepts, see Summerfield, 'Culture and Composure'.

6 Dawson, *Soldier Heroes*, p. 25.

7 Thomson, *Anzac Memories*, p. 8 and generally.

8 (PI) Ray Atkins (pseud.), 23 March 2000 (99).

9 Correspondence, Victor S. Waterhouse, November 1999 (43).

10 Correspondence, Nigel Grey, January 2000 (29).

11 Correspondence, Tex Laws, 3 May 2000 (44).

12 Popular Memory Group, 'Popular Memory', p. 211.

13 (PI) Atkins (633); with regard to the feelings of personal satisfaction and enhanced self-esteem achieved from such recollection, see Summerfield, 'Culture and Composure', pp. 69–70.

14 Correspondence, Bill Trueman, 25 February 2000 (76).

15 Christopher Redmond (pseud), 13 March 2000 (692).

16 (PI) Frank Whittard, 1 March 2000 (99–100). These class distinctions in the workplace were marked by differences in the working hours and dress of the two groups.

17 (PI) Whittard (1157–1169, 55). Whittard attributed his boss's leadership role mainly to his First World War military experience rather than social privilege.

18 (PI) George Nicholson, 18 May 2000 (755).

19 (PI) Cyril Hall, 28 October 1999 (198–204).

20 (PI) Kendall, 27 October 1999 (110, 117).

21 (PI) Kendall (131).

22 (PI) Kendall (161, 193).

23 (PI) Arthur Brown, 1 October 1999 (525).

24 (PI) Brown (545, 537, 566).

25 (PI) Brown (436).

26 (PI) Brown (553–4). Brown's depiction of the Shropshire Home Guards – wherever they originated from – echoed the criticisms of Home Guard 'slackers' and 'Sunday soldiers' voiced by those campaigning for greater military discipline in the force during 1941. See Chapter 2, 'Conscription'.

27 (PI) Alfred Claxton, 12 May 2000 (1378).

28 (PI) Leslie Revill, 29 November 1999 (53).

29 (PI) Revill (8, 89).

30 (PI) Revill (10).

31 (PI) Revill (129–131).

32 (PI) Revill (133–135).

33 (PI) Revill (337).

34 (PI) Revill (63).

35 (PI) Revill (111); Len Hill also said that everybody 'hated the Lewis gun': IWM, SA, 11234, Len Hill, 1990.

36 (PI) Revill (91).

37 (PI) Revill (171).

38 (PI) Revill (298).

39 (PI) Revill (157).

40 (PI) Revill (324).

41 Brophy, *Britain's Home Guard*, p. 5; also George VI, 'Stand-Down' speech, 3 December 1944, *Speeches and Replies*, pp. 53–54.

42 Correspondence, John Lewis, April 2000 (33).

43 Correspondence, F. J. Lusted, 2 December 1999 (51).

44 (PI) Redmond, 13 March 2000 (776)

45 (PI) Redmond (228).

46 (PI) Atkins (127, 131).

47 Correspondence, John Best, 29 February 2000 (24); he also stated: 'In fact we were better equipped than those who had returned from Dunkerque', 18 December 1999 (32).

48 Correspondence, Bill Trueman, 25 February 2000 (31).

49 Correspondence, Martin Maunder, 18 January 2000 (74).

50 (PI) Kendall (181).

51 IWM, SA, 18615, Norman Griffin, 18 November 1998.

52 (PI) Atkins (127).

53 IWM, SA, 11350, Frederick Cardy, 22 October 1989.

54 Correspondence, Nigel Grey, January 2000 (27).

55 This is not to say that none of the men told critical stories of exercises: Frank Whittard described one exercise that was 'a bit of a farce' because the Home Guard was 'arrested' by a Regular Army officer before the engagement had begun: (PI) Whittard (63–67).

56 He concluded an account of being taken prisoner by commando-style army tactics: 'I think the whole weekend was one glorious learning process if you like': (PI) Atkins (385).

57 IWM, SA, 18615, Norman Griffin, 18 November 1998. Similar comments were made in interview by Brown (690), Fred Bailey, 15 February 2000 (34) and Ron Smith, 11 May 2000 (1617).

58 The 16-year-old, 6-foot Tex Laws, as well as his friends, were taunted in the street: '"Bloody great boys. Ought to be in the Guards"... so eventually I became a Home Guard', before call-up: Correspondence, Tex Laws, 3 May 2000 (28).

59 (PI) R. Smith (1493–1497). Similar comments: IWM, SA, 5561, Robert Rosamond, April 1981; 11456, Gerard Walgate, 13 August 1990.

60 (PI) R. Smith (1513).

61 (PI) R. Smith (765).

62 (PI) R. Smith (765–777). Irony characterised other memories of anticipating invasion: 'there was me with a double bore shotgun, and four cartridges. So that would have fixed the German army good and proper': IWM, SA, 15788, William Callan, 1989.

63 (PI) Alfred Claxton, 12 May 2000 (1196).

64 (PI) Atkins (111).
65 IWM, SA, 8337, John Graham, 6 August 1984.
66 (PI) Claxton (317, 337).
67 (PI) Claxton (337).
68 (PI) Brown (436, 444).
69 IWM, SA, 11234, Len Hill, 1990.
70 Portelli, *Battle*, p. xi.
71 Brophy, *Britain's Home Guard*, p. 5.
72 (PI) R. Smith, 11 May 2000 (1669).
73 (PI) John Shuttleworth, 21 March 2000 (221).
74 See Mass Observation, *The Pub and the People: A Worktown Study* (London: Cresset Library, 1987 [1943]), Chapter 9, for the pub as a site of male camaraderie and fraternity in the 1930s.
75 (PI) Shuttleworth (221).
76 IWM, SA, 11229, Arthur Ambler, 1990.
77 (PI) Brown (501).
78 IWM, SA, 15882, Reginald B. J. Lewis, 1989; correspondence, F. J. Lusted, 2 December 1999 (33); (PI) Whittard (39); (PI) Nicholson (263, 277).
79 A mass-observer in Worcestershire in 1940 made the general observation: 'It seems to be a sign of manliness to be a member of the Guard': MOA, TC 66, Town and District Survey 1938–49, Box 22, Worcester Village, August-September 1940.
80 Interviews: Claxton (250–257); Nicholson (283); Redmond (572). In contrast, 14-year-old Dennis Smith was excluded as too young: (PI) D. Smith, 11 May 2000 (522–555).
81 (PI) Atkins (649).
82 (PI) R. Smith (1521, 1525).
83 (PI) R. Smith (1537).
84 (PI) Kendall (382); he did not remember when they joined, and thought they did not wear uniforms or learn to shoot.
85 (PI) Atkins: 'I was surprised at that question, when I saw it written down, because as far as I know there was no women in the Home Guard' (445); (PI) Nicholson: 'No, no, they didn't have women in then, I suppose. This day and age they probably would, but not then' (423).
86 (PI) Nicholson (953–965).
87 (PI) Nicholson (743).
88 Correspondence, Nicholson, 15 December 1999. There is contemporary evidence that women were in fact well aware of such ploys: See MOA, TC 29, Box 4 29/4/H, Stand-Down Parade of the Home Guard, 3 December 1944, L.B.
89 (PI) D. Smith (328). Respondents recalled that the few differences (e.g. belts and gaiters made of leather rather than non-reflective webbing) detracted from the sense of being a real soldier in the Home Guard: (PI) Brown (242–244, 652–653); (PI) Hall, 28 October 1999 (236–240); correspondence, Nigel Grey, n.d. (1999–2000) (48).

90 Correspondence, Lusted, 2 December 1999 (24). Military status was enhanced by the cap badge which denoted attachment to the local army regiment.

91 Correspondence, Laws, 3 May 2000 (32).

92 (PI) Redmond (76). On the origins of the dissemination of white feathers signifying cowardice, see N. Gullace, 'White Feathers and Wounded Men: Female Patriotism and the Memory of the Great War', *Journal of British Studies*, 36:2 (1997), pp. 178–206. Redmond's 'masquerade' is discussed in Summerfield, 'Culture and Composure', pp. 72–74.

93 (PI) Redmond (72).

94 (PI) Redmond (204, 208).

95 (PI) Redmond (256, 260).

96 (PI) Redmond (288).

97 (PI) Redmond (284, 312, 348).

98 (PI) Redmond (76, 312–328).

99 (PI) Shuttleworth (589).

100 (PI) Shuttleworth (597). Atkins (525, 681) spoke in the same vein of 'girl-pulling badges' from magnificent army regiments. .

101 IWM, SA, 18076, Ted Petty, 1 November 1989; also 17673, David Hopkins, 1985; 18615, Norman Griffin, 18 November 1998; correspondence, Mike Riley, 8 March 2000 (12).

102 (PI) Kendall (515).

103 This was true of the Imperial War Museum interviews, undertaken between 1981 and 1998, as well as of our interviews, undertaken between 1998 and 2000.

104 Correspondence, Tex Laws, 22 June 2000 (not indexed).

105 *Dad's Army*, Episode 80, 'Never Too Old', 13 November 1977.

106 Correspondence, Nigel Grey, n.d. (88), and Bill Trueman, 25 February 2000 (81).

107 Correspondence, Trueman, 25 February 2000 (81).

108 Correspondence, Nigel Grey, 17 April 2000 (88).

109 Correspondence, Bill Trueman, 25 February 2000 (81).

110 Correspondence, Bill Trueman, 25 February 2000 (81).

111 (PI) Redmond (776).

112 T. G. Ashplant, 'Anecdotes as Narrative Resource in Working-Class Life Stories: Parody, Dramatization and Sequence', in M. Chamberlain and P. Thompson (eds), *Narrative and Genre* (Routledge, London, 1998), pp. 99–113.

113 (PI) Kendall (169).

114 (PI) Kendall (169, 177, 272).

115 Correspondence, Nigel Grey, January 2000 (31).

116 Correspondence, Grey, January 2000 (34); 'stupid boy' was what Mainwaring called Pike.

117 Correspondence, Grey, 17 April 2000 (25). Respondents attached their memories to other *Dad's Army* catch-phrases, too, notably Jones's 'Don't panic!'

118 (PI) Redmond (232).
119 Correspondence: D. E. Brundrett, 26 February 2000 (107); John Best, 29 February 2000 (61).
120 (PI) Shuttleworth (521).
121 Correspondence, Fred Bailey, 15 February 2000 (95).
122 Correspondence, John Lewis, 17 April 2000 (197–200).
123 IWM, SA, 9366, Frederick W. Johnes, May 1986.
124 (PI) Brown (288–332).
125 (PI) D. Smith (651); he repeated: 'It was serious. It was serious' (633–635).
126 Correspondence, David Jones, 26 February 2000 (81–84).
127 The respondents referred to here who enrolled aged 16 were Ray Atkins, Nigel Grey, Arthur Brown, Alfred Claxton, John Lewis, D. E. Brundrett, and David Jones; Norman Griffin and Mike Riley enrolled aged 15 and Dennis Smith aged 14.

8

Women, memory and home defence

The history of women and wartime home defence is, as we have seen, distinct from that of men. Summerskill's struggles in the political arena for women's membership of the Home Guard were of a different order from Wintringham's challenges to the organisation's military and political direction. Both campaigners were outsiders, he for his politics and she because of her gender, but Wintringham's school was adopted by the War Office and he was given an inside role in training, whereas Summerskill and her organisation were always officially excluded. Representations of women's contribution to home defence were almost entirely absent from wartime popular culture, whereas men's involvement was the focus of an enormous amount of interest, serious and comic, supportive and satirical. Even so, post-war culture almost forgot men's part in the Home Guard until the advent of *Dad's Army*: perhaps not surprisingly, then, it entirely forgot women's roles in home defence. *Dad's Army*'s inclusion of women recruits in one episode did not end the neglect: on the contrary, it confirmed the prevailing impression that women had no place in the force. Even though accounts of local Home Guard battalions published during and soon after the war referred to women's involvement, by the 1980s it was possible for men who had served in those same battalions to have no memory of women's presence.[1] The history of women's part in home defence is little known, and the consequences for personal recall are profound. Testimony to women's membership, when available, constitutes valuable historical evidence, but the processes of recalling and composing accounts of personal involvement in a hidden history are problematic.

In reconstructing the contest over women in the Home Guard in Chapter 3, we supplemented official records with personal testimony.

Published and unpublished memoirs, diaries and oral histories[2] complemented the evidence found in the conventional political record, such as
Hansard, War Office files and the press. In this chapter we explore further
the revelations concerning women's participation in the Home Guard and
the WHD that personal testimony offers. We also discuss the problematic
aspects of women's memories of involvement in home defence, using the
concepts of the cultural circuit, composure and intersubjectivity which
we outlined in Chapter 7.

Revelations: fathers, weapons and uniforms

As Chapter 3 demonstrated, a variety of sources suggested that women
were recruited to the Home Guard not only from April 1943, but earlier,
during the period of the War Office's ban on women's membership.
LDV and Home-Guard units were evidently keen to have these women.
Personal testimony indicates that some were recruited by friends, siblings,
colleagues and even by their Home Guard fathers, while others responded
to appeals for help in the press or cinema. Gwendoline Taylor, a 19-year-
old clerk at the time, recalled going with her younger sister to the local
cinema in Tatton, south Manchester, where they saw 'a notice on the
screen to say that Home Guard Auxiliaries, ladies of a certain age, I think
it was probably 18, were wanted'. So she and her sister, who was only 14
but who saw this as her chance to do 'her bit of war duty', insisted on
joining together or not at all.[3]

Fathers might have been expected to have been at one with the War
Office in opposing women's membership of the Home Guard. The
evidence of sons such as George Nicholson, reviewed in the previous
chapter, was of fathers who (like the left-wing journalist and Home
Guard CO John Langdon-Davies) relished the exclusively male company
of the force and regarded home defence as a man's job.[4] But oral history
accounts indicate that some fathers, on the contrary, actively recruited
their daughters. Kaitlin Wells described her father's tactics. He was a bank
manager and local community dignitary in Workington, Cumberland.
He had strong military leanings, having fought in India in the First World
War until invalided out of the army and was a member of the Home
Guard from its formation.[5]

> He … came home and said: 'We want … some typists! Want some typists. I
> thought you could … rally a few of your friends around', he said, 'to … see
> if you can get a little group of lady Home Guarders.' And of course it was
> mostly girls that I knew in the bank.[6]

Home Guard fathers such as Kaitlin's, whose overt motive was to recruit women to help with paperwork, also regarded it as appropriate for the women to train with the Home Guard for functions such as intelligence work (coding and decoding), map-reading, signals (such as use of field telephones and morse code), driving, drilling and parading.[7] Combat was not necessarily excluded, in spite of the strict prohibition issued by the War Office which banned the involvement of the Home Guard in training women to bear arms. We have seen that Ann Godden's father took her with him to the police station in Sunningdale, Berkshire, after Eden's broadcast announcing the formation of the LDV in May 1940, and insisted that she be accepted on the grounds that she could already shoot. With his approval, she honed her combat skills in the Home Guard, learning to use an array of weapons, and went on exercises with the Home Guard and the Regular Army, as well as doing guard duties in the locality.[8] Kaitlin Wells, in contrast, had no prior experience of martial arts. Her father initially undertook to train her himself. He began teaching her to use his First World War revolver in their back garden 'so that my mother and I could defend ourselves if the Germans landed, you know', until a neighbour, fearing that the sounds of shooting indicated that the Germans had indeed landed, alerted the authorities who put a stop to it. Subsequently, Kaitlin learned to shoot with the Home Guard, under the instruction of the Workington post master, on the floor of the central sorting office.[9]

These women joined Home Guard units in their localities, and their inclusion in both the Home Guard and its weapons training might be explained by family and friendship networks coupled with local assumptions that women as well as men should learn armed defence. But other women joined independently of their locality and friends. Yvette Baynes, a factory secretary at D. F. Tayler & Co., a Birmingham munitions firm, remembered that five women responded to an invitation to help the factory Home Guard 'with the clerical side'; although the women were thus to be auxiliaries, they were given the full Home Guard training. The women learned map-reading, tracking and plotting troop movements, and went out on exercises with the men, which involved the use of flour-bombs and required sleeping overnight on the ground in sleeping-bags. However, rifle drill was suddenly cancelled, to Yvette's regret: 'We were going to use rifles but then suddenly they disbanded the Home Guard.'[10] The dates are vague, a problem to which we return, but we have seen that the War Office never regarded weapons training for women as appropriate, explicitly banned it in November 1941 and reiterated the prohibition in April 1943. Nevertheless, of the 35 women in our 'archive' who worked with the Home Guard, 22, or nearly two-thirds, were trained in the use of weapons.

Women who had joined the WHD frequently mis-remembered its name, complicating the identification of the organisation to which they were recruited, Home Guard or WHD, an issue to which we return shortly. Nevertheless, nine women can be identified as having been WHD members, attracted in ways similar to those in which women were recruited to the Home Guard, by friends, through work and by public announcement of one sort or another, except that fathers did not feature in their accounts as recruiters, but figured rather (if at all) as role models who were already in the Home Guard.[11] But although the introduction to the WHD was usually made by women friends or colleagues, such as the woman veterinarian who took her 16-year-old assistant Jeanne Gale Sharp to her first meeting in Oxford,[12] it was not *always* women who recruited for the WHD.

Vida Staples, who spoke of joining 'the Home Guard' in Chatham, Kent, explained that one of the managing-directors of Wingates, the firm for which she and her sister worked, initiated the recruitment of thirty women who would specifically train to bear arms, 'soon after Dunkirk':

> He said he wanted … some women to volunteer to be armed … If they were willing, could we sound out the right type of person and see what the response was. So his secretary joined, my sister joined, and she asked me, and so I said yes, OK, so I joined. My very great friend who was at the college with me, she joined because she became the CO's secretary.[13]

This man was a JP: as we saw in Chapter 3, the War Office acknowledged that if two JPs authorised it, there was nothing illegal about the formation of an armed group of civilians, men or women.[14] As a man of local power and influence, he used the same type of informal 'club' to form a women's Home Guard as men like himself used in the formation of the men's Home Guard. But he did not take Vida and her friends and colleagues straight into the male Home Guard: Vida said that she initially joined the 'W.H.D.', continuing, 'then soon afterwards, as I say, we were into the Home Guard', although her membership of the 'W.H.D.' continued.[15] The role of the WHD in Vida's recruitment speaks to the effectiveness of the alliance that Summerskill had made with male sympathisers, and the close links between her organisation and the Home Guard.[16]

The explicit intention of the WHD was, from the outset, to be an armed organisation, as its badge, featuring crossed rifles and a revolver, signified. The ten women in our 'archive' whose WHD membership we were able to establish were trained by members of the Home Guard: they learned to fire rifles and to use a range of other weapons, including hand-grenades, sticky bombs, mortar-bombs and machine-guns, and were also taught military techniques including unarmed combat.[17] Kathleen Holmes, who joined the WHD in Leytonstone after attending a public meeting addressed by Summerskill,[18] said in response to the question 'Who taught you to shoot?':

> Oh, the soldiers, the fellows. They were young men. I mean, you see their photograph, they're young. I don't know why they were there … they couldn't have been in the army I shouldn't think. They must have been Home Guard. Perhaps they were rejected or something and – I don't know – but they were really quite tough on us. We used to go to Eton Manor, which was like a boys' club … And we used to go there quite regularly and learn to shoot. Because I used to show my husband my targets, which were really quite good he thought. … It was the Lee Enfield rifle, and we used to disarm and put them together and then lay on our tummies and shoot, and we, you know, it was really, you did get quite an impact on your shoulder from them, but, we did that all the time, and then we learnt how to handle hand-grenades.[19]

It was not the case that every woman relished her training in the way that Kathleen evidently did ('my targets … were really quite good'). Some found the Lee Enfield rifle too heavy or they lacked confidence about using it.[20] Others wondered whether they would really have been able to use the 'dirty methods' they were taught, such as how to decapitate an invader with a cheese wire, something Audrey Simpson thought would be especially difficult, given her height: she joked that she would have to ask him to bend down first.[21] The point, however, is that the oral testimony constitutes clear evidence that, in spite of the ban, WHD members

Figure 19 Leytonstone WHD. Kathleen Holmes is standing in the second row, fourth from right

learned, under Home Guard auspices, to use both the regular and irregular weapons of the Home Guard.

We saw in Chapter 3 that uniforms for women Home Guards were also forbidden by the War Office. However, oral evidence indicates that some women in the Home Guard as well as the WHD wore *both* badges, and also improvised uniform. Six of the women who joined the Home Guard said they were given, or were asked to adapt, a military uniform: Mary Warschauer and Lois Baker, working in the Air Ministry Home Guard, wore navy-blue RAF dungarees and Glengarrie-type hats;[22] Winifred Watson, full-time Home Guard secretary in Wingham, Kent, wore an ATS-style tunic and skirt;[23] Eunice Lowden's unit in the City of London wore dark trousers, white shirts with epaulettes and shoulder flashes, dark ties and forage caps, their round badges pinned to their chests;[24] and Mollie Dale in Smethwick and Jeanne Townend in Goole, new entrants after 'recognition', wore ATS-style greatcoats and army trousers, and a battle-dress top.[25] Jeanne Townend, whose father, the local mayor and fishmonger, had recruited her, said: 'Probably my father ... had asked for it, 'cause we used to do manoeuvres and marching and – I suppose really you needed it'.[26] Even members of the WHD were, in some places, issued with military uniforms. Louie White, in the Leeds WHD, was given a denim battledress by the Home Guard, as she recorded in her diary for 1943:

> Nov 21 In the morning went to HG and Barbara and I got our uniforms. They are only Denims but we will alter them and make them fit. During the afternoon I altered the trousers.
>
> Dec 4 Stayed in at night and finished my uniform.
>
> Dec 5 Had to go out bombing with the home guard. Went in my uniform and corporal thought I looked nice.[27]

In February 1944 she was issued with a beret and a Home Guard badge.[28]

Women who received no such garments improvised with their own 'dark trousers and a dark top' or 'slacks'.[29] They remembered the pleasure of going to the training meetings in trousers and simple pullovers, which were practical for lying on the ground during rifle drill, in an era when it was still relatively unusual, and not altogether respectable, for women to be seen in trousers.[30] Those in authority sometimes justified such attire in terms of propriety, as Gwendoline Taylor explained. The Cheadle Home Guard meetings were held in a hayloft over a stable, and her CO became concerned:

He'd say 'Now come up to the office', and as we went up the ladder, he said, 'Oh ladies, I'm going to have to ask you to wear trousers, or the men may be seeing more than they should.' So we had to wear trousers to climb the ladder (*laughs*).[31]

Another of those who improvised, however, recalled more serious reasons for needing a uniform. Vida Staples in Chatham remembered being told that the Government had refused to authorise uniforms for women working with the Home Guard, and that the implications for armed women were serious. This was because, in the event of an invasion, civilian combatants would not be taken prisoner by the enemy but would be dealt with summarily. We saw in Chapter 3 that, although the issue was contested in the press, Summerskill believed this to be so,[32] as did some COs. Vida Staples recalled Major Miller summoning the WHD members to see him, to explain:

[W]e all gathered round the table and he said, 'Well I have to put it to you', he said, 'that we can't get any uniforms. The War Office will just not accept it', he said, 'so I have to tell you, that if you're caught with fire-arms, you'll be shot. And so if you want to retract, you know, you can do so.' But none of us did.[33]

Vida was one of several women who said she 'always turned up in slacks', with a jersey top, 'so you were ready for anything'.[34] The oral evidence supports MPs' contentions, in Parliament in March 1944, that women Home Guards felt the need for uniforms and provided their own unofficial versions, while Sir James Grigg, as he put it himself, turned a blind eye.[35]

Dates, names, badges and photographs

Oral history has frequently been criticised on the grounds of the fallibility of memory. With specific reference to the history of the Home Guard, S. P. MacKenzie rejected it on the grounds that 'the passage of time has blurred memories' of specifics such as the weapons used and the dates of events, and that 'the best historical evidence … is evidence recorded at the time'.[36] The response of recovery historians committed to oral testimony is that some aspects of the past simply were not 'recorded at the time', or that, if they were, the record is brief or ambiguous; oral history fills gaps and amplifies such cases: thus oral and documentary types of source can be used together to advantage. Chapter 3 showed that oral evidence about women's recruitment by the men of the Home Guard is supported by local COs' accounts of the formation and activities of their units, quoted in the appendix to Graves's 1943 history of the force. Likewise, oral testimony concerning the Home Guard's co-operation with the WHD is validated by the files of Wallasey WHD in the Wirral archives, which testify to close links between the two organisations. More specifically, the memories of Kaitlin Wells, who was recruited to the Home Guard by her father in Workington, are borne out by local historical research. Kaitlin said that at least two of the town's Home Guard companies recruited women from 1941 onwards, including 'Headquarters Company' to which she belonged.[37] A website run by local historian R. W. Barnes states that Workington Home Guard did indeed recruit women to both its 'A-Company' and its 'HQ-Company'.[38] In these instances, documentary and oral sources offer mutual confirmation of accounts that might otherwise seem unlikely, given their dissonance with the official version of events.

On the problem of the reliability of memory, it has been claimed that while short-term memory deteriorates with age, long-term memory is not affected in the same way and may even improve,[39] and that while anxiety about memory increases in old age, so too does the motivation to recall the distant past.[40] Defenders of oral history have also pointed out that individuals' memories of routines and particular incidents are often strong, even if recalling more abstract information such as dates, particularly of public as opposed to personal events, is harder.[41] This was evident in the personal testimony: both male and female interviewees asked for help with wartime dates, such as the declaration of war and the retreat from Dunkirk. Vida Staples summed up the problem for many, 'I have an awful job with chronological order these days.'[42] But men were more often able to pinpoint the moment they joined the Home Guard in relation to the date they left school, started a new job or received their call-up papers. Women were more likely to lack such clear landmarks. In exploring their difficulties, we are not *criticising* the women's capacity to remember; on the contrary, we are seeking to identify the gendered reasons for these problems of memory and to recuperate women's partial and imperfect memories as historical evidence.

Many of the interviews bear the imprint of the mutual struggles of interviewee and interviewer to clarify dates. Ellen Baxter said that, on receiving her call-up papers with other women born in 1921, she went to the Employment Exchange to enlist, but was informed that her job of pay-roll clerk with London Transport was a reserved occupation. This meant that she could not join the Women's Royal Naval Service, as she had wished, so she joined the 'Women's Home Guard' instead: she was uncertain, but thought this was at the start of the war, in 1939, when she was 18.[43] However, in contrast to the conscription of men, which began at the start of the war in 1939, the conscription of young single women was not introduced until December 1941, and the call-up of women born in 1921 began in 1942. This would suggest that Ellen was enrolled in the 'Women's Home Guard' in 1942. But as we saw in Chapter 3, women were officially permitted to join the Home Guard for the first time in April 1943; and it was initially tempting to impose that date on this apparently insecure chronology.[44] There was, however, sufficient corroborating evidence, in Ellen's and other cases, to make it clear that this was inappropriate: women's personal testimonies described an alternative reality to that which could be derived from the official files, and it could not be ignored.

Part of this evidence concerned the identity of the organisations joined by the interviewees, although that, too, was problematic. They agreed to be interviewed on the grounds that they had something to say about women and the Home Guard, but the specifics of the organisations joined were frequently difficult for them to remember. However, their recall of organisational names was coloured by their possession or recollection of items of material culture such as badges and photographs.

The complexity of these interactions is illustrated by the case of Louie White (later Louie Williams) whose personal testimony took a variety of forms: a diary, photographs, letters and telephone conversations. She had deposited her wartime diary, a rare example of evidence of women's Home Guard involvement 'recorded at the time', in the Imperial War Museum in 1983. Having consulted it, we contacted Louie,[45] and she corresponded with us and sent us photographs, and we spoke several times on the 'phone. Thus we were able to compare her wartime account of her experiences with her recent memories. On the subject of organisational affiliation, she referred in correspondence to the 'Home Guard', but she also wrote and spoke of a number of badges, providing material evidence of the groups she had joined.

She said in the first telephone call that she remembered being given a badge with a horse on it, the regimental badge of the 9th West Riding Battalion Home Guard unit. She also remembered that she had a round, plastic Home Guard badge that was 'just for the women', who wore it pinned to the berets with which they were issued (in addition to military uniform) by the Home Guard. Louie recalled sadly that she had lost her round badge. In addition she remembered getting 'a little shield' that she thought had the initials LDV on it, which she had given to the Imperial War Museum with the diary in the early 1980s. Two days later, Louie called

Figure 20 Louie White, seated second from the left, with Leeds Home Guard

back to say that she had remembered that the shield was enamel, had crossed rifles on it, possibly said 'WHD' rather than 'LDV' and that she had acquired it at a meeting in Leeds, addressed by Edith Summerskill.[46] There is no direct reference in the diary to this badge; nor is it visible in the photographs that Louie sent, but the details in the diary support the inference that the 'little shield' was the WHD badge: on 4 November 1942 she received 'an answer to my request about Women's Home Defence' and from 10 November 1942 to 1 December 1944 entries chronicle her active involvement in the WHD. As well as using its full name, Louie referred in the diary to the Women's Home Defence as both 'W.H.' and 'H.D.' from November 1942 to March 1943, and then as 'H.G.' or 'Home Guard' from March 1943 to December 1944. The diary substantiates Louie's possession of the round, plastic Home Guard badge and records its loss on 20 October 1944.[47] The omission in the diary of any direct reference to the WHD shield emphasises, however, that even 'evidence recorded at the time' is not necessarily complete. The undated wartime photographs that Louie sent, of herself and three other women on manoeuvres with the men of the Home Guard, show the women wearing the regimental badge pinned over the top-left pocket of their army battledress, with the Home Guard badge on their berets.

Taken together, Louie White's diary, her spoken memories and her photographs, constitute significant evidence of organisational affiliation which transgressed the official rules. They confirm and elaborate the close links of the Home Guard with the WHD. The nomenclature and acronyms used in the diary, and the photographs and badges, suggest that organisational boundaries in Leeds became increasingly permeable. The Leeds Home Guard accepted members of the WHD as Women Home Guard Auxiliaries. But they were not only involved as 'nominated women', whose contribution was supposed to be cooking, typing and driving and who were entitled to wear the round 'HG' badge but no uniform; they were also included as Home Guards proper, who wore the official badge of the army regiment to which the Leeds Home Guard battalion belonged and who went out on exercises with the men, dressed in almost identical military uniforms.

This account of Louie's memory of the WHD and the Home Guard could be read as an exercise in 'triangulation', using a combination of personal testimony and material culture to establish the validity of her account.[48] The objectives here, however, are to emphasise the difficulties that women had in remembering which organisation(s) they had belonged to during the war (in comparison to the relatively simple issue for men of remembering LDV and Home Guard affiliation), and also, despite the problems, the importance of their evidence for the recovery of the history in which they participated. A case in point is Jeanne Gale Sharp, whose notice in the personal column of *Saga Magazine* in 1997, indicated that it might be possible to find women with memories of their involvement in home defence. Jeanne was well motivated to remember. She was a campaigner: her purpose in placing the notice was to attract support for the inclusion of women former Home Guards in Remembrance Day parades.[49] She still possessed a badge, a signifier of her membership, which she showed to the interviewer. But Jeanne's memory of the name of the organisation to which it referred was confused:

JGS: And I was given, well I suppose given, probably had to buy it, knowing them, I was given this badge.

PS: Oh, great. (*A brief digression follows.*)

JGS: This is one of my treasured possessions, my badge. That's it.

PS: I'm sure. WHD.

JGS: Yes, Women's Home Division, not Guard.

PS: Right.

JGS: I found out, we were always called 'Women's Home Guard' but I realise that they've put 'Division' on that.

PS: Right, it's got crossed rifles, and, and a revolver.

JGS: Yes, and we were taught how to shoot those, you see.[50]

This was in fact the WHD badge, but Jeanne Gale-Sharp had not retained a memory of that name. She recalled that the women were known as Women Home Guards – as it seems likely they were – and imposed on the initials on the badge a plausible, although inaccurate, interpretation.[51]

Why was it hard for WHD members to remember the name of the organisation they joined, in spite of its striking badge? The explanation of unreliable memories is not an issue that recovery historians tend to address, being disposed to overlook evidence subject to such apparent weaknesses, and to emphasise instead whatever can be declared as valid. In contrast, such mis-remembering is regarded by those who adopt the cultural memory approach as an important aspect of the history under scrutiny, relevant in particular to the subjective meanings of that history to its participants. Thus, for example, Alistair Thomson discusses the account of an Australian First World War veteran, Percy Bird, of witnessing the seizing of the German ship *Holtz* on the River Yarra, in Melbourne in August 1914, from the train on which he was a passenger at the time. Thomson demonstrates that the geography of Melbourne is such that it would have been impossible to see the ship from the train. But he treats this mis-remembering not as a mistake or invention on Percy's part, to be disregarded by the historian, but as a key 'memory' that functioned significantly in Percy's narrative as an explanation for volunteering to fight in the war, in personal circumstances that were not conducive to his doing so.[52]

In the case of Percy Bird's unreliable memory, the historian's task was to suggest a reason for the inaccurate account that he supplied, and it was possible to do so in relation to the meanings communicated by his narrative as a whole. In a similar vein, as far as women's membership of the WHD is concerned, our task is to explain why women have forgotten the name and, by implication, the status of the organisation they joined. There are a number of ways of approaching this issue.[53] Those that we explore here concern, broadly, the circuit between memory and culture, and, specifically, two types of intersubjectivity: the relationship between personal memory and the audiences for reminiscence and that between memories and cultural representations of the past.

Women's memories and *Dad's Army*

Women with memories of Home Guard involvement told us they had difficulty finding receptive audiences. The absence of intersubjective opportunities was a problem since it denied the women casual, quotidien chances to talk about their Home Guard experiences, and thereby to keep the memory of them alive in the same ways as men. There was a consensus among the women respondents that there was no possibility of telling friends and family about their wartime experiences with the Home Guard. Audrey Simpson, who joined the Leytonstone WHD with her friend Kathleen Holmes, said at a moment in the interview when she was finding it hard to remember: 'Do you know, I never talk to my children about it?' The interviewer later asked her more about this: 'They haven't been interested you know. When I showed my daughter this [interviewer's letter] and told her what was going to happen, she, you know, said, "Ooh. What're you bothering with that for? It's a long time ago". Because they don't know anything about it, you see.'[54] Several women referred to being laughed at when they mentioned that they were women Home Guards – a response not conducive to 'composure'.[55] Even contemporaries, including their husbands, were sceptical rather than encouraging. Audrey's friend Kathleen Holmes described taking a photograph of the Leytonstone WHD unit with her when visiting Audrey:

> And she said to her husband, 'There you are, you see, John.' She said, 'That proves it, doesn't it?' because I don't think he believed her. Nobody believed us, and of course when we said we did rifle shooting, I'm sure they didn't believe us, our friends, you know, really. But, because they'd never heard of it, nobody – it had never been mentioned in all the war bits or anything about the war.[56]

Kathleen's reference to the absence of representations of women's participation in the Home Guard in 'anything about the war', and her use of this as an explanation for the indifference of local and familial audiences ('Nobody believed us') gives rise to the wider question of the relationship of reminiscence to cultural representations of the past. Kathleen was arguing in effect that the lack of audience for women's memories was not surprising: this history was absent from everyday knowledge gained from present-day coverage of the war ('all the war bits') on television and in the press. Lois Baker, who joined the Air Ministry Auxiliary to the Home Guard, made the same point, and added to it a reminder that, even at the time, there was an absence of public accounts of women in the Home Guard: 'Have they ever shown anywhere that there were women? Have they ever shown any of these films? I mean they have had references to the Home Guard forming, well it was the L.D.V. to start with. They have had that, because I've seen it. But we were isolated, or insulated. I don't think we knew that there were any other ladies anywhere doing anything of that nature. How could we have known?'[57] One of the satisfactions for women of participating in the project was to discover that they were not alone.[58] However, the absence of women in the Home Guard from popular representations, in the present or the past, to which Kathleen and Lois drew attention, was still problematic for individual memory.

We have used the concept of the cultural circuit to refer to the process by which individual stories of experience are given public form and, as a result, the subject (if not the detail) of such stories is perpetuated in popular memory. As we said in the previous chapter, such public accounts both facilitate and constrain recall. Audiences, whether small and casual or larger and more formal, play a crucial part in the circuit. They tend to affirm accounts that they recognise, from sources such as film and television, but are less receptive to those that bear little resemblance to what they know; unresponsive audiences thus act as 'circuit-breakers'. With men's accounts of their pasts in mind, theorists of popular memory such as Alistair Thomson suggest that audience recognition and affirmation lead narrators to emphasise some aspects of their story at the expense of others: notably, in Thomson's research, to emphasise aspects that conformed to 'the Anzac legend' as opposed to those that did not. But in the case of histories that have been entirely hidden, and about which there is no legend, audiences' non-recognition of the subject matter is likely to be profound, and to have a powerful silencing effect that works to the detriment of memory.

As we have seen, the men of the Home Guard were well embedded in popular memory as a result of their representation both in wartime and in late twentieth-century popular culture. *Dad's Army* generated a dominant image of the Home Guard that was at the same time supportive of an heroic interpretation of the war effort *and* sceptical about the Home Guard's military – and masculine – capacity. In contrast, the women of the Home Guard were practically invisible. Exceptional roles in home defence were given briefly to women in a small number of high-profile wartime films; but, those excesses aside, combatant women were not compatible with the norms of femininity, and otherwise women had no more than a marginal relationship to organised home defence, as commentators on the sidelines. Women Home Guards were eclipsed both by the legend of the male membership and by the representation alongside it of the conventional, non-military, female figure.

Dad's Army was as important a reference point for the women who were interviewed as it was for the men. All the women felt that *Dad's Army* satirised the Home Guard, but, like the men, they responded to this representation in two different ways. Some compared *Dad's Army* approvingly with their personal memories: it confirmed their impression of the Home Guard as inept and comical. Others contrasted *Dad's Army* unfavourably with memories of a force that was not ridiculous.

Of the women who took the view that the Home Guard was as comic as *Dad's Army* suggested, Lois Baker made the most emphatic and categorical statement.[59] In response to a question about whether the Home Guard could have been effective in action, she said: 'It would have been a farce, the whole thing would have been a farce, I'm sure. I mean when I see *Dad's Army* on here I think that is it to a T, I really do. A lot of self-important men.'[60] She went on to bracket herself and the other women Home Guards with these pretentious men, when reflecting on the origins of her own membership: 'How it actually came about I don't know, but I suspect, as all girls together, we said, "Well that's a good thing. We can dress ourselves up and perform."'[61] Yet in every instance in which women asserted that *Dad's Army* was 'it to a T', there were qualifications, and even, as we show, again in the case of Lois Baker, a complete contradiction.

Several of the women who saw *Dad's Army* as an accurate representation delighted in likening the Home Guard members with whom they worked to *Dad's Army* characters, in ways similar to male interviewees. Gwendoline Taylor, who told the story about being instructed to wear trousers, said that her Home Guard captain 'was very much ex-First World War army, he was a very, very military man, he was Captain Ginger … and he looked all the world like a little, round Captain Mainwaring … He was very self-important, he used to bristle, you know'.[62] A description of her work, in response to a question about whether she drilled with the men, led her to enlarge on the similarities to the *Dad's Army* characters, as well as evoking the achievement of social unity from diversity that was a feature of the sitcom:

> All we did was be in the office and type the reports and type the drills and type the rotas, answer letters. And Captain Ginger, as I say, very much like Captain Mainwaring, and he used to make a lot of work as well (*laughs*) and it had to be documented you know. Oh he loved being in charge … they were nearly all elderly, they weren't likely to be called up. We didn't have anybody like Lavender who was a bit thick, but even the sort of, well, labourer type of chaps, they were all, all so polite and so genuinely nice.[63]

Mainwaring provided a template for authoritarian, militaristic – and comical – Home Guard leaders, whether male or female. Kathleen Holmes and Audrey Simpson compared their woman leader in the WHD with Mainwaring. Holmes said 'now they've had *Dad's Army*, she was absolutely like Captain Mainwaring, only a woman'. She was 'dumpy and fair, and little glasses, and only small, and plump'. Simpson added to the description, '[she was] a very bossy woman'.[64] Others of the seven leading characters were also reference points, including the callow Frank Pike, referred to above, the antique and incontinent Charles Godfrey, and the well-bred and insouciant Sergeant Wilson.[65]

But although these women attested to the verisimilitude of *Dad's Army*, they also qualified their assertions. Gwendolyn Taylor said: 'I mean, obviously that's a caricature because it was far more serious.'[66] The dictates of 'sitcom' made the programme different from documentary and other representations of history. Kaitlin Wells, who said that the programme was 'typical' added 'of course that is a comedy programme ... I think the television series was much more angled at making it humorous, making a serious situation very humorous. I mean, they couldn't very well do anything else, could they?'[67] Wells, however, struggled with the issue of typicality: 'The, all sorts of people involved in it, you know. The opportunist and the patriotic ... It was reasonably true to life, I think. Although we never had anything like that happening.'[68] We show later how Wells sought to reconcile the tension between her statements that the programme was 'true to life' and that 'nothing like that happened' in her experience.

Ann Godden had a clear sense of the difference, and the interplay, between television comedy and real life: '*Dad's Army* to a certain extent pokes fun, but I don't mind that, I think that's fine. I mean, if you can get a laugh out of these things I'm all for it. I love the programmes. I think they are splendid and quite a lot of it is true.' She went on, reflectively, to suggest that there was a consonance between the fun of *Dad's Army* and views of the Home Guard at the time: 'there was a humorous side. I mean, I don't think we could have coped if we hadn't laughed at things and ourselves as well as everything else. And I think it's fine.'[69] Her comment obliquely evokes the wealth of self-deprecating wartime Home Guard humour reviewed in Chapter 4, which can be seen as part of just such a strategy of wartime coping.[70] She was well aware that the comic image of the Home Guard was not the only story, either in wartime or in the era of the television show: 'I mean, those who really knew a bit about it realise we were serious and we were doing our best, and the others, well let them get some fun out of it, if there's any going, fine.'[71]

The women referred to above subscribed to the view that the Home Guard was, at least in part, ridiculous, and that *Dad's Army* reconstructed it as such. In focusing on the 'pathetic' and 'comic' elements of the Home Guard in the television rendering, they (apart from Godden) overlooked the 'valorous' components. But even they acknowledged that the Home Guard as they had known it had a serious side as well. Rather than maintain both viewpoints at once, as 4 of these 5 women did, Lois Baker moved during the interview from the one to the other. As we have seen, she asserted early on that the Home Guard was a 'farce' and that 'Dad's Army' represented it 'to a T', that is, to perfection. However, after a further hour of reminiscence she reversed her claim that *Dad's Army* was an accurate representation of the Home Guard: 'I would say, of course, that the men that we had in the Home Guard weren't as stupid or disorganised as they are shown to be on television. No, of course they weren't. They were intelligent men who thought they could do a good job, and I suppose we were the same.'[72] The interview process carried her back in time, imaginatively, and gradually enabled her to think outside the powerful received view, 'as shown ... on television', to re-evaluate the meaning of her experience.

Other women were consistently critical of the show: *Dad's Army* misrepresented the Home Guard which did not deserve to be ridiculed. They were forgiving towards the programme as entertainment, making the same distinction as the first group between sitcom and experience, but they were emphatic that the comedy was a misrepresentation. 'I enjoy it because it's a laugh, and, Mainwaring and all those sort of people, they are a laugh. But they really became very proficient' said Marion Bourne.[73] It was generally felt, as Marion implied, that *Dad's Army* overlooked the changes that had occurred in the Home Guard from the early, ill-equipped and untrained days to the creation of an efficient part-time army.[74] Vida Staples stated that she loved the programme, but then responded to the question 'Was it like that?' with 'No! (*Laughs*) Not from my point of view. But you can see that you could make a farce of it, quite easily.' She referred to shortages of equipment, and the perplexity experienced by Home Guards on exercises, as 'situations that could be exploited', but declared that over time the 'able-bodied men' of the Home Guard, under Churchill's inspirational leadership, 'really got themselves going and got their resources together'.[75]

Joan Hardy, who had worked for a succession of Home Guard COs at the War Office in London, took a harder line on the farcical representation of the force than the other women in this group. Even though she enjoyed likening some of the men of the Home Guard that she knew to characters in *Dad's Army*,[76] she explained that she had been so infuriated by a letter in the *Daily Mail*, in August 1993, saying that the Home Guard was a joke that she wrote to the paper to protest. The main points of her letter, which was published and a copy of which she had kept, were as follows:

members of the Home Guard took the place of Grenadier Guardsmen stationed at the Admiralty Arch in London who were killed by bombing, and a number of Home Guard leaders known to her lost sons in the war. She thus emphasised the heroism of the men of the Home Guard, albeit by vicarious means: substituting for the 'real' army; suffering the deaths of sons in war. She also stated proudly that Churchill, when inspecting the Home Guard, had called her 'Number One Lady Home Guard',[77] thereby claiming official recognition at the highest level for her own role. Writing the letter to the *Daily Mail* was one way of asserting that women too 'were there'.

Women who had been involved in home defence made two further kinds of references to *Dad's Army*. In one, they challenged women's invisibility in the popular memory of the Home Guard and suggested that women Home Guards should also have been included in the show as part of its comedy. Kaitlin Wells argued that the inclusion of women would have enhanced the comic interpretation: 'I'm surprised that he never had any women's Home Guard section because it could have been developed into quite a useful offshoot of his comedy show, you know.'[78] With this in mind, she retold as a *Dad's Army* vignette the story of her own recruitment to the Workington company by her bank-manager father.[79] Of course, as we have seen, one *Dad's Army* episode out of eighty did feature women as members. But its focus was on the unlikely romance that arose between Captain Mainwaring and one of the volunteers, and the only message of the episode seemed to be that the recruitment of women was a disastrous experiment. But the regular inclusion of women members in the comedy series would have secured for women members of the Home Guard a place in collective memory. In doing so, it would have contributed to the rehabilitation of Kaitlin's personal experience. As it was, Kaitlin did not believe she could find a receptive audience for her memories: 'I keep quiet about it because I, I think people would just laugh, you know, and say "what was the Home Guard?"'[80]

Kaitlin would evidently have been content with the inclusion of women as part of the 'pathetic' and 'comic' version of the Home Guard portrayed by *Dad's Army* . But several of the women who took a critical view of the *Dad's Army* representation felt that its treatment of the men of the Home Guard had produced a public image of a ridiculous (all-male) force that made it even more difficult to speak of their own experiences. When asked if she talked to her son and his family about her wartime experiences, Winnie Watson said: 'Well, he don't ask much about it really, they don't ask. Well, actually, *Dad's Army* done it a bit. I mean, if you say you were in the Home Guard, it's a bit of a joke, isn't it?'[81] Lois Baker made a similar statement with reference to her friends. As we have seen, early in the interview she said that *Dad's Army* represented the Home Guard 'to a T', but she took a different view later, asserting its seriousness. At this point in the interview, she was critical not just of the programme but of its effects on popular attitudes to the Home Guard:

> LB: I was telling people I swim with about this [interview], and they thought I must be mad.
> CPB: Why?
> LB: I don't know. I think they regard it as all rather a joke, you see, because people have only seen *Dad's Army*, and they think it's a joke.[82]

For some women such disappointment with, or even outrage at, comic misrespresentation, was strengthened by the awareness that women's part in the Home Guard had been overlooked in history. Jeanne Gale Sharp was adamant that the history of the women's Home Guard had been ignored or suppressed: 'they quietly and conveniently forgot about us, and sat on what they knew, didn't they? … I mean, people up here say, "Well there wasn't one" and I say "Oh yes there was, because I was in it", you know …But "Oh no" and if you talk to any men about it they think it's a *huge* joke, huge joke.' The effect of *Dad's Army* was to reinforce this vulnerability to ridicule: 'It's not done us any favours really. Not really. I mean, it was, it's a great show and I've laughed as well as anybody but it hasn't done [them] any favours, it hasn't done us any favours either, because it makes the whole thing look rather foolish and ineffectual.'[83] In her view, the programme had damaged the popular memory of the Home Guard.

The power of the Home Guard legend created by *Dad's Army* was thus acknowledged in the women's interviews, as it was in the men's. It was endorsed in some accounts, albeit with reservations which recognised that a sitcom obeyed rules different from those of 'history-making'. It was lamented in others, by women who felt it was an unfair implantation in the popular mind, and who were, or became, critical of the legend, believing that the warping of popular knowledge of the Home Guard by the successful television programme made it all the harder for them to insert their own past experiences within its history. Their point of view contrasts with one of the criticisms of oral history referred to in the previous chapter: to these women, popular historical and ideological interpretations do not distort personal memory: they contaminate the public reception of memory stories.

Anecdotes and epics

Clearly, the problems of unreceptive audiences and cultural distortions contributed to women narrators' difficulties in achieving *composure* from reminiscence. However, the oral history interviews provided them with interested and sympathetic audiences that specifically invited them to compose stories about their Home Guard experiences and to integrate them into their life stories. Crucial to this process of narration and self-realisation was women's use of available narrative forms.

Anecdotes featured in most of the women's oral history accounts, as they did in the men's. They took the form of amusing or dramatic accounts of single incidents concerning the narrator and/or others, told in the expectation that the audience would recognise the subject matter. Some of the anecdotes that peppered the women's oral testimony have already been referred to or quoted: Kaitlin Wells's story of her father teaching her to shoot in the back garden, until a neighbour mistook the noise for the invasion and raised the alarm; Audrey Simpson's account of being trained to garrotte Germans with a cheesewire, having asked them to bend down first; and Gwendoline Taylor's story of 'Captain Ginger' making the women Home Guards wear trousers, so that the male Home Guards would not 'see more than they should' as the women climbed the ladder to the office. Each of these 'snapshots' encapsulated a subjective truth about war, the Home Guard, gender and the British. There was an element of transgression in each of them: women bore weapons in two and wore trousers in the third. Another example is Ellen Baxter's account of the preparations she had to take before she used her rifle, a story which she had included in the notes she was using to aid her memory:

> It was quite funny, I had to wear – I can only wink with that eye. I can't wink with that. And of course when we used to have to do our rifle duties, I had to have an eye-shield on because I couldn't wink! And I put here – it was quite funny – I had to wear an eye-shield on my left eye as I couldn't wink. This caused a great deal of amusement. They said I would have to tell the Germans to wait while I put my eye-shield on![84]

This single anecdote caught the essence of Ellen's Home Guard experiences. It had two facets, the second of which was dominant. The first constructed Ellen's wartime subjectivity as a valiant woman who joined the WHD and learned to use a rifle alongside the men of the Home Guard, experiences to which, as we have seen, present-day audiences tended to be unable to relate. But its other facet communicated the meaning of the Home Guard and the war effort in ways familiar to a British audience, accustomed to jokes about the incompetence of the Home Guard and the improbability of victory, had the British depended on them. The punchline is a good example of the ironic British wartime humour reviewed in Chapter 4 concerning both the enemy (who would not have waited for anyone) and British defence capability (reliant on defenders with all sorts of deficiencies, such as an inability to wink). Humour cloaks the force of any implied critique, but the anecdote still suggests that Ellen's membership was a relatively futile, if sincerely meant, gesture, and that, by implication, so too was the formation of the Home Guard as a whole.

Such Home Guard anecdotes followed the course of the wartime humorous sketches about the Home Guard that we reviewed in Chapter 4. By the same token, they resembled the stories based on personal experience that were sent to the BBC by the first viewers of *Dad's Army*, which we reviewed in Chapter 6, and which contributed to the creative and experiential flow that nourished the series. The plots of numerous *Dad's Army* episodes were built on such stories. There was a cultural connection at the level of narrative form, for women as for men, between the short, humorous anecdotes that punctuated the interviews and the comic incidents of which *Dad's Army* episodes were constructed. This link was explicit in some of the interviews with women, just as it was in some of those with men.

When asked whether *Dad's Army* portrayed the Home Guard accurately, Kaitlin Wells repeated two anecdotes that she had told earlier in the interview, in response to a question about whether 'you could have defended yourself if the Germans had invaded then'[85] The immediate prompt for the repetition was her own struggle with the 'typicality' of *Dad's Army*, referred to earlier in this chapter: 'It was reasonably true to life, I think. Although we never had anything like that happening.'[86] The two repeated stories were about the Clifton Home Guard company, to which the local coal-miners belonged. They indicated that these Home Guards were not incompetent, and although they were comic, they were in earnest. In the first, Kaitlin recounted that when performing mock battles as training exercises, the miners frequently refused to play 'dead'. Mimicking the miners' speech, she explained that the Clifton Home Guard

> used to have exercises on a Sunday, you know, and very often … people were supposed to have been shot and they were dead: 'Naw Arter, tho's deid.' 'Ah isn't, Ah isn't.' 'Ah told tha, tho's deid,' you know, and he wouldn't, he was supposed to have been shot and would, he wouldn't admit that he was dead! 'Ah's not deid.' They were very tough. I wouldn't like to have been any German that had got into their hands.[87]

The other repeated anecdote substantiated this last point. German prisoners of war were favoured by the local farmers as a source of free labour, but occasionally they used the opportunity to escape, in which case the Clifton Home Guard went after them:

> The farmers used to feed them up like mad ...They were falling over themselves to volunteer to work on the farms. And we used to see truckloads of them going. We always used to stick our tongues out at them, which was stupid really. But, once or twice ... one or two escaped, and I don't know where they thought they could go but they escaped, and of course the Home Guard, their blood was up, you know, hunting down these chaps. They got them, of course, and brought them back![88]

The story portrayed the farmers as opportunists, the Germans as enemies to be routinely insulted, and the Clifton miners as patriotic and coura- geous Home Guards.

Kaitlin's use of these anecdotes to broker between what she felt to be the true-to-life qualities of *Dad's Army* and her memory that 'we never had anything like that happening' suggests that *Dad's Army* established its own 'typicality' which shaped the imaginative possibilities open to individuals to recall and recount Home Guard experiences. This is not to say that Kaitlin invented her anecdotes under the influence of *Dad's Army*. But her reiteration of them in the context of her discussion of the television series suggests that she identified them as suitable Home Guard stories. They offered the kind of typicality associated with *Dad's Army*, because of their conformity to the spirit of its episodes, specifically the combination of 'pathetic, comic yet valorous' qualities. It is notable, however, and consistent with *Dad's Army*'s treatment of women, that Kaitlin herself did not feature in them as a participant in home defence. In contrast to the anecdotes that *Dad's Army* inspired men such as James Kendall to tell, it did not facilitate Kaitlin's reconstruction of her own subjectivity as a member of the Home Guard.[89]

Men made more extensive use of the anecdotal form than did women: 'swinging the lamp', the term Ray Atkins used for swapping stories over a drink, is an established male form of social interaction. But oral history accounts rarely consist entirely of anecdotes: the unwritten contract of the oral history interview is that the interviewee is prepared and able to produce a narrative, laden with personal and historical significance, that places themselves at the centre as the subject.[90] Men's recall of wartime experience was given shape, in many cases, by a well-established narra- tive of a young man's encounters with the military on his journey into adulthood during wartime. The Home Guard was included, either as a stepping-stone to the goal of full military enlistment or as an alternative to it. Such accounts often contained epic elements of striving to overcome obstacles on the way to a morally sanctioned goal. In this respect, they revealed a key difference from women, who, even in the Second World War, did not share this journey towards combat: this was a male model of narration.

However, wartime films such as *The Gentle Sex* and *Millions Like Us*, both released in 1943, adapted the male narrative to support the participation of young single women in the war effort. These officially sponsored films suggested that women's recruitment to, respectively, the women's auxiliary services and a munitions factory, paralleled that of men, even though it excluded the training for combat that was central to men's military experience. Both films emphasised women's responsibilities towards the military war, and *The Gentle Sex*, which depicted ATS searchlight operators on a mixed anti-aircraft battery, emphasised servicewomen's involvement in battle.[91] Such stories of women's mobilisation were under-represented in popular memory after the war, but research in the 1990s on women's memories of their wartime experiences showed that some women drew on just such narratives to depict their wartime lives. Their accounts were built on stories of call-up or volunteering, the support or opposition of parents, leaving home, initiation into war work and its proximity to 'the front line', experiences on and off the job, and transition into post-war life and work. Accounts that borrowed most heavily from the male model of narration were 'heroic': that is, imbued with a spirit of feminine patriotism that welcomed the altered gender roles consequent for women upon 'doing one's bit' for the war effort. In contrast, other accounts rejected a heroic interpretation. They were 'stoic': that is permeated by a sense of endurance and of 'just getting on with it' until the exceptional circumstances of war were over and a return to normal life, including familiar gender relations, was possible.[92]

The wider story of women's mobilisation for war offered women with Home Guard experiences a general reference point, even though they, like the men, were not literally mobilised, either because they were below call-up age (which was set at 19 for women in December 1941) or because they were in reserved occupations. But there were significant omissions in the versions of this narrative in popular memory: neither women in combat nor women in the Home Guard featured.

Some of the Home Guard women presented themselves as frustrated 'heroes' who were excluded from the range of new wartime experiences available to women. Their ambition to join one of the women's services was thwarted by the practice of 'reservation' or by their employers' manipulation of the reservation regulations. As with men, joining the Home Guard was in such cases a way of compensating for a sense of marginalisation from the war effort.[93] Whether or not Home Guard membership involved weapons' training, it was spoken of by this group of women as a serious contribution to the war effort, especially in contrast to work that caused them to be 'reserved' but which seemed less directly relevant to the war, or even wholly futile. Thus Gwendoline Taylor was called up into the National Fire Service as a clerical worker. She found her form-filling job deeply unsatisfying, but because this was a reserved occupation she was unable to leave. While in the Fire Service, she became a member of the Home Guard, where she also did clerical work, which, in contrast, she enjoyed. She finally precipitated a confrontation with her Fire Service employer and was abruptly transferred to the Ministry of Health. She evaluated this employment history as follows: 'So that was the end of my ignoble war service, and it didn't shorten the war by that [much] (*laughs*). But, working for the Home Guard, you really felt you were doing something, you were making that effort, you know, you were being of some use.'[94] Similar accounts of the patriotic meaning of belonging to the Home Guard were offered by other women in reserved occupations. Like the men, they used the language of the war effort. Ellen Baxter, a London Transport pay clerk, said of her membership of the WHD that 'we all felt we were doing our bit',[95] and Vida Staples, clerical worker at Chatham Town Hall, emphasised her sense of solidarity with fighting men: 'All the chaps were going, they were all doing their bit, and it was a question that, you know, we want volunteers, I mean it was natural, you stood alongside the fellows.'[96]

Ironically, however, in one case it was employment in the Home Guard itself that thwarted a woman's ambitions to be more closely involved in the war effort and deprived her of her chance to stand 'alongside the fellows'. Winnie Watson worked as a full-time secretary for a Home Guard colonel. The heroic story of women's mobilisation became an explicit reference point in the interview: Winnie became defensive about how little she appeared to have done during the war, citing the Land Girls in comparison, and explained: 'I wanted to go in the forces, all my friends were in uniform and I wanted to be in uniform really.'[97] However, her Home Guard colonel would not have it. Winnie regularly received notification from the Employment Exchange that she should report to them because she was of call-up age:

Every time I had that, the Colonel used to tell me I was to take it in to him. And every time I took it in, of course, he said 'Oh no, no, no, you're not going.' And then in the end I myself said I wanted to go. And he said 'Now look, if you really say you want to go, I am going to tell you I'm going to fight you, because you were here from the beginning, and you are going to stay with us until we stand down.' That was all history. Nothing more. I was only a young girl of eighteen, twenty.[98]

The three final sentences constitute a cryptic postscript. Winnie possibly meant that if things had been otherwise, she would have had a mobilisation story to tell. But she was 'only a young girl', and hence no match for the colonel who had more power than she to determine 'history'. There was 'nothing more' she could do to secure herself a place in the war effort, or to create for herself the history she would have liked to have. Her frustration parallels that of other women and men denied the conscription they desired, yet the compensations of Home-Guard membership were, for Winnie, sadly limited.

The rectitude of standing alongside the men in wartime was, as we have seen, given by Vida Staples as her reason for joining the Home Guard. In her account, the need for wartime solidarity overrode gender difference and division. But a markedly gendered reason for participation was articulated by some of the other women. It was based on the idea that the threat of invasion held special horrors for women, which, as we saw in Chapter 2, was articulated by some newspaper commentators.[99] In these accounts, 'defending ourselves if the Germans landed' had terrifying meanings. Kaitlin Wells, who used this phrase, was one of several women who revealed that fathers recruited their daughters to the Home Guard in part because of fears of what an invading German army might do to them. Kaitlin explained: 'You see, at the time, we thought that they were going to come armed to the teeth and that all women would be raped or something.' Her father had never discussed this possibility with her, but she understood it to be 'his greatest fear'.[100] Dorothy Williams's father communicated the same anxiety. He recruited Dorothy to his Home Guard unit at Shotley Bridge in County Durham, but rather than equipping her to defend herself, he told her that he would end her life and those of her two sisters if the Germans invaded:

My father said that if the Germans did land, that there'd be pillage, rape, and he just wouldn't *ever* allow us to be subject to anything. Having said pillage and rape, he didn't exactly use those words, because one did not in those days talk about rape ... But I knew that it was something that he would never allow us to be submitted to. And he said if they ever landed he would *kill* us all rather than us ever fall into their hands. That frightened us a little bit, too. We didn't know which was going to be the worse of the two (*laughter*).

Q: Did you believe he meant it?
A: Oh, he meant it. He certainly meant it at the time he said it … He had been right through the previous war, always abroad, and he had seen a lot, obviously had grounds for what he was saying. I think a lot of men felt that way, where they were protective towards their families.[101]

Such a patriarchal interpretation of the lengths to which 'protection' should be taken left women little scope for agency. Certainly, the idea that a German invasion threatened women in a special, sexualised way was prevalent at the time, as it had been in the First World War.[102] Some of the women who joined the Home Guard and received weapons training recalled the motivating power of the special threat to women represented by the imagined invasion without mentioning their fathers. Vida Staples was given the option by the Chatham Home Guard *not* to learn to shoot because of the 'franc tireur' problem. However,

VS: There was never any doubt because really, when we thought about it, we didn't think there was any choice actually. We thought we'd be shot or raped or any, it didn't matter, it didn't matter. It was immaterial, yes.
PS: So you thought you might as well have a gun?
VS: Yes, that's what we thought, yes, we thought that was rather like Churchill said, you know? We'd take one with us if we didn't do anything else! Yes, yes.
PS: And … you knew about rape, did you, when you were a young woman in your twenties? You sort of knew that that was a possibility?
VS: Oh yes, oh yes, quite. As I say, we knew there was no quarter. Oh yes, yes, yes, yes.[103]

The anxieties of Kaitlin Wells, in Cumberland, were elaborated and coloured by her understanding of Nazi ideology and reproductive policy: 'I had long ash-blonde hair, and I was terrified that I'd be carried off with some German, you know! To some, you know, they had these baby factories to make a pure Aryan race.' This specific fear – that the occupation of the country implied the invasion of the female body – was remembered within a more generalised context of apprehension and motivation. The touchstone of memory for Kaitlin Wells was, as for Vida, Churchillian rhetoric. She continued:

But, I don't know, you were just apprehensive, because you didn't know what it was going to mean. But when we listened to Mr Churchill you know, with, 'We shall fight on the beaches and we shall … never give in!' (*mimicking*

Churchill) I mean, it fired you up. I think everybody, I mean if they'd come, everybody would have been ready for them, even if they'd fought with the kitchen sink.[104]

The Second World War had a specific meaning for women in these memories that has become muted in the popular memory of the British war effort, although it is present in the memory of that war in other participant countries, just as it is in understandings of modern 'dirty' wars.[105] Rather than figuring as a 'just war', which the allies could not lose and which they fought determinedly and even cheerfully against an evil enemy, the Second World War was remembered, in this account, as a war in which there was a real possibility of occupation by an enemy that used degenerate means of warfare which would have had special consequences for women. In view of such fears, an active, even combatant, role made more sense than the conventional women's role of 'watching and waiting': it was preferable for women to adopt the solution offered by Churchill, the father-figure and patriot who (in the same way as some actual fathers, including Kaitlin's) offered inclusive action rather than selective passivity.

Conclusion

Personal testimony makes a significant and distinctive contribution to the study of women and home defence. It reveals women's recruitment at times and in ways that flew in the face of government policy. Women were enlisted not only by other women, but also by fathers and by a number of Home Guard COs who co-operated with the WHD despite the ban: some of them required of the women they recruited more than the officially approved cooking, driving and typing. They taught women a full range of military skills, including signalling, intelligence and also the use of weapons. One transgression led to another: women trained in such ways were needed in military exercises, and this required them to have the practical and symbolic protection of military uniform. This is not to say that all women in home defence bore arms and wore unofficial uniforms: oral evidence also shows that some Home Guard units followed official policy, recruiting women only after April 1943, equipping them with no more than the round Home Guard badge, and involving them only in 'feminine' activities. Others, as men's reminiscences indicate, recruited no women at all.

But if personal testimony reveals a history of women and home defence that is hidden, that very concealment constitutes a problem for memory.

Women who wanted to recall this part of their past nevertheless forgot both the dates and the names of the organisations they joined. Their omissions and mis-rememberings are symptomatic of the absence of a place in popular memory for the WHD specifically and for women and the Home Guard more generally – lacunae confirmed and reinforced by the treatment of women and gender relations in *Dad's Army*. The lack of representation of women and home defence in popular culture contributed to the unreceptiveness of familiar and local audiences, whose discouraging responses to women's attempts to recall their experiences in home defence did nothing to assist composure and keep these memories alive. Women invited to reach back in memory to personal histories, and ways of understanding them, that were so profoundly forgotten, had immense bridges to build from the present to the past. It is hardly surprising that some barely recognised the Home Guard selves they reconstructed. As Kaitlin Wells said: 'When I look back on it, it all seems so long ago, you know, as though it never really happened, as though it probably happened to somebody else really, more than me.'[106]

Nevertheless, women as well as men used narrative forms in which the meanings of the Home Guard and the Second World War have been passed down since the war, notably the comic anecdote and the mobilisation story. Women's anecdotes added a specific feminine component to the satirical treatment of the war and the Home Guard that we have reviewed earlier in the book. The gendered story of mobilisation for war constituted a point of reference even for women whose recall and narration it did not assist. It implied that successful home defence depended on unity, within which solidarity across genders (and other social divides) was a vital component: men and women needed to bear arms together as citizens united against the common foe. Women's part in home defence was also understood in relation to an even more muted narrative, according to which defensive solidarity was the appropriate response to a threat posed by an enemy who would differentiate profoundly between men and women. According to that story, women needed to be armed primarily because they were women rather than because they were citizens.

Personal testimony

Notes

1 BCL, WA, YPX/75, 1359/8, *The History of the Cheshire Home Guard: From L.D.V. Formation to Stand-Down, 1940–1944* (Aldershot: Gale & Polden, 1950) states: 'When Women Auxiliaries were permitted these were recruited ... from the Local Women's Home Defence under the direction of Mrs Edith Roberts. Altogether, 145 women enrolled ... in the Wallasey Battalion'. In the summer of 1986, *Wallasey News* published 'Recollections' of the Wallasey Home Guard by Trevor Eynon which made no mention of the Women Auxiliaries. Mrs Edith Roberts wrote to Eynon reminding him of women's membership of the 16th Cheshire Battalion, but he replied on behalf of himself and friends in the same platoon: 'This was news to all of us': correspondence, August–September 1986.

2 See Chapter 7, n. 1, for details.

3 (PI) Gwendoline Taylor, 21 February 2000 (14); officially, 'nominated women' should have been over 45 years of age.

4 See Chapter 7: (PI) George Nicholson (959–961); J. Langdon-Davies, 'Home Guard Parade', *Sunday Pictorial*, 24 November 1940.

5 (PI) Kaitlin Wells (pseud.), 19 May 2000 (17).

6 (PI) Wells (88).

7 Five women were introduced to the Home Guard by their fathers: Mollie Dale, Ann Godden, Jeanne Townend, Kaitlin Wells and Dorothy Williams, of whom Dale, Godden and Wells learned combatant skills.

8 (PI) Ann Godden, 30 March 2000 (385, 389, 467, 471, 689, 721).

9 (PI) Wells (59, 88–90); she also trained with the Home Guard in the Hippodrome Cinema, Workington.

10 ESRC Project on Gender Training and Employment (GTE Project), interview, Yvette Baynes (pseud.), 21 November 1991 (324–348). Photograph of Yvette Baynes with her Home Guard unit; see also n. 44, below.

11 As in the case of Ellen Baxter's father, a keen member of the Home Guard: (PI) Baxter (pseud.), 30 July 1998 (382).

12 (PI) Jeanne Gale Sharp, 8 January 1998 (105).

13 (PI) Vida Staples (pseud.), 26 May 2000 (110–112).

14 NA, WO, 32/9423, Minute by Frederick Bovenschen, 22 April 1942.

15 (PI) Staples (118–122).

16 (PI) Staples (327); Vida Staples thought that her WHD organiser was married to the CO of the Chatham Home Guard, with which the WHD worked.

17 Jean Barber (Ilkeston and District Local History Society Newsletter, September 1984); (PI) Baxter (384); (PI) Marion Bourne, 3 May 2000 (735, 861, 869, 790); (PI) Gale Sharp (105, 133, 735–59); (PI) Kathleen Holmes, 25 May 1999 (463, 483, 521, 535) and Audrey Simpson, 28 July 1999 (530–550); Rhona Morgan (writing as R. D. Havis), *The Green Pullover* (Braunton, Devon: Merlin Books, 1988), p. 9; (PI) Staples (225, 247); IWM, DD, 86/54/1, Diary, Louie White; IWM, SA, 11227, Barbara Wynne, 1990.

18 (PI) Holmes (439).

19 (PI) Holmes (483).
20 (PI) Lois Baker, 16 December 1999 (534–546); IWM, SA, 11227, Barbara Wynne; Morgan (Havis), *Green Pullover*, p. 9.
21 She explained that they were given cheesewires, 'and we were told that if ever they came we were to crawl up behind them – mind you, I mean, the Germans were much taller than me – and decapitate them! … whether I'd ever got it off with this cheesewire, I don't know (*laughs*). I don't think I would': (PI) Simpson (274–278).
22 IWM, SA, 16762, Mary Warschauer, reel 3, 1996; Baker (558 and photograph).
23 (PI) Winifred (Winnie) Watson (pseud.), 31 March 2000 (26–42 and photograph).
24 Correspondence, Eunice Lowden, 6 February 1998.
25 Mollie Dale (photograph), 2 May 2000; (PI) Jeanne Townend, 3 April 1998 (251–3 and photograph).
26 (PI) Townend (251–3).
27 IWM, DD, 86/54/1, Diary, Louie White, 21 November–5 December 1943. Denim battledress was made of thick khaki fabric.
28 IWM, DD, 86/54/1, Diary, White, 13 February 1944.
29 (PI) Baxter (460); (PI) Staples (283); (PI) Holmes (635).
30 (PI) Holmes (635–653).
31 (PI) Taylor (14); this justification for women wearing trousers is a recurring theme in wartime humour.
32 Hansard, vol. 391, cols 2117–2118, 3 August 1943.
33 (PI) Staples (285).
34 (PI) Staples (283).
35 Hansard, vol. 398, col. 1223, Oral Answers, 28 March 1944.
36 Mackenzie, *Home Guard*, p. 186.
37 (PI) Wells (92).
38 R. W. Barnes, 'The Defence of Workington during World War II', online: http://www.users.globalnet.co.uk/~rwbarnes/defence/hg1.htm (accessed October 2001).
39 Thompson, *Voice of the Past*, pp. 136–137; Lummis, *Listening*, pp. 117–118.
40 See P. Coleman, 'Creating a Life Story: The Task of Reconciliation', *Gerontologist*, 39:2 (1999), pp. 133–139. Coleman notes that disinclination to reminisce may be caused by: lack of a habit of reminiscence and interested audiences; avoidance of disturbing episodes in the past.
41 Thompson, *Voice*, pp. 158–159; Lummis, *Listening*, p. 125.
42 (PI) Staples (76).
43 (PI) Baxter (74, 485–496).
44 For other 'insecure chronologies' see (GTE PI) Yvette Baynes (342, 353–356); (PI) Staples (110–112).
45 Thanks to Sonya Rose; IWM, DD, 86/54/1, Diary of Louie White (now Louie Williams).

46 Louie Williams, telephone conversation, 7 February 2004.

47 IWM, DD, 86/54/1, Diary of Louie White, 20 October 1944.

48 'Triangulation' refers to the use of multiple research methods, data sources or theoretical perspectives to investigate the same phenomenon: see N. Denzin, *The Research Act: A Theoretical Introduction to Sociological Methods* (London: Butterworth, 1970), pp. 300–301.

49 The 'March Past' is organised by the Royal British Legion which only recently included male Home Guards in the parade. The Home Guard Association was formed in 2002 by Michael Burkenshaw to press it to do so, and secured the participation of men *and* women in November 2002. However, the website states: 'Officially, there were never any women in the Home Guard', while referring to WHGAs working 'in an administrative capacity, with the Home Guard': http://www.home-guard.org.uk/ (accessed February 2004).

50 (PI) Jeanne Gale Sharp (105–125).

51 Ellen Baxter likewise referred to the Women's Home Guard: she had both the WHD badge and the round Home Guard badge, recalled joining the 'Women's Home Guard' after going to one of Summerskill's meetings, but did not remember the name 'Women's Home Defence' nor that the organisation was separate from the Home Guard: (PI) Baxter (382, 440).

52 Thomson, 'Unreliable Memories?'

53 See Summerfield, 'Culture and Composure', pp. 65–93, which refers to some of the cases discussed here.

54 (PI) Audrey Simpson (438 and 694).

55 (PI) Gale Sharp (167–173); (PI) Holmes (177).

56 (PI) Holmes (968).

57 (PI) Baker (1088).

58 (PI) Holmes described her response to seeing the *Saga* notice: 'I thought, "Good God, there's more than just two"' (968).

59 (PI) Taylor (609); (PI) Wells (326); (PI) Godden (937); (PI) Betty Bowers, 13 April 2000 (49); (PI) Baker (514).

60 (PI) Baker (514).

61 (PI) Baker (518).

62 (PI) Taylor (14).

63 (PI) Taylor (40). Pike in *Dad's Army* was played by Ian Lavender.

64 (PI) Holmes (443–447); (PI) Audrey Simpson (390).

65 (PI) Godden (1847); (PI) Joan Hardy, 27 July 1998 (535). Godden (572) evoked the British values sent up in the series, regarding the capture of a downed German airman by a neighbouring platoon: 'Several people said they should have killed him but others said, "No, it wouldn't really be very sporting"', and linked this implicitly with *Dad's Army*.

66 (PI) Taylor (609); (PI) Simpson (390, 921–925, 953–955).

67 (PI) Wells (326).

68 (PI) Wells (326).

69 (PI) Godden (1847–1855).

70 See *Journal of European Studies*, 31: 3–4 (2001), Special Issue, 'Humour as a Strategy in War'.
71 (PI) Godden (1847–1855).
72 (PI) Baker (1040).
73 (PI) Marion Bourne (1037).
74 Mollie Dale said: 'There was … talk of them as 'Dad's Army' efforts, and, quite honestly, I don't think that's true … they weren't that stupid! … They were much more dedicated': (PI) Dale (420–422).
75 (PI) Staples (701–705); see also Townend (432–436) and Watson (278, 1184).
76 Notably Wilson: (PI) Hardy (535).
77 (PI) Hardy (181).
78 (PI) Wells (179).
79 (PI) Wells (179).
80 (PI) Wells (177).
81 (PI) Watson (1180).
82 (PI) Baker (1036–1040).
83 (PI) Gale Sharp (170–173, 181).
84 (PI) Baxter (384).
85 (PI) Wells (64).
86 (PI) Wells (326).
87 (PI) Wells (75, repeated 326).
88 (PI) Wells (75, repeated 326).
89 This was not, however, always the case for women. Jean Barber, 'in the Dale Abbey detachment of the Women's Home Defence', described being called out, weapons at the ready, to halt the advance of 'a column of German soldiers' who turned out to be Italian prisoners-of-war, an outcome 'worthy of Captain Mainwaring': Ilkeston & District Local History Society Newsletter, September 1984.
90 M.-F. Chanfrault-Duchet, 'Narrative Structures, Social Models and Symbolic Representation in the Life Story', in S. B. Gluck and D. Patai (eds), *Women's Words: The Feminist Practice of Oral History* (London: Routledge, 1991), pp. 77–92.
91 *The Gentle Sex* (Leslie Howard, 1943, UK, Two Cities–Concanen); *Millions Like Us* (Frank Launder and Sidney Gilliat, 1943, UK, Gainsborough Pictures).
92 Summerfield, *Reconstructing*, Chapter 3.
93 For example Kaitlin Wells wanted to join the WRNS but was compelled to remain a bank clerk: (PI) Wells (118).
94 (PI) Taylor (35–36).
95 (PI) Baxter (384).
96 (PI) Staples (221). Some narratives were more ambivalent about 'standing alongside the men'. GTE PI, Yvette Baynes (687–690).
97 (PI) Watson (894).
98 (PI) Watson (78).
99 Admiral Sir Reginald Bacon, *Sunday Express*, 17 May 1942.

100 (PI) Wells (69, 254–256).
101 IWM, SA, 9940, Dorothy Williams.
102 N. Gullace, 'Sexual Violence and Family Honor: British Propaganda and International Law during the First World War', *American Historical Review*, 102 (1997), pp. 714–747.
103 (PI) Staples (287–291).
104 (PI) Wells (75).
105 Hsu-Ming Teo, 'The Continuum of Sexual Violence in Occupied Germany, 1945–1949', *Women's History Review*, 5:2 (1996), pp. 191–218; M. Kaldor, *New and Old Wars: Organized Violence in a Global Era* (Oxford: Blackwell, 2001), especially pp. 31, 52, 53, 56, 62, 100.
106 (PI) Wells (360).

9

Conclusion

To return to our opening question: what does British home defence in the Second World War signify? The history of men, women and the Home Guard traced here could be read as a case study of the triumph of male power over women, involving not only their exclusion from the Home Guard but also their erasure from popular and personal memory. The vigorous campaign waged by Summerskill and the WHD did not entirely succeed: the compromise of April 1943 did not recognise the WHD and the values of feminine armed patriotism for which it stood. Thereafter, the campaign and the compromise were almost completely forgotten. The Home Guard was marked as male in both popular culture and the historiography of home defence.

Why was there this amnesia? Should it be seen as implicit in the operation of patriarchy, working to obliterate from popular memory a development that destabilised the masculine–feminine binary? We have reviewed much evidence in favour of such an interpretation. Even though the Home Guard was a subject of enormous interest in wartime popular culture, the representation of women as members was fleeting in the extreme. *Dad's Army* gave space to women auxiliaries some thirty years later, only to banish them within the single episode that introduced them, having demonstrated the inappropriateness of their presence. Depictions of women as active and armed defenders of the home (in the three wartime films discussed in Chapter 5) located them in domestic settings and showed them acting individually; there was no connection with, or even passing reference to, the organisation and training of women for home defence.

Popular culture represented the Home Guard as an all-male association, but within those parameters it explored the force from a variety of angles. Accounts emanating from politicians and from the MoI, as well as non-official representations that supported them, stressed the Home Guard's qualities of unity in diversity and, in particular, of a solidarity that was both enthusiastic and voluntaristic across class, age and regional boundaries. In this lay the Home Guard's qualification to stand for the British people at war. But such imagery was problematic in view of evidence, highlighted in Parliament and the press, of a recruitment policy that was both selective and at times coercive. Moreover, in the absence of an invasion, official representations that continued to emphasise the supposed strength of the Home Guard as a counter-invasion force began to imply its redundancy. In any case, the use of tradition and the pastoral metaphor in official representations suggested that the Home Guard was essentially rural and backward-looking. The construction of this almost pre-modern identity contradicted the highly industrialised war effort of which the Home Guard was in fact a part. In particular these representations overlooked the development of the Home Guard as an adjunct of the army, engaging in training and taking over defence functions at strategic points all over the country, including large cities. From 1942 onwards, recruitment and training films and broadcasts were adapted to stress such aspects. But most official and non-official accounts continued to oversimplify the Home Guard's role and character, while a rich vein of satire exploited those oversimplifications.

Because the producers of popular culture uncritically accepted the official definition of the all-male Home Guard, the masculinities situated within it were a key target. Sceptical and satirical accounts explored their interrelation with social status and class, with age and physique, with military leadership and efficiency, and with local and regional loyalties that challenged the larger unity of the force and the nation. Those accounts also engaged with the dynamics of the Home Guard and the home: depictions of Home Guard members in domestic settings, and particularly at the centre of domestic tensions and marital strife, emphasised gender difference while questioning the Home Guard's role in the war effort. The location of Home Guards in the all-male venue of the pub reinforced the message. The class dimensions of those depictions should not be overlooked: they contributed to the construction of the Home Guard as a 'people's army', though without the radical implications of that term. John Tosh has observed, for an earlier period, that the middle-class conceptualisation of men of the lower classes as skivers who got drunk, abused their wives and assaulted each other served to confirm middle-class identity and its (supposedly) different masculine code.[1] Depictions of the Home Guard were, on the whole, more affectionate and somewhat less polarised than this: they subscribed to the official view of a period characterised by unprecedented social mixing that set a high premium on co-operation; but they nevertheless characterised the Home Guard as the product of a familiar class society.

In any case, representations of the Home Guard in wartime were not only and entirely about the deflation of virility. Humour and irony were also used in support of the force. They were deployed to criticise the Government for failing to equip the Home Guard appropriately; they were also used to reveal the loyalty, courage and commitment of Home Guard members and to document the changes that took place over time. However, in spite of the varied registers in which the Home Guard was recorded, women's roles, other than conventional ones on the sidelines of the force (from which vantage points women might offer both support and sardonic comment), escaped attention. A fascination with the Home Guard as an all-male association evidently gripped almost all those who wrote, drew or sang about it.

Depictions of women and femininity were, of course, plentiful in wartime popular culture, and included representations of women playing novel roles in wartime. However, research has identified a strong normalising current in film, literature and advertising: women were undertaking exceptional tasks cheerfully and effectively, but only for the duration; they would preserve their femininity while they performed them (with the help of wartime cosmetics and Make-Do and Mend); and once the war was over they would swap them for their conventional roles at work and at home.[2] Why were women Home Guards not included within such an interpretative genre? The existence of a privately produced and circulated collection of cartoons of life in a Home Guard platoon, one that did include women as members, makes the lacuna seem all the more odd. However, Captain Saxon's purpose was not to explore the complexities and tensions of gender in the Home Guard, but to expose the 'trials of the Home Guard' from the point of view of a CO seeking to negotiate the plethora of Army Council Instructions, the twists and turns of policy, and the tangle of red tape that confronted him and his colleagues. The various restrictions and requirements affecting women offered irresistible grist to this mill.[3]

Nonetheless, the presence in the Home Guard of men like Captain Saxon complicates the view with which this chapter opened – of Home Guard history as a straightforward victory for patriarchy over a forceful feminist challenge to the political and social order. We have seen how Home Guard COs such as Saxon willingly accepted women as members, including those already organised in the WHD, and involved them in all aspects of Home Guard training, including rifle practice and other types of weapons training, at least until they were ordered not to do so by the War Office, and in some cases even afterwards. How could they get away with such apparent defiance?

Firstly, even though War Office instructions unequivocally prohibited women from training to use weapons in the Home Guard, there was ambiguity about women's permitted roles. There were numerous signs of this, including the partial approval of women 'helping' the Home Guard – unofficially and unpaid – while they were still officially excluded in the period before formal 'recognition'; the lack of clarity about the role of the WVS before and after April 1943; the grudging acceptance by the Secretary of State of the – forbidden – practice of women wearing uniforms after 1943; the confusion over the name by which women Home Guards should be known: 'nominated women' or 'auxiliaries'. More abstractly, a major source of ambiguity was the impossibility of precise differentiation between combatant and non-combatant roles.

Secondly, the local and voluntary character of the Home Guard lent itself to a habit of relative autonomy. This was particularly strong in the first eighteen months of its existence, but remained intrinsic to its identity even after the introduction of conscription and military discipline following legislation in December 1941. The use of the Home Guard as an adjunct of the army demanded its assimilation into army structures and procedures; but this was always in tension with the part-time and voluntaristic character of the force, which did what it could when it could, depending on its members' availability, commitment and enthusiasm, and drawing on their capacity for improvisation. From the early months onwards, it made good sense to some COs to make up numbers and secure much-needed services by bending the rules: admitting over-age and under-age men and, of course, women. It also made sense to train all these individuals to perform all the functions that might be required of them – which in the view of numerous COs meant that women, along with the rest, needed combat training.

The issue of local autonomy brings us to another question raised by this research. Was the Home Guard a radical or even, potentially, a revolutionary organisation? George Orwell and Tom Wintringham imagined it to be so: for them the huge flood of volunteers in the first four weeks not only expressed an unprecedented determination to defy a totalitarian power, but demonstrated a new form of popular democracy in action. Wintringham was not alone in likening the Home Guard to the People's Militia which had taken up the Republican cause against the Francoist Right in the Spanish Civil War. Both Orwell and Wintringham believed that the Home Guard would not tolerate a bid for peace by the British Government in 1940, in spite of the odds against Britain at that stage of the war. But although Wintringham did not shed his view of the Home Guard's origins as the British manifestation of an international anti-fascist guerrilla movement, he despaired of the direction in which the War Office insisted on taking it: towards static defence and to the exclusion of left-wing radicals not just from training and leadership roles but even from ordinary membership. Both men thought that the War Office was determined to ensure that the Home Guard was led by 'blimps' – officers drawn from the traditional social strata that had generated previous army leaders, but who were also committed to outdated military strategy. Both suspected the Government of deliberate efforts to suppress the popular radicalism that they believed pervaded the force. But if Orwell began by believing that the Home Guard represented an armed people, politicised by wartime unity and the fascist threat, by 1944 he had concluded that it had never been inspired by more than a local and nationalist repugnance towards invasion and occupation.[4] And after resigning from Denbies, Wintringham, though a popular lecturer and broadcaster on Home Guard and army matters, shifted his central focus to the political struggle for a better world after the war, joining the Common Wealth Party and standing as its candidate at a wartime by-election and in the general election of 1945.[5]

British patriotism in the Second World War was complex: as Miles Taylor has argued, the war was an occasion when the Left – for the first time – aligned itself with the nationalist cause, and it did so under Churchill's deeply conservative leadership.[6] But this does not mean that the patriotisms of the Right and the Left were identical: on the contrary, that of the Left (including non-communists) was suffused with enthusiasm for Britain's Russian ally and inspired by expectations of egalitarian social reconstruction, to be achieved by a Labour Government after the war. As we saw in Chapter 2, the Home Guard succeeded in embracing men who identified with this type of patriotism, as well as those to whom patriotism meant the preservation of the traditional social order. It also offered, to men who could not – at that moment – be full members of the armed forces, similar opportunities to those which Tosh ascribes to nineteenth-century imperialism: 'adventure, male comradeship and licensed aggression'.[7] It was happily remembered by some men who (retrospectively) valued their service in it for giving them just those experiences. Unsurprisingly, however, men's memories varied widely, both in register and in detail. The irksome constraints which Saxon's satirical critique of army red tape had highlighted were also recalled by some of the more critical respondents. Memories of division jostled with those of social solidarity; assertions that the Home Guard became an effective fighting force competed with views (albeit sometimes ambivalent ones) that the force was never effective in military terms. Such memories can be read in relation to wartime representations: official as well as sceptical and satirical. But they were also mediated by the representation that has defined the Home Guard since 1968: *Dad's Army.*

Dad's Army presents a distinctive and memorable view of the Home Guard and its Second World War setting, yet there is no unanimity about the interpretation it offers. Men and women interviewed about their service in the Home Guard have generally seen the show as a send-up: but while some have found its portrayal accurate, others have complained that the Home Guard was not really such a joke. Women interviewees have felt that *Dad's Army*'s comic image of the Home Guard makes it even more difficult to find comprehending audiences for their memories of joining the organisation. Similarly, men who have challenged the accuracy of the show have stressed that *Dad's Army* ignored key aspects of the Home Guard, notably its development as a serious endeavour which had an important place in the formation of young soldiers. This is to simplify: even within individual accounts there is some slippage from a supportive view, endorsing the *Dad's Army* representation, to the second, more critical, viewpoint. Whatever their response to the sitcom, however, those looking back at their Home Guard experiences have not been able to evade it: for participants and their audiences alike, *Dad's Army* has provided the dominant version of the Home Guard and the British war effort during the last quarter of the twentieth century, and continues to do so to this day.

Dad's Army, we have argued, offers simultaneously a 'loyal' representation of the Home Guard as a pillar of British home defence, inspired by the most patriotic of motives, and a satirical view that treats this sceptically. The embodiment of the key qualities of the Home Guard – and by extension of Britain at war – in the well-intentioned but inept and unfit Captain Mainwaring, emphasises the ambiguity. Superbly portrayed by Arthur Lowe, Mainwaring is both the figure of incompetent military authority and the loyal patriot, courageous and self-sacrificing. However, his conservatism and class-consciousness position him – and through him the Home Guard – on the Right, behind Churchill, rather than on the Left, with Orwell and Wintringham. Mainwaring would not have voted Labour in the general election of 1945. His conservatism extends to gender and nationality as well as to class. But Mainwaring's socio-political position and stance are always vulnerable: there is a comic counterpoint to every manifestation of Mainwaring's character. The same is true of the men he leads: in addition to their roles as Mainwaring's foils, they embody different types of masculine Britishness in their own right. Whether youthful or elderly, Scottish or southern, crooked or straight, their capacity to fulfill the requirements of the Home Guard is always in (comic) question. Can they cohere socially, in spite of the tensions? Can they meet the standards required of a military force? Can they triumph in confrontations with 'the enemy', whether that enemy is the Eastgate Platoon, the army, the ARP, the vicar and his verger, or, scarcely more seriously, the Nazi forces themselves?

At first glance, *Dad's Army* presents the Home Guard, and by analogy Britain at war, as muddling through, triumphing against the odds over an enemy who is well disciplined and equipped and highly efficient. Victory is secured not because the Home Guard and Britain have attained superiority in these, ultimately contingent, respects, but because the British are, somehow, intrinsically better. Even that message, however, is ambiguous: it can be read with, as well as without, irony. Comments made by Gina Wisker about a very different television sitcom, *Goodness Gracious Me*, can be adapted to the case of *Dad's Army*. It 'manages ironic twists and turns which give … viewers … ways into negotiations between the mythic histories people construct for each other, and the contradictions and potentials of the present'.[8] Ultimately the avoidance of a single simple message accounts for the huge, diverse and ongoing appeal of *Dad's Army*; the 'ironic twists and turns' of the scripts mean that the show neither buys into Calder's 'myth of the Blitz' – the idea of a united wartime Britain with the capacity to endure – nor does it ignore it. *Dad's Army* has been received both as satire and as a celebration of British values, as simultaneously a damning critique of Britain at war and a source of deep nostalgia for just that period of British history. Wisker's formulation helps us to view this straddling of apparently opposed interpretative viewpoints, not as a disabling contradiction, but as offering productive – and seemingly unending – potential for the negotiation of preferred meanings.

This is not to suggest that *Dad's Army* is unselective: numerous political messages, including those of Wintringham and the Spanish Civil War,

Summerskill and the WHD, were well and truly written out. A show that claimed to pride itself on historical authenticity rejected a whole set of references that deviated from the mainstream. It is, of course, arguable that wartime dissent would have complicated its message, and any hint of didacticism would have detracted from the comedy. It remains the case, however, that the exclusion of the left-wing and the feminist challenges has contributed to their obliteration from the popular history of the Home Guard. By the same token, the presentation of the Home Guard as a never-to-be-effective group of would-be soldiers, in a benign Britain which held together and triumphed in spite of social tensions and gross inefficiencies, has been firmly inscribed on popular memory.

The aim of this book has been to contribute to the destabilisation of such a comfortable vision, not only of the Home Guard but of the Second World War as a whole. It has emphasised the variety of wartime interpretations of the 'People's War' and the contestations to which they gave rise. Enthusiasm for redefined citizenship strained against habits of gendered social selectivity; objectives that encompassed profound changes in the social and political order, nationally and internationally, competed with war aims focused primarily on the achievement of victory rather than the creation of a new society. In the largely cultural task of maintaining wartime national unity, official representations acknowledged the radical implications of the all-inclusive British war effort, while neutralising them with comforting visions of the endurance of traditional British ways of life. Non-official popular culture, at greater liberty to parody the British at war, avoided devastatingly critical satire, and, while observing and recording numerous wartime changes, ultimately promoted social harmony rather than radical alterations of class and gender relations. Above all wartime popular culture reinforced the notion that self-reflexive humour is the key to British national identity. The ground was thus laid for selective amnesia about the more challenging wartime developments, with compelling consequences for subsequent understandings of the meaning of the war. This book, it is hoped, will prompt further questions about the complex interactions of official discourse, popular culture and personal testimony in the wartime and postwar construction of the popular memory of Britain – and other countries – at war.

Notes

1 J. Tosh, 'Masculinities in an Industrialising Society: Britain 1800–1914', *Journal of British Studies*, 44:2 (2005), p. 342.
2 Gledhill and Swanson, *Nationalising Femininity*.
3 IWM, DD, 75/35/1 T, Papers of Captain F. C. Saxon.
4 G Orwell 'Home Guard Lessons for the Future', *Observer*, 15 October, 1944.
5 Purcell, *Last English Revolutionary*, pp. 216–217.
6 Taylor, 'Patriotism', pp. 971–987.
7 Tosh, 'Masculinities', p. 342.
8 G. Wisker, 'Negotiating Passages: Asian and Black Women's Writing in Britain', *Hecate: An Interdisciplinary Journal of Women's Liberation*, 30:1 (2004), p. 11. *Goodness Gracious Me* was created by Meera Syal, and broadcast on BBC2 in 1998, 2000 and 2001.

Appendices

Appendix 1: women's personal testimony

Project interviews

Name	Year of birth	War work	Home defence (and date/year where known)	Date of interview or correspondence
Lois Baker	1922	Clerk, Air Ministry 1939–44	HG, Air Ministry, Auxiliary Section, Central London 1940/1–45	16 December 1999
Ellen Baxter (pseud.)	1921	Pay-roll clerk, London Transport	WHD/WHGA, Hammersmith, London c.1942–44	30 July 1998
Yvette Baynes (pseud.)	1925	Office worker at various companies 1939–47	Factory HG unit, D. F. Tayler, Birmingham c.1942/3	21 November 1991
Marion Bourne	1923	Clerk 1939–40; typist, Ministry of Aircraft Production 1940–44; clerk 1944–45; typist 1945–51	WHD, Ministry of Aircraft Production, Central London c.1941–44	3 May 2000
Mollie Dale	1923	Clerk, Ministry of Health 1940–48	WHGA, Smethwick, South Staffordshire 1943–44	2 May 2000

Jeanne Gale Sharp	1926	Schoolgirl –1941; civil defence 1941–42; veterinary assistant 1942–43; library assistant 1943–44; Royal Observer Corps 1944; munitions worker 1944–45	WHD/WHGA, Oxford c. 1942–44	8 January 1998
Ann Godden	1926	Secretary, gas company	LDV/HG/WHGA, Sunningdale, Berkshire 1940–44	30 March 2000
Joan Hardy	1916	Secretary, War Office	Secretary to CO, LDV/HG/WHGA, War Office 1940–May 1944	27 July 1998
Kathleen Holmes	1919	Telephone switch-board operator, General Post Office	WHD, Leyton-stone, East London c.1940/1–44	25 May 1999
Mary Johnston	1911	Shorthand typist, tea merchants, 1931–47	Railway HG, Edinburgh c.1940–44	28 November 1998
Audrey Simpson	1920	Factory worker	WHD, Leyton-stone c. 1941–44	28 July 1999
Vida Staples (pseud.)	1920	Clerical worker, Chatham Town Hall	WHD/WHGA, Chatham, Kent 1940–44	26 May 2000
Gwendoline Taylor	c.1924	Office worker for various companies c.1939–43; Fire Service c.1943–44; Ministry of Health c.1944–45	HG/WHGA, Gatley, South Manchester c.1942/3–44	21 February 2000
Jeanne Townend (and husband Michael Townend)	1927	Schoolgirl	HG/WHGA, Goole, East Riding of Yorkshire c.1942/3–44	3 April 1998
Winifred Watson (pseud.)	1921	Office worker, HG	LDV/HG/WHGA, Wingham, Kent 1940–44	31 March 2000

| Kaitlin Wells (pseud.) | 1923 | Bank clerk | LDV/HG/WHGA, Workington, Cumberland c.1940–44 | 19 May 2000 |
| Barbara Wetherley | 1917 | Clerical worker, Railways | Railway HG, Edinburgh 1942–44 | 7 January 1999 |

Project correspondents

Name	Year of birth	War work	Home defence (and date/year where known)	Date of interview or correspondence
Betty Bowers	1924	Office worker	LDV/HG/WHGA, Sunningdale, Berkshire c.1940–44	13 April 2000
Phyllis Burr	1927	Schoolgirl	HG/WHGA, Gatley, South Manchester c.1942/3–44	7 March 2000
Peggy Hugo	c.1926	Shorthand typist: Plymouth Garrison Command HQ; Plymouth Sector HG HQ	HG, Plymouth c.1943–4	10 December 1999; 13 January 2000
Eunice Lowden	c.1914 (d. 1998)	Chief clerk, insurance office 1939–45; senior Red Cross officer 1945–	HG/WHGA, City of London, –1945[a]	6 February 1998
A. O. Milner	1925	Factory worker (product for aircraft de-icing)	HG, Bamber Bridge, Lancashire c.1940–44	1999–2000
Rhona D. Morgan (wrote as R. D. Havis)	c.1920	Office worker: Civil Defence Control Centre; Ministry of Food	WHD, Bexley, Kent c.1940–44	24 March 2000 (enclosing *The Green Pullover*)
Patricia Neale	c.1921	Clerical assistant: City of London office; Eltham HG HQ; WAAF	HG, Eltham, Kent [a]	14 February 2000

Marjorie Tomlinson	1921	Shorthand typist, Royal Engineers; Battalion Secretary, Rochester HG 1940–45; ATS	Battalion Secretary, Rochester HG 1940–45	29 January 2002
Louie Williams (see also Louie White, IWM, DD)	1918	Shop assistant, 1931–41; munitions worker/aircraft inspector, Leeds c.1940–45; nurse, Epsom, Surrey 1945–	HG/WHD, Moortown, Leeds c.1942–44	30 November 2001; 4, 6 February 2002; 5 February 2004

Imperial War Museum, Sound Archive (IWM, SA)

Name	Year of birth	War work	Home defence (and date/year where known)	Date of interview or correspondence
Patricia Crampton (17426)	1925	Schoolgirl –1943; university student 1943–46	HG, Beaconsfield, Buckinghamshire 1940	1997
Edna Selwyn (11228)	–	Secretary, steel firm; HG HQ, Birmingham	Secretary to Zone Commander, HG, Birmingham c.1940–44	1990
Mary Warschauer (16762)	1920	Typist/teleprinter Operator, Air Ministry 1938–45	HG, Air Ministry, Central London c.1940–44	1996
Dorothy Williams (9940)	c.1923	Book-keeper, solicitor's office 1939–41; wireless operator, WAAF 1941–45; Coastal Transport Command 1945	HG, Shotley Bridge, County Durham c.1940–41	1986
Barbara Wynne (11227)	–	–	WHD, Beeston, Leeds[a]	1990

Erewash Museum Service, Ilkeston, Derbyshire

Name	Year of birth	War work	Home defence (and date/year where known)	Date of interview/ correspondence
Jean Barber	–	–	WHD, Dale Abbey, Derbyshire[a]	Ilkeston and District Local History Society Newsletter, September 1984

Note:[a] Date or location unknown or uncertain.

Appendix 2: men's personal testimony

Project interviews

Name	Year of birth	War work	Home Defence (HG unless otherwise stated)	Date of interview/ correspondence
Ray Atkins (pseud.)	1925	Publicity officer, Co-Operative Wholesale Society; British Army 1943–47	Manchester 1941–43	23 March 2000
Arthur Brown	1925	Commis chef; store-keeper, Royal Ordnance Factory; British Army	Central London and Shropshire 1941–43	1 October 1999
Alfred Claxton	1923	Messenger boy; RAF 1942–46	East London 1940–42	12 May 2000
Cyril Hall	1913	Baker; Army	Gainsborough 1940–41	28 October 1999
James Kendall	1910	Machine fitter, munitions factory	Gainsborough 1940–44	27 October 1999
George Nicholson	1924	Apprentice bricklayer; Royal Navy 1942–46	Near York 1941–42	18 May 2000
Christopher Redmond (pseud.)	1925	Apprentice draughtsman, 1939–43; engineering course 1943–45; naval cadet 1945–46	Wootton, Oxfordshire 1940, 1941–43; Wolverhampton 1943–45	13 March 2000
Lesley Revill	c.1923	Agricultural labourer	Lincolnshire 1940–44	29 November 1999

John Shuttle-worth	1922	Electrical contractor's assitant; munitions worker; R.A.F. 1941–46	Great Barr, Birmingham 1940–41	21 March 2000
Dennis Smith	1926	Schoolboy; technical college student; REME 1944–47	Kent 1940–41	11 May 2000
Ron Smith	1923	Labourer, building trade; factory worker; Royal Navy 1942–46	Leicestershire c. 1941–42	11 May 2000
Fred Whitlow	1920	Apprentice draftsman, Mersey Power Company; RAF	Liverpool c.1940–41	1 March 2000

Project correspondents

Name	Year of birth	War work	Home defence (and date/year where known)	Date of interview or correspondence
Fred Bailey	c.1924	Colne Valley Water Co.; British Army	Watford 1940–41	15 February 2000
Ronald Berry	c.1924	Apprentice aircraft fitter, A. V. Roe; aircraft fitter, Shorts Bros; British Army 1944–	Chadderton, Lancashire 1940–42; Swindon, Wiltshire 1942–44	2 January 2000
John Best	1922	Printer; Navy 1941–46	Withington, Manchester 1940–41	18 December 1999; 29 February 2000
Philip Blakey	c.1922	Schoolboy; Navy	Doncaster 1940	19 March 2000
D. E. Brundrett	1925	Technical college student; techni-cian, Croydon Gas Co.; British Army 1943–47	Purley, Surrey 1941/2–43	26 February 2000
Norman Field	1917	British Army	HGA, Kent 1940–41	30 January 2000

Nigel Grey	1924	Tailor	Hounslow, Middlesex 1940–42	January 2000; 17 April 2000
David Jones	1924	Coal-miner; British Army	Nantyffyllon, Glamorgan 1940–41	16 February 2000
Lyndon Jones	1920	Music student, pianist; sports reporter; RAF 1940	Pontypool, Monmouthshire 1940	3 January 2000; 5 April 2000
F. A. L. (Tex) Laws	1924	Post Office messenger, 1939–42; British Army	Battersea 1941–42	3 May 2000; 20 June 2000
John Lewis	1926	Schoolboy; farm worker	Gloucestershire c. 1942–44	Email, April 2000
F. J. Lusted	1922	Grocer's errand-boy; British Army 1942–46	Burwash, Sussex 1940–42	2 December 1999
Martin Maunder	1923	Schoolboy; British Army 1942–47	Tavistock, Devon 1940–42	Email 9 December 1999; 1, 18, 19, 21 January 2000
Mike Riley	1926	Schoolboy, Dulwich College; Royal Marines 1943–47	Bromley, Kent 1941–43	8 March, 7 June, 18 July 2000
Donald Russell	1923	Farm worker; British Army 1943–	1941–43[a]	6 November 1999
Bill Trueman	1924	Errand boy; rivet heater; apprentice wagon-builder, Great Western Railway Works	Swindon, Wiltshire 1941–44	29 December 1999; 25 February 2000
Stan Weeks	1922	'Countryman'; Royal Navy 1941–42	Bishopsworth, Somerset 1940–41; 1942–44	June 2000
Bertram Charles Waterhouse	1925	Farm labourer; British Army	Burwash, Sussex 1940 – call-up	9 November 1999
Victor Stanley Waterhouse	1924	Building worker, family business	Burwash, Sussex 1941–44	November 1999

Appendices

IWM, SA

Name	Year of birth	War work	Home defence (and date/year where known)	Date of interview or correspondence
Arthur Ambler (11229)	c.1920	Draftsman	Littleborough, Lancashire 1941–44	1990
Richard Body (14751)	1904 (d. 1997)	Farmer; armed services	HGA, Kent 1940–44	1994
William Brighouse (11230)	c.1923	Shop worker, Lewis's, Liverpool; railway foot-plate worker	Liverpool c.1940–42	1990
William Callan (15788)	1923	Gardener, RAF c.1941	Gravesend, Kent c.1940–41	1989
Frederick George Richard Cardy (11350)	–	Railway worker	Railway HG, Colchester c.1940–44	1989
Percy Clark (13612)	–	–	HGA, Kent	1990
Colin S. Cuthbert (15803)	1922 (d. 1992)	Family business; RAF	Margate, RAF 1940	1990
Edwin Joseph Embleton (16340)	1907	Ministry of Information 1939–45	MoI, City of London	1995
George E. Freeland (15826)	–	Farmer	Tenterton, Kent 1940; HGA 1940	1989
Ron Freeman (11226)	–	Assistant professional, golf club, Leeds; armed services 1942–	Leeds, 1940–42	1990
Jack French (14758)	–	Farmer	Kingston, Kent, c.1940–42; HGA, Kent 1942–44	1994
Harold W. G. Gower (10966)	–	Office worker, St James's Park, London	Amersham, Buckinghamshire 1940–	1989
John Graham (8337)	1923	British Army (1941)	Isle of Wight 1940–41	1984

Name (ID)				
Norman Griffin (18615)	1925	Technical College; British Army (1942)	Blackpool 1940–42	1998
James Robert Marland Heppell (16778)	1922	Trainee solicitor; British Army (1941)	Preston, Lancashire 1940–41	1996
Len Hill (11234)	c.1912	–	Scraptoft, Leicestershire 1940–44	1990
Edward Hillison (9581)	–	Salesman	Cosham, Hampshire 1940–44	1987
Klaus Ernst Hinrichsen (3789)	1912	Interned	For eleven months after release from internment	1978
Harold Edwin Watts Hodder (11360)	1925	–	Portesham, Dorset c.1940–41	1990
Harold Holttum (10459)	1896	Family business (market garden machinery)	Willingham, Cambridgeshire 1940–44	1988
David Hopkins (17673)	1904	Hovis Van and Motor Works 1939–45	Shirley, near Birmingham c.1940–44	1985
Frederick William Johnes (9366)	–	Apprentice draughtsman	Anti-Aircraft HG, Sydenham, Kent c.1943–44	1986
Gerhard Kraus (4420)	1919	Interned; forestry worker; laboratory worker; coal-miner	Keswick c.1941–42	1979
Fred Lewis (15883)	–	Aircraft worker	Rochester, Kent c.1940–43	1989
Reginald Bert Lewis (15882)	– (d. 1993)	Farm worker	Kent and Essex[a]	1989
Martin Mason (15894)	c.1922	Factory worker	Kent c.1940–44	1989
Tom Miller (15888)	–	Fruit farmer	HGA, Betteshanger[a]	1989/1990
Denis Bernard Oliver (12167)	1922	Apprentice painter; Royal Navy	East Hull c.1940–41	1991

Joe Pascall (11236)	–	Apprentice marine fitter and turner	Falmouth[a]	1990
Ted Petty (18076)	1919	Aircraft worker	Weybridge, Surrey c.1940–44	1989
William Charles Scott (11233)	c.1925	RAF	Ruislip, Middlesex c.1942–43	1990
Gerard Patrick Walgate (11456)	–	Tannery worker; Royal Navy	Hull 1940–42	1990
Norman Webber (15974)	–	Clerk, local government	Canterbury c.1940	1989/90
Henry Weston (11235)	–	–	East Derbyshire 1940–44	1990
Harry Wharton (8322)	–	Farmer	Mautby, Norfolk 1940; HGA c.1940–44	1984
John Wheeler (6204)	–	Temporary civil servant; British Army	Purton, Wiltshire 1940–42	1982
Peter Williams (11231)	–	Farm labourer	Lymm, Cheshire 1940–44	1990

Note: [a] Date or location unknown or uncertain.

Select bibliography

Primary sources

Birkenhead Central Library (BCL)
Wirral Archives (WA), YPX/75, 1359/1–8, Wallasey Women's Home Defence Unit, Papers of Mrs E Roberts

BBC, Written Archives Centre (BBC, WAC)
R19/509 Entertainment Home Guard 1940–43
R51/231 Talks: HG 1940–44
T12/880/1 Dad's Army, General and External Correspondence, 1968

Imperial War Museum, Documents Department (IWM, DD)
75/35/1 T Captain F. C. Saxon, Unpublished Memoir and Trials of the Home Guard 1940–1944
77/165/1 Brigadier W. Carden Roe, Papers
86/54/1 Mrs Louie White (later Williams), Wartime Diary

IWM, Photograph Archive (IWM, PA)
H5869–5871 The Home Guard 1939–1945
HU 18501 1940 Local Defence Volunteer and 1944 Home Guard.
HU 36270 Amazons barred from LDV
HU 36277 A member of the local Home Guard gives rifle instruction to a member of the Watford Women's Home Defence Unit
HU 83511 Louie White with the Leeds Home Guard

Imperial War Museum, Sound Archive (IWM, SA)
Radio broadcasts
431, 432 Winston Churchill (1940, 1943)

Select bibliography

7386 (Various) *Descent at Dawn* (c. 1943/4)
11225 Jimmy Perry (15 May 1990)
13921 Robb Wilton, *The Day War Broke Out* (n.d.)
17697 Anthony Eden (14 May 1940)

King's College London Archive (KCLA)
LH10/1941 'Home Guard Warfare' and other articles 1941
LH10/1942 Articles on Home Guard 1942
LH15/4/335 Handbook and LDV Training Instructions 1940
LH15/4/336 Newspaper items 1940–45
LH 15/4/337–8 Correspondence and Intelligence 1941–50
THW 1/34 Correspondence 1940–42
THW 2/1 *Picture Post* articles 1940
THW 2/2 'The Home Guard Can Fight' 1940
THW 3/32 Correspondence, lectures, talks 1939–42
THW 5/25 Osterley Park 1940

National Archives (NA)
HO 45/25009 Parts One and Two, Home Guard
WO 32/9423 Home Guard, use of women as auxiliaries, 1940–44
WO 165/92 Inspectorate of L.D.V.: Meetings
WO 199/3237 Regulations and instructions: LDV and HG
WO 199/3238 History of HG
WO 199/3243 History of Formation and Organisation of HG

University of Kent at Canterbury Cartoon Database (UKCCD)
Cartoons in *Daily Express, Daily Mail, Evening News, Evening Standard* http://library.ukc.ac.uk/cartoons/collect.html (accessed 1999–2004)

Official films
Citizen Army (Ivan Moffat, 1940, GB, Strand)
Miss Grant Goes to the Door (Brian Desmond Hurst, 1940, GB, Denham and Pinewood Studios)
One Man, Two Jobs (Gerald Sanger, 1944, GB, British Movietone News)
The Dawn Guard (Roy Boulting, 1941, GB, Charter)

Commercial films
Dad's Army: The Movie (Norman Cohen, 1971, UK, Norcon)
Get Cracking (Marcel Vernel, 1943, UK, Columbia British)
Mrs Miniver (William Wyler, 1942, USA, Metro-Goldwyn-Mayer)
The Life and Death of Colonel Blimp (Michael Powell, Emeric Pressburger, 1943, UK, The Archers)
Went the Day Well? (Alberto Cavalcanti, 1942, UK, Ealing Studios)
Whisky Galore (Alexander Mackendrick, 1949, UK, Ealing Studios)

Select bibliography

Television programme
Dad's Army (BBC1, 1968–77)

Printed sources

Newspapers
Colliers Weekly, Daily Express, Daily Herald, Daily Mail, Daily Telegraph, Defence, Evening Standard, John O'London's Weekly, Lake District Herald, Listener, Manchester Guardian, News Chronicle, News of the World, Observer, Picture Post, Punch, Reynolds News, Sunday Chronicle, Sunday Dispatch, Sunday Express, Sunday Graphic, Sunday Pictorial, Sunday Times, The Times, Wallasey News, War, War Pictorial News

Women's magazines
Home Chat, Modern Woman and Modern Home, My Home, My Weekly, Weekly Welcome and Woman's Way, Woman, Woman and Home, Woman's Illustrated, Woman's Own, Woman's Weekly

Official publications
Central Statistical Office, Fighting with Figures: A Statistical Digest of the Second World War (London: HMSO, 1995)

Hansard, Parliamentary Debates, House of Commons, vols 351–424 (London: HMSO, 1939–46)

Ministry of Labour and National Service, Report for the Years 1939–1946, Cmd. 7225 (London: HMSO, 1947)

Parliamentary Papers, Home Guard: Memorandum on the Principal Measures to Be Provided for by Defence Regulations, Cmd. 6324 (London: HMSO, 1941)

Speeches and Replies to Addresses by His Majesty King George VI. December 1936–February 1952 (Office of the Private Secretary to Her Majesty, H&S, n.d.)

Books and articles (pre-1955)
Adam, R., Murder in the Home Guard (London: Chapman & Hall, 1942)

Boothroyd, B., Home Guard Goings On from 'Punch' 1940–41 (London: Allen & Unwin, 1941)

Brophy, J., Britain's Home Guard: A Character Study (London: Harrap and Co., 1945)

Churchill, W. S., The Second World War, vols 1–6 (London: Cassell, 1948–54)

'Cilias' (pseud.), Home Guard Rhymes (London: no. pub., 1942)

Cobb, G. B., Home Guard Mystery (London: Longmans, 1941)

Crompton, R. William at War: A Collection of Just William's Wartime Adventures (London: Macmillan, 1995 [1939–45]).

Graves, C., The Home Guard of Britain (London: Hutchinson, 1943)

Graves, C., Women in Green: The Story of the Women's Voluntary Service (London: Heinemann, 1948)

Langdon-Davies, J. *Parachutes Over Britain* (London: Pilot Press, 1940)

Langdon-Davies, J. *Home Guard Fieldcraft Manual* (London: John Murray, 1942)

Liddell Hart, B., *Dynamic Defence* (London: Faber & Faber, 1940)

Mackenzie, C., *Keep the Home Guard Turning* (London: Chatto & Windus, 1943)

Mackenzie, C., *Whisky Galore* (London: Chatto & Windus, 1947)

Priestley, J. B., *Postscripts* (London: Heinemann, 1940)

Radnor, J., *It All Happened Before: The Home Guard through the Centuries* (London: Harrap, 1945)

Slater, H., *Home Guard for Victory: An Essay on Strategy, Tactics, and Training* (London: Gollancz, 1941)

Smith, H., *Bureaucrats in Battledress: A History of the Ministry of Food Home Guard* (Conway: R. E. Jones & Bros, 1945)

Spencer, G., *John Bull's Home Guard* (London: Artists' International Association, 1944)

Street, A. G., *From Dusk Till Dawn: The Sedgebury Wallop Home Guard Platoon Prepare for War* (London: Blandford Press, 1946 [1943])

Thomas, S. E., *Laughs with the Home Guard* (London: Harrap, 1942)

Uttley, A., *Hare Joins the Home Guard* (London: Collins, 1941)

Watkins, A. H., *Home Guard Rhymes: The Home Guard in 'Di-Verse' Moods* (Salisbury Square: Practical Press, 1943)

Wintringham, T., *Armies of Freemen* (London: Routledge, 1940)

Wintringham, T., *Mutiny: Being a Survey of Mutinies from Spartacus to Invergordon* (London: Stanley Nott, 1936)

Wintringham, T., *New Ways of War* (Harmondsworth: Penguin, 1940)

Wintringham, T., *People's War* (Harmondsworth: Penguin, 1942)

Books and articles (post-1955)

Aldgate, A. and Richards, J,. *Best of British: Cinema and Society from 1930 to the Present* (London: I. B. Tauris, 1999 [1983])

Aldgate, A. and Richards, J, *Britain Can Take It: The British Cinema in the Second World War* (Edinburgh: Edinburgh University Press, 1994 [1986])

Bryant, M., 'Crusader, White Rabbit or Organ-Grinder's Monkey? Leslie Illingworth and the British Political Cartoon in World War II', *Journal of European Studies*, 31:3–4 (2001), pp. 345–366.

Calder, A., *The Myth of the Blitz* (London: Jonathan Cape, 1991)

Calder, A., *The People's War: Britain 1939–1945* (London: Pimlico, 2000 [1969])

Campbell, D'Ann, 'Women in Combat: The World War II Experience in the United States, Great Britain, Germany and the Soviet Union', in G. Martel (ed.), *The World War Two Reader* (London: Routledge, 2004)

Cannadine, D. (ed.), *What Is History Now?* (Basingstoke: Palgrave Macmillan, 2002)

Chapman, J., *The British at War: Cinema, State and Propaganda, 1939–1945* (London: I. B.Tauris, 1998)

Select bibliography

Connelly, M., *We Can Take It: Britain and the Memory of the Second World War* (Harlow: Pearson Education, 2004)

Crang, J., *The British Army and the People's War 1939–1945* (Manchester: Manchester University Press, 2000)

Dawson, G., *Soldier Heroes: British Adventure, Empire and the Imagining of Masculinities* (London: Routledge, 1994)

Eley, G., 'Finding the People's War: Film, British Collective Memory, and World War II', *American Historical Review* 106:3 (2001), pp. 818–838

Fisk, R., *In Time of War: Ireland, Ulster and the Price of Neutrality 1939–45* (London: Deutsch, 1983)

Gledhill C. and Swanson G. (eds), *Nationalising Femininity: culture, sexuality and British cinema in the Second World War* (Manchester: Manchester University Press, 1996)

Gluck S. B. and Patai, D. (eds) *Women's Words: The Feminist Practice of Oral History* (London: Routledge, 1991)

Hinton, J., *Women, Social Leadership and the Second World War: Continuities of Class* (Oxford: Oxford University Press, 2002)

Holmes, C., *John Bull's Island: Immigration and British Society 1871–1971* (London: Macmillan, 1988)

Kushner, T., *The Persistence of Prejudice: Antisemitism in British Society during the Second World War* (Manchester: Manchester University Press, 1989)

Longmate, N., *The Real Dad's Army: The Story of the Home Guard* (London: Arrow Books, 1974)

Mackay, R., *Half the Battle: Civilian Morale in Britain during the Second World War* (Manchester: Manchester University Press, 2002)

MacKenzie, S. P., *The Home Guard: A Military and Political History* (Oxford: Oxford University Press, 1995)

MacKenzie, S. P., 'The Real *Dad's Army*: The British Home Guard, 1940–1944', in P. Addison and A. Calder (eds), *Time to Kill: The Soldier's Experience of War in the West, 1939–1945* (London: Pimlico, 1997)

McCann, G., *Dad's Army: The Story of a Classic Television Show* (London: Fourth Estate, 2001)

Orwell, S. and Angus, I. (eds), *The Collected Essays, Journalism and Letters of George Orwell*, vols 2 and 3 (London: Secker & Warburg, 1968 and 1969)

Peniston-Bird, C. and Summerfield, P., '"Hey, You're Dead!": The Multiple Uses of Humour in Representations of British National Defence in the Second World War', *Journal of European Studies*, 31 (2001), pp. 413–435

Perry, J., *A Stupid Boy: The Autobiography of the Creator of 'Dad's Army'* (London: Century, 2002)

Perry, J. and Croft, D., *Dad's Army: The Lost Episodes* (London: Virgin, 1998)

Popular Memory Group, 'Popular Memory: Theory, Politics, Method', in R. Johnson, D. Sutton and G. McLennan (eds), *Making Histories: Studies in History-Writing and Politics* (London: Hutchinson, 1982)

Purcell, H., *The Last English Revolutionary: Tom Wintringham 1898–1949* (Stroud:

Sutton Publishing, 2004)

Richards, J., *Films and British National Identity: From Dickens to Dad's Army* (Manchester: Manchester University Press, 1997)

Rose, S., *Which People's War? National Identity and Citizenship in Britain 1939–1945* (Oxford: Oxford University Press, 2003)

Summerfield, P., *Reconstructing Women's Wartime Lives: discourse and subjectivity in oral histories of the Second World War* (Manchester: Manchester University Press, 1998)

Summerfield, P., 'Culture and Composure: Creating Narratives of the Gendered Self in Oral History Interviews', *Cultural and Social History*, 1:1 (2004), pp. 65–93

Summerfield, P., '"Our Amazonian Colleague": Edith Summerskill's Problematic Reputation', in R. Toye and J. Gottlieb (eds), *Making Reputations: Power, Persuasion and the Individual in Modern British Politics* (London: I. B.Tauris, 2005)

Summerskill, E., *A Woman's World* (London: Heinemann, 1967)

Taylor, M., 'Patriotism, History and the Left in Twentieth-Century Britain', *Historical Journal*, 33:4 (1990), pp. 971–987

Thomson, A., *Anzac Memories: Living with the Legend* (Melbourne: Oxford University Press Australia, 1994)

Webber, R., *Dad's Army: A Celebration* (London: Virgin, 1999)

Yelton, D. K., 'British Public Opinion, the Home Guard and the Defence of Great Britain, 1940–1944', *Journal of Military History*, 58 (July 1994), pp. 461–480

Index

Note: 'n.' after a page reference indicates the number of a note on that page. Page numbers in *italics* refer to illustrations.

McKechnie, James 129
Mackendrick, Alexander 172
Mackenzie, Compton 112, 172,
    198n.10
MacKenzie, S. Paul 6, 8, 24n.67, 42,
    80–1, 246
Madoc, Philip 185
Mainwaring, Elizabeth 181, 200n.45
Mainwaring, George 170, 171, 175–89,
    192–6, 202n.70, 227, 230, 254,
    256, 257, 278–9
Manchester Guardian 32
Margesson, Henry David Reginald 68,
    76, 99n.133
Marshall-Cornwall, Sir James 46
Martin, K. J. 81
Mata Hari 152–3, 168n.32
media 3, 14, 26, 27, 104, 105, 170
medical inspections 53, 61n.147, 131,
    209
medical support 15, 75, 96n.77
memory 2, 6, 11–16, 19, 92, 123, 171,
    172, 207–8, 226–32, 234, 240,
    246–7, 273
    popular 7, 11–13, 15, 20, 51, 172,
    253, 257, 258, 262, 266–7, 273,
    280
Mesurier, John Le 170, 194–5
MI5 *see* Security Service (MI5)
Miles, Bernard 109
military effectiveness 5–6, 28, 41, 52,
    73, 91, 115, 120, 122, 124, 133,
    177, 184, 206, 215–21, 233–4,
    254, 278, 280
military exercises *see* training,
    exercises
Military Training Act (May 1939)
    22n.29
Miller, Kristine 154–5
Milligan, Spike 188
Millions Like Us 262
Mills, Michael 177–8, 183, 184, 185,
    186, 189
Ministry of Information 37, 43,

104–5, 109, 114–16, 130, 133,
    274
Miss Grant Goes to the Door 115, 117,
    155–7, 158–62, 166
mobile role 44–7, 50, 53
mobilisation 1, 11, 15, 68, 154, 166,
    262, 263, 264, 267
Moore, Thomas 87, 88
morale 5–6, 17, 46, 47, 53, 104,
    114–16, 130, 164, 215
Morrison, Herbert 9, 71, 72–3, 94n.28
Mrs Miniver 110, 147, 155, 161–6
Murder in the Home Guard 110,
    154–5, 161, 166
music hall 150, 165
myths 3–5, 6–7, 191, 203n.88, 221, 279

NAAFI *see* Navy, Army and Air Force
    Institute (NAAFI)
National Fire Service 8, 263
national identity, British 4, 11, 27–8,
    49, 52, 104, 112, 117, 133, 149,
    155, 190, 206, 280
national service 174, 175, 194, 209
National Service (Armed Forces) Act
    (2 September 1939), 22n.29, 30
National Service (No.2) Act (18
    December 1941) 22n.29, 47, 51,
    68, 93n.23
national unity 3, 18, 19, 26–30, 32,
    37, 89, 104, 107–9, 111, 114,
    140, 178, 190, 196, 206, 209–15,
    221–4, 280
National Viewers' and Listeners' As-
    sociation 184
navy *see* Royal Navy
Navy, Army and Air Force Institute
    (NAAFI) 147
Nazi (National Socialist) 5, 9, 31–3,
    43, 109, 111, 116, 118, 130,
    156–7, 160–1, 164, 170, 179,
    185, 232, 265, 279
'Neb' *see* Niebour, Ronald
New Model Army 40

Index

women 64–5, 67–79, 82, 83, 86–7, 141, 144, 161, 242–4, 266
'transformation' of the Home Guard 50, 119–29, 133, 192, 230
triangulation 250, 270n.48

Ulster Defence Force 31
unarmed combat 46, 72, 123, 219, 244
Unarmed Combat 137n.62
uniforms, meaning of 15–16, 53, 131, 149, 224–6, 234, 237n.89
  for women 70, 74, 87–90, 142–4, 245–6
United States of America (USA) 5, 10, 121, 155, 162
Union of Soviet Socialist Republics (USSR) 34, 37, 48, 50, 58n.107
  see also Russia
Uttley, Alison 125–6, 137n.69, 147–8

veterans *see* ex-servicemen
Volkssturm 58n.107
voluntarism 26, 28, 39, 49–53, 60n.141, 84

Walbrook, Anton 129
Wales 28, 36, 77, 108, 112, 219
Walker, Joe 170, 177, 179, 181, 183, 184, 186, 194, 199n.32, 200n.42
Wallasey News 79
Walmington-on-Sea 170, 183
Walsh, Percy 109
War Office 8, 36, 38, 42–3, 65–7, 71, 76–8, 91, 130, 157, 241, 242, 256
Watching Post 107
Watkins, A. H. 'Cilias' 151–2, 199n.22
Went the Day Well? 116–18, 119, 147, 155, 157–62, 164, 166, 169n.42, 198n.9
weapons training 46–7, 64–6, 70, 73, 77–9, 82, 86, 87, 141, 144–5, 157, 166, 242–4, 263, 265, 276
WHD *see* Women's Home Defence (WHD)

Whisky Galore 172–3
White, Jack 32, 52
White, Stanley 41
Whitehouse, Mary 184
Whitty, May 162
Who do you think you are kidding Mr Hitler? 183
Wicked Lady, The 160
Wilson, Arthur 170, 171, 176–7, 180, 183, 184, 186, 187, 194, 255
Wilton, Robb 150–1, 165, 222
Wingate, Orde 41
Wintringham, Tom 16, 40–5, 50, 58n.103, 75, 106, 110, 122, 126, 130, 134, 217, 240, 276–7, 279
Wisker, Gina 279
wives of the Home Guard 95n.51, 132, 141–2, 147–52, 163, 165, 167n.19, 173, 192, 224
Women's Auxiliary Forces 11, 15, 16, 68, 85, 262
  see also Auxiliary Territory Service
Women's Home Defence (WHD) 63, 66, 68–87, 92, 141, 165–6, 182, 207, 243–52, 254, 259, 263, 266–7, 273, 276, 280
  recruitment 241–4
Women's Home Guard Auxiliary 83, 89, 90, 141, 144, 165, 166, 223, 268n.1
  recruitment 241–4
women's non-combatant status 65–76, 81–3, 86–7, 91–2, 141, 276
Women's Voluntary Services (WVS) 69, 70, 71, 80, 83–6, 92, 99n.124, 131–2, 139n.90, 141, 147, 165, 223, 276
World War I *see* First World War
Wright, Teresa 162
Wynne-Candy, Clive 129, 130, 138n.79, 172, 187

Yelton, David 5–6
Yeomanry 28, 40